Charles Wyllys Betts

American colonial History illustrated by contemporary Medals

Charles Wyllys Betts

American colonial History illustrated by contemporary Medals

ISBN/EAN: 9783337152840

Printed in Europe, USA, Canada, Australia, Japan

Cover: Foto ©ninafisch / pixelio.de

More available books at **www.hansebooks.com**

The Hon.ble Edward Vernon Esq.r Vice Admeral of the Blue
And Comander in Cheif of all His Majesties Ships in the WEST-INDIES

AMERICAN

COLONIAL HISTORY

ILLUSTRATED BY

CONTEMPORARY MEDALS

BY THE LATE

C. WYLLYS BETTS

MEMBER OF THE AMERICAN NUMISMATIC AND ARCHAEOLOGICAL SOC.

EDITED, WITH NOTES, BY

WILLIAM T. R. MARVIN, A. M.

MEMBER OF THE BOSTON NUMISMATIC SOC.; HON. MEMBER AMERICAN NUMIS. AND ARCH'L
SOC.; COR. MEMBER NUMIS. AND ANTIQ. SOC., PHILADELPHIA; FOREIGN
ASSOCIATE SOCIÉTÉ ROYALE DE NUMISMATIQUE DE BELGIQUE,

AND

LYMAN HAYNES LOW

MEMBER OF THE AMERICAN NUMIS. AND ARCH'L. SOC., AND OF THE NUMIS. SOC. OF LONDON;
COR. MEMBER NUMIS. AND ANTIQ. SOC., PHILADELPHIA.

NEW YORK
SCOTT STAMP AND COIN COMPANY, L'D
18 EAST 23D STREET
1894

T.R. MARVIN & SON
PRINTERS.

PREFACE.

THE accompanying descriptions of Medals illustrating American Colonial History, were compiled by my brother, C. WYLLYS BETTS, of New York, whose death, in 1887, in the early maturity of an active and useful life, put an end to labors in more than one line of interesting research.

The value of coins and Medals, as enduring records of events, has often been emphasized. All original documents and contemporary accounts of occurrences are of peculiar importance to the conscientious historian. Medals are original documents in metal. In studying them we study history at its source. As contributions to the knowledge of the history of portraiture, dress and habits, as indices of then existing information in architecture, geography and the natural sciences, and as means of restoring the knowledge of structures long destroyed, Medals are not to be under-estimated. Medals are a "body of history," or, perhaps, a " collection of pictures in miniature," or "so many maps for explaining ancient geography." One is to look upon a cabinet of Medals "as a treasure, not of money, but of knowledge," and as the means by which a conqueror has sometimes 'discharged a debt to posterity, after he has ruined or defaced a strong place, by delivering a model of it, as it stood whole and entire, so as in some measure to repair the mischiefs of his bombs and cannon.' *

* Addison's Dialogues on Medals.

As an intelligent student of history, my late brother was not
unconscious, also, of those unintended teachings often to be derived
from contemporary Medals, which, perhaps, sometimes enable us
to realize as vividly the feelings, beliefs and conditions of the past.
as do the purposed labors of chroniclers. "It is safer," it has
been said, "to quote a Medal than a historian."

Thus, observance of the fact that there was no immediate
commemoration, by the enduring medium of Medals, of what is
now realized as the stupendous event of the Discovery of America, and that, for more than half a century after a new continent
had been added to the Spanish domains, none of its names were
deemed worthy of addition to the titles of its Sovereign, is apt
to modify the ideas previously entertained, regarding the recognition of the importance of that event at the time of its occur-
rence.

The mistaken devices which sometimes adorn Medals bring to
us, also, surprising indications of the lack of accurate knowledge
on subjects concerning which it now seems impossible that the
world could have been then in doubt. Such are the instances
of the representation on a Medal, as late as 1581,* of the figure
of a camel among the emblems of the spoils of the Western
Indies, and of palm-trees on Medals relating to Canada, as late
as 1751 and 1776.†

The change of national feeling in England from the despon-
dency which existed in the early part of the eighteenth century,
over what was supposed to be the decline of national prestige
under a peace-loving administration, to that of enthusiasm over
the revival of glory by the capture of Porto Bello and Carthagena from the Spaniards, by Admiral Vernon, in 1739, could
not be better recalled nor illustrated than is done by the vast

---

* See No. 12.

† See Nos. 385 and 539; while the latter does not name Canada, it can hardly
have any other reference.

number and variety of Medals commemorating these now almost forgotten events, and attesting the phases of popular temper by the mottoes with which they are inscribed.

These, and many more instances which might be cited, indicate the indirect as well as the direct historical uses which contemporary Medals subserve, and which caused them to become objects of absorbing interest to my brother.

At the time he left us, his work was chiefly in manuscript, a small part only having been tentatively put in print, and it was almost presumptuous on my part even to attempt the completion of that which he had left unfinished. But the obligations of affection, which seemed to bid me preserve the record of his labors, and the hope that his work might, in some degree, subserve the ends for which it was designed, impelled me to undertake the task.

So much, however, remained to be done when my brother's papers devolved upon me, that I should scarcely have ventured to assemble and prepare their contents, had it not been for the generous interest manifested by Mr. Lyman H. Low, of New York, and Mr. William T. R. Marvin, of Boston. To their exhaustive knowledge, their scholarly views as to the proper interpretations of designs and inscriptions, and careful revision of the work, are alone due the completeness and accuracy of its presentation, and they are entitled to the assurance of my heartfelt gratitude. To my son, Wyllys Rosseter Betts, mention is also due for much patience and care in the preliminary preparation of his uncle's manuscript for printing.

FREDERIC H. BETTS.

NEW YORK, January 1. 1894.

EDITORS' PREFACE.

HAVING been intrusted with the supervision of the publication of the MS. of the late Mr. Betts, we desire to state that we are conscious that his work contains descriptions of a few Medals the connection of which with America is considered doubtful; of some, the date of which is uncertain; and of others, which, if the date when they were actually issued were alone considered, might be excluded; but the number of these is so small that it seems needless to particularize them, and our own opinions concerning them are given in the Notes. In one or two instances it has been found necessary to allude in the text rather than in the Notes, to historical events which have occurred since the death of Mr. Betts, and to refer to issues of the *American Journal of Numismatics* of a later date.

Should any errors in description or attribution be noticed, we must beg the reader to consider the difficulties of verifying Mr. Betts's descriptions, after the pieces under his inspection, and the authorities which he consulted, had been dispersed; and especially as he had not completed his own final revision of his work, when his early and lamented death put an end to his labors.

Our thanks are due to Mr. Addison Van Name, of Yale University, keeper of the Cabinet of Medals bequeathed to that institution by Mr. Betts, for his kindly interest and assistance; and to Mr. William S. Appleton, of Boston, and to Mr. Benjamin Betts, of Brooklyn, N. Y., for valuable information, and the opportunity, in several instances, of comparing pieces in their collections with the MS. descriptions. For our notes on the die-cutters, we have frequently been indebted to the excellent work of Messrs. Hawkins, Franks and Grueber, referred to as " Medallic Illustrations," the full title of which will be found on a subsequent page, and to " Münz-Abkürzungen " by Schlickeysen and Pallmann.

WM. T. R. MARVIN,
LYMAN H. LOW.

CONTENTS.

LIST OF ABBREVIATIONS

AND WORKS CONSULTED.

A. J. N.—American Journal of Numismatics. [Published quarterly at Boston, Mass.]

ALEXI.—Jno. Law und sein System: [A contribution to the history of finance and coinage; with two heliotype plates and three tables.] By S. Alexi. Berlin, 1885.

B.—Catalogue of American Coins and Medals of Chas. I. Bushnell. [Chapmans' Sale in New York, June, 1882.] Philadelphia, 1882.

B. N.—Bibliotheque Nationale, France. [The collection of Coins in the National Library, at Paris.]

C.—S. S. Crosby. The Early Coins of America, and the Laws governing their issue, comprising also descriptions of the Washington Pieces, the Anglo-American Tokens, many pieces of unknown origin of the Seventeenth and Eighteenth Centuries, etc. By Sylvester S. Crosby. Boston, 1875.

C. M.—Catalogue des Poincons, Coins et Medailles du Musee Monetaire de la Commission des Monnaies et Medailles. Paris, 1833.

F.—Die Jules Fonrobert'sche Sammlung uberseeische Munzen und Medaillen (compiled by A. Weyl). Berlin, 1878.

H.—Medallas de Proclamaciones y Juras de los Reyes de Espana. Por Adolf Herrera.

K.—Johann David Kohlers wochentlich herausgegebener Historischer Munz-Belustigung. Nurnberg, 1733–88.

L.—The Medallic History of the United States of America, 1776–1876. By J. F. Loubat, LL. D. . . . New York, 1878.

McL.—Canadian Numismatics: A Catalogue of the Coins, Medals, and Tokens of the Dominion of Canada. By R. W. McLachlan. [Reprinted from American Journal of Numismatics: completed 1885.]

MED. ILL.—Medallic Illustrations of the History of Great Britain and Ireland to the Death of George II. By Messrs. Hawkins, Franks and Grueber. London, 1885.

M. H.—Medalische Historie der Republyk. . . . Amsterdam, 1690.

O'C.—Catalogue of the Collection of Don Pedro Alonso O'Crowley [Spanish] . . . Madrid, 1794.

T. N.—Tresor de Numismatique et de Glyptique. Paris, 1836.

S.—Coins, Tokens and Medals of the Dominion of Canada. By Alfred Sandham. Montreal, 1869.

V. L.—Histoire Metallique des XVII Provinces des Pays-Bas. . . . Gerard Van Loon. La Haye, 1732.

V. L., SUP.—Beschrijving van Nederlandsche Historie-Penningen, . . . Amsterdam, Vol. I, 1821, and Vol. II, 1861.

AMERICAN COLONIAL HISTORY

ILLUSTRATED BY CONTEMPORARY MEDALS.

CHAPTER I.

THE PERIOD OF DISCOVERY.

OR many years after the discovery of the American continent, its existence had little or no influence upon the political or social condition of the Old World, and, hence, no allusion to it is found upon contemporary Medals. The deeds of Columbus and Vespucius and Cabot were never thus commemorated during the period of which this history treats.

The wealth of Mexico and Peru, poured into the treasury of Spain, gave to that nation for a time controlling influence in the affairs of Europe; but even Cortez and Pizarro, whose conquests secured it, are not immortalized by Medals. Although events of much less moment and names of far less renown are inscribed upon these enduring memorials, yet for more than a century after 1492 there does not appear upon them a single name directly connected with the New World. Perhaps this is a just retribution. The lust of power and greed of gold alone tempted adventurers to cross the ocean in those early days; and the rulers, at whose bidding they sailed, thought only of the wealth which was to aid their schemes of aggrandizement at home. It is not surprising, therefore, to find the first medallic allusion to America, among the titles of Philip II, of Spain, on the pieces struck to commemorate his accession, and the abdication of Charles V, his father, more than sixty years after the discovery.[*]

PHILIP II, "KING OF THE NEW WORLD."

1. 1556. *Obv.* PHILIPPVS · HISPANIAR · ET · NOVI ORBIS OCCIDVI · REX (Philip, King of Spain and of the New Western World.)   Armored bust of the King to the left.

Rev. IMP · CAES · CAROLVS · V · AVG · (Charles V, Emperor, Cæsar, Augustus.)   Laureated bust of the Emperor to the right, in armor.

Silver, cast.   Size 22.   H. 6.   V. L., I, 8.

2. 1556. *Obv.* PHILIP . ET . MARIA . D . G . R . ANG . FR . NEA . PER . HISPAN .   (Philip and Mary, by the grace of God, King and Queen [*Reges*] of England, France, Naples, Peru, Spain.)   Busts of Philip and Mary.

Rev. PHILIPPVS . HISPAN . REX.   The royal arms of Spain.

Silver.   H. 1.   No cut of this medal is given by Herrera, and probably no specimen is now in existence.   It is described in a manuscript in the National Academy of Madrid as struck in silver upon the proclamation of Philip II in Peru.

3. 1559. *Obv.* PHILIPPVS HISPANIAR ' ET NOVI ORBIS OCCI-DVI REX [Translated above.]   Armored bust of Philip II to left ; under truncation, I . PAVL . POG . F . (for Giovanni Paolo Poggini, fecit).

Rev. PACE · TERRA · MARIQ . COMPOSITA.   In exergue M · D · LIX.   (Peace established by land and sea 1559.)   Temple of

---

[*] The earliest numismatic reference to America is probably on the coins of Charles V, struck in Flanders in 1519, when he changed the motto NON PLUS ULTRA to PLUS ULTRA, and on his coins struck in 1555 with title REX INDIARVM. For comments on these see Mr. Brevoort's articles in A. J. N., XVI, and succeeding volumes, also "Descripcion Generale de las Monedas Hispano-Cristianas, etc.," by Alois Heiss, Madrid, 1865.   Charles abdicated October 25, 1555, retaining only the imperial titles used by the rulers of the " Holy Roman Empire."   Philip then succeeded as King in the Netherlands, and in Spain, February 5, 1556, which approximately fixes the date of these pieces.   Van Loon places them under 1555—the year 1555 Old Style, ending in March, 1556.—EDS.

Janus closed, before which Peace, laureated, and holding a cornucopia in her left hand and a torch in her right, is burning the trophies of war.

Silver. Size 25. V. L., I, 27. This Medal celebrates the Peace of Cambrai (Cateau-Cambresis), April 2, 1559.

4. 1559. *Obv.* Same legend and design, but apparently from a different die by the same engraver.

Rev. FELICITAS TEMPORVM Two right hands joined issuing from clouds; below the hands and across the field REGVM CONCORDIA. (The peace of kings is the happiness of the age.) Size 25. V. L., I, 27. Alludes to the same event.

5. 1559. *Obv.* PHILIPPVS · II · HISPAN · ET · NOVI ORBIS OCCIDVI · REX · [Translation above.] Bust to left in armor, draped; resembling preceding, but from still different dies.

Rev. · ISABELLA · VALES · PHILIPPI · II · HISP · REGIS · VX · (Isabella of Valois, wife of Philip II, King of Spain.) Bust to right in dress of the period, her hair richly dressed : under the bust, I · PAVL · PRC She was his third wife.

Silver. Size 22. V. L., I, 30. Commemorating their marriage, June 22, 1559 — the first fruits of the Peace.

6. 1559. *Obv.* PHILIPPVS HISPANIAR ET NOVI ORBIS OCCIDVI REX [Translation above.] Bust to left in armor, draped.

Rev. MARGARETHA · AB · (*in mon.*) · AVSTRIA · D · P · ET · P · GERM · INFER · G ·; on truncation ÆT · 43 : (Margaret of Austria, Duchess of Parma and Plaisance, Ruler [*gubernatrix*] of the Netherlands. Aged 43). Bust to right in close cap and dress.

Silver. Size 22. V. L., I, 38. This Princess, the natural daughter of the Emperor Charles V, was made ruler over Holland by her brother Philip, to conciliate the people, who had a great regard for the memory of that Emperor.

7. 1570. *Obv.* PHILIPPVS · II · HISPAN · ET · NOVI · ORBIS · OCCIDVI · REX [Translation above.] Similar design to 5.

Rev. ANNA · REGINA · PHILIPPI · II · HISPAN · REGIS · CATHOL · (Anne, Queen of Philip II, Catholic King of Spain). Bust to right in high ruff and cap of the period.

Silver. Size 26. V. L., I, 131.

8.   1570.   *Obv.* Same legend and design as the preceding.

Rev. ANNA · AVSTRIACA · PHILYPPI · CATHOL : (Anne of Austria, wife of Philip the Catholic :) on truncation of arm, ÆT. 21. (Aged 21.) Similar design and on the same event as the preceding ; the Queen wears a necklace of gems.

Silver.   Size 24.   V. L., I, 131.   Commemorates the fourth marriage of Philip, celebrated at Segovia, Nov. 12, 1570.

SIR FRANCIS DRAKE'S VOYAGE.

9.   1580.   *Obv.* D. F. DRA . EXITUS ANNO 1557 . ID . DEC^E —— REDITUS ANNO 1580 . 4 . CAL . OCT   (The departure of Sir Francis Drake in the year 1577 on the ides of December [Dec. 13] —— Return in the year 1580 on the 4th before the calends of October [Sept. 28].)   Map of North and South America, the course of Drake being indicated by a dotted line ; the map contains the following names and legends : AMERICA ; *meta incognita innenta ab Anglis* 1576 (unknown limits discovered by the English 1576); N. FRANC. ; *Virginia ;* FLORIDA ; NOVA ALBION *ab Anglis* 1580 *innenta* (New Albion discovered by the English 1580); CALIFORNIA ; BACALLAOS *ab Ang.* 1496; N. HISPANIA ; *Mexico ; Cuba ; Spaniola ; Jamaica ; Panama ;* CARIBANA ; *Lima ;* PERU ; AMERICA ; BRAZILIA ; *Chili ; Patagonis.*

Rev. A map of the Eastern Hemisphere, with the course of Drake indicated by a dotted line and the word *Reditus ;* the Cape of Good Hope marked BONA SPES.

Silver.   Struck in intaglio to imitate engraving.   Size 42. Med. Ill. Eliz., 83.   Brit. Mus. [The Viscount Dillon Collection, sold at auction 1892.]   Rare.

PORTUGUESE POSSESSIONS IN AMERICA TRANSFERRED TO SPAIN.

10.   1581.   *Obv.* PHILLIP · II · HISP · ET · NOVI · ORBIS · REX · (Philip II, King of Spain and of the New World.)   Bust of Philip II, three-quarters to right, wearing hat, cloak and ruff.

Rev. NON · SVFFICIT · ORBIS (One world is not enough.)   A horse leaping from a globe representing the earth.

Silver.   Size 32.   V. L., I, 282.

11. 1581. *Obv.* Same legend and design as the preceding.

Rev. RELIQVVM · DATVR. (The remainder is given.) A globe: the upper portion shows the meridians and parallels, and a band with zodiacal signs runs diagonally from the centre to the upper left circumference: the lower portion is plain.

Silver. Size 31. V. L., I, 282.

This and the preceding Medal were struck to commemorate the conquest of Portugal, by which the possessions of that kingdom in the New World fell into the hands of Philip. The line of division on the globe refers to the partition made by agreement between Spain and Portugal as to new discoveries, now abolished by the union of the two crowns, Sept. 2, 1580; the globe is said to hint at Philip's ambition to become the ruler of Christendom, still further disclosed on the next following Medals.

12. 1581. *Obv.* PHILIPPVS · II · HISPAN · ET · NOVI · ORBIS · OCCIDVI · REX · [Translated above.] Bust of Philip II, to left, in armor, draped, similar to those preceding.

Rev. RELIQVVM DATVRA. In exergue, INDIA (India about to give the remainder.) A woman typifying the Indies, followed by a camel (!) and a group of figures, representing other nations, offers a terrestrial globe to a ship symbolizing Spanish commerce.

Silver, cast and chased. Size 23. V. L., I, 283.

13. 1581. *Obv.* Similar to last: a knot of ribbon on the shoulder. I · PAVL · POG · F under truncation* (see 3).

Rev. HISPANIA · VTRIVSQ · ORBIS REGNATRIX · (Spain the mistress of both worlds). A woman in armor representing Spain, seated on a trophy of arms: a man upon one knee offers to her two keys, representing the East and the West Indies; Fame at left, flies towards her, and blows a trumpet above.

Silver. Size 23. V. L., I, 283.

---

* The I for Johannes, the Latin equivalent of Giovanni. John Paul Poggini was a Florentine medallist, from 1540–59, when he entered the service of Philip II; he probably died at Madrid about 1580.

14.   1581.   *Obv.* Same legend and design as the preceding ;
I . PAVL . POG . F (Giovanni Paolo Poggini, fecit) on truncation.*

Rev. Same as the preceding.

Copper.   Cast and chased.   Size 23.   Brit. Mus.

RALEIGH'S PLANTATION (?).

15.   1584. (?) *Obv.* ∗ AS ˙ SOONE ˙ AS ˙ WEE ˙ TO ˙ BEE . BEGVNN :
| ∗ WE ˙ DID ˙ BEGIN ˙ TO ˙ BE ˙ VNDONN :˙ :. in two circles
separated by lines, surrounding a full blown rose upon a stem
having two leaves.

Rev. A boy reclining to the right, his elbow upon a large
skull ; at his feet a rose growing ; behind him a bush, and a
house with three gables (?) in the distance.   No legend.

Brass, rude.   Size 18.   Very rare.   F. 3728.†

This Medal has been said to refer to Sir Walter Raleigh's unsuccessful attempt in 1584 to establish a colony on the coast
of North Carolina, under a patent from the Queen.   Its application to Raleigh or America is however extremely doubtful.

AMERICAN COMMERCE.

16.   1596.   *Obv.* SIDERE PROFICIANT DEXTRO NEPTVNIA
REGNA ✠   (May the kingdoms of the sea prosper beneath a
fortunate constellation.)   The legend is punctuated with small

---

* The difference between 13 and 14 appears to be chiefly in the place of the
die-cutter's name.   We do not find this mentioned in Med. Illus. — EDS.

† The engraving is not exactly correct, as we learn there was a serpent devouring its tail surrounding the reverse of the piece in F.   An engraving of a
similar reverse is given in Withers' Emblems (London, 1635, p. 45).   F., and
Atkins in his "Coins and Tokens of the Possessions and Colonies of the British Empire" (p. 250), attribute it to Raleigh : F., however (*loc. cit.*), seems to
doubt, for that gives the date as 1660, with a query, which is very likely correct ;
but if so, it can of course have no reference to America. — EDS.

quatrefoils.   Neptune seated on a dolphin, holding a trident in his right hand.   In the distance are two vessels under sail, and a city illumined by rays of glory proceding from יהוה [the name of JEHOVAH in Hebrew characters].

Rev. INSIGNIA FRISIÆ CISRHENANÆ   (Arms of Cis-Rhenic Frisia).   The arms of seven cities of Holland on small shields, with their names on scrolls between the devices on an outer circle; * in the field two lions holding a crown above the arms of West Frisia, azure billety gold, two lions passant gold.

Silver.   Size 29.   V. L., I, 447 [who gives the date 1596 in his description, which is not in his engraving].

17.   1596.   *Obv.* NVNC SPE NVNC METV 1596   (Now filled with hope, and now with fear) *m.m.* a castle.   Arion seated on a dolphin † playing a harp ; in the distance, a galley at the left and a city on the right ; in the field above, ARION.

Rev. LVCTOR ET EMERGO   (I strive and emerge); *m.m.* a castle.   Arms of Zealand (a demi-lion crowned over three bars wavy).   The legends on obverse and reverse are punc-tuated with small quatrefoils.

Silver.   Size 18.   V. L., I, 477.

This and the preceding commemorate the flourishing com-merce that began in 1696 by reason of prizes offered by the State for the discovery of a route to China.   The vessels of Holland visited Brazil, and returned laden with wood ; and the Island of St. Thomas, returning with cargoes of sugar.

VOYAGES TO AMERICA.

18.   1598.   *Obv.* SACRA ' ANCHORA ' CHRISTVS ✛   (Christ our Holy Anchor.)   Crowned arms of the Marine Council of West Frisia upon two anchors crossed.   P P P in the field, at

---

* The Cities are Alckmaar, Hoorn, Enckhuysen, Medemblick, Edam, Monick-endam, and Purmerend, the seven principal market cities. — EDS.

† The signification seems to be that as Arion was carried to the shore by a dolphin, after his companions had thrown him into the sea, so the Dutch voyagers might hope, in spite of their fears, for equal good fortune. — EDS.

right and left and below the anchor flukes. (For *Pugno pro patria*, I fight for fatherland.)

Rev. o ✠ o | QVI · NAVIGᴬT · | MARE · NARRANT · | PERICVLVM · EIVS · | QVOD · AVDIENTES · | AVRIB' · NOSTRIS · | ADMIRAMVR · | CIƆ · IC · XCVIII ·   (Those who navigate the sea relate its danger; hearing this with our ears, we wonder. 1598*). Inscription in seven lines beside the ornament at the top.

Silver.   Size 18.   V. L., I, 490.

A jeton struck by the Admiralty of North Holland to commemorate the voyages to the coast of America and Africa, and to China by the Straits of Magellan, and the wonders of those countries which filled all men's thoughts upon the return of the vessels.   The device denotes that as the anchor was the last resort of the mariner, so Christ was the last refuge of the Admiralty.   The legend of the reverse is from the Apocrypha (Ecclus. xliii : 26).

CAPTURE OF ST. THOMAS.

19.   1599.   *Obv.* MAVRITIVS · P · AVR · CO · NASS · CAT · MARC · VER · ET · VLIS · (Maurice, Prince of Orange, Count of Nassau, of Catzenellebogen, Marquis of Vere and of Flessingen.) Armored bust of Maurice, Prince of Orange, to right ; below, completing the legend, in small letters, C · FRIS · C · M · perhaps for Count of Frisia and Moers.

Rev. Fortune holding a sail which swells at her left, standing on a globe in the sea ; behind her, Neptune in his chariot ; in the distance, a city in flames.

Silver.   Size 20.   V. L., I, 519.

Struck to commemorate the victories of Admiral Van der Does, who sailed with sixty-six vessels to the Canaries, then belonging to Spain, and after their conquest sailed for Brazil. Having captured many Spanish merchantmen he proceeded to St. Thomas, and captured the City of Pavoasan (now Charlotte Amalie) with its forts.   Then loading the fleet with booty he was about to proceed upon other conquests, when he was seized with fever and died, together with about a

---

* It is IC not IƆ in Van Loon's engraving. — EDS.

thousand of his troops. Maurice, Prince of Orange, as Admiral-General, had planned this expedition, and receives the credit upon this medal and the following jeton.

20. 1599. *Obv.* EN · ALTERA · QVÆ · VEHAT · ARGO (See what [heroes*] the second Argo carries). The "Argo" or ship of Jason. יְהוָֹה [the name JEHOVAH] on the sail in Hebrew letters. On the waves beneath the ship, s. c.

Rev. SIC · NESCIA · CEDERE · FATA · CIƆ IƆ IC ● (Thus the Fates who know not how to yield, *i. e.* destiny cannot be changed. 1599). A landscape with islands and cities, among which stand two Termini or gods of boundaries; between them the Hebrew letters for JEHOVAH. The device represents the islands of Bommel and Thiel, and the deities denote that divine power had set a limit to Spanish dominion in the new world.

Size 17. V. L., I, 519.

Jeton struck to commemorate the same victories, and comparing the Holland Admiral to Jason.

HOLLAND COVETS SPANISH AMERICA.

21. 1602. *Obv.* POSSVNT QVÆ POSSE VIDENTVR 16 MARTY · 1602 · (They are able to do what seems to be possible; March

---

* The hemistich in Virgil, Eclog. IV: v. 34, supplies the missing word "heroes."— EDS.

16, 1602.) The Spanish galleon St. Jago between two Dutch ships, alluding to a naval combat when the Dutch drove the Spanish galleon ashore, at St. Helena, at the close of 1601.

Rev. NON SVFFICIT ORBIS (One world does not suffice,) on a ribbon.   A horse, with tail erect, leaping from a globe; [the device and motto* of Philip II of Spain, indicating his American possessions].   On the right of the horse and behind him, the lion of Zealand is leaping out of the sea.   On a ribbon behind the lion are the words : QVO SALTAS INSEQVAR (Whither thou leapest I will follow) ; a castle (mint mark of Tournay) between the ribbons, at the top.

The device of the reverse intimates the persistent rivalry of Holland and Spain in the New World.   The emblems are explained at length by Van Loon, who says that the motto of Philip, who by the conquest of Portugal had gained control of the commerce of both the Indies [see 11], was found by Drake, embroidered in gold on the throne of the Viceroy in San Domingo.

Silver.   Size 32.   V. L., I, 548.

PERU AND BRAZIL, DUTCH NAVAL VICTORIES.

22.   1624.   *Obv. Mauritius D. G. Princeps Auriacæ . Com. Nafs : &c., Prov: confœ Gub.* [Maurice, by the grace of God Prince of Orange, Count of Nassau, and Governor of the United Provinces.] Bust three-quarters right, nearly facing, in armor, with ruff and broad scarf, separated by a circle from an outer border of ornamental shields bearing the arms of the seven United Provinces ; and with the names GROENI . GELRIA . TRANSI . HOLLAN . FRISIA . ZEELAN . on ribbons, between the shields, and TRAIEC under the lowest one.   At the top, two hands clasped, and tied by a ribbon, hold a sheaf of seven arrows, alluding to the seven Provinces.   The legend as engraved, is in italic letters, within the bordering circle.

---

* From Juvenal, Satire X, v. 168.

Rev. Ie Maintiendray (I will maintain), on a tablet below the arms; at the bottom, very small, 16 *Cum Privil* 24. Within a laurel-wreath of two branches, alluding to the two victories, a crowned shield bearing the arms of Maurice, with inscription of the Order of the Garter (Honi · soit, etc.) of which he was a member.

Silver. Size 42. V. L., II, 155. Med. Ill. Jas. I., 91.

A Dutch medal, struck to commemorate the two victories gained in 1624 by the Dutch fleet, one over that of Spain, off Lima, Peru, under Admiral L.'Hermite, and the other on the coast of Brazil, under Admiral Willens.

CAPTURE OF TREASURE, MATANZAS.

23. 1628. *Obv.* GENTES · SERVIENT · EI · DONEC · VENIAT · TEMPUS · QUO · EADEM · AB · IPSO · SERVITUTEM · EXIGENT · *Jer. 27, v. 7.* ·:· (The nations shall serve him until the time come in which they shall serve themselves of him.* Jeremiah xxvii, 7.) Map of the Western Hemisphere, as conceived in the beginning of the 17th century, inscribed TROP CANC | LINEA ÆQUIN | TROPI CAPRICO.

Rev. VI · ID · SEPT · CIƆ · IƆ · CXXVIII · AVSPIC · | FOED · REGIM · BELG · SOCIET · IND· | OCCID · DUCTU · P · P · HEYNI · POTITA | EST · IN · ET · SUB · MATANZA · | SINU · CUBA · INS · REGIA · | CLASSE · ARGENTEA · | · REGNI · NOVAE · HISP. (On September 8th, 1628, the West India Company, under the auspices of the United Provinces of the Netherlands and under the command of Peter Heyn, the son of Peter, captured near Matanzas, a bay of the Island of Cuba, the royal silver [treasure] fleet of the Kingdom of New Spain.) Inscription in seven lines on the field below the device. Around the border FILIA · BABIL · QUASI · AREA · CALCABITUR · AB · AQUILONE · TEMPORE · MESSIS · EIUS · *Jerem. 51, v. 33 et 48.* (The daughter of Babylon is as a threshing floor; she shall be threshed

---

* Eadem for Eandem, but the line over the A, denoting the omitted N is lacking in the engraving. Mr. Betts gives the Bible version; more literally, "shall require the same service from him."—EDS.

[by the spoilers] from the north, in the time of her harvest.
Jeremiah li, v. 33 and 48.)   View of engagement between the
Dutch and Spanish fleets off Matanzas, Cuba, in which the
former captured the entire Spanish treasure fleet on its way
from Mexico to Spain.   [The allusion to "the spoilers from
the north" refers to the geographic position of the Dutch.]
    Silver.   Size 41.   V. L. II, 171.

24. 1629. *Obv.* NON FERRO TANTVM HISPANVS QVANTVM ·
VALET · AVRO : AVRVM · AVFER · FERRO · NON SVPERABIT IBER.
(The Spaniard is not so strong with the sword as with gold :
take away the gold, the Iberian will no longer win with the
sword.)* View of the Spanish treasure ships pursued into the
bay of Matanzas ; seventeen vessels and ten launches being
shown.
    Rev. INDICA CLASSE | INTERCEPTA, PAR- | TISQ. SINE ·
SANGVINE | OPVLENTISSIMIS · SPO- | LIIS, AD CVBÆ PORTVM, |
HISPANORVM NVNC DA- | MNIS QVAM OLIM CÆDE, | NOBILIOREM,
FOEDERATÆ | BELGICO—GERMANIÆ | PROCERES E. GAZA · CA- |
PTIVA · MONVMENTVM | CVDI FECERVNT . | CIↃ DC XXIX. | *Cum
Privil.* (The fleet of the Indies being cut off, and very rich
booty taken without bloodshed, at the Bay of Cuba, now more
celebrated by the [pecuniary] loss of the Spaniards than formerly by their defeat, the chiefs of the United Provinces of
the Netherlands have caused this medal to be struck from
the captured silver. 1629. With privilege.) Inscription in
thirteen lines, a cross crosslet at the top.
    Silver.   Size 37.   V. L., II, 171.
    Commemorates the same event ; the date is that of striking.

25. 1629. *Obv.* Same legend as last, and similar design,
but execution different, seventeen vessels and five launches
being shown, and the shore being less rocky.
    Rev. Same legend and arrangement as last, but from a dif-
ferent die.
    Silver.   Size 37.   (Not in V. L.)

---

* This legend is an elegiac distich, the first verse ending with AVRO.—EDS.

PETER HEYN, VICTOR AT MATANZAS.

26. 1629. *Obv.* PET : PETRI : HEINIVS . FOED : BELG : ORD : ARCHITHALASS . (Peter Heyn, the son of Peter, Admiral of the United States of the Netherlands).   Bust of Heyn facing, in ornate armor and wearing a ruff and quadruple chain.

Rev. HEINIAD NVP SENSIT SPOLIATA MATANCA (Pillaged Matanzas has lately felt the power of the nation of Heyn,)

1628 in exergue, date of the victory. View of the capture of
the Spanish galleons ; a large number of vessels and a few
boats being shown.

Silver. Size 37. V. L., II, 171.

27. 1629. *Obv.* NOCH SILVER GOVT NOCH STAET DE DEVGT
TE BOVEN GAET • (Neither silver, gold nor rank, surpass courage, — a rhyming couplet in the original.) Bust of Heyn facing, similar to last, but different style of ruff ; the chain he
wears, was a gift from the States.

Rev. SILVERVLOOT | 1628 (Silver-fleet) on an ornamental
tablet under a view of the fleet entering the harbor of Matanzas.

Silver. Size 29. V. L., II, 171.

28. 1629. *Obv.* AFBEELDINGE V . VERMAERDEN HELT
PIETER PIETERZ HEYN. (Portrait of the famous hero Peter
Heyn, the son of Peter.) Half length figure of Heyn facing,
in armor and ruff, leaning upon a lance ; in the field at his
left, AD (Admiral) engraved, and 16–99 deeply stamped with
punches.

Rev. View of the Admiral's ship between two vessels of
the enemy entering a harbor, [Dunkirk] four castles on a hill,
enclosed within a circle ; above the circle, view of two ships,
a schooner and two small boats ;* around the lower part of
the circle are nine smaller circles, one containing the arms of
Orange or Nassau, and the others have lions rampant, a griffin,
a pelican, a falcon, Neptune, etc. ; no legend.

Struck upon the death of Heyn, who fell in battle with the
enemy's fleet off Dunkirk in June, 1629.

Silver, cast and chased, the legend on obv. and the views
on rev. being engraved , the date, 1699, being deeply stamped
with punches, on the impression examined, doubtless at a later
period.   Size 30.

---

* This description is apparently of a medal examined by Mr. Betts, and unknown to us, for it varies in some particulars from that engraved by Van Loon.
—EDS.

29. *Obv.* Similar to the preceding, but without the date.

Rev. Similar to the preceding; five vessels entering a harbor, with houses and fortifications: a circle surrounds the view, at the top of which is a fleet, the sterns of the ships showing; and around the remaining portion of the enclosing circle are small circular tablets, bearing armorial devices, as described in the previous number, which Van Loon supposes to be the arms of the officers of the fleet engaged.

' Silver. Size 30. V. L., II, 183.

CAPTURE OF PERNAMBUCO.

30. *Obv.* AUREA CONDET | SÆCULA (He founds the golden age). on a tablet upheld by a cherub. Bust of Frederic Henry, Prince of Orange, three-quarters to the right, in a cartouche, or ornate tablet; the Prince in armor, wears a square collar trimmed with broad lace; MARS on the left who holds a blazoned shield, and VICTORIA on the right holding a palm branch in her left hand, support a crown of laurel above. Below, view of a city, SHERTOGHENBOS | . 1629. — 16 — 30 . A . VD . WILGE .

Rev. The Belgian lion on shield, supported by Prudence who holds a serpent, and Constancy leaning on a column; angels hold wreath above. Below are four cartouches, representing views of three cities and a sea fight, inscribed 1627 GROL.; 1629 WESEL.; 1628 SYLVER VLOOT ; 1630 PERNAMBVCO. Above is the legend AVSPICIIS ADSIT VICTRIX CONCORDIA, (May victorious peace be present with her [favoring] auspices); the Hebrew letters for Jehovah divide the legend at the top; CVM PREVII. (with privilege) *sic*, at the bottom.

Commemorates the capture of Pernambuco in Brazil by the Spanish, and the other victories named, by reason of which the Dutch considered themselves masters not only of Brazil, but of all America.

31. 1631. *Obv. Aurea Condet Sæcula* (italic). Similar design to preceding, but with VICTORI instead of VICTORIA under the figure on the right, and SHERTOGENBOS, and with A.VD.

[in monogram] W. in exergue on obverse. For A. Van Der Wilge, the die-cutter's initials, as appears from the preceding.

Rev. Similar design, but the dates are *below* the names in the cartouches, and the date 16–31 appears in the field.

Silver.   Size 42.   V. L., II, 190.

VICTORY AT BAY OF ALL SAINTS.

32. 1631.   *Obv.* PHILIP · IIII · HISP · INDIAR · REX · CATH-OLICVS (Philip IV, Catholic King of Spain and the Indies). Bust to left, armored, draped and with ruff; below bust ƆIIƆCXXXI.

Rev. DVLCIA · SIC · MERVIT (Thus he deserved joys). Samson rending the lion.   On a stone below, 1631.

Medal and copper jeton.   The device is the same on both pieces, but there are slight differences in the dies.   The letters on the jeton are a little larger, as engraved by Van Loon; there is a mint mark (?) after DVLCIA on the reverse, and the position of the date and the bottom of the bust also differ slightly.   Both, size 18.   V. L., II, 192.

Commemorating victory over Dutch ships at the Bay of All Saints; the lion typifies the device of Holland.

DUTCH NAVAL VICTORY IN AMERICA.

33. 1631.   *Obv.* FREDER · HENR · D · G · PRINCEPS · AVRIAC · COM · NASS   (Frederic Henry, by the grace of God, Prince of

Orange, Count of Nassau).   Bust in profile to right, armored, with falling, broad lace collar.

Rev. HERCVLEAS   VLTRA EXTV   LIT COLV̄NAS   Between the base of the pillars CONCVSSIT | VTRAM- | QVE and in exergue 1631   (He has extended [his bounds] beyond the columns of Hercules ; he has struck each of them).   The columns of Hercules, one of which the Belgian lion is pulling from its place.   The capitals of the columns extend into the legend.

Size 31.   V. L., II, 198.

CHAPTER II.

A GRANT was made by James I, in 1606, to the London Company and the Bristol Company, of all the land lying between the thirty-fourth and forty-fifth parallels, from the Atlantic Ocean westward. Both Companies immediately commenced adventures, the London Company south of the Chesapeake Bay, and the Bristol Company eastward at the Kennebec. In 1620 the Bristol Company received a new charter with the name, The Council of Plymouth in New England, and it made grants of land under the name, The New England Company.

James also granted to George Calvert, the first Lord Baltimore, an extensive territory in Newfoundland, where in 1621 that nobleman planted a Colony which he called Avalonia, and not only sustained it at large expense for many years, but gave it his personal supervision. The curious blunder of a writer in the *American Historical Magazine*, who thought the so-called Avalonia token was an issue for this Colony, and elaborated his theory in a very learned paper, but which was only a Glastonbury (England) token, should be mentioned in passing. The absurdity of this theory has been so clearly shown by Mr. William S. Appleton and others, in the *American Journal of Numismatics** and elsewhere, that further reference is unnecessary.

Sir William Alexander, the Earl of Stirling, received a Charter in 1621, for the territory of Nova Scotia, and struck some copper coins, which circulated for a time in Scotland.† Possibly he may have designed that these should also be used in his Colony, but this coinage and the Baltimore money are not properly within the limits of this work.

Carolina was created by Charles I, in 1630, by a grant to Sir Robert Heath of all the land between the thirty-first and thirty-sixth parallels, and from the Atlantic to the South Seas. In 1635 the London and New England Companies surrendered their patents, and new grants were afterwards procured ; but during the Civil War the settlements were made without reference to these grants. Upon the restoration, Charles II gave charters to the various Colonies, and, among other grants, he gave to several noblemen and gentlemen all the country between 31° and 36° 30′ north latitude, and from ocean to ocean, under the name of Carolina. The old patent to Heath under this same name does not seem to have been surrendered, and Sir Daniel Cox attempted to revive it in 1698.

The London, New England and Carolina Companies thus appear to have been the chief agents in the English settlement of America, and the three medals bearing the prayer for their preservation, to be described below, are thought by many to be commemorative of this fact. The elephant, if cut for the reverse, as there is reason to doubt, is very remarkable. There is excellent ground for believing that the suggestion made by Snelling in 1769, — "that the Elephant tokens" were originally struck in 1694, in memory of the visitation of the plague in 1665,‡ and that the prayer was really for the preservation of the "Lords Proprietors" from that terrible disease — is the true explanation. If this be the case, the

---

tokens have no allusion in any way to the unknown beasts of the New World; but the mastodon mounds at the west, and the remains of such creatures discovered in New Jersey, seem to show that after all the device did not lack, however unconscious of the fact those who used it may have been, a certain appropriateness.

The French made their first settlement in Canada in 1541, under Jacques Cartier, who gave its name to the St. Lawrence; but the first permanent settlement of " New France " was made in 1608, on the present site of Quebec, — and the first French Medal which relates to their possessions, properly belonging to this period, is that of the Viceroy D'Ampville, struck in 1658.

MARYLAND SETTLED.

34. 1632. *Obv.* DMS . CÆCILIVS . BARO . DE . BALTEMORE . ABSOLV . DMS . TERRÆMARIÆ . ET . AVALONIÆ . &c. (Lord Cecil, Baron Baltimore, Lord Paramount of Maryland and Avalon, &c.). Bust of Lord Baltimore, three-quarters right, in armor.* Mint-mark, Cross.

Rev. DNA . ANNA . ARVNDELIA . PVLCHERRIMA ET . OPTIMA . CONIVX . CÆCILII . PREDICTI . (Lady Anne Arundel, the most beautiful and excellent wife of the said Cecil). Bust of Lady Baltimore, three-quarters right. Mint-mark, Cross.

Silver, cast and chased, with ring. Size 29½. Very rare. Med. Ill. Chas. I, 52.

35. 1632. *Obv.* ✠ CÆCILIVS : BALTEMOREVS. ✠ • Bust of Lord Baltimore to left in armor with scarf.

Rev. ✠ VT : SOL : LVCEBIS : AMERICÆ (As the sun thou shalt illumine America). TERAMARIÆ (Maryland). Map of Maryland, showing the Chesapeake and Potomac and trees upon the land : the sun above ; the arms of Calvert crowned above the centre of the map.

---

* Baltemore on the Medal. Cecil, the first proprietor and second Lord Baltimore, was the son of George Calvert, who died before the grant was legally executed. Lady Anne was the daughter of Thomas, first Lord Arundel of Wardour. The rosette after the cross on obverse of 35 is a mint-mark. — EDS.

Silver, cast and chased.*   Elliptical, size 21 x 24.   Med. Ill. Chas. I, 53.

36.   1632.   *Obv.* EGO CORPORA IVNGAT CORDA DEVS (I [unite] their bodies ; may God unite their hearts).   CÆCILIVS on a ribbon binding six arrows.   VIS . VNITA . FORTIOR . (United power is stronger) on a band below.

Rev. CÆCILIVS BALTEMOREVS ET ANNA ARVNDELIA VXOR EIVS ∴ (Cecil Baltimore and Anne Arundel his wife).   On a band COR . VNVM . ET . ANIMA . VNA (One heart and one mind).   Field plain for inscribing name of recipient.

Silver, with ring : R. 1.   Size 30.   Med. Ill.† Chas. I, 54.

CAPTURE OF LARRAYAL, BRAZIL.

37.   1637.   *Obv.* VICTRICEM ACCIPE LAVRVM above, and HOSTIS HISPAN' PROFLIGAT below (Accept the laurel of victory ; the Spanish enemies are vanquished).   Trophy of arms upon a column, with shield of Portugal, erected to Artischofski for his capture of Fort Larrayal, in Brazil ; behind it a view of the fort and encampment.

Rev. Inscription in thirteen lines, a space between the seventh and eighth,‡ HEROI | GENERIS NOBILITATE | ARMO-

---

* The expression "cast and chased" is adopted by Mr. Betts from " Medallic Illustrations."   It is applied to Medals which were cast, (not struck), and then "worked over with sand-paper or some fine instrument, and in many cases a graving-tool was used to emphasize the outlines, or to reproduce the finer lines, such as the indications of hair which could hardly be left distinct after the casting.   When this additional process has been used, the Medal is described as cast and chased." — EDS.

† The specimen in the British Museum is an electrotype from a silver original, possibly unique, in Sir W. Eden's collection.   Designed for presentation. — EDS.

‡ Artischofski was a Pole of noble family, who served the States of Holland for three years.   Fort Larrayal was a Portuguese strong-hold on a high hill called " Autero del Conde," near Affogados, and the river of that name (now called Capibaribe).   By its capture he freed the possessions of Holland in Brazil from Portuguese interference, and a monument of stone was erected in honor of the event.   We follow the capitals and punctuation of the engraving, which is not uniform.   REB in line 6 (for Rebus) is improperly united with the preceding word in the engraving. — EDS.

RUM . ET . LITTERARUM | SCIENTIA LONGE PRÆSTANTISSIMO |
CHRISTOPH : AB ARTISCHAU ARCI | SZEWSKIREB IN BRAZILIA
PER TRIENNI | PRUDENTISS : FORTISS. FELICISS. GESTIS | SO-
CIETAS · AMERICANA | SVÆ GRATITUDINIS · ET IPSIUS | FOR-
TITUDINIS · AC FIDEI · HOC | MONUMENTUM ESSE VOLUIT | ANNO
A CHR. NATO | clɔ Iɔc · XXXVII (The affairs of Brazil having
been most prudently, bravely and happily managed for three
years by Christopher Artischofski Arciszewski, a hero most
distinguished in nobility of race and in knowledge of arms
and letters ; the American Company has desired this [medal]
to be a monument of its gratitude and his valor and fidelity.
In the year from the birth of Christ 1637.)

Size 39½.   V. L., II, 235.

DUTCH VICTORY AT PARIBA.

38.   1640.   *Obv.* I · MAVRITS · GRAEF · VAN · NASSAV · GEN-
ERAEL. · VAN BRAZIL · (John Maurice, Count of Nassau, Governor General of [the AN of VAN in monogram] Brazil.)
Bust of Maurice, in armor and broad lace collar and sash,
three-quarters to right, nearly facing.

Rev. GOD . SLOEG. S VIANDS HOOGMOED · DEN. 12 . 13 . 14.
17 IAN. ● (God has destroyed the pride of the enemy, Jan. 12,
etc., 1640.)   View of naval engagement.   In the field, above,
1640.

Size 29 x 25½, elliptical.   V. L., II, 247.

Medal struck to commemorate the victory of the Dutch
Admirals William Loos and James Huygens, with forty-one
ships over the Spanish Admiral Ferdinand Mascarenhas,
with ninety-three ships, before Pas Amorelle and on the coast
of Pariba.   In the first day of the battle which lasted four
days, Loos was killed, and Huygens took command.

We pass several gold pieces, struck by the West India
Company in 1646, for Brazil, described and illustrated by Van
Loon, II, 283, as being money of necessity, and not Medals,
and the well known pieces referring to Carthagena, in Spain,

struck by Louis XIV, which, because they bear the name Nova Carthagena, have been erroneously thought to relate to the City of Carthagena in South America.*

DAMPVILLE, VICEROY OF AMERICA.

39. 1658. *Obv.* · FR · CHRIST · DE · LEVI · D · DAMPVILLE · P · FRANC · PROREX · AMERICAE · I · HARDY · F · 1658 · (Francis Christopher de Levi, Duke of Dampville, Peer of France. Viceroy of America). Bust in armor to the right, with long hair streaming over the shoulders.

Rev. · EX · TE · ENIM · EXIET · DVX · QVI · REGAT · POPVLVM · MEVM · (For out of thee shall come a governor who shall rule my people). Arms quartered on an ermine mantle surmounted by a ducal coronet.†

Silver and copper. Size 32. T. N., Pt. III, pl. 6. A. J. N., IX, 70; XIV, 44; Cana. Ant. and Num. Jour., Oct., 1874, McL., XV. This has been restruck in both metals.

---

* Even the compiler of the Fonrobert Catalogue fell into this error. — EDS.

† The blazon of the arms and some account of De Levi are given in the American and Canadian Journals, *loc. cit.* The legend of the reverse is from Micah v : 2, Vulgate. — EDS.

‡ We may here mention that many of the French Medals herein described have been restruck; these may be known by the edge, where the name of the metal is incused. — EDS.

COMPANY OF THE INDIES.

40. 1664. *Obv.* LUDOVICUS XIIII · REX CHRISTIANISSIMUS · J · MAVGER · F · (Louis XIV, Most Christian King). Bust to right, undraped.

Rev. JUGENDIS COMMERCIO GENTIBUS · In exergue SOCIE-TATES NEGOTIATORUM | IN UTRAMQUE INDIAM · | M · DC · LXIV · (Nations united by Commerce. The Societies of Merchants to both Indies, 1664). Mercury standing with the caduceus in his right hand, and in his left a bag of money ; in the background bales of merchandise and a blazing altar with banner ; two ships under sail at left.

Silver and bronze. Size 26.

41. 1664. *Obv.* LUDOVICUS MAGNUS REX CHRISTIANISSIMUS. (Louis the Great, etc.). Bust of the King to the right, undraped.

Rev. Same design and legend as last.

Size 40. No specimen known. Med. Louis le Grand, p. 82. Die not now in the mint.

CONQUEST OF ST. CHRISTOPHER.

42. 1666. *Obv.* LUDOVICUS XIIII · REX CHRISTIANISSIMUS · ——— I · MAVGER · F · Bust of the King to right, without drapery.

Rev. COLONIA FR · STABILITA · In exergue ANGL · EX INSULA ST · CHRISTOP · | EXTURBAT · | M · DC · LXVI · (The French colony established. England driven from the Island of St.

Christopher, 1666). An Indian queen seated upon a rock, holding the shield of France, and the shield of Britain at her feet ; at her left a tobacco plant.*

Silver, B. N., and copper. Size 26.

FAIRFAX, VIRGINIA.

43. 1665. *Obv.* HENRY FAYRFAX. ✠ Shield with arms of Fairfax, and crescent indicating the second son.

Rev. Crest, a lion's head erased on a wreath ; scroll border.

Size 24. Electrotype in British Museum ; original not known. Med. Ill. Chas. II, 153.

Henry, fourth Lord Fairfax, emigrated to America, and Fairfax County, Virginia, was named in honor of the family.†

COLONIZATION MEDAL.

44. 1670. *Obv.* CAROLVS · ET · CATHARINA · REX · ET · REGINA. (Charles and Catharine, King and Queen). Busts of King and Queen conjoined to right.

Rev. DIFFVSVS · IN · ORBE · BRITANNVS ✠ 1670 (The Briton dispersed over the globe). Globe, with portions of all four continents. By his marriage with Catharine of Portugal, the King of England gained a foothold in the East Indies and South America, which are prominent on the Medal.

Gold and silver. Size 26. Med. Ill. Chas. II, 203.

Colonization medal by Roettier.

---

* This, like most of the Medals of the period, has been restruck, muled with a younger bust, unless that is the original, as seems more probable.—EDS.

† The date is that assigned with a query in Med. Ill.— EDS.

INDIAN MEDALS, VIRGINIA.

These three medals, 45, 46, 47, are, we suppose, engraved, and were badges required to be worn by Indians coming within the limits of the white settlements.* [See Henning's Statutes at Large, II, 141.]

45. *Obv.* CHARLES II KING OF ENGLAND SCOTLAND FRANCE IRELAND AND VIRGINIA. Shield with royal arms, and in one corner a tobacco (?) plant ; the ribbon of the garter surrounding the shield with motto HONI SOIT QUI MAL Y PENSE (Evil to him who evil thinks); above is the royal crown, below in an oblong surface, THE QUEEN OF PAMUNKY.†

• *Rev.* Plain with five rings for attaching the medal.

Silver, oblong and central convex disk. Size 4 x 6 in. A. J. N., V, 82 ; X, 86. Collection of Dr. M. P. Scott, Baltimore.

46. *Obv.* Same as the last, except that the inscription in the oblong space is YE KING OF PAMUNKEE.

Rev. Same as the last.

Silver, oblong and convex, as the last. Size 4 x 6 in. A. J. N., V, 82 ; [See Willis's Current Notes, London, 1862.] Virginia Historical Society.

47. *Obv.* YE KING OF   A tobacco plant.

Rev. PATOMACK.   A tobacco plant.

"Irregular shape." A. J. N., II, 84; V, 82. Formerly in the possession of the Virginia Historical Society.‡   •

---

* The descriptions of these three Indian Medals are approximate only. The Indians of the different tribes probably wore them on these visits to indicate who were their chiefs, as these were held responsible for any pilfering, etc.—EDS.

† "The 'Pamunkeys' were a tribe of Indians in Virginia, 1722. See 'Byrd Papers,' Richmond, 1866." A. J. N., VI : 47. The conventional translation of the motto of the Order of the Garter is here given. Any discussion on its correctness by us would be out of place. See Force's Tracts, I : Tract 8, "The Beginning, Progress and Conclusion of Bacon's Rebellion in Virginia, 1675-76," on page 14 of which is an interesting account of the Queen of Pamunkey.—EDS.

‡ The citations in A. J. N. leave it uncertain whether the words there, — "the inscription, 'Ye King of Patomeck' divided, a part on each side of the medal, on which is . . . . a tobacco plant "—refer to the obverse and reverse, or to the sides of the face of the medal, the plant dividing the inscription. — EDS.

VICTORY AT MARTINIQUE.

48.   1674. *Obv.* LUDOVICUS MAGNUS REX CHRISTIANISSIMUS.
Under decollation ﹐·ᴍᴀᴠɢᴇʀ·ᴘ· Bust to right, without drapery,
and long flowing hair.*

Rev. COLONIA FRANCORUM AMERICANA VICTRIX . In exergue
BATAVIS AD MARTINICAM | CAESIS AC FUGATIS · | M · DC ·
LXXIIII . (The American Colony of the French victorious ;
the Dutch slain and put to flight at Martinique, 1674).   An
Indian crowned, with bow and quiver at his back, stands
astonished beside a wounded female captive, typifying the
Dutch Republic ; Fame flying above, holding a wreath in her
left hand and a trumpet in her right ; the stern of a galley
at the left, a flag, an anchor [not shown in the cut], etc., in
background.

Gold, silver and copper.   Size 26.   V. L., III, 148.

49.   1674. *Obv.* Design and legend similar to last.
Rev. As last, except error in date, given M . DC . LXIV.
Size 26.   Med. Louis le Grand, Ed. 1723, 138.   No such
medal known ; no such dies now exist in the Paris mint.

Admiral Ruyter made his attack in the latter part of July,
1674, but found the fort so well protected that he was unable
to carry it by assault ; and his principal officers and a large
number of his troops having been wounded or slain, he left
the island by night and returned to Holland.

---

* Jean Mauger worked at Paris, 1664–1722 ; but little is known of him. — EDS.

RECOVERY OF CAYENNE.

50.   1676. *Obv.* LUDOVICUS MAGNUS REX CHRISTIANISSIMUS. Under truncation, I·MAVGER·F· Bust of the King to right, with long flowing hair, and undraped ; similar to 48, but from a different die.

Rev. BATAVIS CAESIS. In exergue, in two lines curving upward, CAYANA RECUPERATA. | M ·DC ·LXXVI. (The Dutch slain, Cayenne recovered, 1676). Neptune rising from the sea driving four sea-horses and seated in a shell, holding aloft a trident in his right hand and in his left the banner of France ; in the distance a castle on the shore.

Gold, silver and copper. Size 26. B. N. Med. Louis le Grand, Ed. 1702, 158. V. L., III, 188.

51. 1676. *Obv.* Similar legend and design, without engraver's name.

Rev. Similar design and same legend, except in exergue, which is CAYANA RECUPERATA | MENSE DECEMBRI. | M. DC. LXXVI. (Cayenne recovered, in the month of December, 1676.)

Size —. Med. Louis le Grand, 157. No specimen known ; no such dies now exist in the Paris mint.

Cayenne was colonized by the French in 1664; captured by the Dutch, 1675 ; and recovered by the French in 1676. Count d'Estrées arrived Dec. 17, in that year, and landing 800 men, summoned the garrison to surrender, and upon its refusal he took the place by a night assault.

VICTORY AT TABAGO.

52. 1677. *Obv.* LUDOVICUS MAGNUS REX CHRISTIANISSI-
MUS. Under truncation, J. MAVGER. F. Similar to 50.

Rev. INCENSA BATAVORUM CLASSE. (The fleet of the Dutch
burned). Female figure (Victory) alighting on galley, with
torch (? or thunderbolt) in her right hand, and in her left a
palm branch; a paddle at the left. Her face is turned to
the left. In exergue, AD INS . TABAGO . | M . DC . LXXVII.
(At the Island of Tobago. 1677.)

Silver and copper. Size 26. V. L., III, 208.

53. 1677. *Obv.* LVDOVICVS ' MAGNVS ' REX CHRISTIANISSI-
MVS ' Under truncation, ANT . MEYBVSCH . F. Bust of the King to
the right, draped.*

Rev. INCENSA ' BATAVORVM ' CLASSE ' In exergue, TABAGO. |
. MDCLXXVII . (The fleet of the Dutch burned. Tobago,
1677). Similar design to last, except that Victory holds a
cluster of arrows, her face is turned toward the right, clouds
are behind her; her drapery floats to the right instead of the
left, as on the preceding; the galley is floating on the sea, and
the paddle is omitted.

Gold and silver; and in copper cast with ring for suspension. Size 43. B. N. V. L., III, 208.

54. 1677. *Obv.* Similar to last, but from different die;
bust without armor, draped; R. below the bust.

---

* Meybusch was a Dane, but worked at Paris with Roettier and others about
1677 to 1690, when he returned to Copenhagen, and died in 1701. — EDM.

Rev. Same die as last.

Bronze. Size 43. B. N. (Not mentioned by Van Loon.)

55. 1677. *Obv.* Design and legend same as last, but without name of maker.

Rev. Design and legend same as last, except that the inscription in exergue is AD INSULAM TABAGO | III . MARTI | M . DC . LXXVII . (At the island of Tobago, March 3, 1677.).

Size —. Med. Louis le Grand, 158. No specimen known ; no such dies now exist in the Paris mint.

56. 1677. *Obv.* LVDOVICVS MAG : REX CHRISTIANISS : Under the bust, A . MEYBUSCH F . Bust of the King to right, without drapery.

Rev. INCENSA BATAVORVM CLASSE. In exergue, TABAGO . | 1677. (The fleet of the Dutch burned at Tobago, 1677.) Design similar to last.

Silver. Size 18. V. L., III, 208.

57. 1677. *Obv.* LVDOVICVS · MAGNVS · REX. Under the bust, N. (Nyris, a French die-sinker, 1675–95.) Bust of King to right, without drapery.

Rev. * INCENSA * BATAVORVM * CLASSE * Similar to the preceding ; but no water is indicated beneath the galley.

Brass counter. Size 16.

58. 1677. *Obv.* LVDOVICVS · MAGNVS · Under the bust, LGL · (Lazarus Gottlieb Laufer, mint-master in Nuremberg, 1670–90.) Design similar to last.

Rev. INCENSA · BATAVORVM · CLASSE · Design similar to last. Exergue plain.

Brass counter. Size 16. V. L., III, 208.

59. 1677. *Obv.* Similar to 50.

Rev. TABAGUM EXPUGNATUM   In exergue curving upwards,
M · DC · LXXVII (Tobago taken by assault, 1677.)   View of
Tobago attacked by eleven vessels, and the magazine explod-
ing by a bomb thrown from a mortar on the shore at the left

Silver and copper.   Size 26.   V. L., III, 210.*

60. 1677. *Obv.* Similar to 59: no engraver's name.

Rev. Design and legend same as last, except that the
inscription in exergue is XII . DECEMBRIS . | M . DC . LXXVII .

Size —.   Med. Louis le Grand, 166.   No specimen is
known ; no such dies are now in the Paris mint.

61. 1677. *Obv.* LOVIS · XIV · ROY · DE · FR · ET · DE · NAV
(Louis XIV, King of France and Navarre.)   Bust of the
King to right, in armor.

Rev. IGNIBVS · ICTVS · CONGEMINAT ·   In exergue, 1677.
(He combines fire with his assaults.)   A mortar in the foreground throwing a bomb into the fort of Tobago.

Size 16.   V. L., III, 210.

---

* The fort at Tabago was under the command of Binkes, and was resolutely
defended against Count d'Estrees, who the year before had stormed and retaken
Cayenne (see 50, 51); on the 9th December, 1677, he summoned it to surrender,
but Binkes was determined to hold it to the last.   The Count opened fire on the
place two days later, and finding his ships insufficient to reduce the fort, he
erected a mortar battery on the shore; the third bomb which was thrown, fell
on the magazine of the Dutch, which exploded, burying in its ruins the brave
commander and nearly all his officers : the French stormed the fort in the confusion which followed, but even then the defence was so stubborn that the Dutch
were able to gain terms from the Count, as a condition of the surrender of the
position.   The fortunate shot is commemorated on the medal.—EDS.

RELIGIOUS MEDALS FOR THE INDIANS.

62. 1682. *Obv.* N . S . D . GVADALVPE . DE .   Below, MEX-
ICO . OR . PR . N . ROMA . (*For* Nuestra Señora de Guadalupe,
etc., Ora Pro Nobis : Our Lady of Guadalupe of Mexico, pray
for us.) The Virgin standing upon a crescent and clouds,
and surrounded by a glory.   In field, 16 — 82.

Rev. SAN | FRANCESCO . O . P . [? N.] (St. Francis, pray for
us.) Bust of St. Francis to right in monk's dress gazing
upward ; his hands crossed ; a halo surrounding his head.

Brass, with loop and ring for suspension ; elliptical.   Size
29 x 24.   Originally struck for Mexican Indians. (?)

63. 1687. *Obv.* SANTA . ROSA . DE . LIMA . ORD . (ROM . ?)
Bust of female saint facing the right.

Rev. DE PAVL   Bust of St. Paul facing the left, with arms
crossed and holding the [crucifix ?] in his left hand.

Elliptical, with loop for suspension.   Size 10 x 8.

Found on the site of an Indian village at Scipioville, Cayuga County, N. Y.   The Cayuga Mission was begun in 1656,
and lasted to 1687.   The village at Scipioville was probably
of captive Hurons.   A large number of other religious medals
and several crosses were found on the same site ; but no
others have reference in their legends to America.*   This
seems to have been struck for Peruvians.

---

* We do not know the precise causes which led Mr Betts to place these
two pieces (62, 63) here, and we have been unable to verify his descriptions. To
us these seem to belong to the religious medals of the Roman Church, and to
a much later period, but we do not feel at liberty to exclude them. St. Rose of
Lima, the patroness of that city, is a popular Saint among the French Cana-
dians, even to the present day, and " Delima," the closing portion of her title,
is frequently used as a baptismal name. Mr. Betts very properly excludes two
Medals described as Canadian by Leroux ; one of Cardinal Richelieu (302),
whose only claim rests on the fact that he is said to have organized a Canadian
Trading Company, and to have been " the protector of the Colony ; " the other,
(304), is of Jean Varin, struck in 1684, who, he says, " was the first Intendant
General of Canada." He was a famous engraver of dies, and Superintendent of
the French Mint. We can find nothing to show that he ever had anything to do
with Canadian affairs, and believe that Leroux was misled by his reading of the
obverse legend. — EDS.

DUTCH WEST INDIA COMPANY.

64. 1683. *Obv.* SOCIETAT . IND . OCCID . DIRECTORES . GRON . ET ˙ OM • (The Directors of the Company of the West Indies for Groningen and Ommelande) G W C V G O (abbreviation for " Geoctroieerde Westindische Camer Van Groninge en de Ommelanden " — Incorporated West India Company, Chamber of Groningen and of Ommelande) in monogram in the centre, surrounded by twelve crowned shields bearing the arms of the Directors, within a beaded circle.

Rev. FVLCRA . NON . MINIMA . 1683. • S. G. DEL MINA (? Not the smallest support. St. George Del Mina) in the field at the left, above a view of that fort, with banner flying from its citadel ; on the right a town upon the hill ; in the foreground a ship sailing to left.*

Gold and silver.   Size 27.   V. L., III, 284.

---

* The meaning of this legend is not evident.   The word on the Medal is clearly Fulgra (Fulgura ?) as engraved by Van Loon, but he translates it as if Fulcra — the point on which the lever turns (*De puissans soutiens*, i. e., The upholder of the power.)   If we read Fulgra, instead of Fulcra, "Not the least brilliant," would perhaps be intended.   The Medal had its origin in a quarrel between two rival mercantile corporations, and this was struck by the successful one.   Van Loon, however, does not profess to explain it entirely, and remarks that some believe it to have been originally struck from gold left by the Governor General of Del Mina in his will, to the Directors of the Company named, and distributed among them.   The twelve shields bear the arms of the twelve Directors, whose names are given by Van Loon.—EDS.

MORTUARY MEDAL, CURACOA.

65. 1687. *Obv. Salic syn | die Dooden | die in den Heere | sterve | want sy Riisten Van | Horen | ar | Beyt.* (Blessed are the dead who die in the Lord, for they rest from their labors). A skull, crowned with laurel, and cross-bones supporting a winged hour-glass, behind which are two scythes crossed ; the legend being upon a ribbon floating around them ; below the skull in an oval space with a wreath of grasses *Homo | Memento | Mori* (Man, remember that thou must die.)

Rev. Ter Gedachtenis | *Van | Ariana Toffeten | Huysvrou van Mattys Gerkens | Bottelier | op Curason | obiit den* 12 *Juli | A*? 1687 (To the memory of Ariana Toffeten, wife of Matthias Gerkens Bottelier, at Curacoa. Died July 12, 1687).

Silver, cast and chased, with loop for suspension. Elliptical. Size 38 x 31.

ALBEMARLE, GOVERNOR OF JAMAICA.

66. 1687. *Obv.* CHRISTOPHORVS '. ALBEMARLIÆ . DVX . IAMAICÆ . LOC . TEN . GEN . GVB . GEN . (Christopher, Duke of Albemarle, Lieutenant-General and Governor-General of Jamaica). Bust to right of the Duke of Albemarle in decorated armor and in rich costume, draped ; on truncation, G. B. F. (George Bower[*] fecit).

Rev. EX . AQUA . OMNIA (All things from water). Neptune reclining, to the left, on the shore, rests his arm on an urn, and holds a trident ; two ships in the distance.

Silver. Size 29. Med. Ill. Jas. II, 34. Very rare.

Son of General Monke, appointed Governor of Jamaica, 1687, chief promoter of Sir William Phipps's scheme by which £300,000 in silver was recovered from a Spanish wreck off St. Domingo ; Albemarle's share being £90,000 ; he died in Jamaica, 1688 ; Phipps received £20,000, and was knighted Thus the prosperity of the Duke as well as of Sir William was due to what they brought "out of the water."

---

[*] Bower was one of the engravers in the Royal Mint, 1664–90.—EDS.

RECOVERY OF TREASURE, ST. DOMINGO.

67. 1687. *Obv.* IACOBVS · II · ET · MARIA · D · G · MAG · BRI · FRAN · ET · HIB · REX · ET · REGINA · (James II and Mary, by the grace of God, King and Queen of Great Britain, France and Ireland.) Busts of King and Queen conjoined to right; the King laureate, in scale armor, draped; the Queen draped. Under truncation, G. B. (for George Bower).

Rev. · SEMPER TIBI PENDEAT HAMUS · (Let thy hook always hang,* i. e. Persevere.) In exergue, NAVFRAGA REPERTA | 1687. (Shipwrecked [wealth] recovered.) A ship in the distance and a boat in the foreground fishing over a wreck.

Gold and silver. Size 33. Med. Ill., Jas. II, 33 ; (see also V. L., III, 317.)

Commemorating the same enterprise. Presented to the officers and promoters of Sir Wm. Phipps's expedition.

QUEBEC ATTACKED.

68. 1690. *Obv.* LUDOVICUS MAGNUS REX CHRISTIANISSIMUS. I . MAVGER . F . Head of Louis XIV, to right with flowing hair.

Rev. FRANCIA IN NOVO ORBE VICTRIX . In exergue, KEBECA LIBERATA | M.DC.XC. (France victorious in the New World; Quebec liberated, 1690.) Quebec murally crowned, to left,

---

* The legend is from Ovid, Art. Amor. III, 425.—EDS.

seated on a rock, resting her left arm on a shield with arms of France; on either side, behind, banners (one of England), and a shield at her feet. At the foot of the rock on the right is a river god (the St. Lawrence), while a beaver crawls down the rock from right to left, in front. Behind her are pine trees.

Silver and copper. Size 26. Med. Ill., Wm. and Mary, 150. A. J. N.,* IX, 2; XIV, 44. McL., 16.

The outbreak of the small-pox among his forces obliged Sir William Phipps to abandon the siege of Quebec.

69. 1690. *Obv.* Similar to last; a slight difference in the arrangement of the hair. In exergue, j. mavger f.

Rev. Same as last.

Copper. Size 26. A. J. N., XIV, 44. McL., 17.

70. 1690. *Obv.* Similar to last, hair much fuller. In exergue, R.

Rev. Same as last.†

Copper. Size 26. A. J. N., XIV, 44. McL., 18.

71. 1690. *Obv.* LUDOVICUS MAGNUS REX CHRISTIANISSIMUS. [Mint-mark of Lille.] Bust similar to last.

Rev. Same as last.

Copper. Size 26.

---

* See Plate in A. J. N., IX, facing page 1. McLachlan says, A. J. N., XIV, 44, "on the Medal it is at the right, crawling downward," and implies that there is no such Medal as these described. The engraving in the Journal is from Shea's translation of Charlevoix (6 vols.), where the Medal is also mentioned. The description of 74 below, however, conforms to the engraving, and seems to show that McLachlan may have been in error.—Eds.

† It is not certain whether R denotes Joseph Roettier, Chief Engraver of the Mint at Paris, from the death of Varin in 1672, until 1703, or Henri Roussel, a "medallist of considerable merit, much engaged on the medallic series of Louis XIV. His works date from 1654 to 1711, or even later. As he excelled in portraiture he confined his attention chiefly to the execution of the obverses of Medals." See Med. Ill., II, 738, from which it seems most probable that this is the initial of the latter engraver. Some of these busts are those known as "old heads," others as "young heads," but we have not attempted to distinguish them, as the Medals have been frequently restruck with each. This note applies also to 54.—Eds.

72. 1690. *Obv.* LUDOVICUS MAGNUS REX CHRISTIANISSIMUS.
DOLLIN F. (A die-sinker in Paris.)   Bust similar to last.
Rev. Same as last.
Copper.   Size 26.   McL., 16.

73. 1690. *Obv.* LUDOVICUS XIIII . REX CHRISTIANISSIMUS +
Bust similar to last.
Rev. Same as last.
Copper.   Size 26.

74. 1690. *Obv.* LVDOVICVS . MAGNVS . REX . CHRISTIANISSI-
MVS •   Bust of the King to right, without drapery, in a de-
pressed circle.
Rev. FRANCIA IN NOVO ORBE VICTRIX .   In exergue, KE-
BECA . LIBERATA | M . DC . XC .   (Translation under 68.)   De-
sign similar to last, but the beaver is crawling *up* the rock at
the *left.*
Size 32.   S. 1.   Med. Louis le Grand, Ed. 1723, 234.
A. J. N., IX, 1.   [See note on 68.]

FRENCH-INDIAN MEDAL.

75. 1693. *Obv.* LUDOVICUS MAGNUS REX CHRISTIANISSIMUS.
Bust of King to right undraped, laureated.   H . ROVSSEL . F .   be-
low bust.
Rev. FELICITAS DOMUS AUGUSTAE. (The pride of the Royal
house.)   At the top, bust of the Dauphin to left, SEREN .
DELPH . beneath. (His Serene Highness, the Dauphin).   Bust
of the Duke of Burgundy to the right, . LUD . D . BVRG .
beneath. (Louis, Duke of Burgundy).   Bust of the Duke
d'Anjou to left, . PHIL . D . ANJ . beneath. (Philip, Duke of
Anjou.)   Bust of the Duke de Berri, at the bottom, . CAR . D .
BITUR . beneath. (Charles, Duke of Berri.)   The busts of
Louis and Philip face each other.   All are in profile with
flowing hair.   In exergue, M.DC.XCIII.   H. ROVSSEL. IN.
Silver and copper.   Size 48.   Laval Univ. (Canada).   Le
Roux,* 300.

---

* Le Medaillier du Canada, par Jos. Le Roux, M. D., Montreal, 1888.

This medal was used for presentation to the Indian Chiefs, although not originally struck for that purpose.*

76. *Obv.* Similar to the preceding.

Rev. Similar to the preceding, reduced in size; the busts are differently arranged and the date is 1686.

Silver and bronze.   Size 26.   Le Roux, Sup., p. 13.

REPULSE OF FRENCH FROM JAMAICA.

77. 1694. A gold medal known only from the following account : "Captain Elliott, who first gave notice of this invasion, had a medal and chain given him of £100 value, and £500 in money."

See A New History of Jamaica, London, 1740, 261.

On June 17, 1694, the French fleet of twenty sail, under Du Casse, landed at Cow Bay, in Jamaica. They afterwards landed 1,500 men in Carlisle Bay and captured a breastwork defended by 200 English ; but the English, being reinforced by five companies of foot and some horse, compelled the French to retreat with a loss of 700 men, and to reëmbark in the night. [Probably an engraved Medal.]

CAROLINA COMPANY.

78. 1694. *Obv.* GOD : PRESERVE : CAROLINA : AND THE : LORDS : PROPRIETERS. (*sic.*)   1694. in six parallel lines.

Rev. An elephant facing the left.   Edge milled.

Copper.   Size 18½.   C. 338, pl. 9, I.

---

* The busts on the reverse are those of the Dauphin, Louis, [son of Louis XIV and Maria Theresa, born 1661,] and his sons, Louis, Duke of Burgundy (which had been annexed to the Crown of France in 1678); Philip, Duke of Anjou, and by the will of Charles II, heir to the Spanish crown to which he succeeded as Philip V, 1701 ; and Charles, Duke of Berri. The Dauphin died before his father, and his grandson, son of the Duke of Burgundy, succeeded Louis XIV (his great grandfather) as Louis XV. Aside from the fact that this is said to have been presented to Indian chiefs by the French officials in Canada, it has no reference to America. This Medal and the next have been restruck. Leroux 300, describing the obverse says, " H. Roussel, Jr.," doubtless an error, as we find no " Junior," and the letters on his engraving are IN. He mentions in his Supplement that it was also struck sizes 20 and 22, but we have seen no examples of those sizes, and as Mr. Betts omitted them, we also pass them with this reference.—EDS.

79. 1694. *Obv.* Same design, but with the inscription corrected to PROPRIETORS.

Rev. Same design, but the elephant's tusks almost touch the milling.

Copper. Size 18½. C. 338, pl. 9, II.

NEW ENGLAND COMPANY.

80. 1694. *Obv.* GOD : PRESERVE : NEW : ENGLAND : 1694.
Rev. Same as last. Edge plain.
Copper. Size 18½. C. 338, pl. 9, III.

LONDON COMPANY.

81. 1694 (?). *Obv.* LONDON : GOD : PRESERVE : ✱ A shield, with cross, and a sword in one of the quarterings.* (Arms of the city of London.)

Rev. Same as last. Edge plain.
Copper. Size 18½. See C., 337.

82. 1694 (?). *Obv.* LON DON Arms as last.
Rev. Same as last.
Copper. Size 18½.

---

* The dies of the Medal were preserved in the Tower of London for many years, and Snelling says the piece "appears to be the work of Rotiers "— but whether John Roettier (as Med. Ill. spells the name), or one of his sons — James or Norbert, who were all in the mint at the time this was struck, does not appear. Snelling further says, various "opinions concerning the intent of uttering this piece" have been held ; "as that it was for the London Workhouse....And we have likewise heard it was intended to be made current at Tangier in Africa, but never took place."—EDS.

CARTHAGENA CAPTURED.

83. 1697. *Obv.* LUDOVICUS MAGNVS REX CHRISTIANISSI-
MUS. Under decollation, ɪ . MAVGER . F . Bust of the King to
right, without drapery.

Rev. HISPANORUM THESAURI DIREPTI. In exergue, CARTH-
AGO AMERICANA | VI CAPTA. | M . DC . XCVII. (The treasure of
the Spaniards carried away; the American Carthage taken
by storm. 1697.) A female reclining at the foot of a palm-
tree; at her left an overturned urn of money.

Gold, silver and copper. Size 26. F. 8182.

84. 1697. *Obv.* Similar legend and design, but without
engraver's name.

Rev. Similar legend and design, except that the inscription
in exergue is CARTHAGO AMERICANA VI | CAPTA | IV . MAII
M . DC . XCVII . (Translated on 83.)

Med. Louis le Grand, Ed. 1723, 267. No specimen known;
no such dies now exist in the Paris mint.

85. 1697. *Obv.* Similar design and legend to the preceding.

Rev. VICTORIA COMES FRANCORUM. In exergue, MDCXCVII.
(Victory the companion of the French, 1697.) A palm-tree
supporting three shields upon which Victory is writing, on
one AD | CAR | THAGE | NEM | NO | VI | ORBIS On another,
AD | ATHAM | FLAN | DRIÆ and on the third, AD | BAR |

CINO | NEM | HIS | PANI | Æ　　(At Carthagena* in the New World ; at Atham in Flanders ; at Barcelona in Spain.)
Gold and copper.　Size 26.

86. 1697.　*Obv.* Similar design and legend ; ɪ. ᴍᴀᴠɢᴇʀ below head.　(Different die.)

Rev. Same as last.

Copper.　Size 26.

87. 1697.　*Obv.* Similar design and legend.

Rev. Same legend and design, but the words inscribed by Victory upon the shields are AD | CARTH | NOVI | ORBIS and AD | ATHAM | FLAN | DRIÆ and AD | BARCI | NONEM | HISPA | NIÆ.　(Translation under 85.)

Size —.　Med. Louis le Grand, 268.　No specimen known ; no such dies now exist in the Paris mint.†

SCOTCH COLONY AT DARIEN.

88. 1700.　*Obv.* QUID NON PRO PATRIA on a ribbon, issuing from a compass.　In exergue, TOUBOCANTI UBI 1600 HISPAN

---

* The word is given Carthaginen in C. M., 149, No. 336, and the date is spaced M DC XCVII. The description in the text, however, corresponds with the engraving furnished us. [See 86.] As stated in our Preface, we have not been able to compare the original Manuscript with the Medals in all cases, and the death of Mr. Betts prevented his completing its final revision. A few other instances of a similar character will be found, but with this explanation we leave them. It is also proper to remark that as Mr. Betts seems to have sometimes used the words *head* and *bust* interchangeably, we have not attempted to distinguish between them, as for instance on 83.—EDS.

† We pass without numbering, a mule in this series, obverse of 84 and reverse of 83. [C. M., 149, No. 334.]—EDS.

FUDIT DUX ALEXANDER CAMPBELL . MDCC . 8 . FEBR . (What [will] not [one do] for fatherland? At Toubucan, where Captain Alexander Campbell put to flight 1600 Spaniards, February 8, 1700.) M. S. (Martin Smeltzing.*) A Highlander in scale armor, holding sword, and shield with unicorn, advancing to attack a fort in the background.

Rev. QUA PANDITUR ORBIS on a ribbon above; below, VIS UNITA FORTIOR. (Wherever the world extends. Power is stronger united.) Shield, bearing the arms of the African and Indian Company of Scotland ;† with helmet, crest and supporters.

Gold, silver gilt and silver. Size 35. Med. Ill., Wm. III, 529.

PROCLAMATION OF PHILIP V, IN MEXICO.

89. 1701. *Obv.* ·: PHILIP : V : DG : HISPANIARVM : REX : AN : 1701. (Philip V, by the grace of God, King of Spain,‡ 1701.) Bust of King (in profile) to right in armor, draped.

Rev. IMPERATOR ✶ INDIARVM. (Emperor of the Indies.) In the field MEX   ICO on each side of a castle, supported by two lions, alluding to Castile and Leon, and supporting an eagle seated on a cactus, the castle resting on waves. [Called the Arms of Mexico, by Van Loon.]

Silver, cast. Size 19. H. 6. V. L., IV, 327.

---

* Martin Smeltzing was the son of Arend, and younger brother of Jan Smeltzing; all were well-known die-engravers. Martin lived at Amsterdam (Med. Ill.), or according to other authorities at Leyden, 1696–1712, and died in 1713. His works are inferior to those of his brother Jan.—EDS.

† This Medal alludes to an attempt to establish a British Colony at Darien, for which purpose two parties of about 1200 persons each, left Scotland. They were nearly overcome by famine and disease, and a Spanish force numbering 1600, encamped at Toubucan, were only awaiting the arrival of a fleet, before attacking the Scotch. Captain Campbell arrived before the fleet, and stormed the camp of the Spaniards; he was, however, unable to establish the Colony on a safe footing, notwithstanding his success, and it finally capitulated on highly honorable terms. On his return to Scotland, Campbell was presented by the African Company with an impression of this Medal in gold, and a grant of supporters to his arms, a Spaniard and an Indian, was made to him, with an inescutcheon of the Company's arms. See Med. Ill. *loc. cit.*—EDS.

‡ See note on 75.

PROCLAMATION AT LIMA.

90. 1701. *Obv.* PHILIPPVS V DEI GRATIA HISPANIARVM ET INDIARVM REX. ANN 1701. (Philip V, by the grace of God, King of Spain and of the Indies, 1701). Said to be described in a manuscript in the National Library as silver *money* struck in Lima upon proclamation of Philip V.*

Rev. Not described.

H. 5 ; no illustration given.

PROCLAMATION IN VERA CRUZ.

91. 1701. *Obv.* PHILIP : V : DG : HISPANIARVM : REX : AN : 1701. Bust of King to right in armor.

Rev. PRO —— ET REGE on each side of a cross supported by a castle with three turrets.†

Silver, cast. Size 19. H. 7.

SPAIN PROTECTS HER AMERICAN POSSESSIONS.

92. 1702. *Obv.* ANDEGAV. D. PHIL. V. HISP. ET IND. R. In exergue, M DCCII. (The Duke of Anjou, Philip V, King of Spain and of the Indies, 1702.) A female figure at the left, representing Spain, on a platform, draped, placing a crown on the head of Philip, Duke of Anjou, who stands in armor and mantle at the right, facing her ; his right hand holds a globe, his left a sceptre, and his right foot is resting on the platform. Behind the female, the two pillars, a crown resting on their capitals, the arms of Spain on a shield between them and PLUS | ULTRA (more beyond) beneath.

---

* This is the Prince commemorated on 75. Since that page was printed we find in a letter from Rev. A. Rheaume, of Laval University, in A. J. N., XI: 93, corroboration of the fact that 75 was struck for presentation to Indian Chiefs for bravery, while 76, although used for the same purpose, was originally struck on the birth of the Duke of Berri. On this the name and title are wanting below every bust but his, while to his name and title is added the date of his birth. The Medal is extremely rare. Sandham and McLachlan do not give it, and Mr. Betts and the Editors have never seen it. Leroux describes it as our 76, but does not mention the variations. We therefore note the differences.—EDS.

† The inscription may perhaps signify " For the Church and the King," or " For Castile and the King," according to the weight the reader chooses to give to the device.—EDS.

Rev. VIGILANS ELUDIT HIANTEM. (Watching he foils the spoiler.) The golden fleece hanging from a fruited tree, of which there are several growing beside a high fence : on rocks washed by waves is a dragon with expanded wings.[*]

Silver. Size 30. V. L., IV, 326.

AMERICAN TREASURE CAPTURED AT VIGO.

93. 1702. *Obv.* On the left, outside a cable border, MEM . INC . CATAPLI . AMER . HISP . ET . CLASS . GALL . AD . VIGOS . and on the right, III NOSTRI REDITUS EXPECTATIQUE TRIUMPHI. On an inner circle on the field, near the edge, TROPÆO HÆC . on the left, and CÆTERA FLAMMIS . on the right. (In memory of the burning of the Spanish-American galleons, and the French fleet at Vigo ; these are our returns and our promised triumphs ;[†] these for a trophy, the rest for the flames.) ANNO | LIBERTATIS | TRIUMPHALI | MDCCII . (In the triumphant year of Liberty 1702) upon the base of a rostral column surmounted by Victory, with trumpet and wreath, trampling upon standards ; two captives chained below ; in the background the English fleet capturing the Spanish and French fleets near land marked REDONDELLA . VIGOS . CANNAS .

Rev. TELA ROSA ET MAGNI IOVIS ALES SIC TIBI GALLE GORGONA DEMONSTRANT SIC ET IBERE TIBI ✳ (The arrows, the rose, and the bird of mighty Jove thus show to you, O Frenchmen, the Gorgon's head, and to you too, O Spaniards.) M. S. (Martin Smeltzing.) A trophy of prows, castles and standards ; above a bunch of arrows, a rose, and eagle, denoting

---

[*] This Medal, says Van Loon, appears to him to have been struck by France, who had seized certain Spanish possessions in Holland. Others have held that aside from the direct allusion, in the title of the King, to the West Indies, the emblems of the golden fleece (see 99), the garden of the Hesperides, and its watchful dragon with the sea in front, on the reverse, refer to his possessions beyond the Western ocean, and to the care which Philip (who was, as has been mentioned under 75, a prince of the French house) would maintain over his American possessions which had proved so fruitful a source of wealth. It has also been remarked that he is represented as receiving not the royal "orb" surmounted by a cross, but a globe. For these reasons it is believed to be properly included here. [Hiantem, literally, the yawning one.]—EDS.

[†] Hi nostri, etc., from Virgil, Aen. XI: 54.—EDS.

Holland, England and Germany, united by the shield of Minerva with Gorgon's head; forked lightnings around it; the base supported by the English unicorn, the German eagle and the lion of Holland.

Silver. Size 37. V. L., IV, 360. Med. Ill. Anne, 24.

94. 1702. *Obv.* HIS MILITAT ÆTHER. In exergue, OB CLASSEM HOSTIVM DELETAM | GAZASQVE INDICAS EREPTAS | IN PORTV AD VIGOS | D . 22 OCT. CIƆ IƆCCII . (Heaven fights for these. For the fleet of the enemy destroyed and the wealth of the Indies captured in the harbor at Vigo, October 22d, 1702.) Neptune driving over the sea toward the right, holding a trident in his left hand, and in his right receiving a scroll from Victory flying above, bearing the following list of the captured galleons: NAVES GALL. | ET HISP | LE FORT . IN | LE PROMT OC . | L'ASSURE . OC | L'ESPERANCE . S | LE BOURBON . O . | LA SIRENE . SU . | LE SOLIDE . INC | LE FERME . OCC | LE PRUDENT . INC | LE MODERE . OCC . | LE SUPERBE . SUB . | LA DAUPHINE . IN . | LE VOLUNTAIRE | LE TRITON . OCC . | L'ENFLAME . INC | L'ENTREPREN . IN . | LE FAVORI . INC . | LA CROQUANTE . I . | 3 CORVETTES IN . | 17 CARAVELLES . IN | 9 GALIONE OCC . | 2 GALIONE SU. The inscription gives the names of the vessels burnt INC. for *incensae*), sunk (SV. or SVB. for *submersae*), or captured (OCC. for *occupatae*). It seems unnecessary to anglicize the names which are probably taken from the official report in the London Gazette. Around the car of Neptune three Nereids bear the shields of the Emperor, England and Holland. G. F. N. for Georg Friedrich Nurnberger,* and on the chariot G. H. for Georg Hautsch.

* Georg Friedrich Nurnberger was Engraver and Master of the Mint at Nuremberg, 1682-1724. He also engraved dies for the City of Halle. Georg Hautsch was a native of Nuremberg and worked from 1683 to 1712, at that city and at Vienna. His private mark was a star or asterisk. The date on the Medal is not that of the engagement, but of the day before, when the allied fleets were drawn up outside the harbor. No German force was present, but the Emperor was a member of the Alliance, which is the reason his emblem is given. In Van Loon's engraving the letter U is given in the names of the ships, but the corresponding letter in the exergue is V.—EDS.

Rev. ET CONIVRATI VENIVNT AD CLASSICA VENTI . (And the confederate winds come to the call of the fleet.) Passage adapted from Claud. De III Cons. Honor., 98. View of the bay of Vigo, with a double chain across the entrance, defended by a fort on each side ; in the foreground a fleet of nine vessels in line advancing to attack the vessels in the harbor.

Silver. Size 20. V. L., IV. 360. Med. Ill. Anne, 17.

95. 1702. *Obv.* ANNA. D. G. MAG. BR. FR. ET. HIB. R. (Anna, by the grace of God, Queen of Great Britain, France and Ireland.) Bust without crown, to left. Below bust L. G. L. (Lazarus Gottlieb Laufer.)

Rev. ANGLOR. ET. BATAV. VIRTVTE. (By the bravery of the English and Dutch). In exergue, INCENS. CLASSE OPES | AMERIC. INTER | CEPT. 1702. (The fleet burned, and American treasure captured). Naval engagement in perspective below map of land and harbor with fort marked VIGOS, and other places marked REDOND ; BOC ; CONG.

Copper and brass.* Size 16. Med. Ill., Anne, 23. V. L., IV, 363. A. J. N., IV, 44.

96. 1702. *Obv.* ANNA . D G . MAG . BR . FR . ET . HIB . REGINA . Bust of the Queen to left, uncrowned, love-lock on right shoulder. Below, I . BOSKAM . F . curving to conform to the edge.

Rev. GALL : HISP . Q . CLASS . EXPUG . COMB . CAPT . (The French and Spanish fleets defeated, burnt [*combusta*] and captured.) In exergue, BRIT . BATV . Q . EXPEO (*sic.*) . AD . VIGOS . MDCCII . (The British and Dutch Expedition to Vigo, 1702.) A fleet attacking boats and ships in Vigo harbor.

Silver. Size 28. V. L., IV, 363. Med. Ill., Anne, 20.

---

* This Medalet is a "Nuremberg Counter." The obverse is copied from 98, and the reverse from 102, described below. The dies were cut by Lazarus Gottlieb Laufer, perhaps a son of the Chief Warden of the Nuremberg mint, of the same name, who flourished from 1670 to 1690. The younger Laufer worked in the early part of the last century as we learn from Med. Ill. II, 730. The piece is engraved in the February number of the American Historical Record, for 1873.—EDS.

The dies for this Medal were cut in Holland, by Jan Boskam.* The portrait of the Queen is from a coronation Medal by Croker. This Medal represents the position of the belligerents in the heat of the battle ; 94 and 95 their places before and at the beginning of the fight, and 97 the victory won.

97. 1702. *Obv.* ANNA . DEI . GRA : MAG : BRI : FRA : ET . HIB : REGINA Bust of the Queen to left, crowned, a long curl or love-lock falling on her left shoulder, her dress fastened with a brooch in front.

Rev CAPTA . ET . INCENSA . GAL : ET . HISP : CLASSE . (The French and Spanish fleets taken and burnt.) In exergue, AD . VIGVM . XII . OCT . | MDCCII . (At Vigo, Oct. 12, 1702.) [This is the date in Old Style.†] View of Vigo harbor ; vessels burning inside ; ships before the entrance, near a fort.

Silver and copper. Size 24. V. L., IV, 363. Med. Ill., Anne, 18.

The dies of this Medal were by John Croker ; and there were three pairs made to strike it, all slightly varying, and one with FR. in place of FRA. in obverse legend.

98. 1702. *Obv.* ANNA . D . G . M . BRIT . FRAN . ET . HIB . REGINA . Bust similar to the preceding.

Rev CAPTA . ET . INCENSA . GAL . ET . HISP . CLAS . In exergue, AD . VIGUM . XII . OCT . MDCCII . View of Vigo harbor. similar to the preceding.

Silver. Size 26. Med. Ill., Anne, 19.

These dies are thought to have been cut by Christian Wermuth, after the preceding one ; the medal is in higher relief, and of coarser work.

---

* Boskam was a native of Nymwegen, and a successful engraver. He executed a large number of Medals for William III, but none relating to America. In 1703 he removed to Berlin, and returned to Amsterdam in 1706. He was working as late as 1708, but the date of his death is not known. See Med. Ill., II, 721.—EDS.

† See note on 94.—EDS.

99. 1702.   *Obv.* Bust of Queen Anne, to left, as on 96, with the same legend.

Rev. NON DOLO NEC ARTE SED APERTO MARTE (Not by deceit nor by stratagem, but by open war.) In exergue, MDCCII. Hercules stepping from the sea, plants his foot upon the neck of a prostrate dragon, and arrests the flight of a French soldier, who is striving to carry off the Golden Fleece.

Silver.   Size 28.   Med. Ill., Anne, 21.   V. L., IV, 363.

Sir George Rooke, the commander of the English forces, as Hercules or Jason, destroys the Spanish dragon, and rescues the Golden Fleece from its guardian, Aetes, repre-sented by Louis XIV, who was striving to obtain the Spanish wealth and dominion in the West Indies and South Amer-ica.   Louis had equipped a fleet sufficiently powerful, as he hoped, to protect the treasure and bring it home in safety, in order that it might be devoted to the necessities of the State, then very pressing, and was anxiously expecting its arrival.   The naval power of France did not recover, during the war, from this crushing blow.   This victory occasioned great rejoicing as it was by far the most important gained by the Confederates against France, up to that time, and entirely defeated the French plan of campaign.

100.   1702.   *Obv.* LIBERTAS . NEOMAGI . INTUS . ET . EXTRA . (The Liberty of Nymwegen, within and without.)   In exergue, I. B. F. (Jan Boskam fecit.)   Nymwegen, typified by a female figure to left, wearing a Liberty cap, holds a book with three seals and the Gorgon shield; her left foot tramples the serpent of Discord ; on the right are a curule chair and two fasces, the latter with a sword, rests against the base of two draped columns.

Rev. From the same die as the preceding.*

Silver.   Size 28.   Med. Ill., Anne, 25.

---

* The obverse has no reference to America ; the reverse however has such an allusion.   The Dutch Commander at Vigo Bay was Van der Goes.—EDS.

101. 1702. *Obv.* SPES ET VIRES HOSTIUM FRACTAE In exergue, INCENSA GALLOR CLASSE · | HISPAN · OPES AMERIC · | · INTERCEPT · (The hope and strength of the enemy broken. The French fleet burnt, and the American treasures of Spain intercepted.) Victory placing a crown upon a trophy of arms, flags, bales of merchandise, etc.

Rev. ANGLORVM ET BATAVORVM VIRTVTE. In exergue, AD VIGOS PORT . | GALLICIAE . | 1702. (By the valor of the English and Dutch, at Vigo Bay, in Spain, 1702.) Similar design to 95 ; the places on the map are marked REDONDELLE ; VIGOS ; BOCES ; CANGAS. On edge, DECIDIT IN CASSES PRÆDA PETITA MEOS . OVID . ✠ (The prey sought for is fallen into my nets).*

Silver and tin. Size 25. V. L., IV, 160. Med. Ill., Anne, 22.

102. 1703. *Obv.* G. ROOKE EQ⁵ & DUX CLASSIS ANGLIÆ. MAGNA EST VERITAS & PRÆVALEBIT. (George Rooke, knight [eques] and Commander of the English fleet. Truth is mighty and will prevail.) Bust to right, long, flowing hair, and no drapery.

Rev. MARIA ROOKE. Bust of Lady Rooke to right, hair compactly arranged, except one loose lock behind, and slight drapery.

Silver. Size 32. Med Ill., Anne, 37.

Sir George Rooke was the Admiral of the fleet which captured the Treasure fleet at Vigo Bay; he had been sent to

---

* The edge inscription is from Ovid, Art. Amor. II : 2.—EDS.

take possession of Cadiz, but the Spaniards refusing to surrender, and his Dutch allies not permitting an attack, he
sailed for home, and on the 12th October, O. S., 23d, N. S.,
1702, took the fleet of the French and Spanish, commanded
by Chateau Renault, at Vigo, Spain. The war was that of
the "Spanish succession" so-called. Lady Rooke, whose
portrait is on the reverse, was his second wife, and the
daughter of Col. Francis Luttrell.

AMERICAN CENTURY PLANT.

103. 1700. *Obv.* ALOEN AMERIC . ANNOR . 28 ALTAM PED .
24 . RAMIS 35 FL . PROTRUDERE 5138 in an outer circle, and
LIPSIÆ VIDIT HORTUS BOSIANUS . in inner circle. In exergue,
MDCC (The Bosian Garden at Leipsic in 1700 saw the American Aloe of twenty-eight years reach a height of twenty-four
feet, with thirty-five branches, and blossom with five thous-
and one hundred and thirty-eight flowers.) The Agave in
bloom; two of the leaves being inscribed* CULTORE E : PEIN.

Rev. SIC LIPSIA FLOREAT USQVE . (So may Leipsic ever
flourish.) View of Leipsic surrounded by a wall; fields, and
a village in the foreground, and I . K. upon a stone.†

Silver. Size 24. Yale University Cabinet.

---

* 'E. Pein' the name of the gardener, Elias Pein. The plant budded in
May, and blossomed Aug. 13. The die of the obverse cracked. —Eds.

† The letters I . K. may be for Johann Kühnlein, a Mint-master at Lange-
nargen, Wurtemberg, 1696–1724; another well-known engraver with the same
initials, Johann Koch, Mint-master at Dresden, 1688–98, probably died before
this die was cut.—Eds.

104.   1701.   *Obv.* NATVRA SEMEL MEMORIA SEMPER. (Once in nature; always in memory.)   The Agave in bloom in the foreground, growing from an ornamented box, on which is G the initial of the engraver Grosskurt; in middle distance, rocky cliffs on each side, upon which the Muses are sitting; on the top of one is Pegasus, and on the top of the other Apollo, with a glory around his head; from each rock water spouts into a basin behind the plant; and between them appears a distant view of hills.

Rev. • | IN HORTIS | VALLIS SALINÆ | II · LAP . A . CAST . GVELPHER . | ALOE AMERICANA | ANNOR . XXIII . | ALTA XXXVI . PED . | RAMIS XL . | CALICVLIS . VIMCLXVI | EFFLORVIT . V . NON . OC . | MDCCI . | •   (The American Aloe [or Century plant], of [the age of] twenty-three years, in the gardens of Salzdal, two miles* from the Castle of Wolfenbuttel; height thirty-six feet, forty branches, bloomed with six thousand one hundred and sixty-six flowers, on the fifth day before the nones [i. e. the third] of October, 1701.)

Silver.   Size 37.   In the Yale University Cabinet.

105.   1701.   *Obv.* FINIS CORONAT OPVS . (The end crowns the work.)   In exergue, G in a scroll.   Design very similar to last, except that a double row of shrubs extends in front of

---

* LAP. for Lapidibus [stones, or mile stones]. GUELPHER for Guelpher-bytano. The Agave, of which the chief species is the Maguey or "Century plant," so called from the idea formerly held that it blossomed but once in a century, and incorrectly styled an Aloe (see Webster's International Dictionary, *sub voce*), is that represented on this Medal. The descriptions and engravings are from originals now in the Cabinet of Yale University, presented to that institution by Mr. Betts. From a rare work on Medals, entitled " Historische Gedächtniss-Muntzen," etc., [Latin title, Thesavrvs Nvmismatvm Modernorvm Ilvivs Secvli....ab anno MDCC, *et cet.*] printed at Nuremberg early in the last century in Latin and German in parallel columns, a copy of which we have found in the Library of the American Numismatic and Archæological Society, New York, we learn that the "rocky cliffs on each side" allude to a quaint conceit in the garden of the Duke (where this plant flowered) intended to represent the double peak of Parnassus and its neighbor, whence flowed the Castalian spring. An engraving and description of this Medal is given in Vol. I, p. 136 of the work cited; 103 is also illustrated in the same work, p. 43.—EDS.

the cliffs on each side ; the rocks are steeper, and the water falls more perpendicularly. [A nearer view than the preceding.]*

Rev. Same inscription and arrangement of lines as last, except OCT. instead of OC.

Silver. Size 26. In the Yale University Cabinet.

106. 1709. *Obv.* CAROLVS · XII · D · G · REX · SVE · (Charles XII, by the grace of God, King of Sweden.) Bust in profile to right, in armor.

Rev. STVPENDOS DEBVIT STVPENDO FLORES in outer circle ; AB AC (in monograms) 1708 IN on the left and SEQUENTEM on the right, in a letter resembling script, in an inner circle. (It owed stupendous flowers to a stupendous man. [It bloomed] from the year 1708 until the following [year].) A flowering Agave or Century plant with five blooming stalks, and numerous leaves at its base, growing from a box on the ground.

Silver. Size 17. In the Yale University Cabinet.†

---

* The legend alludes to the compensation the flowers make for their long delay in blooming, and to the popular idea that the death of the plant followed the flowering. G is the initial of Heinrich Peter Grosskurt, die-cutter at Berlin and Dresden, 1694–1734. He also signs H. P. G. It is described and engraved in Hist. Ged. (*ut sup.*) p. 137, pl. XLIV.—EDS.

† This also was among those presented to Yale University by Mr. Betts, and was probably acquired by him after his Manuscript was prepared, as he did not mention it ; Charles XII invaded Saxony in September, 1707, after his numerous victories in Poland, and dictated peace to the Elector, who then renounced the crown of Poland. In September, 1707, he marched with a large army to dethrone the Czar of Russia, and in June, 1708, he gained some advantages, but there his career was soon checked ; his subsequent history need not be mentioned, but it was probably about this time, "following" his departure from Leipsic, that the Medal was struck, before the star of Charles had passed its zenith : this suggests a possible double meaning for *in sequentem.* Dr. Storer,

107.   1710.   *Obv.* MVnDI . sIC . transIt . gLorIa . LenIs.
At the bottom, c . wermuth . f .   (Thus passes away the fleeting
glory of the world. 1710. Date in chronogram.)   The Agave
blooming in a garden ; hills in the distance.

Rev. SPECTATOR . | MIRARE . MIRANDAM . | ALOES . AMERI-
CANAE . FIGVRAM . | NVMEROSIS . FRVCTIBVS . ORNATAE | RARAM .
NON . MINVS . QVAM . CVRIOSAM . | QVAE . SOLO . EXTERO .
ANNOS . XXXIII . | RIGATA . AC . ENVTRITA . | OMINE . NON .
VANO . | FAXIT . SVMMVS . FAVSTO . | IN . HORTO . QVI . GOTHAE .
VIGET . | SERENISS . SAXONIAE . DVCIS . AC . HEROIS.   FRIDER-
ICI . NVMERVM . LIBERORVM . HVIVS . SERENISSIMAE . DOMVS . |
PROLIFERAE . | NON . MINVS . AC . HVIVS . SAECVLI . ANNORVM . |
PER . DECEM . CAVLES . | EX . RADICE . EXSVRGENTES . | AEMV-
LATVR . AVT . IMITATVR . | HAEC . | RAMIS . CC . ET . RAMICVLIS . |
HINC . PROTRUSIS . M . | FLORIBVS . VLTRA . XXX . M | QVI .
NVNC . APPARENT . | MIRIFICE . SVPERBIT . | FLORET . MENSE . |
SEPTEMBR . ET . OCTOBR .   (Beholder, admire the wonderful
likeness of the American Aloe, adorned with many fruits, not
less rare than curious, which has been watered and nourished
in foreign soil for thirty-three years : may the result be no
vain omen, but rather a propitious one, of the most Serene
and heroic Frederic,* Duke of Saxony, who flourishes in the

---

of Newport, R. I., informs us that this Medal is mentioned "by Carl Reinhard
Berch, in his Beskrifning Oefwer Swenska Mynt, Upsala, 1773, 4to, an authorita-
tive work published under the auspices of the Royal Academy of Upsala, (p. 334,
No. 86.)....Johann Hieronymus Lochner, in a brief list of Medals by pupils of
Arvid Karlstén, of Stockholm, in the preface (No. LXXXVI) of Vol. III, 1739,
of his ' Samlung merkwürdiger medaillen,' abbreviates the legend on reverse to
STVPEND . DEEVIT . STVPENDO . FLOR . and then continues, with an error of
date, AB A . 1700 . IN SEQVENTEM ."   If that description is exact, there would seem
to be another reverse die. Lochner says that the Medal was to commemorate
the first blooming of an Aloe in Sweden.—Eds.

 * The Duke alluded to, on this Medal, was Frederic II, of Saxe-Coburg-
Gotha (1691-1732) ; the arrangement of the punctuation on the Medal leaves it
somewhat doubtful whether the "ten stalks" allude to the number of children
descending from Frederic, the "root," or to the number of stems from the plant
itself. There seems to be some confusion in the Latin. The Agave puts out
large leaves at the bottom, and when it blossoms, shoots out a large number
of flowering branches from a spike which springs to a great height ; it has no
boughs or branches, in the ordinary sense of those words.—Eds.

garden of Gotha ; the number of descendants of whose Serene
House, not less fruitful than this plant of a hundred years,
through the ten stalks rising from the root, rivals or resembles it.　This plant, with two hundred boughs and branches,
and a thousand blooming flowers, beside thirty-thousand more
which are now appearing, flourished wonderfully, and flowered
in the months of September and October.)

Silver.　Size 27.　In the Yale University Cabinet.

108.　1711.　*Obv.* ALOEN AMERIC . ANNOR . 26 ALTAM PED .
28 RAMIS 37 . FL . PROTRUDERE 6486 in an outer circle, and
LIPSIÆ VIDIT HORTUS BOSIANVS . Aᵒ . 1711 . in an inner
circle.　(The Bosian Garden at Leipsic, in the year 1711, saw
the American Aloe, in twenty-six years, reach the height of
twenty-eight feet, with thirty-seven branches, and blossom
with six thousand four hundred and eighty-six flowers.)　The
Agave in bloom ; a man in a court costume standing beside
it at the right.

Rev. Legend and design as obverse of 103 : different die.
Silver.　Size 24.　Yale University Cabinet.

109.　1720.　*Obv.* FLORERE SATIS　(To bloom [or flower
out] is sufficient.)　The Agave in bloom ; a plant on each side,
and a building in the background extending across the field.

Rev. NOVA | ALOES AMERICANÆ | ANNOR : XXIV PROGENIES |
IN HORTIS SALTZDAL : | SVB CAL : MAII CALAMVM | INDE GEM-
MAS TRVDENS | CIRCA NONAS AUGUSTI | AD XXV PED : SUR-
REXIT | COMATA RAMIS XXXVIII | ET SERT : MCCCIV FLORIBVS |

REDIVIVI FLORIS | A. W. (in monogram) PRÆSAGA | MDCCXX . (The new offspring of the American Aloe in the garden of Salzdal, in its twenty-fourth year, put out a spike about the Calends [the 1st] of May ; then issuing buds about the Nones [the 5th] of August, it rose to the height of twenty-five feet, crowned with thirty-eight branches and adorned with one thousand three hundred and four flowers. The presage of a reviving flower,* A. W., 1720.)

Tin. Size 30. Yale University Cabinet.

110. 1726. *Obv.* CVNCTANDO EXSVPERAT. In exergue, SIC CAROLI SEXTI STIRPS | FLOREAT OMINE | FAVSTO . (It succeeds by delaying. So by this happy omen may the race of Charles the Sixth† flourish.) The Agave in bloom upon a terrace above a garden surrounded by a high hedge ; mountains beyond ; the top of the plant divides the legend ; upon the box containing the Agave MDCCXX | VI . and upon the ground of the terrace p. p. w. (Peter Paul Werner.‡)

Rev. B . F . | ALOES | AMERICANÆ | AN . AER . CUR . MDCCXXVI | NVREMBERGAE | IN VIRIDARIO SVBVRBANO | EFFLORESCENTIS | VEGETA ANN . XXVI AETATE | FOLIIS . LXXVIII | THYRSO XXVI PED . ALTO | SCAPIS XXXIX | CALICVLIS VIII MCCLXVI | SPECTABILIS MEMORIAM | POSTERITATI CONSECRAT | IOII . . M. VOLCAMER. (Freely rendered, The plant of the American Aloe in the year 1726 of the Christian era, blooming in the suburban garden of Nuremberg, in the twenty-sixth year of its age, with seventy-eight leaves, a spike twenty-six feet in height with thirty-nine branches and eight thousand

---

* A W is probably for Augustus Wilhelm, Duke of Brunswick-Wolfenbuttel 1714–31. The "presage" perhaps alludes to a recovery from sickness about the time the plant bloomed, or there may be some hidden political allusion to Polish matters. See note on 106. — EDS.

† Charles VI of Germany (Hapsburg), the Electorate of Bavaria having then been virtually suppressed.—EDS.

‡ Werner was "a clever medallist born at Nuremberg in 1689 and died there in 1771. As early as 1712 he was well known as an engraver, and in the course of his long life he was successively in the service of nearly all the different German Courts. His works are very numerous." Med. Ill., II, 744.—EDS.

two hundred and sixty-six flowers. John M. Volcamer strikes this [literally consecrates] for posterity in memory of its beauty. B. F. in the first line may be for BONA FORTUNA, By good fortune.) A small ornament below.

Silver. Size 31. In the cabinets of Dr. H. R. Storer, Newport, R. I., and Yale University.

There are other "Century plant Medals" beside the foregoing. They are, however, of a date too late to entitle them to a place in this volume, or the plant is of a different species and not of American origin.

SOCIETY OF MERCHANTS.

111. 1715. *Obv.* LUDOVICUS XV . D . G . FR . ET NAV . REX . (Louis XV, by the grace of God King of France and Navarre.) Under decollation, DUVIVIER. Youthful bust to right, laureate ; no drapery.

Rev. TOTUS MIIII PERVIUS ORBIS. In exergue, INSTITUTO MERCATORUM | COLLEGIO INSULIS | 1715. (All the world is open to me. Society of Merchants founded for the islands, 1715.) A ship under full sail advancing to left.

Copper. Size 22. B. N.

COMPANY OF THE INDIES.

112. 1723. *Obv.* FLOREBO QUO FERAR* (I shall flourish wherever [*quo* for *quocumque*] I am carried.) 17 23 at the

---

* "The Compagnie des Indes Occidentales" was formed by Letters Patent in 1664; Louis XIV granted them "the right to trade all over the mainland of America, from the Amazon to the Orinoco, in Newfoundland and other northern islands; and in the country that extends from Canada to Virginia and Florida ; also on the African coasts," etc. (Zay, p. 39.) Zay says (p. 40) it was suppressed by an edict of December, 1670, but on p. 271 gives the date as 1674. The "Compagnie des Indes Orientales " was also founded in 1664, and continued until 1719, when it was united with the "Compagnie d'Occident " for commerce with Louisiana. The following year it was entitled "Compagnie perpétuelle des Indes," and John Law became its Director. It passed through various vicissitudes and a new "Compagnie des Indes" was formed in 1785, which had a brief existence ; the older Company seems to have usually omitted the word *perpétuelle* from its name. The Company of 1664 bore for its arms a round or ornamental escutcheon, having a field azure (blue), charged with a fleur-de-lis or (gold), enwreathed

top. A crowned shield with horizontal lines denoting blue, and charged with three fleur-de-lis.

Rev. No legend. Crowned arms of the "Compagnie des Indes;" Indians as supporters, the one on the right seated, the other leaning on the top of the shield. COMP. DES INDES on a scroll below.

Lead. Size 12, nearly. Zay, 271.

Apparently used as a tag on the manufactures of the Company.

There is another metallic tag, used by the same Company, illustrated by Zay, but as it can hardly be classed among Medals, no description seems necessary. Other issues of a later date will be found in a subsequent chapter.

113. 1723. *Obv.* No legend. In exergue, COMPAGNIE DES INDES 1723 (Company of the Indies, 1723.) A shield which, in an inverted "pile," bears a river-god seated, with a paddle uplifted in his right hand, and leaning on a horn of plenty. A chief azure (blue) sprinkled with fleurs-de-lis or (of gold); the field is vert (green); the shield is surmounted by a crown, and supported by two Indians, each holding a bow.

Rev. SPEM AUGET OPESQUE PARAT. (It increases hope and prepares wealth.) A ship under full sail to left.

Size 20. Zay, 272.

---

with two branches, one of palm, the other of olive, joined at the base and surmounted by another fleur-de-lis, or (gold). Motto, *Florebo quocumque ferar* (I shall flourish wherever I am carried.) The Company of 1719 also used this motto. Supporters, Two figures, one of Peace, the other of Plenty. The second Company bore an escutcheon of which the field was green (*sinople*), with a "point undée" argent (silver), on which is a river-god proper, with chief and supporters, as on 113; the chief is separated from the field, in Zay's engraving, by a single "bar" of gold, too narrow to be a fess (a very uncommon device); in Art. LIV, of the decree defining the privileges of the Company, the charge is called a fess; the "point" is also an ordinary not known to English heralds; it somewhat resembles the device "parti per chevron" except that the ends of the chevron rest on the lower part of the shield, instead of the sides, — or like the wedge-shaped ordinary called a pile, reversed, as described in the text, and the border lines of the "point" are wavy.—EDS.

JOHN LAW AND THE MISSISSIPPI COMPANY.

114.   1720.   *Obv.* LOVISIANA | EST EST | BANCO ET | MONETA |
(Louisiana is [? valuable as] a Bank and a Mint), upon a
scroll or lottery ticket in the right hand of John Law,* who
stands in cocked hat, wig, and court dress, before a cave, in
which sits Envy; Law holds a ship in his left hand; above,
at the left, Fame blows two trumpets; from the upper one
come the words LAVS IN ASTRIS, and from the other, LAVS IN
TERRIS. (His praise is in the stars — his praise is throughout
the earth.)   In exergue, INVIDIAM VIRTUTE PARTAM | GLORIAM
NON INVIDIAM | IVDICO . | CIC . P . CAT . I . C . 13. (The envy
which is born of virtue [i. e. which has its birth because of
virtue in another,] I consider to be glory not envy.   Cicero's
First Oration against the Prætor Catiline, chapter 12.)

Rev. * | *INVIDIA * | LVCRIPETAS ALLICIS | VANAE VENDITIONE
SPEI | LAVS | QVOD VERVM EST . LATEAT | QUAMVIS . ALIQVAN-
DO PATEBIT. | INVIDIA | AVRIFEROS VENDIS MONTES : | POTIERIS
AHENIS! | LAWS | QVICQVID SVB TERRA EST, IN | APRICVM PRO-

---

* John Law, the promoter of various speculative enterprises, was born in
Scotland, April 21, 1671. Driven from his native country because he killed his
opponent in a duel, he wandered about Italy, and turned up in Paris in 1715,
where he began his famous career. At first his schemes were very successful,
and he was appointed to several positions of importance in connection with
banking. His connection with America properly dates from the year 1719, when
he floated the Mississippi Company, but the bubble burst and thousands were
ruined. He was obliged to quit France, and resided for a time at Brussels and
afterwards at Venice, where he died in poverty, March 21, 1729.—EDS.

FERET AETAS . | HORAT . 1 . EP . 6 | AVTOR | PASCITVR IN VIVIS LIVOR ; | POST FATA QVIESCIT ; | TVNC SVVS EX MERITO | QVOQVE TVETVR HONOS . | OVID . 1 . AMOR . 15 . | ARG . STRAESB . F . | 1720. in parallel lines. The inscription is a dialogue between the two figures on the obverse, Envy or Spite, and Law, i. e. Praise, its opposite, concluding with a quotation appended as a sort of commentary, by the designer. (Envy : "You entice those who seek wealth by the sale of a worthless hope." Law : "That which is true, although concealed, will sometime be disclosed." Envy : "You offer for sale gold-bearing mountains; you possess nothing but brass." Law : "Whatever is under the earth, time will bring to light." Horace, Epistles, I. 6 (line 24). Author : "Malice feeds on the living; after death, it rests. Then every one will receive honor according to his deserts." Ovid, Art. Amor. i : 15. Made at Strassburg, in silver, 1720.)

Silver. Size 28. Alexi I.*

115. 1720. *Obv.* CREDIT ist mausetodt. (Credit is as dead as a rat.) A man lying dead on rocky ground, grasping a winged caduceus in his right hand, and in his left a packet,

---

* This Medal is a good example of the satirical jests at the expense of Law, which characterize nearly all of these pieces, and therefore may receive a more extended notice. The word *est*, for instance, means "eats," as well as "is." Its duplication therefore suggests the alternative translation, " Louisiana operations eat up one's money;" its repetition is also a sort of chaffing assertion, implying the exact reverse of the statement, as well as an emphatic way of putting it ; for instance, we sometimes hear the slang expression " You're a nice man, *you* are," meaning that the person addressed is just the opposite. The same repetition will be found on another, described below, with a similar meaning. In this connection we may note the fact that in French the name is pronounced *Lass*, a nearer approach to the Latin word *Laus*, i. e. praise. The pun on his name thus becomes more sarcastic when Fame declares that Law's praises are heard throughout the universe. It is noticeable that the last time his name occurs it is given Laws, as if to prevent any doubt who is meant. The accounts of Louisiana published by the promoters, describe its " Mountains of gold and silver." Alexi, who illustrates eleven of these pieces, remarks "they offer little that is attractive to the lover of art ; they are mostly wretched pieces of work of a South German die-cutter, and are, except the first [our 114], satirical." We think there can be no doubt this is fully as satirical as any. We believe it is found in silver only. — EDS.

inscribed WEXL BRIEFE (Letters of Exchange) his cocked hat
has fallen near him.   On the end of the rocks, near his left
hand, MDCCI (an error in the die for MDCCXX).

Rev. BANQVERODT ist A LA MODE!   (Bankruptcy is the
fashion.*)   Half length figure of Law in cocked hat, with his
back towards the observer, between the words VISIBILIS
INVISIBILIS (Visible, Invisible).

Copper.   Size 22.   Med. Ill., Geo. I, 59.   Alexi X (1.)

116.   1720.   *Obv.* As the preceding, but MDCCII (for 1720).
Rev. As the preceding, but WEXEL.

Silver and lead.   Size 22.   Alexi X (2).   This variety is
the one shown in his illustration.

117.   1720.   *Obv.* MELAC REDIVIVVS SINE IGNE ET
LIGNO GRASSANS, | IN CRVMENAS EVROPAE CASSAS ET
TOTAS EXENTERANDAS in two circles.   (Melac making a raid
without fire or wood, on the purses of Europe, now utterly
empty and turned inside out.)   Bust of John Law facing;
below bust, ERGO on the left, on the coat, and IEAN LAW on
the right;   below, HIC NIHIL | EXPECTES.   (Therefore, John

---

* Struck on Law's flight from France. The dies by Christian Wermuth.
The obverse, especially, indicates the downfall of credit resulting from his
schemes, and the caduceus its effect on commerce and business; while the
reverse motto "Now you see it, and now you don't," and Law's figure, with his
face invisible, intimating that he could not face the consequences,—points at the
specious arguments by which he had deceived the public through his System.—
EDS.

Law you need not expect anything here.) The dates 1720 and 1721 in chronograms.

Rev. IN ACTIIS MISSISIPPEIS ET BILLETIS above, and CAETERA TEXTVS HABET below. Inscription, GALLI | NARRARVNT | ET NOS | NARRAVIMVS OMNES | ANGLVS ET HOLLANDVS | FRANKFVRT NORIBERGAQ | ET HAMBVRG | AVGSPVRG ET SVA QVI | VOLVERVNT | DAMNA | SILERI. (In regard to the shares and notes of the Mississippi Company, the French have told us, and we all have repeated the story, the Englishman and the Hollander, Frankfort and Nuremburg, Hamburg and Augsburg, and those who have wished that their losses might be kept quiet. As to the rest, the scheme has it.*)

Silver. Size 26. Alexi II.

118. 1720. *Obv.* WER SICH DVRCH DIESEN WIND DEN GELDGEITZ LÄSSET FÜHREN. (Who, in his avarice, will allow himself to be carried away by this wind?) Law walking to right, with a pair of bellows, from which are flying certificates; a scroll issuing from his mouth, to the right, on which WER KAVFT ACTIEN. (Who buys shares?) In exergue, SEI KLVG V. WITZIG IN | VERKEHREN. (Be prudent and cautious in your transactions.)†

Rev. DER KAN VERWIRRVNGS VOLL | SEIN HAAB. V. GVTH VERLIEREN. (One who gets confused may lose the goods and possessions he has.) A dog crossing a bridge over a stream, snaps at his shadow in the water, and thereby drops a bundle

---

* It is clearly impossible to give a rendering of the legends and inscriptions on these various pieces, which will convey their full meaning as appreciated when they were struck. On many of them the "Latin" is anything but Latin, and the words are frequently incorrectly spelled; the dies were evidently cut, as mentioned above, by some careless or incompetent hand; the inscriptions were composed by one ignorant of the language, or are wrong by intention. On the piece under notice, Melac was the name given to a barbarian who seems to have ravaged Europe, much after the style of the "bummers" in the late Civil War. *Textus,* which probably means the famous "System," signifies literally something that is woven, and hints at the skill with which Law had evolved his schemes, (as a spider weaves his web,) and caught his victims, and there is nothing now but the certificate of stock to show for the investment.—EDS.

† Med. Ill. gives in the exergue SEV for SEI and WIZIG for WITZIG.—EDS.

of billets. In exergue, SOLL DICH ESOPI HVND | NICHT LEHREN, 1720. (Shall not Esop's dog teach you a lesson?)*

Silver and copper. Size 22. Alexi, VII. Med. Ill., Geo. I, 58.

119. 1720. *Obv.* QUI MODO CROESUS ERAT * IRUS ET EST SUBITO. (He who but now was [the wealthy] Croesus, is [the beggar] Irus, and that suddenly.) * * * PARIS . | MISSISIP-PISCHER . | ACTIEN | GENERAL-DIRECTOR | EST, EST, | LAWS | SCOTUS EDENBURGICUS . | MERCATOR | MONETARIUS | INTRICA-TISSIMUS | BANQUIER & GENERAL | CONTROLLEUR . | FINAN-CIER | TRES-RAFFINÉ | MDCCXX. (Laws is the Manager-General of the stock of the Mississippi Company, of Paris, he is; the Edinboro' Scotchman, the merchant, the capitalist, the most skillful banker and Comptroller-General, and an extremely acute financier, 1720.)

Rev. * FURIAE GALLIARUM NATURA * above, and QUOD CITO FIT, CITO PERIT below. (Madness is the natural characteristic of the French: whatever is made quickly perishes quickly.) Inscription on the field, • * • | TOLLUNTUR | IN | ALTUM | UT | LAPSU | GRAVIORE | RUANT . | ... (They are raised up on high that they may be destroyed by a greater fall.)

Silver, copper and lead. Size 19. Alexi XI.

120. 1720. *Obv.* GELD IST DIE LOSUNG. (Money's the thing.) Two soldiers, with sword and spontoon; one, holding his hat, whispers something in the ear of the other, whose back is turned to observer; the latter seems to hear him; he

---

* These dies were by Wermuth.—EDS.

holds his hat under his arm, and a purse behind him. In
exergue, ABER (But).

Rev. WIE'S KOMMT SO GEHT'S. (As it comes so it goes.)
A speculator holds in his uplifted left hand a tattered purse,
from which money is falling ; with his right he points to the
wasted wealth behind him. In exergue, NULLA BLEIBT ÜBRIG.
(Nothing at all is left.)*

Silver. Size 38. Alexi XIX. Extremely rare.

121. 1720. *Obv.* PARISER | WEST-INDISCH — | LOUISIAN-
ISCHER | COMPAGNIE | ACTIEN | ODER | BANCO-BILLETS | IEDES
A | 500 . LIVRES OD . 166⅔ THL . | VON 1 . IAN . 1717 . | MIT IV
PRO CENT ZU | VERINTERESSIREN | AO . 1720 . AUT . 2 . PR . 100 .
(Shares or certificates of stock of the Parisian West Indian-
Louisiana Company were valued at 500 livres each, or 166⅔
thalers, on Jan. 1, 1717, and yielding four per cent interest :
in 1720, two shares† for 100 livres.) Below, curving, (these
these lines are upside down with the rest) SIND INCONFIS-
CABEL | UND SEMPER FREY • | IN FINE VIDEBITUR | CVIVS |
TONI. (They cannot be confiscated and are always free. In
the end it will be seen what is the value of this story.)

Rev. ALLES LIEGT AM GLÜCK UND AN DER ZEIT • (Everything depends on luck and time.) Inscription on the field,

---

* The obverse legend is a proverb, but the word LOSUNG also signifies a
watchword, which meaning is suggested by the device. The reverse legend is
to be read as a continuation of the obverse. The Medal has no date, but was
undoubtedly struck about 1720. The introduction of the Latin *nulla* in the
exergue, mingled for no special reason with the German, is another instance of
the characteristic *abandon* which marks these pieces.—EDS.

† Shares which sold for 18,000 francs in 1719 were worth only 200 in
October, 1720, a far greater depreciation than that noted on the Medal. See
Fiske's Memoir of John Law, p. 185.—EDS.

SO | VERSICHERTS | LAWS | UND SPRICHT : | DIESES GLAUB ICH |
ANDERS NICHT | MANCHER | DOCH MIT THOMA | SPRICHT : | ICH
GLAUB ES | NOCH LANGE | NICHT . | 1720 . (So Laws de-
clares and says ; I hold exactly this belief : many a one, however, says with Thomas, I do not yet believe it entirely [i. e.,
I doubt it.])*

Silver, tin and lead. Size 17. Alexi XII.

122. 1720. *Obv.* Mʳ DE LAWS, COMTE DE TANCKERVILLE,
CONSEILLER DU ROY DANS TOUTS SES CONSEILS, SURINTEND-
ANT ET CONTROLLEUR GENERAL DES FINANCES DU ROYAUME
DE FRANCE. (Mons. de Laws, Count of Tanckerville, Adviser
of the King in all his Councils, Superintendent and Comp-
troller General of the Finances of the Kingdom of France.)
Half-length figure of Law, three-quarters to right, his head
facing ; his hair long ; he wears a cocked hat and an embroidered coat, and the badge of the Order of the St. Esprit
attached to a ribbon ; in his right hand he holds a paper
inscribed ACTIEN BILLETS . (Shares in notes.)

Rev. DIMANCHE : NOUS VIDONS PAR LES BILLETS DE
BANCQVE TOUTES LES BOURSES . | LUNDI : NOUS ACHETTONS
DES ACTIONS, | MARDI : NOUS AVONS DES MILLIONS, | MER-
CREDI : NOUS REGLONS NOTRE MENAGE, | IEUDI : NOUS NOUS
METTONS EN EQUIPAGE, | VENDREDI : NOUS ALLONS AU BALL, |
ET SAMEDI : A L'HOPITAL . | 1720 . (Sunday, by the notes of
the Bank we empty all the purses. Monday, we buy our
shares ; Tuesday, we are millionaires ; Wednesday, we arrange
our *menage ;* Thursday, we start our equipage ; Friday, we go
to the ball, and Saturday, we go the Hospital, i. e., the Poor-
house.)

---

* The crash of Law's " System " swamped the Company of the Indies, which,
as stated in a previous note, he had united in his Mississippi Company, and the
stock proved worthless; *cuius toni,* literally, of whose tone, referring to the
inscription on the reverse, i. e., " It remains to be seen whether the credulous
believer in Law, or the doubting Thomas, was right." The obverse has such a
mixture of French, Latin and German that one can only guess to which language
the abbreviations belong, hence their meaning is somewhat doubtful ; the reverse
inscription is a jingle of four lines, *spricht* and *nicht* rhyming alternately.—EDS.

Silver and tin.   Size 21.   V. L., Supp. III, 31.   Med. Ill.,
Geo. I, 55.*   Alexi V.

123.   1720.   *Obv.* Half-length figure of Law, as the preceding (122), with the same legend, etc.

Rev. KWIA MVNTVS FULD TEZIBI | NICHT LUSCHT MEHR
HAT ZUR LOTTERIE, | SO SCHAFFT VOR BILLETS *ACTIEN* HER, |
IN DIE KREUZ UND IN DIE QUER, | NACH DER IETZ'GEN WELT
BEGEHR . | 1720 .   (Because the world wishes to be deceived !
it takes delight no longer in lotteries, and so purchases shares
for tickets in all directions according to its present desire.)†
Silver.   Size 21.   Med. Ill., Geo. I, 56.   B. N.

124.   1720.   *Obv.* Half-length figure of Law; apparently
the same die as 122.

Rev. DURCH | ACTIEN | CREDIT . TEICH, | GAERTEN, LOT-
TERIE, | KUX, LIB'ROS, BILLETS, | WIE AUCH DURCH ALCHYMIE, |
KOMMT MAN | ZUMS | LIEBE GELT, | UND WEIS SO GARNICHT |
WIE | IN ANNO QVO : | DEFICIENTE PECV | NOS FVGIT
OMNE | NIA. (Through stocks, credit, pools, gardens, lotteries,
mining shares, children, notes, as well as by alchemy, a man
comes to love gold, and thereby falls into trouble, as in the

---

* The description and translation are taken from Med. Ill. The dies were
by Christian Wermuth, of Gotha, and cut soon after the bubble burst. It is a
very rare Medal. The experiences of the week, as here described, are hardly an
exaggeration of the wild speculation which preceded the catastrophe. Alexi
gives this (V), but apparently had not seen it; he does not separate the lines,
and puts DIMANCHE,....BOURSES at close, before the date. He also has V for
U. We have not seen the piece to compare it; the text follows Med. Ill.
Alexi cites Adam, Numoph. Mansbg., fol. 975, and Rolas du Rosay, No. 2939.
"An unheard of number of equipages paraded the capital, and the streets....
were so blocked up by the carriages of rich Mississippians that the merchants
complained to the Regent that they seriously interfered with business." Fiske,
Memoir of John Law, p. 112.—EDS.

† The dies of this piece, the obverse certainly, and it is believed the reverse,
were cut by Wermuth; the spelling of several of the words, if the attribution is
correct, was clearly intentionally wrong, in order to add ridicule to the device.
The first line, for instance, is for *Quia Mundus vult decipi.* In der Kreuz, etc.,
literally in the cross-roads, or market places, and in the cross-streets, or by-ways.
This piece is also extremely rare.—EDS.

year 1720, in which money being wanting, everything escaped
us.   The date in chronogram.)*

Silver.   Size 21.   Alexi III.

125.   1720.   *Obv.*   LUDOVICUS XV . D . G . FR . ET . NAV .
REX .   (Louis XV, by the grace of God, King of France and
Navarre.)   Armored bust of the King, in profile to right ;
youthful head, with long and flowing curls.   On truncation,
J. LE BLANC. F. (die-cutter.†)

Rev. VINDEX AVARAE FRAUDIS.   (The avenger of avarici-
ous fraud,) on a ribbon at the top of the field.   Hercules, in
lion-skin, his club in his right hand, with his left drags Cacus
from his cavern‡ on Mount Aventine ; rocks at the left and
above.   In exergue, CHAMBRE DE JUSTICE | 1716.   (Chamber
of Justice, 1716.)   On the field, at the right, near the heel
of Hercules, DV. (Du Vivier.†)

Silver.   Size 25.   Alexi XVIII.

---

* This reverse inscription is a *salmagundi* of German, French and Latin.
The last line is a part of the word at the end of the last line but two — *pecunia*.
Gärten furnishes opportunity for various conjectures ; it may hint at the tulip-
mania of Holland the previous century, or to the returns expected from the fertile Southern lands, so glowingly described in his Mississippi scheme, or to the
name assumed by Law — M. du Jardin — on his flight to Brussels. — EDS.

† Le Blanc, the engraver of the obverse die, flourished at Paris, 1715-1725.
Jean Du Vivier, born at Liege, 1687, died at Paris, 1761 ; he was a member of
the Academy. — EDS.

‡ Cacus, the son of Vulcan, and a famous robber, had stolen some of the
cows of Hercules, and dragged them backward into his cave to prevent discovery.   Cacus thus represents the usurious robbers of the French treasury, who
had taken advantage of the necessities of the Kingdom in the long wars under
Louis XIV, to loan him money at their own terms, while Hercules typifies the
power of the realm asserting itself when the opportunity came.   By the "Chamber of Justice" is meant a special tribunal popularly called by the French *cham-
bre ardente* (literally a burning chamber, i. e. the chamber in which by the custom
of the Roman church in France, the coffin of a deceased person was placed, surrounded with burning tapers).   When Noailles, the French Minister of Finance,
took office, he found the public debt so enormous that the interest thereon
absorbed half the revenue; by an arbitrary decree he scaled it down, and in
March, 1716, by a "chamber of justice" a special commission which examined
the various securities, and reduced their face value, he deprived the holders of the
public debt of a large proportion of their property, and then issued paper money
to represent what remained.   In this and his subsequent steps he followed the
advice of Law. See Alexi p. 5.—EDS.

126. 1720. *Obv.* BEETER IN DE WYDE WERELT; ALS IN DE NAUE BUYK *of* KIST. (Better in the wide world, than in the narrow stomach, or chest.) A man, partially undressed, lighting his pipe with a bundle of script, is emitting coins, some of which, provided with wings, are flying away; above, NVMMVS VBI LOQVITVR. (Money, where he speaks.) In exergue, NOOIT BREEKT YSER . 22 PRO CENT (Necessity breaks iron; i. e. knows no law. 22 per cent.) The chronogrammatic date in the legend and exergue combined, is 1714, about which time Law began his operations.*

Rev. KOMT SEHT DAS FRANTZVOLCK AN! HERR LAVV THVT GROSSE THATEN! (Come, behold the people of France. Mr. Law doeth great things.) Inscription: EN MAGNAS DAT OPES CELEBER LAVV FOENORE QVESTVS. (Behold, the renowned Law, by usury of gain, gives great wealth.) The dates in the legend and inscription are chronogrammatic, and each make 1720.

Silver. Size 20. Med. Ill., Geo. I, 57.

127. 1720. *Obv.* As the preceding, except NOVIT instead of NOOIT.

Rev. AVT DESERVNT NOS AVT DESERIMVS ILLOS. (They either leave us or we leave them.) Inscription: DIS | TING | VEND | VM. (A distinction must be made.)

Silver. Size 20. Alexi XVI ;† Adam, Numoph. Mansbg. p. 967.

128. 1720. *Obv.* VERGROESSERVNGS GLAS THVTS HIER VND AN SO VIELEN ENDEN | DAS SICH DIE THOREN AVCH DIE GELDSVCHT LASSEN | BLEN DEN, in three semi-circular lines above. (The magnifying glass makes these seem close at hand, and a great amount; so also the pursuit of gold suffers itself to be

---

* The description and translations are from Med. Ill.: Alexi gives this obverse combined with another reverse (see 127). Med. Ill. has NOOIT where Alexi gives NOVIT. If the latter is correct, as seems probable, the date would be 1719, nearer Law's period of speculation.—EDS.

† It will be observed that four dies only, make Nos. 126, 127, and 130; Alexi notes but two combinations, viz.: IX and XVI.—EDS.

blinded by folly.*)   A man in cocked hat and court costume, and turning to the left, holds in his right hand a magnifying glass,—which bears the figures 100,—through which he is looking at various bank-bills, one marked 1,000, others, 100, which are lying on a table before him ; his left hand is extended behind him towards an open chest, filled with money. In exergue, DER ACTIEN BETRVG | VND LIST.   (Bills are a fraud and deceit.)

Rev. DAS SPIEL IST NVN ENDECKT DAS BLAT HAT SICH GEWEND V SO MACHT | DE BETRVG EIN SCHRECKENVOLLES END.   (The game is now ended ; the tables are turned, and the deception has wrought a fearful end.)   Beside a river stands a leafless tree ; a man has hung himself upon it ; his wig, hat and sword lie at the foot ; a second has thrown himself into the stream ; a third, at the left, full of despair, seems ready to follow him, while a fourth, at the right, is running away.   In exergue, DER GANZEN WELT EIN | DENKMAL IST. 1720.   (The whole world is a monument [i. e. of the folly of the hour].)

Copper.   Size 24½.   Alexi VIII.

129. (1720.) *Obv.* Law, in court costume, is shouting, to left, AVS. KVNST. ALLES. GEWONEN.   (By skill all things are gained.)

Rev. AVS. VNGLICK. ALLES. VERLOHREN.   (By bad luck all things are lost.)   A mourning woman (France ?) seated by a table.†

Silver.   Size 17.

130.   1720.   *Obv.* LES RICHESSES DES FRANCE.   (The wealth of France.)   A windmill on a post, driven by a blast, marked LOVIS-DORS, which proceeds from the mouth of Law, whose head is seen near the edge at the right.   The four

---

* The hat of the man divides the last word BLENDEN of the obverse legend, which, like that of the reverse, as will be seen, is a rhyming couplet.—EDS.

† This Medal has no date, but evidently belongs to 1720 or 1721 ; it was unknown to Alexi. We take the description from Numismatische Correspondenz, 104/6, No. 189, to complete as far as possible the list of the Law Medals.—EDS.

arms of the windmill have horns of plenty attached ; from the upper left arm fly rings, jewels, Orders, etc.; from the upper right arm, bank-notes and the word BILLETS ; from the lower left, certificates of stock, marked ACTIEN ; and from the lower right, coins,* some of them winged, and flying away. In exergue, 1720.

Rev. As reverse of 126.

Silver and tin.   Size 20.   Alexi IX.

131.   1720.   *Obv.* As 121, but without AUT . 2 . PR . 100.
Rev. MANN . SETZ . SICH . NICHT . FUR . MAASS . NOCH . ZIEL . *
(Man sets neither limits nor bounds to himself [i. e. puts no restraint on his desire for money.])   Inscription, DIE | DA | REICH | WERDEN | WOLLEN | FALL . IN . | VERSUCHUNG | I TIMOT VI . V 9 10 | 1720.(They that will be rich will fall into temptation.   I Tim. Chap. vi : verses 9, 10.   1720.)

Silver.   Size 27.   Alexi XIII.

132.   1720.   *Obv.* As obverse of 117.
Rev. LaVs tIbI et IMpostor CorVos eLVDIs hIantes. (Praise to you [Law] who art also an imposter, you have escaped the eager ravens. 1720. Date in chronogram.) Inscription on the field : ITA | ACTVM EST | CVM IIS QVI | AVGENDÆ PECVNIA CAVSA | ACTIORVM NOMINE | CHARTAS CAPTABANT PECVNIATAS | LITTERATA CHARTÆ OSORES | INGNIOSÆ PE-CVNIÆ CONTEMTOR | PRO AVCTO TANDEM ACTVS CENSV | CREDITORVM CENSVRAM | PRO PECVNIA CHARTAS | PRO LAQVE-ARIH. LAQVEOS HABENT | ET DVM PAVLVM NON | SED SAVLVM AVDIVNT | IVDAM SEQVNTVR | ET CVM HOC FIVNT | LITTERA | LONGA.   (This is the result with those who, for the sake of increasing their money, eagerly seek for moneyed papers, under the names of stocks ; haters of literary papers, despisers of honest money.   Instead of gaining an increased property they win the censure of their creditors ; paper instead of

---

* Alexi calls the objects which are falling from one arm, bombs and grenades ; but in his engraving they seem rather to be winged coins. He does not mention the combination of dies given as 126. — EDS.

money ; snares instead of panelled ceilings ; and while they hear not Paul, but Saul, they follow Judas, and with him become a long letter.   [i. e. I.])*

Tin.   Size 26.   Benj. Betts's collection.

133.   1720.   *Obv.*   QVVM TV SCHADEN HABES, NEC OPVS EST SORGERE SPOTTEN. (Since you have met with the loss, there is no need to worry over the ridicule.)   An invalid scated in a chair, which stands on low wheels, with a support for the feet in front ; his arms are folded ; at the left, on a couch, is a woman, slightly draped, a crown on her head, and apparently conversing with the invalid.   At the right, behind the man, is a fury walking to the right, with a sword in her right hand, a torch in her left, and a plumed chapeau on her

---

* For an engraving of the reverse of this Medal, from which this description is given, we are indebted to Mr. Benjamin Betts (the original owner of the Law Medals, which passed to Mr. Wyllys Betts), who had collected nearly all the known Law Medals, and several undescribed till now; and he has kindly furnished us with the description of several in his cabinet, which were unknown to Alexi and other writers on these pieces, although himself having in preparation a monograph on the subject; so that the list of them now printed may embrace all so far as known. For his generosity in the matter the grateful thanks of the Numismatic fraternity are certainly due. It will be observed that there are several errors in the Latin words on this piece. The legend properly follows, in reading, the inscription. It is not possible in a translation to give the contrasts in sound of the Latin words; but the following may properly be noted. ACTVM is used for its similarity with *Aetien*, the word denoting stocks; PECUNIATAS CHARTAS, *moneyed* papers, i. e. bank bills, is contrasted with LITTERATA[S] CHARTAS, *lettered* papers, i. e. books; the first three letters of INGENIOSÆ are in monogram, and E is omitted; CONTEMTOR for CONTEMPTORES; PRO AVCTO CENSV, literally, "instead of an increased rating of property," where census, "the rating," is contrasted with censure. LAQUEARIB[US] "panelled ceilings," as adornments of a palace, contrasted with LAQUEOS, "snares," and alluding to the duty of rich men, as declared by St. Paul to Timothy, (see 131) which is also hinted at in the next line of the inscription, DVM PAVVLM, etc. LITTERA LONGA, i. e. the letter I is used as an emblem of the body of Judas, who hung himself. SEQVNTVR for SEQVVNTVR. SAVL seems to have a double meaning,—an anagram of LAVS (as on 134), and an allusion to his seeking counsel of a necromancer, instead of the Prophet of God, just before his destruction ; and finally, LAVS TIBI in the legend, alludes to the response in the service of the Church, after the reading of the Gospel. Here it might well be rendered, "Lucky for you." The Medal is in many respects one of the most remarkable of the series.—EDS.

head ; she turns backward to the others ; in the background
a table with glasses, and in the foreground, crutches. Over
the group, SVSTINE | VEL | ABSTINE (Sustain or abstain.)*

Rev. CERTE PODAGRA above, and ANNO QVO AVTOREM
EXERCEBAT below. (In the year 1720 [date in chronogram],
in which the gout certainly was afflicting the author.) In-
scription, AVLA | SVVM | SERVAT NOCTESQ. | DIESQ. | TENO-
REM, | POTARE INVITI | COGIMVR ABSQ. SITI ; | MORIBVS ET
PODAGRA. SI | SIC VENIEMVS AD ASTRA, | FRVSTRA SE CRVCIANT |
SOBRIETATE | PII : (The Court holds on the tenor of its way
by night and by day. Unwilling to drink, we are yet compelled to, by thirst, by the customs of the time, and by the
gout : if by such a course we reach heaven, in vain do the
pious torture themselves by sobriety.)

Silver. Size 21. Benj. Betts's collection.

134. 1720. *Obv.* As obverse of preceding. (The same
die.)

Rev. PODAGRA | VAN DE KONINGLYKE | FRANSCHE BEURS |
GEPROIECTEERT EN | GETRANSPLANTEERT | IN DE BEURSES |
VAN DE | MISSISSIPISCHE- | ZUIDE- EN | GENERALE -ASSUREN-
TIE- | COMPAGNIES | DOOR | LAVS | Managr. | SAVL . (The
gout of the Royal French Treasury injected and transplanted
into the treasuries† of the Mississippi, the South, and the

---

* For our knowledge of this and the two following pieces we are indebted to
Mr. Benjamin Betts. The obverse legend, like so many others of the class, is a
mixture of bad Latin and German, a macaronic rendering of popular slang :—
" Brace up or let up," would be a version in accord with the spirit of the piece.
SORGERE is a German word Latinized. The gout, and the wheeled chair, showing the inability of the sufferer to walk, evidently allude to the crippled state of
the finances of the kingdom ; the crowned woman, stripped of everything, to
France, and the other figure with her cocked hat, the absurdity of the popular
frenzy.—EDS.

† The crippled condition of the French Treasury before the rise of Law's
schemes, followed by the bankruptcy of his various enterprises, is the motive of
this Medal. Its peculiarities need no special explanation. This and the preceding were unknown to Alexi, and we believe have never before been described,
which increases our indebtedness to the owner, who has so kindly consented to
allow them to be given here to complete the series, in advance of the appearance
of his own work.—EDS.

General Assurance Companies, by Law [LAUS], Manager. Saul.) NOMINA on the margin at the left, OMINA at the right, and HABENT at the bottom. (Names have omens.)

Silver.   Size 21.   Benj. Betts's collection.

135.   1721.   *Obv.*   BEATVM DIC sINe ACtIIs PATERNA RVRA | QVI AGItAT. (Call him happy who cultivates his paternal fields without shares.)   A ploughman, who swings a whip in his right hand, drives two horses attached to a plough to the left, over a field ; the sky is clouded.   In exergue, POST NVBILA PHOEBVS | DVM ABIIT LAW A PARIS | IN SOLSTITIO LVNAE | D . XIX DECR | XX. (The sun appeared from behind the clouds while* Law went away from Paris on the winter solstice of the moon, Dec. 19, 20, 1721.   Date in chronogram.)

Rev.   Inscription, SPES | MaLa | DAt laqVEos | AVCtIs | PRO | REDVs AVaro | I. TIM. VI. | V. 6. *incl.* 12. | 17. 18. 19. | c. w. (An evil hope proves a snare instead of increased riches, to an avaricious man.   1 Timothy, Chap. vi, verse 6 (?9), including 12, etc.   C. W. for Christian Wermuth.   Date in chronogram, 1721.)

Silver.   Size 20.   Alexi VI.

136.   *Obv.*   RISIT STVLTITIAM TEMPORIS ILLE SVI.   (He laughed at the folly of his times.)   The head, facing, and shoulders, of a man laughing, whose face slightly turned to the right, has a sinister expression ; his head is partly bald, his beard full, and his arms folded on his breast, but concealed

---

* D of DVM in obverse exergue is so near the edge, that the word may be meant for QUUM (when).   The Latin seems to have a double meaning, of which the second one is more sarcastic than that given in the text, i. e., The sun was behind the clouds, so long as (dum) Law was absent from Paris.   The expression the "solstice of the *moon*" seems to allude to the popular belief that the moon causes lunacy, and the date, which is that of the night of Dec. 19-20 (just before the winter solstice, Dec. 21), that Law took himself off "between two days," as the saying is.   The 6th verse of the chapter quoted, has no allusion to the inscription, and is probably an error for the 9th, which contains the thought expressed.   The other verses referred to, are those which describe the duties incumbent on rich men, "to be rich in good works, ready to distribute," etc. Law fled to Brussels, where he arrived on the morning of Dec. 22, 1720.—EDS.

by a portion of a globe, showing parts of the Eastern and Western Continents, the meridians and parallels; the pole to the right near the edge.

Rev. TEMPORIS ILLE SVI CASVS ET CRIMINA FLEVIT. (He wept over the misfortunes and crimes of his times.) The head and shoulders of a younger man, in similar attitude to that on obverse, facing, but slightly turned to the left, and having a doleful expression. The portion of the globe in front of him shows a part of both Continents, meridians, etc., but the pole is erect.

Silver. Size 18. Collection of Daniel Parish, Jr.*

137. 1720. *Obv.* PARTURIUNT MONTES NASCETUR TRALA-LARALA. INSIGNE TOUT LA COMPAGNIE (The mountains are in labor; Tralalarala [Nothing but a sound], is born. The emblem [or arms] of the entire company.) A shield, bearing a blazon. In exergue, MANN SCHICKE SICH NUN NUR IN DIESE NEUE ZEIT. (A man can do nothing under present circumstances but go with the times.)†

Rev. As 131. (MANN SETZ, etc.)

Tin. Size 27. Alexi XIV. Hauschild, 2834.

138. 1720. *Obv.* Three figures. In exergue, o CONSTI-TUTION o ACTIEN (Oh Constitution, Oh Stocks.)

---

* This has no date, but may belong to the Law series. The portion of the globe, which it bears, seems to entitle it to be placed in this work. Since the descriptions of 133 and 134 were printed, we have been informed by Mr. Betts that those are not in his collection, but in that of Mr. Daniel Parish, Jr.—EDS.

† Mr. Wyllys Betts obtained the description of this Medal from Alexi, *loc. cit.*, who does not describe the arms, and we infer he had not seen it. Mr. Benj. Betts also advises us that he has never seen it, and we are unable after various inquiries to complete the description. The piece, as will be noticed, is a "mule." Its connection with the Law series therefore depends on Alexi's authority, and on the association of the obverse with a die belonging to that series. We learn from Alexi (note on p. 59), that the devices of several of these Medals were taken from a Dutch work entitled "Tafereel der Dwaasheid." Among them are his IX (130), X (115, 116), XIII (131)—of which the inscription is found with the 51st Caricature in that work—and XVI (127); the inscriptions on the obverse of XIV (137), and the reverse of XI (119), are from a Poem on page 25 of the same work, and the inscription on reverse of V (122), he adds, is a satirical saying of the Parisians, of the time.—EDS.

Rev. PAX PAX DICENTES TAMEN NVLLA PAX IER. VI
14. (Saying Peace, Peace ; yet there is no peace. Jeremiah
vi : 14 ; date 1736, in chronogram.) Inscription on the field,
· 2 · | SCHAV PFENNIG | GROSCHEN | FIAT | IVSTITIA | AVT |
PEREAT MVNDVS | ₀ (Two medallic groschen. Let justice
be done, or the world perish.). Edge with broad milling.
Copper, bronzed. Size 22. Alexi XVII.*

139. 1720. *Obv.* As obverse of 115. (CREDIT IST, etc.)
Rev. As the preceding.
Copper, bronzed. Size 22. Benj. Betts's collection.†

140. 1720. *Obv.* As obverse of 131, but in the seventh
line the words are STAAT BILIETS, and in the eighth IEDE (not
IEDES) on the engraving examined, instead of as on that
number.
Rev. As reverse of 121. (ALLES LIEGT, etc.)
Silver. Size 27. Benj. Betts's collection.‡

---

* This is given by Alexi as a Law Medal, but if so, the obverse is one of the
dies of some rare Medal of the period, of which the full description was unknown
to him,—as it is also to Mr. Benjamin Betts (who supplies us with the reverse, not
given in full by Alexi), and to the Editors,—in combination with a die of a much
later date, as shown by the chronogram. The only claim the piece can have to
be included here, with our present knowledge, rests upon its attribution by so
excellent an authority as Alexi, to Law, which may hereafter be established by a
more complete description of the obverse.—EDS.

† For a knowledge of this combination we are indebted to Mr. Benjamin
Betts; while it is possible that it belongs to the series, we are in accord with his
opinion that it is extremely doubtful whether it be a Law Medal, since the obverse, as he informs us, is also found muled with other reverses, having no connection with Law, which seems to cast a doubt on the statement taken from
Alexi, under 115, that the dates on that and 116, are errors. While Med. Ill.
assigns 115 to Law, it does not mention the error in the date, which is somewhat
obscure on the piece. On the correctness of Alexi, therefore, depends the
attribution.—EDS.

‡ It seems probable, since these obverses so closely resemble each other,
that Alexi may have overlooked the differences noted above, existing in the inscription, to which our attention has been called by Mr. Benj. Betts, and that
the obverse die of 131 is really the same with this ; in that case this piece would
seem to be the same as noted by Alexi, under his XII, as a variety of that Medal.
It should, however, properly be given a distinct number, an account of the essen-
tial differences in the two obverse dies, and also because it is another combination. We know of it only through Mr. Betts's kindness.—EDS.

141.   1721.   *Obv.* ʀᴇDDᴇɴDᴀ ᴇX ᴀCᴛIs LᴀVs LᴀVsᴏ (Praise should be rendered to Law, from his acts.)   In exergue, ʀᴏᴍᴀᴍ ᴄᴠᴍ ᴘᴇᴛᴇʀᴇᴛ ɪᴀ | ɴᴠᴀʀɪᴏ ᴍ . ᴍɪssɪᴏɴɪs | ᴀᴍᴇʀɪᴄᴀɴᴀᴇ ᴀᴠᴛᴏʀ | ᴀᴄᴛᴏʀ ᴇᴛ | ꜰᴀᴄᴛᴏʀ.   (When the author, the promoter and the operator of the American Scheme sought Rome, in the month of January, 1721.   Date in chronogram in the legend.)   A staff erect, and bearing a banner inscribed ᴀʙ | ᴀᴄᴛɪs | ᴀD | ꜰᴀᴄᴛᴀ.   (From acts to facts, i. e. from the promise of stocks to deeds.)*

---

* This Medal was struck after Law reached Rome, whither he went shortly after leaving Brussels, following his flight from Paris: and to understand the full significance of the piece, which is rather abstruse without a knowledge of the history of the adventurer, it must be remembered that Law, who was by early education a Protestant, became a Roman Catholic when his schemes were beginning to fail, in order that he might win sympathy not otherwise to be gained; the Latin *acta* and *actis* have a double meaning; "acts" as shown by several of the preceding Medals, being the word used for stocks.   In substance the legends, etc., seem to imply that praise ought to be given to Law, since the author of the American Mission (i. e. the Mississippi Scheme) went to Rome, as if on a mission to obtain the aid of the Church in forwarding his plans, which his prospectus had declared included christianizing the Indians of Louisiana, as had been attempted in the earlier French colonization of Canada; if *facta*, which literally means things accomplished, be translated *deeds*, — evidences of real property — we have the nearest possible rendering of the double meaning of the Medal.   The reverse is still more sarcastic, and intimates that Law, who at the height of his success was deemed a far-seeing man, had scattered his paper money, which he claimed would, by the guarantee of the Government, be equally valuable with specie — a theory which was the foundation of his "System," — in the hope that it would bring returns in gold and silver; and that Louis, the "Most Christian King," might succeed in making Christians out of the Indians, but would have to labor zealously to accomplish it, a result as difficult of attainment as for Law's schemes to return material wealth.   Alexi, who had not seen this piece, gives a partial description under XV, from Hauschild, 2839.—Eᴅs.

Rev. • | SPARSVS | IN ORBEM | VT REDEAT NVMMVS, | PRO-
VIDVS ILLE FACIT : | AVREVS ATQVE ARGENTEVS | ET LVDOVICVS
ET INDOS | CHRISTIANOS | FACIAT, | SEDVLVS | EFFICIET . | •
(Money is scattered throughout the world, that it may return
in gold and silver; the prudent man [i. e. Law] does this!
And Louis may even make the Indians Christians; if he is
zealous, he will accomplish this.)

Tin.   Size 22.

The foregoing comprise all which have come under our
notice, that seem entitled to be classed among the " Law
Medals," and hence to be more or less remotely connected
with America.   There are indeed a few others, which by
some authorities are erroneously reckoned among them,—
notably one with a burlesque coat of arms, having monkeys
as supporters,—but which is doubtless of an earlier date.*

LOUISBURG FOUNDED.

142.   1720.   *Obv.* LUDOVICUS XV . REX CHRISTIANISSIMUS.
DU VIVIER F. on arm.†   Youthful bust of King to left, in armor.

---

* The piece alluded to in the text is described in the American Journal of
Numismatics (XXIII, p. 88), which Mons. Alphonse de Witte, of the Royal Belgian Numismatic Society, there shows to have been struck towards the close of
the reign of Louis XIV.   It is engraved in Plate XIII of the Revue Belge de
Numismatique, for 1847, and is described on page 404 of that volume.   It certainly is not a Law Medal.—EDS.

† See note on 125.—EDS.

Rev. LUDOVICOBURGUM FUNDATUM ET MUNITUM . In exergue, M . DCC . XX . (Louisburg founded and fortified. 1720.)
View of the fort of Louisburg with a large building in the
centre having a cross; houses grouped around the fort; a
point of land with lake and grove of firs extends to the foreground, where are wharfs, warehouses and ships in a harbor;
at the left a strait leads to the open sea, where appear two
ships and three sloops.
Gold.   Size 26.   B. N.

143.   1720.   *Obv.* LUDOVICUS XV. D. G. FR. ET NAV. REX.
(Louis XV, by the grace of God King of France and Navarre.)
Under bust, DU VIVIER. Young laureated bust of Louis to right,
in toga.
Rev. Same as 142.
Copper.   Size 26.   McL., XIX.   Leroux 308.

144.   1720.   *Obv.* Same legend and design, but without
name of engraver.
Rev. Same as 142.
Silver and copper.   Size 26.

145.   1720.   *Obv.* Same legend but with period after ET.
and with I . LE BLANC F . upon truncation.   Youthful bust of the
King facing right in armor and draped, but not laureate.
Rev. Same as 142.
Silver and copper.   Size 26.

146.   1720.   *Obv.* LUDOVICUS XV . REX CHRISTIANISS . (Louis
XV, Most Christian King.)   On truncation, DUVIVIER . F . Bust
of the King to right, without drapery; the neck very long.
· *Rev.* Same as 142.
Silver and copper.   Size 26.

147.   1720.   *Obv.* LUDOVICUS XV . REX CHRISTIANISSIMUS .
Older bust of the King to right, laureate.
Rev. Same as 142.
Silver and copper.   Size 26.   McL., XII.

GUADALOUPE FORTIFED.

148. 1721. *Obv.* LUDOVICUS XV. D. G. FRAN. ET NAV. REX Laureated bust to right in antique armor, with hair floating over the shoulders and below the bust. On truncation of arm, DU VIVIER F.

Rev. Two large and twelve small islands at the left ; above, a dart, the point downward, adorned with lilies. In exergue, GUADALUPA INSULA MUNITA, | PHILIPPO REGENTE . | M . DCC . XXI . (Guadaloupe fortified in 1721, Philip, Regent.)

Copper. Size 26. C. M., p. 216, the abbreviation FR appearing in the legend instead of FRAN.

PROCLAMATION OF LOUIS I, OF SPAIN, IN CHOLULA.

149. 1724. *Obv.* LVDOV . I . D . G HISPANIAR . R . (Louis I, by the grace of God King of Spain.) Profile bust of King Louis to right, draped, within a circle, the hair and upper part of the head extending into the outer circle.

Rev. CHOLVLA. 1724. A church upon a hill, with a banner on each side ; a trumpet or cornet, in the foreground ; all within a circle.

Silver, cast. Size 20. H., Luis I, 18.

PROCLAMATION IN MEXICO.

150. 1724. *Obv.* LUDOUICUS . I . D . G . HISPANIARUM . REX . ANO . 1724 ✦ (Louis I, etc., in the year 1724.) Bust of the King in profile to right, with Order-chain of the Golden Fleece, and draped.

Rev. IMPERATOR . INDIARUM. (Emperor of the Indies.) In the field, MEX ICO at the sides of a castle of two stories, which rests upon waves, and is supported by two lions ; and upon which is an eagle seated on a cactus.

Silver, cast. Size 25. H., Luis I, 19.

151. *Obv.* ✦ LUDOUICUS . I . D . G . HISPANIARUM . REX . ✦ Bust of the King to right in armor, draped.

Rev. INPERATOR (*sic*) . INDIARVM. In the field, MEX ICO. Similar design to last.

Silver, cast. Size 20. H., Luis I, 20.

PROCLAMATION IN PANAMA.

152. 1724. *Obv.* ✶ LVDOVICVS . I . D . G . HISPANIARVM REX ✶ Bust of the King in profile to right, draped, within a circle.

Rev. N . C . PANAMENSIS TE AMAT CORDE TE CLAMAT · ORE : (N. C. for (?) *nostra civitas*, Our city of Panama loves thee with its heart, and proclaims thee with its lips.) [The first N in Panamensis is reversed.] A shield divided per fess; in chief a ship sailing to sinister, a star at right; in base another ship sailing in the opposite direction, but the star is at the left; a border of castles and lions (for Spain); surmounted by a crown; columns entwined with scrolls, and bearing globes at the sides; all within a circle.

Silver. Size 22. H., Luis I, 21.

PROCLAMATION IN SAN FELIPE.

153. 1724. *Obv.* LUDOUICVS . I . D. G. HISPANIARUM . REX . ANO . 1724   Louis I, etc., in the year 1724.) Bust of the King to right, clothed, and wearing an Order-chain.

Rev. IMPERATOR INDIARUM (Emperor of the Indies). A shield bearing a rampant lion regardant in the first and fourth quarters, and a castle in the second and third; a crown above. Across the field below the shield, S . PHE . EL REAL. (San Felipe el Real.)

Silver, cast. Size 23. H., App. 25.

PROCLAMATION IN SANTA FE DE BOGOTA.

154. 1724. *Obv.* LVDV : : : : L. D. G. ✕ followed by a Teutonic, or "crutch-cross." Bust of the King to left, laureated, in a circle of dots.

Rev. HISPAN : : : : : REX. 724. An eagle displayed, his head to left, and wings drooping, within a circle of dots.

Silver. Size 12. H., App. 26.

PROCLAMATION IN VERA CRUZ.

155. 1724. *Obv.* LVDOV . I . D . G . HISPANIAR . R. [The N is reversed.] Bust of the King in profile to right in armor, within a circle; the upper part of his head extends into the outer circle.

Rev. VERACRVCIS . PROCLAMATIO . 1724. (Proclamation of Vera Cruz. 1724.) A castle, with three turrets, standing on waves, and surmounted by a cross ; all except the cross within a circle.

Silver, cast. Size 20. H., Luis I, 22.

PROCLAMATION IN YUCATAN.

156. 1724. *Obv.* S. D. I.. I. 1724. [The 4 reversed.] (Perhaps for "*Senatus Dicavit Ludovicus I,*" The Senate has proclaimed Louis I.) Bust of native, with abundant matted and disordered hair, to right, draped. Beaded border.

Rev. YVCA on the left, TAN on the right of a rude shield, divided in pale, bearing a rampant lion and castles, and surmounted by a coronet. Beaded border.

Silver, cast. Size 16. The letters are engraved. H., Luis I, 23.

PROCLAMATION IN ZACATECAS.

157. 1724. *Obv.* LUDOUICUS . I . D . G . HISPANIARUM . REX . (Louis I, etc.) Bust of the King in profile to left, in armor and draped. Beaded border.

Rev. MINERIA DE above, and in exergue ZACATECAS. (Mines of Zacatecas. TE in monogram.) View of mountains, one with lofty peak, with sun at the left and crescent moon at the right. In the foreground at the left, BVFA (the name of the mountain.)

Silver, cast. Size 20. H., Luis I, 24.

PEACE BETWEEN AUSTRIA AND SPAIN.

158. 1725. *Obv.* PRO SIGNO FOEDERIS ARCUS (The bow for a token of covenant.) The columns of Hercules in the sea, that on the left surmounted by the imperial double-headed eagle, and that on the right by a lion standing, crowned ; three vessels sailing between them, one of which is in front of the left pillar ; a rainbow above, and a city in the distance, beyond the columns.   On the field between the capitals PLUS ULTRA (More beyond.)

Rev. CAROLUS VI · IMPERATOR GLADIOS NUNC PERMUTAVIT OLIVIS · | PAX ConCorDat UtrUMqUe · in two concentric circles (Charles VI, Emperor, has now exchanged the sword for the olive branch.   Peace unites both.* 1725, date in chronogram).   In exergue, PH. on the left, and R. on the right, (Philip Roettiers†).   The Emperor standing at right with a lion crouched at his feet on his left ; and Philip V at the left, holding an orb ; an eagle behind him partly appearing ; both are in Roman costume, and each extends an olive branch to the other ; a double-headed eagle with expanded wings above, places a crown upon the head of each ; in the foreground, on an elliptical tablet, a blazoned shield.

Silver.   Size 34.   V. L., Sup. No. 137, p. 136.

ST. PAUL'S COLLEGE, BERMUDA.

159.   1726.   *Obv.* TO BERKELEY EVERY VIRTUE UNDER HEAVEN.   ST. PAUL'S COLLEGE, BERMUDA.   INCORPORATED A. D. 1726.‡

---

* By this treaty, signed at Vienna, April 30, 1725, his portion of the Spanish possessions was assigned to each of these rulers, and the King of Spain received those in America.—EDS.

† This Philip Roettiers was the son of an elder Philip, and a nephew of the John mentioned in note on page 39.   He resided at Brussels and later at Antwerp, where he died in 1732.   He succeeded his father who had been "at the head of the coinage for Flanders."—EDS.

‡ It has been said that "all his contemporaries agreed with the satirist Pope, in ascribing 'To Berkeley every virtue under heaven.'"   It was his desire to found a college in America "for converting the savage Americans to Christianity," for which he issued proposals and raised a large sum of money by subscription, and also received a grant or promise of £20,000 from the Government. He sailed for Rhode Island in 1728, and just before leaving wrote the poem containing the well-known line —

"Westward the star of empire takes its way."

After spending two years in Newport, R. I., he was compelled to abandon the project of his college, because the British ministry failed to send the promised funds, and returned to England, where he afterwards became Bishop of Cloyne, and died in 1753.   This Medal seems to have been struck in the hope that the college would be founded ; but we cannot learn that such an institution ever was established at Bermuda, and the only reference to the Medal we have discovered is that cited in the text.—EDS.

Rev. GOD HATH MADE ALL MEN OF ONE BLOOD. — *Acts* *xvii.* 26.

"Soft metal." A. J. N., VIII, 45. Said to have been found in Bermuda. Chas. F. Allen's collection, Ithaca, N. Y.

FRENCH-INDIAN MEDAL.

160. *Obv.* LUDOVICUS XV. REX CHRISTIANISSIMUS. (Louis XV, etc.) Bust of King to right, draped and laureated.

Rev. HONOS ET VIRTUS. (Honor and Valor.) Two warriors standing with hands clasped ; one, representing France, on the right, wearing a Roman tunic and holding a spear in his left hand, and the other, representing the Indian allies of France, with loose drapery around his loins and on his left arm, and holding a spear in his left hand.

Size 32. This Medal has been found with LUDOVICUS, etc., erased and GORGE (*sic*) III stamped or engraved in its place.

BRITISH-INDIAN MEDALS.

161. 1714. *Obv.* GEORGE KING OF | GREAT BRITAIN. In exergue, 1714. Laureated bust of George I, in armor, to right.

Rev. An Indian at right drawing bow on a deer, standing at left on a hill, under a tree ; the sun above ; to right of which are three stars, and to left, one.*

Bronze, looped, and brass. Size 26. Bushnell, 255.

This is one of the medals presented by George I to Chiefs of the Six Nations. (See Miner's History of Wyoming, p. 27.) In a Carbondale, Pa., collection, 1858.

162. *Obv.* Same design and legend, but a smaller bust.

Rev. Same design, but the hill lower, the tree higher, and the Indian smaller than the preceding.

Copper, looped. Size 25 x 16. Collection of Rev. H. E. Hayden, Wilkes Barre, Pa.

---

* For a complete description of this number we are indebted to information received from Mr. E. J. Cleveland, of Bridgeport, Conn., and printed in A. J. N., XXVI, p. 83. He mentions that the date 1714 appears in exergue, though it is not shown in the engraving of the piece in Miner's History.. It was found at an Indian burial-place in Wilkes Barre, in 1814, by Chief Justice Gibson, Charles Miner, and Jacob Cist.—EDS.

163. *Obv.* GEORGE KING OF GREAT BRITAIN. Bust of George I, (?) draped and laureated, facing right.

Rev. Large Indian on the right drawing his bow to shoot a deer, which stands on a hill at the left behind a short tree ; flowers and bushes in the background and sun above.

Brass, looped. Size 26. A. J. N., IX, 8. Found at Point Pleasant, Va., on a battle-field of 1774. Rev. H. E. Hayden's collection, Wilkes Barre, Pa.

164. *Obv.* GEORGE KING OF GREAT BRITAIN .˙. * Bust of King to right, with a fillet of twelve laurel leaves.

Rev. A large Indian at right, throwing a spear at a small deer at left ; the sun above.

Brass, very thick. Size 24. Collection of Hon. Steuben Jenkins, of Wyoming, Pa. Copper, thin. Found in 1837, at Tunkhannock, Pa.

165. *Obv.* GEORGE . KING . OF . GREAT . BRITAIN . On truncation, ı c Bust of King to right in armor, draped, laureate.*

Rev. An Indian at right drawing a bow upon a deer, standing at left on a hill beside a tree ; a bush between the Indian and tree ; the sun above.

Copper. Size 26. N. Y. Hist. Soc. collection.

166. *Obv.* GEORGIUS — MAG. BR. FRA. ET. HIB. REX. Bust of George —, laureated, facing left.

Rev. Indian at right, nearly erect, leaning forward under a tree, which follows the curve of the medal, holding a bow at arm's length in left hand, right hand extended a little beyond his body ; at the left, on slightly more elevated ground than the Indian, and under a tree which follows the curve of the medal, a deer is running at full speed ; in foreground, a shrub ; no legend.

---

* ı. c. is doubtless for John Croker "as he styled himself, his name being Johann Crocker ; he was born at Dresden, Oct. 21, 1670, and died in England March 21, 1741. He was Chief Engraver of the English Mint after the death of Harris in 1705," and made the dies for a large number of Medals. See Med. Ill., II, p. 723.—EDS.

Brass, looped.   Size 16.   A. J. N., IX, 8.   Found in 1859, at Point Pleasant, Va.

167. *Obv.* GEORGIUS II. D. G. MAG. BR. FR. ET HIB. REX. Bust of the King to left, laureate, in armor.

Rev. Indian at right beneath a tree, shooting at a deer running away at right beneath a tree.   No legend.

Brass.   Size 15.   Found at Lackawanna, Pa., 1865.

COMPANY OF THE INDIES.

168. 1733. *Obv.* LUDOVICUS XV. REX CHRISTIANISSIMUS. Bust of the King to right in armor, draped.   J. C. BOETTIERS . on the truncation.

Rev. JUGENDIS | AMPLIORI ET FACILIORI | COMMERCIO GENTIBUS | EMPORIUM HOC | A FUNDAMENTIS EXSTRUXIT | SOCIETAS INDIARUM | GALLICA | In exergue, MDCCXXXIII. (The French Society of the Indies has erected this emporium from its foundations, for the purpose of joining the nations by a larger and more easy intercourse.   1723.)   Caduceus and cornucopia crossed.

Gold, silver and copper.   Size 32.   C. M., p. 167.

JERNEGAN CISTERN.

169. 1736. *Obv.* BOTH HANDS FILL'D FOR BRITAIN.   In exergue, GEORGE REIGNING.   Pallas standing amidst emblems of glory, art and industry.   T near palette at the right, for Tanner (the die-cutter).

Rev. GROWING ARTS ADORN EMPIRE; in exergue, CAROLINE PROTECTING | 1736. The Queen, wearing a crown and holding a sceptre, is watering a plantation of young palmettos.

Silver and copper. Size 24. F., 3731. Med. Ill., Geo. II, 72.

This medal is erroneously placed in the Fonrobert catalogue as if having some connection with North Carolina. In reality, it was issued by Henry Jernegan, a goldsmith, the son of Sir Francis Jernegan, also a goldsmith and banker, in Russell Street, Covent Garden, London, and distributed to the purchasers of tickets for the lottery of a silver vase or "cistern," which appears to have been drawn in 1737. The tickets were either five or six shillings, and each purchaser received one of these Medals; about 30,000 were struck in all. The encouragement given by Queen Caroline to Jernegan's undertaking, was the reason for placing her figure on the piece. The only reference to America is in the palmetto trees on the obverse; the design and legend indicating the protection afforded by the Queen to the Plantations and indirectly to the artist.[*]

---

[*] This piece, as Mr. Betts truly remarks, has been frequently and erroneously described by many cataloguers as relating to Carolina, and as it has caused both dealers and collectors so much trouble, it seems proper to give some account of its history. As long ago as 1863, Mr. W. H. Strobridge, in cataloguing the Lilliendahl Collection (sold December 15-17, 1863), said it was "struck by order of the Legislature of North Carolina, to commemorate the separation of the Province into North and South Carolina, in 1736 (Lot 753, p. 44 of Catalogue), and the piece brought sixteen dollars in the sale! That gentleman referred to "Johnson's Traditions and Reminiscences," p. 4. While Johnson certainly confirmed Strobridge, his ignorance of the truth about the piece is only equalled by his absurd description of the reverse, which he says "represents George II in the costume of Minerva, goddess of all the liberal arts," etc.! Professor Anthon, in a paper read before the American Numismatic and Archæological Society, February 27, 1868, and printed in the A. J. N., II, 99, showed the folly of Johnson's statement; but neither he nor the late Mr. Bushnell were then able to place it. It is somewhat remarkable that the author of Medallic Illustrations, under Charles I, 100, describes a medal of 1641, on the marriage of William and Mary, as bearing "William in the form of Pallas, attended by Victory, etc."

Mr. Bushnell, who furnished Strobridge with the reference to Johnson, wrote to the late Henry Cureton, Keeper of the British Museum, for information concerning it, who replied that he knew nothing about it, "except it was always

JAMES OGLETHORPE, FOUNDER OF GEORGIA.

170.   1737.   *Obv.* REVDISSIMUS . IOĦES . TILLOTSONUS . CANT: ARCHIÊPUS . OB : 1694. (The Most Reverend John Tillotson, Archbishop of Canterbury, died 1694.) In exergue, ANGLIA MUNDO (England to the world). Bust of the Archbishop, three-quarters facing to right, in canonicals ; long hair.

Rev. IACOBUS . OGLETHORPEIUS . ARMIGER . ADHUC . VIVUS , 1737. (James Oglethorpe, Esq., still living, 1737.) In exergue, NESCIT CEDERE (knows not how to yield ; [continued from the obverse]). Bust of James Oglethorpe, nearly facing, hair long, in mantle and shirt with open collar.

Archbishop Tillotson, who was born in 1630, succeeded Sancroft, who refused allegiance to William and Mary, and

---

known in England as the 'Cistern Medal.'" But Professor Anthon was not satisfied with this, and pursued his investigations until he found in a catalogue of the collection of Dr. Richard Mead, published in 1755, on p. 202, a description of the piece, to which was added the note: "This is Mr. Jernegan's silver medal, or ticket, for the sale of his famous cistern." Professor Anthon was unable then to learn its origin or previous history; but he asks in his paper, " Was the 'Cistern' a vase, or other large piece of plate, which he could not otherwise dispose of? This is our conjecture, but it may be quite erroneous." The conjecture was very near the truth, and was confirmed by a letter signed J. H. T. (Mr. Taylor) in the A. J. N., III, 68, 69, which referred to Knight's Pictorial London, III, 87, where the matter was fully explained.

Notwithstanding the fact that the history and origin of the piece were thus established, it has, down to a very recent period, been frequently catalogued as "The Carolina Medal." In A. J. N., V, 69, Professor Anthon gave further proof of the correctness of his own attribution by a citation from "Bowyer's Literary Anecdotes of the Eighteenth Century," London : 1812. II, 513, note. And, finally, one of the editors of this volume, in A. J. N., XVIII, p. 91, gave a description of the Cistern, and named its present resting-place — the Hermitage Palace, at St. Petersburg. It had long been lost sight of, and its identity was, we may say, *discovered* by a correspondent of the " London Athenæum " not long before the last article above cited was printed in the " Journal." It is a massive silver wine cistern, " weighing more than a quarter of a ton," made in 1734, 35, and it is described in full, with the circumstances of its discovery, *loc. cit.* The vase was disposed of by lottery, and the "Carolina Medal" was one of the tickets, as Mr. Anthon had conjectured. How it got to Russia has not been ascertained.

The dies were cut by John Sigismund Tanner, a native of Saxe-Gotha, who came to England in 1728, and was made Chief Engraver at the Mint, April, 1741, on the death of Croker. He died March 14, 1775. — EDS.

was therefore deprived. His accession was in April, 1691, and he died Nov. 22, 1694.

A single impression in gold, of the value of ten guineas, was struck,* and impressions in silver and copper are in the British Museum Cabinet. Size 26. Med. Ill., Geo. II, 82. Snelling, XXIX, 8.

---

* This is known as the " Prize Medal," having originally been struck for presentation to the writer of the best poem entitled " The Christian Hero." The obverse was designed to bear the bust of Lady Elizabeth Hastings, but this was prevented by the Lady herself. See Gent. Mag., 1735, p. 778, where an account of the matter is given, and in the same Magazine, November, 1747, is an engraving of the piece. James Edward Oglethorpe was the founder of the Colony of Georgia, so called in honor of the reigning King, George the Second, designed to serve as an asylum for oppressed Protestants from Germany, etc. The first party arrived in January, 1733. This, and his philanthropic efforts for poor debtors in London prisons, made him very popular at that time. The reverse alone has an American allusion.—Eds.

CHAPTER III.

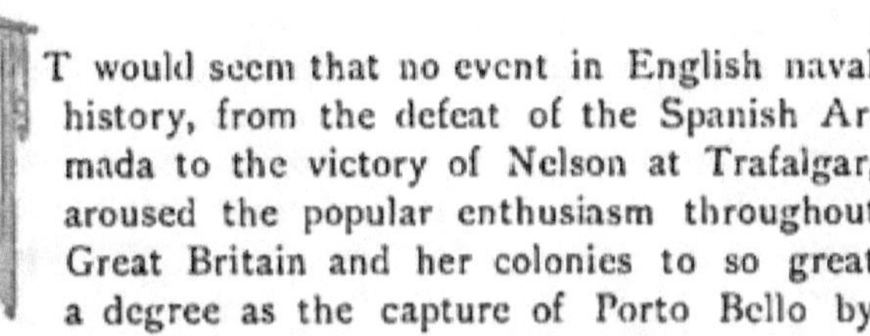

T would seem that no event in English naval history, from the defeat of the Spanish Armada to the victory of Nelson at Trafalgar, aroused the popular enthusiasm throughout Great Britain and her colonies to so great a degree as the capture of Porto Bello by Admiral Edward Vernon in 1739. Certainly no event in English history has evoked so many commemorative Medals. They were worn by all classes, to express the national joy; they were used as tokens, or currency, for card 'counters, and even for playthings by the children, and execrably executed as many of them were, the number sold must have been enormous. In consequence of the large variety of the designs, and the various legends which they bear, as well as the minute differences which distinguish some of the dies, it has seemed advisable to group them in a chapter by themselves.

The scene of the conflict was on the American shores; and the American Colonies, at that time a part of the British Empire, may rightfully claim a share in the glory of the mother country, since Lawrence Washington took part in one of these expeditions, and, as is well known, gave to his estate on the Potomac the name of Mount Vernon, in compliment to the admiral. ,

Before proceeding to describe the Medals, a brief account of the hero whose fame they commemorate, and of the circumstances that led to his gallant exploit, will be of interest, and I shall give it in substance as presented in my paper read before the American Numismatic and Archaeological Society of New York.

Edward Vernon was born November 12, 1684, in Westminster, England. He was the descendant of an ancient family, and at the early age of eighteen he received the commission of second lieutenant in the navy. It was, however, nearly twenty-five years later before he became famous.

The strongly-fortified harbor of Porto Bello for two centuries had been one of the most important outposts of Spain in the New World. Its situation was at the northern point of the great bend of the Isthmus of Panama, and there the galleons filled with treasure from Vera Cruz, took shelter and refitted before beginning their perilous voyage across the ocean. To this port also they sailed from Spain, bringing merchandise for sale or exchange ; and, at their leaving, a great fair was held, lasting many weeks, and attended by the inhabitants of all the surrounding country. It is said that from Panama the bullion was brought in cartloads for the purchase of European luxuries, and laden with this, or with dyestuffs and hides, the galleons returned. Thus for many years the declining monarchy of the Philips had drawn its revenue from America, and every nation with which Spain was at war, turned its eyes to Porto Bello, as one of the chief seats of power in the West, and coveted the riches that centred there, and lay in wait for the silver fleet on its homeward way. Here, too, the *guarda costas*, or Spanish gunboats, congregated, and put to sea in search of prizes, and under the guard of its powerful fortresses they took refuge when they were pursued.

Notwithstanding the importance of its position, and the size and beauty of the harbor, which gave it the name — the Fair Port — the town, early in the eighteenth century, consisted of only about five hundred houses with two churches. Its semicircular harbor, about a mile in diameter, opening toward the west, was defended by a large stone castle, placed upon a high cliff on each side, and by a fort upon a point of land in the middle and near the town.. The castle on the northern shore was called " the Iron Fort," and that on the southern side the castle of " St. Jago de Gloria," while the smaller central battery was called " St. Jeronimo."

At the time of the capture peace had reigned for quarter of a century. To the generation born within that period the " British Glory " was scarcely more than a tradition, and to the older generation Ramillies, and Malplaquet, and Blenheim — the victories of Marlborough — had become a dream of the past. No remarkable action by sea or land had occurred since the Peace of Utrecht, in 1713; and the prospect of distinction for the British arms, under the temporizing and peace-loving administration of Walpole, seemed almost hopeless.

The nation, however, was restless under this long repose, and longed for opportunity to redress real and fancied wrongs inflicted by its neighbors. Spain, in particular, seems to have been the object of popular indignation. The monthly magazines, which alone represented the press, were filled with accounts of Spanish outrages, and Parliament was flooded with petitions, and resounded with speeches denouncing the cruelties inflicted upon English merchantmen upon the high seas, and the searching of British vessels for goods claimed to be contraband.

The Treaty of Breda, in 1667, had permitted "the freedom of searching merchant ships sailing near the ports and in the seas of the respective countries, and of confiscating contraband goods;"* but although this provision was at the time intended to apply to Europe only, and especially to prevent the supply of arms to the Barbary States, yet Spain now claimed that all the ocean lying south of Georgia was her sea, and she actively asserted the right to search all vessels sailing to the British West Indies, or taking a southern passage from the other colonies, and of confiscating both ship and cargo, if any of the products of her colonies were found aboard.

A few extracts from the petitions of the merchants of the time, and from Parliamentary Reports, will show the state of popular feeling, and how closely the coming war affected all the American colonies.

In the Journal of the House of Commons, under date of March 3, 1737, we find a " Petition of Merchants, Planters, and others

---

* Cox's Memoirs of Sir Robert Walpole, quoted in Cobbett's Parliamentary History, X, p. 561.

trading to and interested in the British Plantations in America," which sets forth:

"That application was made to this House in the year 1728 against the many unjust seizures and depredations that had for several years preceding been committed by the *Spaniards in America*," upon which the House resolved, "That from the Peace concluded at Utrecht in the year 1713 to this time the British trade and navigation to and from the several British Colonies of America has been greatly interrupted by the continued Depredations of the Spaniards."

On March 9, 1737, the petition of merchants trading from Liverpool to the British Plantations in America shows:

"That the audacious practice of the Spaniards in boarding, detaining and searching all the British ships that fall in their way in the American sea, under colour of looking for contraband goods, the frivolous pretences on which they carry away and condemn, as Prizes, many of the said ships: the barbarous Treatment the *British* sailors meet with from them in such cases . . . These are such discouragements as must render the American trade very precarious."

On March 30 the Report of Committee of the House formally represented:

"That it is the natural and undoubted right of the British Subjects to sail in their ships on any part of the seas of America . . . and that the Freedom of Navigation and Commerce . . . has been greatly interrupted by the Spaniards, under Pretences altogether groundless and unwarrantable, . . . many unjust Seizures and Captures have been made, and great Depredations committed, by the Spaniards, attended with many instances of unheard of Cruelty and Brutality."

These extracts will be sufficient to indicate the tension of popular feeling, and the fury under which the nation chafed, as news of fresh outrages arrived with every vessel from America. Many more of like character appear on the Journal.

At this time Mr. Edward Vernon was in Parliament, representing Ipswich. He had spent many years in the service of England under Queen Anne, and under the first two Georges. Most of his time had been passed in monotonous cruising in the Mediterranean and Black Seas. In 1706 he commanded the frigate Dolphin on the Lisbon and Mediterranean stations, and in 1707 he was promoted to the frigate Jersey, and sent to the West Indies. There he remained for a number of years engaged in watching the enemy's fleet at Carthagena; but no action of moment is recorded, except in 1711, the capture of a ship of thirty guns, bound for Brest from the French West Indies. Here, however, he acquired that intimate knowledge of the Carribean Seas and of the laws of Spain in that part of the world, which led to all his future greatness. After the Peace of Utrecht he was sent to the Baltic in command of the Assistance, of fifty guns, and we next hear of him at the same station in 1726, with the Grafton, of seventy guns.

His oratorical efforts in Parliament do not seem to have made sufficient impression to be recorded; but his bitter criticisms on what he considered the pusillanimous policy of the Government made him hated by the Ministry, and won the popular applause. I have searched the Journals of the House in vain for mention of him. Even the one utterance that made his fame seems to have produced little impression at the time; and had it not been followed by the striking deeds which the Medals commemorate, it would have sunk into oblivion as the empty boast of a vain and disputatious wrangler. Tradition alone now records it.

Admiral Hosier, with twenty ships, made an unsuccessful attempt to capture Porto Bello, in 1726, and thirteen years after, in a debate on Spanish aggressions, Vernon declared that *with six ships of the line he would take the place.* The earliest mention that I have yet found of this speech is in Campbell's Lives of the British Admirals, in 1785, which, after giving the language quoted above, says : " His offer was echoed by the members of the Opposition, and the whole nation resounded with his praise."

There is no contemporary account of this speech, and the Medals apparently contain the earliest reference to it. The unanimity with which these Medals, struck in a hundred different forms, proclaim that the victory was achieved " with six ships only," shows that England rang with his boast and its fulfillment.

The desired opportunity came not long after. The Ministry were apparently willing to risk defeat if they might crush their opponent. July 9, 1739,* he was made Admiral of the Blue, and July 20 he sailed for the West Indies with nine men-of-war;† but he did not

---

* Gentleman's Magazine, July, 1839, p. 384.

† Campbell's " Lives of the British Admirals."

reach Jamaica until October 23, the very day that war was declared with Spain. On the fifth of November he sailed for Porto Bello, and, as if to carry out his boast, he took with him six ships only, leaving the remainder in Jamaica.

The names of the six ships were: The Burford (flag-ship), the Hampton Court (Commodore Brown), the Norwich, the Worcester, the Strafford, the Louisa. The latter ship was sent by Vernon to cruise off Carthagena, and did not actually take part in the engagement. The account of the battle is best given in the official report of Vernon himself, which was published in the London Gazette, not long after the tidings of the victory reached England, which was on the twelfth of March, 1740, and to which I must refer the reader. The whole nation at once made Vernon and Brown their idols. This was the first victory the British arms had achieved since Marlborough's day, and Vernon who revived the nation's glory, and Vernon who humbled the pride of its hated enemy, was the name upon everybody's lips.

The vast number of Medals struck upon this occasion, not only testify to the extent of the national enthusiasm, but they also make known to us which were the most popular mottoes of the day. It was not the Medal with the legend, " No search upon the seas shall be," that commanded favor, for only one with this device is found ; but the people's cry was for glory and revenge.

" THE BRITISH GLORY REVIV'D."

" THE SPANISH PRIDE HUMBLED."

These were the pieces which commanded readiest sale, and which remain to-day an enduring testimony. In these Vernon Medals we have the best proof of the wild delight that filled England and of the thoughts that were uppermost in every heart.

Vernon's subsequent career was somewhat of a disappointment. In March, 1740, he captured Fort Chagre. In January, 1741, he was largely reinforced by a fleet under Sir Chaloner Ogle, and found himself in command of thirty ships of the line and eighty-five other vessels, aided by 12,000 soldiers, under Gen. Wentworth ; but there was a lack of harmony between the military and naval commanders. It was decided to attack Carthagena, and some successes were gained in the following March. The Admiral sent home a premature despatch announcing his victory, and once more the popular enthusiasm was ablaze, and again the medallists proclaimed his glory; but Fort St. Lazar, the citadel, was too strong for the forces which were brought against it, and the disputes which followed prevented the necessary co-operation of the fleet and the army, and they were obliged to retire.

The Admiral still held a high place in public favor, and the same year was returned to Parliament for Rochester, Penrhyn, and Ipswich, and took his seat as the representative of the last-named constituency. He retained command of the fleet in the West Indies, until October, 1742, but nothing worthy of note was accomplished there. He was then in idleness until April, 1745, when he was promoted to be Admiral of the White, and assigned to the command of the fleet in the North Sea. He succeeded in the duty assigned him — of preventing the arrival of the friends of the Stuart Pretender in England,—but a dispute with the Admiralty in January, 1746, caused him to resign, and in the following year he was cashiered. He lived in retirement the remainder of his life, and died at Nacton, Suffolk, October 29, 1757.*

PLAN OF ARRANGEMENT.

The following List contains upwards of 160 pieces, but it is not claimed that all in existence are here included; indeed, it seems very probable that many more dies were used than are here described, for the authors of some of the works consulted content themselves by mentioning the fact that varieties exist, which they do not describe, and of which I have no other knowledge. Quite a number resemble each other so closely that in some instances it will be very difficult, it must be confessed, for the collector to determine by comparing the description with a piece before him, which of two numbers should be assigned to it, should he desire to place it; but the differences noted, it may be truthfully said, are not imaginary in any case. In preparing this Catalogue, constant reference has been made to the List published by Mr. William S. Appleton, in the American Journal of Numismatics (Vol. II, pp. 46 and 86, and V, p. 64), in which seventy-five Medals are numbered and described; and to that in the second volume of Medallic Illustrations, pp. 530–557, where ninety-two are given, and on subsequent pages of the same volume, five more. The slight differences of the dies (such, for instance, as the punctuation and arrangement of the letters in the legends) are not always noted with sufficient minuteness to enable me to be confident that the numbers correspond in every case; and where doubt

---

* A "Life of Admiral Vernon" was published in London, the year after his death. Campbell, in his "Lives of the British Admirals" as has been mentioned above, and Charnock in "Biographia Navalis" have also very full notices.

exists, a query has usually been inserted, or the possible discrepancy noted. No. 120 in Medallic Illustrations, may be one of several not attributed, and it is therefore not assigned to any in the following List; but all the others have the corresponding numbers given, to the best of my judgment. The same remark applies to the List made by Mr. Appleton; cross-references are made to his numbers, and doubtful cases are noted. It has seemed proper to state these difficulties, to anticipate possible criticism; on the other hand, the effort has been made to note differences with a much greater minuteness than may seem necessary to the general reader, that future investigators, with wider opportunities, may be able by comparison to detect the differences which have here escaped notice.*

In addition to the difficulties noted above, the task of identifying corresponding numbers in other Lists has been rendered still more arduous by continual references to previous numbers; it seems impossible to avoid this entirely, but an attempt has been made to reduce this labor as much as may be by repeating descriptions, as often as seemed necessary, even at the expense of an apparent tautology.

The plan of arrangement which I have endeavored to preserve, as far as circumstances will permit, is as follows: —

    I.   Medals of Vernon naming no event.
    II.   The capture of Porto Bello, Nov. 21–22, 1739.
    III. The capture of Fort Chagre, March 24, 1740.
  IV.   The capture of Forts at Carthagena, April 1, 1741.
    V.   The proposed attack on Havana, July, 1741.

THE PORTO BELLO MEDALS.

The Porto Bello Medals are classified, first, by the legends on the obverse, beginning with those that relate the fact of the capture; second, those that declare the revival of the British glory by Vernon; third, those that associate the name of Commodore Brown with Vernon; fourth, those that bear the British arms on the obverse and the scene of the attack on the reverse. The Medals being thus arranged in groups by their legends, each group is subdivided in accordance with the design. Under the first division will be found the bust of Vernon, facing to right or left, and larger

---

* In his original manuscript Mr. Betts gave as a further reason for his minute descriptions, his hope that collectors might be induced to compare pieces in their cabinets with his list, and advise him of any here omitted; he seems to have been fully aware of the existence of still further varieties which he had been unable to obtain; and evidently contemplated the issue of a Monograph on the subject, before publishing this volume, in the hope of adding greater completeness to the catalogue, but the execution of this plan was prevented by his sudden death. — EDS.

portions of the figure facing three-quarters to left; under the second division, his half-length figure, facing three-quarters to right or left, and also full-length facing to right and to left; under the division that includes Commodore Brown are two full-length figures, and a group of half-length figures.

PORTO BELLO AND FORT CHAGRE.

The Medals of Fort Chagre all refer on their reverses to the capture of Porto Bello. They are subdivided, first, by the legends; second, by the design. Two others follow, voicing the popular dissatisfaction at the course of the Ministry, which it was believed secretly prevented Admiral Haddock from adding glory to the British arms in the Mediterranean.

PORTO BELLO AND CARTHAGENA.

The next group refers to the humbling of Spanish pride by Vernon; all these bear upon the obverse the name of Don Blass, and as this Spanish officer was in command at Carthagena, but not at Porto Bello, I have placed these under the head of Porto Bello and Carthagena.

CARTHAGENA, ETC.

Similar subdivisions are made for the Medals of Carthagena. The contemplated attack on Havana is commemorated by one obverse, which is combined with a reverse of Porto Bello, and also with one of Carthagena, which follows the Porto Bello Medals. These Medals, it has been mentioned, were struck in advance of anticipated victories, but though Vernon had some success at Carthagena, and landed forces on the Island of Cuba, he was compelled by sickness and other difficulties to re-embark them, and returned to Jamaica without assaulting the city.

REVERSE DIFFERENCES.

An attempt has been made to classify all the Medals under each subgroup by differences in punctuation, and in the position of the words; next, by differences in metal, and finally by differences of reverses. A summary will be found at the close of the List, classifying the reverses in order by these differences in legend, punctuation, and design, and also by the position of vessels, number of ships in the harbor, or steeples in the town, and other minutiae, when necessary for exactness, although it has not been found possible to include every piece given, for lack of complete descriptions as to such matters in the works consulted. The statement of the plan suggests also the difficulties which have forbidden its perfect execution. In general the reverses bear a view of Porto Bello, defended on each side by a castle, on a high cliff, and in the centre by a smaller fort; the ships entering the harbor; the city in the distance, and the legend commemorating its capture.

VERNON MADE ADMIRAL.[*]

171. 1741. *Obv.* ADMIRAL . VERNON.　Bust three-quarters to left; beneath it, flags, cannon, balls and canister.

Rev. Plain; no legend or design.　A badge, to be worn in the hat or coat.

Copper.　Size 17.　Med. Ill., Geo. II, 181.

172. *Obv. The Honble* EDW? VERNON *Esq?* VICE ADMIRAL *of the* BLUE.　Bust three-quarters to left, in dress coat and cravat; hair long.

Rev. A large fleet; on a cloud above reclines Fame, blowing a trumpet and holding a branch of laurel; no legend.

Copper.　Size 24.　Med. Ill., Geo. II, 92.　Old England, II, 265.

PORTO BELLO TAKEN.

173. 1739. *Obv.* E . VERNON . VI . AD . OF . TH . BLVE . Bust three-quarters to left, in dress coat and cravat; hair long.

Rev. PORTO BELLO NOV 22.　In exergue, MDCCXXXIX.　Six ships entering Porto Bello harbor.

Silver, cast and chased.　Size 26.　Med. Ill., Geo. II, 93.

174. *Obv.* ADMIRAL VERNON.　In exergue, 1740.　Ship firing a broadside.

Rev. PORTO BELLO.　In exergue,† P. E.　Ships attacking a harbor; all within a laurel wreath.

Pewter.　Size 25.　Med. Ill., Geo. II, 136.

175. *Obv.* BRAVE VERNON MADE US FREE.　Half-length figure to left; baton in his left hand.

Rev. NO SEARCH UPON THE SEAS SHAL (*sic*) BE. In exergue, PORTO BELLO. Six ships entering Porto Bello harbor.*

Copper. Size 16. Med. Ill., Geo. II, 138. Lead. F. 8275.

176. *Obv.* ADMIRAL . VERNON . TOOK . PORTO . BELLO. On truncation T (T. Tibs ?†). Bust to right; hair in twisted queue.

Rev. WITH . SIX . SHIPS . ONLY . NOV . 22 . 1739. Six ships sailing to right, entering Porto Bello harbor.

Brass. Size 24. Med. Ill., Geo. II, 94.

177. *Obv.* ADMIRAL VERNON TOOK PORTO BELLO. Bust to right.

Rev. WITH SIX SHIPS ONLY NOV. 22, 1739. Ships one by one ; three boats.

Brass. Size 24½. A. J. N., V, 65, No. 31.

178. *Obv.* Legend as 177. Bust to left.
Rev. Closely resembling the preceding number.
Copper. Size 24½. A. J. N., V, 65, No. 32.

179. *Obv.* Legend as 176. Bust to left ; head different from last.

Rev. Closely resembling 177 and 178.‡

Copper. Size 24. Med. Ill., Geo. II, ? 95. Prob. A. J. N., V, 65, No. 33.

---

* Great Britain fought to abolish the right of search, when her own merchantmen suffered, but did not hesitate to exercise it herself against others when she had the opportunity. This was one of the chief causes of the War of 1812, between the United States and the mother country, and nearly led to another war in 1842. It was only in 1856 that, by the Treaty of Paris, she consented to relinquish some of her claims, and would no doubt resume them against a weaker power whenever she deemed it for her interest to do so, notwithstanding the popular saying quoted on this Medal.—EDS.

† The dies of this Medal are poorly cut, which fact, with the initial T, leads the editor of Med. Ill. (whom Mr. Betts followed), to believe it the work of Tibs. Little is known of Tibs, except that he engraved from about 1727 to 1745, and that "his Medals are of very inferior workmanship."—EDS.

‡ These three reverses are perhaps identical, except in the size of the planchets ; the differences being in the obverses only.—EDS.

180. *Obv.* ADMIRAL ·:· VERNON ·:· TOOK ·:· PORTO ·:· BELLO. Bust to left; baton in left hand; no line inclosing legend; right hand not shown; hair in twisted queue.

Rev. WITH ·:· SIX ·:· SHIPS ·:· ONLY ·:· NOV ·:· 22 ·:· 1739. Ships **three and three**; first three sailing diagonally to **right**; last three to left; small vessel and two boats; two **steeples** pointing PS and NL; land indicated by lines; water, lines.*

Brass. Size 24.

181. *Obv.* Legend as 176. Half length figure to left; baton in left hand.

Rev. WITH . SIX . SHIPS . ONLY . In exergue, NOV 22 1739. The relative position of the ships is not given by the authority cited.

Silver and copper. Size 25. Med. Ill., Geo. II, 96.

182. Legend as 180. Half length figure to left; line inclosing legend; baton in right hand; fluke of anchor in front.

Rev. WITH ·:· SIX ·:· SHIPS ·:· ONLY In exergue, NOV . 22 . 1739. Ships two and four; two sailing to left; four to right; three boats; one steeple pointing between x and ·:· ; land, chased; water, lines.

Brass (?). A. J. N., II, 48, No. 12. Copper. Size 24. F. 8286. Med. Ill., Geo. II, 115.

183. *Obv.* Legend as 177. Half length figure facing three-quarters to left; baton in left hand.

Rev. WITH SIX SHIPS ONLY In exergue, NOV . 22 . 1739. Ships two and four; small vessel and two boats. (Nearly identical with the preceding reverse.)

Brass. Size 25½. A. J. N., V, 65, No. 35.

184. *Obv.* Similar to preceding number. There are at least four dies of this obverse, differing so minutely that descrip-

---

* The groups of dots used to punctuate the legends have been followed as closely as possible with type; the reproduction is not absolutely perfect, but we believe will be found sufficiently so in most cases to at least assist in identification. In many cases the dots are placed so closely together that they form a cross. It has been found impossible to distinguish them, especially as some of these differences may be only the wear on the dies. This remark applies to all similar cases. — EDS.

tions which would distinguish them cannot be given except at great length, although perceptible on comparison.

Rev. Legend and exergue as 183. Ships entering one by one.

Brass. Size 17. A. J. N., V, 65, where see Nos. 37, 38, 39 and 40.

185. *Obv.* Same as 183.

Rev. WITH SIX SHIPS ONLY NOV 22 In exergue, 1739. Ships entering one by one.

Brass. Size 25. A. J. N., V, 65, where see Nos. 39 and 40.

186. *Obv.* Legend as 176. Half length figure facing three-quarters to left ; baton in left hand ; no line inclosing legend ; his finger points at the first A.

Rev. Legend as 180. Ships one, two and three ; first three diagonally to right; last three diagonally to left; all with three masts ; three boats ; two steeples pointing between P and S and between N and L ; water and land both indicated by lines.

Brass. Size 24. (?) Copper. A. J. N., II, 86, No. 12a.

187. Legend and device as 186, but the Admiral's finger points at D.

Rev. Legend as 180, but there is a group of points before WITH and after the date. Ships one, two and three ; five left ; one right ; no boats ; one steeple pointing to right of I ; no water lines.

Brass. Size 16. The dies of this Medal, it will be observed, are much smaller than those which they resemble.

188. *Obv.* Legend as 180. Half length figure facing three-quarters to left ; baton in left hand ; no line inclosing the legend ; his finger points between D and M.

Rev. Legend as 180. In exergue, NOV 22 1739. Ships two and four ; two left ; four right ; two boats ; two steeples pointing between X and ·:· and I in SHIPS ; land, chased ; water, lines.

Brass. Size 25.

189. *Obv.* Legend as 180, but a group of points at the end. Half length figure facing three-quarters to left ; baton in left hand ; a line inclosing legend ; his finger points between D and M ; field, smooth.

Rev. Legend and exergue as 188. Ships two, one and three ; five left ; one right ; two boats ; one steeple pointing left of s ; land, chased ; water, lines.

Brass and copper. Size 21.

190. *Obv.* Legend as 189. Same die as last, but with the field chased.

Rev. Same reverse die as used on 189.

Brass. Size 21.

191. *Obv.* Legend as 176. Half length figure facing three-quarters to left ; baton in left hand.

Rev. Legend as 176. Device similar to reverse of 176, but a smaller die.

Brass. Size 17. Copper (2 var.) Méd. Ill., Geo. II, 127.

192. *Obv.* Legend as 176. Half length figure facing three-quarters to left ; baton in left hand ; line inclosing legend ; his finger points at D.

Rev. Same die as 187.

Brass and copper. Size 16.

193. *Obv.* Same as 181.

Rev. WITH ✥ SIX ✥ SHIPS ✥ ONLY ✥ NOV . 22 ✥ In exergue, ✥ 1739 ✥ Ships one, two and three ; five left ; one right ; no boats ; two steeples pointing at P and between s and o ; no water lines.

Copper. Apparently the same as Med. Ill., Geo. II, 128.

194. *Obv.* Legend as 176. Half length figure facing three-quarters to left ; baton in left hand ; line inclosing legend ; his finger points at M.

Rev. From the same die as 187.

Brass and copper. Size 16.

195. *Obv.* Same die as 194.

Rev. WITH . SIX . SHIPS . ONLY . 1739   In exergue, NOV . 22.   The relative position of the ships is not given.

Copper.   Size 16.   Apparently Med. Ill., Geo. II, 129.

196. *Obv.* THE . BRITISH : GLORY . REVIV . D . BY . ADMIRAL VERNON.   Half length figure facing left, holding baton ; his finger points at T ; baton at O.

Rev. WHO . TOOK . PORTO . BELLO . WITH . SIX . SHIPS . ONLY   In exergue, NOV. 22, 1739.   Ornament of two leaves with separate stems below date.   Ships two and four ; all sailing left ; no boats ; tower and two steeples pointing at E, O, and T ; no land lines ; no water lines.   This reverse die, more or less worn, is used on Nos. 233, 258 and 297 ; originally the water lines were faint.

Brass and copper.   Size 23.   Med. Ill., Geo. II, 114.

197. *Obv.* THE . BRITISH . GLORY . REVIV . D . BY . ADMIRAL . VERNON.   ∞   Half length figure facing left ; his finger points between IT ; baton at Y.

Rev. HE . TOOK . PORTO . BELLO . WITH . SIX . SHIPS . ONLY In exergue, NOV . 22 . 1739.   Scroll work below.   Ships, two and four ; five sailing right ; one left ; two steeples and one tower pointing at E, O, and I ; no land lines or water lines except within harbor.   Same die as 282, but more worn.

Brass.   Size 23 (?).   Med. Ill., Geo. II, 113.   (Two slightly differing varieties.)

198. *Obv.* THE . BRITISH . GLORY . REVIV . D . BY . AD-MIRAL . VERNON.   Half length figure three-quarters to left ; no line below legend.

Rev. Legend and exergue as 197.   No scroll work.   Ships three and three ; three right, three left ; two boats ; one steeple pointing at W ; no land lines ; water lines below lower ships.

Brass and copper.   Size 23.

199. *Obv.* Apparently the same as the preceding number.

Rev. Legend and exergue as 197.   Ships one, two and three ; five left ; one right ; two boats ; two steeples pointing at first L and T ; no land lines ; water lines below lower ships and forts.

Brass and copper.   Size 23.

200. *Obv.* Legend as 198.   Half length figure three-quarters to left ; line below legend ; his finger points at E ; left elbow at o.

Rev. HE . TOOK . PORTO . BELLO . WITH . SIX . SHIPS . ONLY . 1739 ° In exergue, BY COURAGE . AND | . CONDUCT.   Ships one, one, two and two ; one above, stern on ; three left ; two right ; two small vessels and one larger vessel in harbor, one smaller vessel outside ; one steeple pointing at H ; no land lines ; water lines.

Brass and copper.   Size 24.   (Perhaps Med. Ill., Geo. II, 111.)   See A. J. N., II, p. 36, Nos. 9, 9a, 9b.

Dies with slight differences,* too minute for specification, are found, probably nearest 9a or 9b, as cited above, in copper, and another still, in brass, probably No. 23 in Mr. Appleton's list, A. J. N., V, p. 65.

201. *Obv.* Same as 198.

Rev. HE ·:· TOOK ·:· PORTO ·:· BELLO ·:· WITH ·:· SIX ·:· SHIPS ·:· ONLY . In exergue, BY . COURAGE . AND | CONDUCT. Ships one, one, two and two ; three right ; three left ; one vessel and no boats in harbor ; one steeple pointing between LL ; no land lines ; water lines below.

Brass.   Size 23½.   Possibly one of the varieties mentioned in A. J. N., II, 86, as No. 9a or 9b.

202. *Obv.* Legend as 198.   Half length figure three-quarters to left ; line below legend ; finger points at E ; elbow at last N.

Rev. HE . TOOK . PORTO . BELLO . WITH . SIX . SHIPS . ONLY .   1739.   In exergue, BY COURAGE | AND CONDUCT.

---

* If this be the same as Med. Ill., Geo. II. 111, it is found in lead also ; there are three slightly differing dies mentioned there, but without particular description.—EDS.

Ships one, one, two and two ; one above stern on ; two right ; three left ; three small vessels in harbor, one boat outside ; one tower pointing at o, one steeple at T ; faint land lines, very heavy water lines.

Brass and copper.   Size 23.   A. J. N., II, 48, No. 8.

A variety of this is described, A. J. N., II, 86, No. 7b, as " having very slight differences, but much better in execution."

203. *Obv.* Legend as 198.   Half length figure three-quarters to left ; line below legend ; finger points to left of B, elbow at o.

Rev. WHO . TOOK . PORTO . BELLO . WITH . SIX . MEN . OF . WAR . ONLY   In exergue, NOV 22 . 1739.   Ships two and four ; five right ; one left ; no boats ; ten buildings ; one tower and two steeples pointing at o, w and H ; no land lines ; water lines outside harbor.

Brass and copper.   Size 23.   Perhaps Med. Ill., Geo. II, 112.

204.   *Obv.* Same as 203.

Rev. Legend and exergue as 203, but a period after ONLY. Ships two and four ; five right ; one left ; two small vessels ; one tower and two steeples pointing at second L, w and H ; no land lines ; water lines outside harbor.

Brass and copper.   Size 23.   Perhaps Med. Ill., Geo. II, 112.*

205. *Obv.* Legend as 198.   Half length figure three-quarters to left ; line below legend ; finger points at left of B, elbow below last N.   Closely resembling 202.

Rev. Legend and exergue as 203.   Ships one, one and four ; five right ; one left ; no boats, but one of the six vessels within harbor ; one tower and two steeples pointing at w, H and x ; no land lines ; water lines outside harbor.

Brass.   Size 24.

---

* The minute differences noted here between 203 and 204 are not mentioned in Med. Ill., Geo. II, as cited, and positive identification of either with that is not possible.—EDS.

206. *Obv.* Legend as 198. Half length figure three-quarters to left ; line below legend ; finger points at right of B, elbow at o.

Rev. WHO . TOOK . PORTO . BELLO . WITH . SIX . MEN . OF . WAR . ONLY In exergue, NOV 22 1739 | OH. Ships sailing in acute angle, five to right, and one at right sailing to left ; three boats ; two steeples pointing to right of o and left of T ; land and water lines.

Copper. Size 24.*

207. *Obv.* Legend as 198. Half length figure three-quarters to left ; line below legend ; finger points between BR, baton points at L.

Rev. WHO . TOOK . PORTO . BELLO . WITH . SIX . SHIPS . ONLY . In exergue, NOV . 22 . 1739. No scroll work ; ships two and four ; five right ; one left ; two boats ; one tower and two steeples pointing between I.L, between o and w, and at T ; water lines outside harbor.

Brass. Size 17. Copper, A. J. N., II, 86, No. 10a. Copper ; a variety "almost identical." A. J. N., V, 65, No. 28.

208. *Obv.* Same as 207.

Rev. Legend and exergue as 197. Scroll work below date ; ships two and four ; five sailing right ; one left ; no boats ; one tower and two steeples pointing at E, second L and w ; water lines outside harbor. The same die is used on 227.

Brass. Size 17.

209. *Obv.* Legend as 198. Half length figure three-quarters to left ; line below legend ; his finger points between BR, baton points at o.

Rev. Legend and exergue as 207. Scroll work below date.

Copper, A. J. N., II, 86, No. 10a. Brass. Size 17. Prob. Med. Ill., Geo. II, 130. Copper (2 var.), and lead. Size 17.

---

* We find no previous description of this die-difference, and have not been able to learn who is meant by O. H.—EDS.

210. *Obv.* THE ·:· BRITISH ·:· GLORY ·:· REVIV . D ·:· BY ·:· ADMIRAL ·:· VERNON ∘   Half length figure three-quarters to left ; line below legend ; finger points at R, elbow at R.

Rev. Same die as 201, but face of die slightly worn or turned down, so as to obliterate some of the water lines ; two small houses added at right on water front, and one house and tower at left.   This die as altered is used on 215.

Brass.   Size 23.

211. *Obv.* THE∘ BRITISH∘GLORY∘ REVIV . D∘ BY∘ADMIRAL ∘ VERNON ∘   Half length figure three-quarters to left ; line below legend ;˙finger points between RI, elbow between ON.

Rev. HE . TOOK . PORTO . BELLO . WITH . SIX . SHIPS . ONLY .   In exergue, NOV . 22 . 1739.   Ships irregular, one, one, one, one, at right, and two at left ; three sailing left ; three right ; no boats, and one vessel in harbor ; one steeple pointing at T ; no land lines ; water lines below lower ships.

Brass.   Size 23.   A. J. N., II, 48, No. 17.   This may be Med. Ill., Geo. II, 107.

212. *Obv.* Similar to 210.

Rev. HE . TOOK . PORTO . BELLO . WITH . SIX . SHIPS . ONLY.   In exergue, BY . COURAGE . AND | CONDUCT.   Ships one, one, two and two ; four to left, two to right ; one vessel in harbor ; one steeple pointing at I ; water lines below lower ships.

This may be Med. Ill., Geo. II., 110, which gives six varieties.

213. *Obv.* THE . BRITISH . GLORY . REVIV . D . BY . AD-MIRAL . VERNON : . ∘ (N's reversed).   Half length figure three-quarters to left ; line below legend ; finger points at . between E and B, elbow below last N.

Rev. HE . TOOK . PORTO . BELLO . WITH . SIX . SHIPS . ONLY . 1739 : .   In exergue, BY . COURAGE . AND | CONDUCT (N's reversed).   Ships one, one, two, two ; four left. two right ; four boats in harbor, one outside ; tree on both sides of harbor ; tower and steeple pointing at W and I ; water lines and faint land lines.

Copper.   Size 24.

214. *Obv.* THE . BRITISH . GLORY . REVIV * D * BY . AD-MIRAL . . VERNON *   Half length figure three-quarters to left.

Rev. HE . TOOK * PORTO . BELLO . WITH . SIX . SHIPS . ONLY *   In exergue, NOV . 22 . 1739 .   Seven ships ; three and three, and one at left lower than the upper three ; two small vessels.

Copper.   Size 24.   Probably Med. Ill., Geo. II, 108.

215.   *Obv.*   THE °BRITISH ° GLORY°REVIV°D°BY . ADMIRAL° VERNO ° (*sic*).   Half length figure three-quarters to left ; line below legend ; finger points at E, elbow at E.

Rev. Same die and alterations as 210.

Brass and copper.   Size 23.

216.   *Obv.* Same as 215.

Rev. Same die as 212, but turned down, obliterating one house at left, and recut, adding a mast to large ship at left and enlarging the sail.

Brass and copper.   Size 23.

217.   *Obv.* THE ·:· BRITISH ·:· GLORY ·:· REVIV . D ·:· BY ·:· ADMIRAL ·:· VERNO (*sic*).   Half length figure three-quarters to left ; line below legend ; finger points between E and B, elbow at V.

Rev. Same die and alterations as 212.

Brass, silvered and gilt.   Size 23.

218.   *Obv.* THE . BRITISH . GLORY REVIV D BY . AD VERNON . Half length figure three-quarters to left ; ship at right sailing right ; line below legend.

Rev. HE . TOOK . PORTO . BELO (*sic*).　In exergue, WITH SIX . SHIPS ONLY.　Ships two, one and three ; all sailing right ; two ships in harbor ; eight houses.

Brass, elliptical.　Size 22 x 17 ; made into a key.

219.　*Obv.* THE　BRITISH GLORY　REV . D BY AD VERNON. Half length figure three-quarters to right ; ship at left, cannon at right ; no line below legend.

Rev. As reverse of the preceding (218), of which this is probably the original die.

Brass, elliptical.　Size 23 x 15.

220.　*Obv.* THE . BRITISH . GLORY . REVIV . D . BY . ADMIRAL . VERNON (N's reversed).　Full length figure to left ; sword in his right hand, the left on his hip.　Cannon at left ; no line enclosing legend.

Rev. HE . TOOK . PORTO . BELLO . WITH . SIX . SHIPS : ONLY . In exergue, NO 22 . 1739 (N's reversed).　Ships two, one and three, all sailing right ; no boats ; water lines between ships.

Copper.　Size 17.　Brass, A. J. N., V, 64, No. 15.　Med. Ill., Geo. II, 134.

221.　*Obv.* Legend as 220.　Full length figure to left, standing on platform ; baton in right hand, left on hip.　Line enclosing legend ; cannon at left ; ship at right.

Rev. HE TOOK PORTO BELLO WITH SIX SHIPS ONLY o o　In exergue, NOV . 22 . 1739 .　(Date very small.)　Ships two, one and three, all sailing right ; three small vessels in harbor ; water lines ; one steeple, one tower, pointing at second L and I.

Brass.　Size 25½.　Brass.　Size 25.　Copper, thin.　Size 24.　Copper.　Size 26.　A. J. N., II, 48, No. 6.　Med. Ill., Geo. II, 121.

222.　*Obv.* Same as 221.

Rev. Same die as 221, but recut in exergue with large letters NOV . 22 . 1739 .　The altered die is used on 248.

Brass.　Size 25.　Copper.　Size 24.　Copper.　Size 25.　F. 8279.　A. J. N., V, 64, No. 13.

223. *Obv.* THE . BRITISH . GLORY . REVIVD : BY : ADMIRAL VERNON. Full length figure to left ; baton in left hand. Cannon at left ; anchor at right.

Rev. Legend and exergue as 197. Position of vessels, etc., not given.

Copper. Size 24. Med. Ill., Geo., II, 124.

224. *Obv.* THE . BRITISH : GLORY . REVIV . D . BY . ADMIRAL : VERNON (N's reversed). Full length figure to left, standing on platform ; baton in left hand, right hand extended. Cannon at left ; anchor at right ; line enclosing legend.

Rev. HE TOOK PORTO BELLO WITH SIX SHIPS ONLY In exergue, NOV . 22 . 1739 (N's reversed). Ships two, one and three, all sailing right ; three small vessels in harbor ; water lines below lower ships ; no steeple.

Brass. Size 24. A. J. N., II, 48, No. 7. F. 8280.

225. *Obv.* Legend as 198. Full length figure to left ; sword in right hand, baton in left. Cannon at left hand ; ship at right.

Rev. Legend and exergue as 197. Position of vessels, etc., not given.

Copper. Size 22. Med. Ill., Geo. II, 123.

226. *Obv.* THE . BRITISH . GLORY REVIV . D . BY . ADM . L . VERNON (N's reversed). Full length figure to right, standing on platform ; sword in right hand ; baton in left. Cannon at right ; anchor at left : no line enclosing legend.

Rev. ○ ○ HE . TOOK . PORTO . BELLO . WITH . SIX . SHIPS : ONLY ○ ○ In exergue, NOV . 22 . 1739 (first N reversed). Ships two, one and three ; all sailing right ; three small vessels in harbor ; no steeple ; water indicated below lower ships.

Brass. Size 17. Copper. Med. Ill., Geo. II, 132. A. J. N., V, 64, No. 11.

227. *Obv.* THE . BRITISH . GLORY . REVIVD BY . ADMIRAL . VERNON. Full length figure to right, standing on border of medal ; sword in right hand ; baton in left. Cannon at right ; ship at left ; line enclosing legend.

Rev. Same die as used on 208.

Brass. Size 17. Probably A. J. N., II, 48, No. 5. Copper.

228. *Obv.* Same as the preceding.

Rev. Legend and exergue as 207. No scroll work. Ships two and four, all sailing right ; no boats ; tower and two steeples pointing at LO, W and H ; water lines below lower ships.

Brass. Size 17.

229. *Obv.* THE BRITISH GLORY REVIV ' D BY ADMIRAL VERNON. Full length figure to right, standing on carriage of cannon prolonged into a double leaf ; sword in right hand ; baton in left. Cannon at right ; ship at left ; ornament below, formed of convex shell, with a branch of three leaves on each side ; no line enclosing legend ; bowsprit pointing at I.

Rev. WHO TOOK PORTO BELLO WITH SIX SHIPS ONLY In exergue, NOV 22 *1739.* No line below legend. Ships two, one and three, all sailing left ; no boats ; no steeple ; no water lines or land lines ; double line above date.

Brass and copper. Size 24.

230. *Obv.* Legend as 198. Full length figure to right, standing on the carriage of a cannon prolonged in a single leaf ; sword in right hand, baton in left. Cannon at right ; ship at left ; ornament below, formed of a concave shell, with a fleur-de-lis and a leaf on each side ; line enclosing legend : bowsprit pointing at S.

Rev. WHO ' TOOK ' PORTO ' BELLO ' WITH ' SIX ' SHIPS ' ONLY In exergue NOV ' 22 ' 1739 ' Ornament under date. Ships two and four, all sailing left ; no small vessels or boats ; no land lines ; water lines under ships ; tower and two steeples pointing at E, second L and W.

Brass. Size 23½. ?A. J. N., II, 47, No. 2.*

231. *Obv.* Same die as the preceding.

Rev. WHO . TOOK . PORTO . BELLO . WITH . SIX . SHIPS . ONLY In exergue NOV . 22 . 1739 . Ornament of leaves with two stems crossed, below date. Ships to left and other details as the preceding. This die is used on 261 and 285.

Brass. Size 23. A. J. N., II, 47, No. 2, corresponds, but its size is given as 24.

232. *Obv.* Legend as 198. Full length figure to right, standing on the carriage of a cannon, prolonged into a single leaf ; sword in right hand, baton in left. Cannon at right ; ship at left ; ornament below, formed of a convex shell, with a branch of two large and three small leaves on each side ; line enclosing legend ; bowsprit pointing at H.

Rev. WHO . TOOK . PORTO . BELLO . WITH . SIX . SHIPS : ONLY : In exergue, NOV . 22 . 1739. Ornament below date. Ships two and four, all sailing left ; no boats ; tower and two steeples pointing at O, W and T ; faint water lines below lower ships. Same die as used on 233, 258 and 297, where its condition shows more or less evidence of wear, to which most if not all the differences seem to be due.

Brass. Size 23.

233. *Obv.* Legend as 198. Full length figure at right, standing on carriage of a cannon, prolonged into a quadruple leaf ; sword in right hand, baton in left. Cannon at right ;

---

* Nos. 230 and 231 seem to be identical except in the position of the dots in the reverse legend ; the authority cited does not give these as in the text ; it is possible that the other minute differences mentioned may be due entirely to the condition of the die at different periods, this reverse, if it be the same, as we suspect, having been muled with several obverses. This we cannot determine with our present information. The text agrees with the engraving, drawn from the original.—EDS.

ship at left ; ornament below, formed of a convex shell and a branch of three large and three small leaves on each side ; line enclosing legend ; bowsprit pointing at H.

Rev. Legend and exergue as 196, but no comma after 22. Otherwise apparently from the same die ; this was used on 232, 258 and 297. The ornament below the date has two separate stems. No boats ; tower and two steeples pointing at E, O and T ; faint water lines below lower ships. Probably the original die. [See 232.]

Brass, gilded. Size 23.

234. *Obv.* Legend as 198. Full length figure to right, standing on lines forming ground ; sword in right hand, baton in left. Cannon at right, ship at left ; line enclosing legend extending entirely around ; bowsprit pointing at S.

Rev. Legend and exergue as 207. Ornament below date. Ships two and four, all sailing left ; no boats ; three steeples pointing at first L, O and I ; no water lines.

Brass. Size 23. ?Med. Ill., Geo. II, 116 ; Copper.

235. *Obv.* Same as preceding.

Rev. Legend and exergue as 207. No ornament below the date. Ships two and four, all sailing left.

Brass. Size 23. Med. Ill., Geo. II, 117.

236. *Obv.* THE . BRITISH . GLORY . REVIV . D . BY . ADMIRAL . VERNON . (N's reversed.) Full length figure to right, standing on a solid platform ; sword in his right hand, baton in left. Cannon at right ; ship at left, sailing to left ; small ornament below platform ; a line enclosing legend ; bowsprit points at B ; scabbard projects below coat behind.

Rev. HE TOOK PORTO BELLO WITH SIX SHIPS ONLY In exergue, NOV . 22 . 1739. Ships three and three, five sailing right, one left ; three small vessels in harbor ; one steeple, one tall building and one tower pointing at second L, W and T ; water lines below lower ships and below fort at left.

Brass and lead. Size 25.

237. *Obv.* Legend as 198. Full length figure to right, standing on a solid platform ; sword in right hand, baton in left. Cannon at right ; ship at left, sailing to right, with flag flying toward BR ; no ornament below ; line enclosing legend ; scabbard projects below coat behind.

Rev. Legend and exergue as 224. Ships three and three, five sailing right, one left ; two small vessels in harbor ; one tower pointing between LL ; heavy water lines below the lower ships.

Brass. Size 24.

238. *Obv.* THE . BRITISH . GLORY . REVIV . D . BY . ADMIRAL VERNON (N's reversed). Full length figure to right, standing on a solid platform ; sword in right hand, baton in left. Cannon at right ; ship at left, sailing to right, with flag flying toward T ; small ornament below ; line enclosing the legend ; scabbard projects below coat behind.

Rev. Legend and exergue as 224. Ships two, one and three, all sailing right ; three small vessels in harbor ; no tower or steeple ; large building in centre below LO ; water lines covering harbor ; land chased.

Brass. Size 23. F. 8282. See Med. Ill., Geo. II, 119.

239. *Obv.* THE . BRITISH . GLORY . REVIV'D . BY . ADMIRAL . VERNON (N's reversed). Full length figure to right, standing on a solid platform ; sword in his right hand, baton in left. Cannon at right ; ship at left, sailing to right, with flag flying toward T ; small ornament below ; line enclosing legend ; scabbard projects below coat in front.

Rev. Legend and exergue as 224. Ships two, one and three, five sailing right, one left ; three small vessels in harbor ; no tower or steeple ; large building in centre below W ; water lines covering harbor ; land chased.

Brass and copper. Size 24. Probably A. J. N., II, 47, No. 3.

240. *Obv.* Legend as 198. Full length figure to right, standing on a solid platform ; a sword in his right hand, baton

in left.   Cannon at right ; ship at left ; ornament below plat·
form *in a rim with the legend.*

Rev. Legend and exergue as 197, but a period after ONLY.
Ships two and four, five sailing right, one left.   Apparently
from same die as 197 and 282.

Brass.   Size 23.   A. J. N., II, 47, No. 4

241.   *Obv.* THE . BRITISH . GLORY . REVIV . D . BY . ADM .
L . VERNON   In exergue, I . GILES.   Full length figure three-
quarters to right, standing on a solid platform ; a sword in his
right hand, baton in left.   Cannon at right ; ship at left.

Rev. Legend and exergue as 220, but a colon after NO : and
22 :   Ships two, one and three, all sailing right ; two small
vessels in harbor ; waves throughout harbor.

Brass.   Size 17.   Med. Ill., Geo. II, 133.

VERNON AND WALPOLE.

242.   1741.   *Obv.* THE . BRITISH . GLORY . REVIV . D . BY .
ADMIRAL . VERNON . . .   Full length figure three-quarters to
right, wearing a hat, and standing on a solid platform ; a
sword in his right hand, a baton in his left. Cannon at right ;
ship at left ; three small trees below ship.

Rev. MAKE : ROOM : FOR : SIR : ROBERT   In exergue, NO :
EXCISE.   The devil leading Sir Robert Walpole by a rope
around his neck into the open mouth of a dragon at left,
the legend being on a ribbon proceeding from the devil's
mouth.   A quatrefoil and two dots under Sir Robert's coat.

Brass.   Size 19.   Med. Ill., Geo. II, 192 *rev.*, except the
colon after NO :

243. *Obv.* THE . BRITISH . GLORY . REVIV . D . BY . ADMIRAL VERNON. Full length figure three-quarters to right, wearing a hat, and holding a sword and baton. Cannon at right; a fort at left.

Rev. Legend as preceding. In exergue, NO EXCISE. Device as reverse of preceding.

Copper. Size 19. Med. Ill., Geo. II, 192.

VERNON AND ARGYLE.

244. 1740. *Obv.* THE . BRAVE . ADMIRAL . VERNON. Bust to left, wearing coat; his hair in a twisted queue.

Rev. HIS . GRACE . THE . DUKE . OF . ARGYLE. Bust of the Duke * to right, in armor and mantle; his hair in a twisted queue.

Copper. Size 17. Med. Ill., Geo. II, 189.

245. 1740. *Obv.* NON . DORMIT . QUI . VINCIT (He who conquers does not sleep) In exergue, ADMIRAL . VERNON 1739. | I M. Half length figure three-quarters to right; his right hand rests on a cannon; his left on his sword; before him is a ship.†

Rev. IN . HUNC . INTUENS . CLARUS . ESTO (Be thou distinguished, observing this man.) In exergue, THE DUKE OF ARGYLE. Full length figure of the Duke, three-quarters to right, wearing robes and the collar of the Garter, with the George; he leans upon a column on which is his coronet; behind him is a trophy of arms.

Copper. Size 25. Med. Ill., Geo. II, 188.

VERNON, BROWN AND WALPOLE.

246. 1741. *Obv.* THE . BRITISH . GLORY . REVIV . D : BY . ADM . L . VERNON : COMR . BROWN. Two full length figures;

---

* Vernon and Argyle were at this time prominent opponents of the unpopular ministry of Walpole.—EDS.

† I. M. are doubtless the initials of the engraver, but he has not been identified. While the date on the Medal is 1739, that is merely that of the victory. The piece is placed under 1740, by the Editors of Medallic Illustrations.—EDS.

Vernon at left, facing three-quarters to right, with a sword in his right hand, and his left holding the right hand of Brown who stands at right, facing three-quarters to left ; between them is a crown above and a ship below.

Rev. MAKE ROOM FOR SIR ROBERT.   In exergue, NO : EXCISE.   Device as reverse of 242.

Brass and copper.   Size 23.   Med. Ill., Geo. II, 191. A. J. N., II, 49, No. 31.

247.   1741.   *Obv.*   . THE . GENEROUSE : DUKE : OF : ARGYLE In exergue, NO . .   PENTIONER   The Duke standing, facing ; his right hand on his hip, and his left arm resting on a pedestal, upon which is a crown ; he wears the collar of the Garter ; behind and at his right is a trophy of flags and cannon.   At the end of legend a quatrefoil, etc., as in cut.

Rev. Similar to the preceding, but from a different die.

Silver and brass.*   Size 22 and 23.

247a.   *Obv.*   Legend as 214.   Three-quarter figure facing three-quarters to left ; his right fore-arm extended, and in other respects as device of 217.

Rev. THE . (*sic*) TOOK ● PORTO . BELLO . WITH . SIX . SHPS . (*sic*) ONLY ●   In exergue, NOV . 22, 1739 .   *Seven* ships, six

---

* This mule does not strictly belong to American Medals, but was probably included by Mr. Betts because the reverse die is found with those that do relate to America, and also because of the close relations between Admiral Vernon and the Duke of Argyle, who was a distinguished soldier under Marlborough, and died in 1743.   See also A. J. N., II, 49. No. 31, where it is given as here.—EDS.

of which are in two parallel lines ; those in the lower row are directly beneath those in the upper ; a seventh at the left, a little below the upper three : all before a harbor in the form of a horse-shoe, and described by a line ; a fort at the right, another at the left extending nearly to the centre of the harbor, the town in the distance : two small vessels each with a single mast, in the harbor.

Copper. Size 24. A. J. N., V, 74.*

VERNON AND BROWN.

248. 1739. *Obv.* ADMIRAL ♥ VERNON ♥ AND ♥ COMMODORE ♥ BROWN ♥ Two full length figures ; Vernon at left facing three-quarters to left, but with head turned three-quarters to right, a baton in his right hand extended ; Brown at right facing left, a baton in his left hand ; a cannon at left of both ; line inclosing legend ; field chased.

Rev. Same die as 222, but struck on a slightly larger planchet.

Copper. Size 27. See A. J. N., II, 48, No. 19.

249. *Obv.* ADMIRAL VERNON AND COMMODORE BROWN Two half length figures ; Vernon at left, facing three-quarters to

---

* This is apparently one of the rarest of the series, and we have found no other reference. In the collection of Mr. E. J. Cleveland, formerly of Newark, N. J., now of Hartford, Conn. Although Mr. Betts was aware of this description, having referred to it in another place, (see 252), he did not include it in his MS. by some oversight ; we therefore add it with a *letter*, to avoid disturbing his numerical arrangement.—EDS.

right ; Brown at right, facing left ; both hold batons ; no line inclosing legend.[*]

Rev. TOOK . PORTO . BELLO . WITH . SIX . SHIPS . ONLY . NOV . 22 . 1739 In exergue, BY COURAGE AND | CONDUCT. Ships one, two and three ; four sailing to right, two to left ; one small vessel and one boat in harbor ; one boat below right hand fort ; tower and steeple pointing at T and to right of X ; no water lines ; no line inclosing legend.

Brass.　Size 21.

250.　*Obv.* ADMIRAL . VERNON . AND . COMMODORE . BROWN. Device as 249.

Rev. TOOK . PORTO . BELLO WITH . SIX . SHIPS . ONLY . In exergue, NOV 22 1739. Six ships entering the harbor of Porto Bello. [Positions not given.]

Brass.　Size 23.　Perhaps Med. Ill., Geo. II, 99. †

251.　*Obv.* From the same die as 250.

Rev. WHO TOOK PORTO BELLO WITH SIX SHIPS ONLY　In exergue, NOV 22 1739.　Otherwise as preceding.

Copper.　Size 24.　Med. Ill., Geo. II, 100.

252.　*Obv.* From the same die as 250.

Rev. THE . (*sic*) TOOK . PORTO . BELLO . WITH . SIX . SHIPS . ONLY.　In exergue, NOV 22 1739.　Ships three and three ; three above sailing to left, three below to right ; each lower ship being directly below one of those above ; two small vessels in harbor ; one steeple pointing between LO ; a few hori-

---

[*] All these of Vernon and Brown are placed under 1739 in Med. Ill., Geo. II. The date is simply that which appears on the piece, as they could hardly have been struck so soon.　Brown, as will be remembered, was Vernon's second in command.　Vernon's position at the *left*, on these Medals, is really the more honorable, corresponding as it does to what is called in heraldry the "dexter" or principal side of a "Coat-of-arms."—EDS.

† Medallic Illustrations (*loc. cit.*), quotes Fonrobert ("Weyl, p. 907 "). The reference must be to 8290, but there are no periods in the legend, either in the engraving or description there given, although they appear in Med. Ill. We therefore doubt the correctness of that attribution.—EDS.

zontal water lines below lower ships and the left hand fort, upon which are two flags ; no line inclosing legend.
Brass. Size 23. See A. J. N., V, 74.*

253. *Obv.* From the same die as 250.
Rev. Legend as 252. In exergue, NOV . 22 1739 . Ships three and three ; three above sailing to left, three below to right ; each lower ship being below a gap between the ships and forts ; two small vessels in harbor ; tower and steeple pointing at BE and LO ; a few vertical water lines below lower ships and both forts ; one flag on left hand fort ; no line inclosing legend.
Copper. Size 23.

254. *Obv.* Legend as 249. Two half length figures ; Vernon at left facing three-quarters to right ; Brown at right facing left ; both hold batons ; line inclosing legend.
Rev. Same as preceding.
Copper. Size 22. Med. Ill., Geo. II, 102.

255. *Obv.* Legend as 249. Two half length figures ; Vernon at right facing three-quarters to left, Brown at left facing right ; both hold batons ; line inclosing legend.
Rev. TOOK PORTO BELLO WITH SIX SHIPS ONLY In exergue, NOV 22 1739. Ships one, two and three ; all sailing to right ; two boats and one small vessel in harbor ; one steeple pointing to right of o ; water lines below lower ships.
Brass and copper. Size 23.

256. *Obv.* Legend as 252. Device as 255.
Rev. Legend and exergue as 240. Six ships entering the harbor.
Copper. Size 23. Med. Ill., Geo. II, 101. F. 8291.

---

* This reference clearly does not relate to 252, 253, or 254, as will be found on comparison, though there is a certain similarity between the Medal there described and this reverse. See note on 247a above.—EDS.

257. *Obv*. As 255.

Rev. Legend and exergue as 250. Ships one, two and three; three sailing to right, three to left; three boats in harbor; two steeples pointing to o and T ; water indicated below lower ships.

Brass and copper.   Size 16.   Med. Ill., Geo. II, 135.

258. *Obv*. ADMIRAL . VERNON . AND . COMMODRE (*sic*) . BROWN. Two half length figures facing each other ; both hold a baton ; ornament below of a shell, with a branch of two large and three small leaves on each side ; N and C above heads ; line inclosing legend.

Rev. Same die as 196, 232, 233 and 297, but the period shows after ONLY.   Ornament of leaves with two stems crossed below date.

Brass and copper.   Size 23.

259. *Obv*. Legend and device as the preceding, but the period after N and the first M above their heads ; line inclosing legend.

Rev. Legend and exergue as 258. Ships two and four ; all sailing to left ; no vessels or boats in harbor ; tower and two steeples pointing to left of o, W and T ; ornament of leaves with single stem below date and reaching to V ; faint water lines below lower ships ; large forts with ten guns each.

Brass and copper.   Size 23.   Prob. Med. Ill., Geo. II, 104.

260. *Obv*. Same as 259.

Rev. Legend and exergue as 207. Ships two and four ; all sailing to left ; no vessels or boats in harbor ; tower and two steeples point to right of o and at W and T ; ornament of lines with two stems crossed below date and reaching to o ; faint water lines (scarcely visible upon medal in brass); large forts, with fourteen guns each.   Same die as 288 (but with one steeple added), and 300.

Brass and copper.   Size 23.

261. *Obv.* Legend as 250. Two half length figures facing each other ; both hold batons ; ornament below of shell, with branch of two large leaves on each side ; N and c above heads ; line inclosing legend.

Rev. Legend and exergue as 207. Ships two and four ; all sailing to left ; no small vessels or boats in harbor ; tower and two steeples pointing at first L, between o and w, and at I ; faint water lines below lower ships ; ornament of shell and two leaves below date ; large fort at left with fourteen guns and at right with twelve guns. The die closely resembles 234.

Brass and copper. Size 23. Perhaps Med. Ill., Geo. II, 105.

262. *Obv.* Same as the preceding.

Rev. WHO . TOOK . PORTO . BELLO . WITH . SIX . SHIPS . ONLY (*sic*). In exergue, NOV . 22 . 1739 . Ships two and four ; all sailing to left ; no small vessels or boats in the harbor ; tower and two steeples pointing at E, second L and I ; water lines below lower ships ; ornament of leaves with single stem below date ; fort at left with ten guns and at right with eleven guns. See 284, 298 and 301.

Brass and copper. Size 23.

263. *Obv.* Same as 261.

Rev. Legend and exergue as 262 ; otherwise the same as 230, and probably the original die.

Brass. Size 23.

264. *Obv.* Legend as 250 : device as 261, but the periods after N and the first M are above the heads ; line inclosing legend.

Rev. HE . TOOK . PORTO . BELLO . WITH . SIX . SHIPS . ONLY . (*sic*). In exergue, NOV 22 . 1739. Ships two and four ; five sailing to right, one to left ; no small vessels or boats ; two steeples and one tower pointing at first L, W, and T ; water lines below all ships ; ornament with three stems below the date.

Brass and copper.   Size 23.*

265.   *Obv.* Same as 264.

Rev. Legend and exergue as 240.   Ships entering the harbor.†   Copper.   Size 23.   Perhaps Med. Ill., Geo. II, 103.

266.   *Obv.* Legend as 249.   In exergue, TOOK PORTO | BELLO.   Two half-length figures ; Vernon at right, facing three-quarters to left, and Brown at left facing right ; both hold batons ; no line inclosing legends.

Rev. From the same die as 186.

Brass and copper.   Size 24.   Med. Ill., Geo. II, 97.

267.   *Obv.* Same as the preceding.

Rev. WITH SIX SHIPS ONLY NOV 22 1739   In exergue, GOD . PRESERVE THE | ENGLISH . FLEET.   Ships two and four ; five sailing to right, one to left.   Two steeples, pointing at S and between LY ; three boats.

Brass and copper. Size 24. Med. Ill., Geo. II, 98. A. J. N., II, 49, No. 22.

268.   *Obv.* ✦ OF ✦ ADMIRAL ✦ VERNON ✦ AND ✦ COMMO-
DORE ✦ BROWN   In exergue, . BY . THE . COURAGE . | . AND .

---

* Mr. Betts thought it probable that this was the same as Med. Ill., Geo. II, 103, but that has ONLY [correctly].—EDS.

† Mr. Betts did not describe the reverse of this nor of 256, though he evidently followed Medallic Illustrations (*loc. cit.*) but which gives nothing additional. We are therefore uncertain whether the reverses of 197, 240, 256, 265

CONDUCT. Two half length figures; Vernon at right, facing nearly to the front; Brown at left, facing right; both hold batons; no line inclosing legend.

Rev. PORTO . BELLO . WAS . TAKEN . WITH . SIX . SHIPS . ONLY . NOV. 22 . 1739 ✦ In exergue, I . W . FECIT. Ships one, two and three; the three upper ships being at the extreme right; three sailing to right, three to left; five small vessels in harbor; boat with flag outside; tower and steeples pointing at I and at period after x and the following s; water lines throughout harbor.[*]

Brass and copper. Size 23. Med. Ill., Geo. II, 106. A. J. N., II, 49, No. 24.

269. *Obv.* Same as the preceding.

Rev. Legend as on the preceding. In exergue, I . W . Ships one, two and three; the three upper ships being at the extreme right; four sailing to right, two to left; five small vessels in harbor; boat with flag outside; tower and steeple pointing between TH and between period after x and the following s; water lines throughout harbor.

Copper. Size 23.

270. *Obv.* An oval shield having the arms of Great Britain and Hanover, surrounded by the Garter with motto HONI SOIT QUI MAL Y PENSE, and supported by the lion crowned at left, and the unicorn at right; the royal crown surmounted with a lion as crest above; the letters G R at the sides of the crest; the motto EH | DIEU | ET | MON | DROIT | MON (*sic*) upon a ribbon below; an ornament of leaves and scroll work below the ribbon.

---

and 282 are all from the same die or not. It seems very probable that the Vernon and Brown obverses were muled with quite a number of reverses previously used with obverses of Vernon alone, but of these Mr. Betts was able to identify only a portion.—EDS.

[*] The name of the engraver whose initials appear on this and the three following numbers has not been ascertained. The ornaments in the obverse legend, as given in the text, do not closely correspond to those on the Medal, but are the nearest available.—EDS.

Rev. PORTO . BELLO . TAKEN . BY ADMIRAL . VERNON . WITH . SIX . SHIPS . NOV . 22 . 1739. In exergue, ·:⋮ I. W. ⋮:· (N's reversed).　The harbor of Porto Bello, of semi-circular form, defended by a large fort in the foreground at left, a smaller fort at middle distance at right, and a castle upon a point of land in the middle; the tower in the background; ships entering the harbor sailing three and three, in diagonal lines rising from the left; two sailing to right, four to left; two ships side by side, and five small vessels behind castle; one boat outside; one tower and one steeple pointing at A L and between O N; water lines throughout harbor; trees above left-hand fort.

Copper and brass. Size 24. Med. Ill., Geo. II, 125. A. J. N., II, 87, No. 24*a*.

271.　*Obv.* Same as the preceding.

Rev. PORTO . BELLO . TAKEN . BY . ADMIRAL . VERNON . WITH . SIX . SHIPS . NOV . 22 , 1739. In exergue, I. W. (N's reversed.) Six ships entering harbor, three and three, in diagonal lines; one vessel in harbor.

Brass.　Size 25.　A. J. N., V, 65, No. 60.

272.　*Obv.* Same as 270, but the crest differs, G. R. is omitted and the error in the motto is corrected; roses and thistles near ribbon.

Rev. PORTO . BELLO . TAKEN . BY ADMIRAL VERNON . WITH SIX MEN OF WAR ONLY . NOV . THE . 22 . ANNO DOM . 1739. Six ships entering the harbor, sailing two above and four below, the lower four in a curve following the edge of the medal ; all sailing to right ; four small vessels in harbor ; one tower and one steeple pointing between 1739 and PORTO, and between PORTO and BELLO ; water lines below lower ships.

Brass and copper.   Size 25.

273. *Obv.* Same as 270.

Rev. PORTO . BELLO . TAKEN . BY . ADMIRAL . VERNON . WITH . SIX . MEN . OF . WAR . ONLY . NOV . THE . 22 . ANNO . DOM . 1739. The date stamped in.   Six ships entering Porto Bello harbor.*

Copper.   Size 25.   See Med. Ill., Geo. II, 126, note.

274. *Obv.* PORTO : BELLO : URBS : AB . VERNONO : CLASSIS . ANGLICANŒ : PRŒFECTO : NAVIBUS : SEX : OPPUGNATA : 22 : NOV.RIS : 1739. (The city of Porto Bello attacked by Vernon, Admiral of the English fleet, with six ships, 22 Nov., 1739.) Six ships entering Porto Bello harbor in two lines of three and three, rising diagonally from left to right ; all sailing to right ; four small vessels behind the castle ; one tower and steeple pointing on each side of PORTO ; water lines below lower ships.

Rev. PORTO . BELLO . URBS . AB : CLASSIS : ANGLICANŒ : PRŒFECTO : NAVIBUS : SEX : OPPUGNATA : 22 . NOVEMBRIS : ANNO DOM : 1739. (The city of Porto Bello attacked by the Admiral of the English fleet, 22 Nov., 1739.) Six ships entering Porto Bello harbor in two lines of three and three, rising diagonally from the left ; all sailing to right ; four small vessels behind castle.

Brass and copper.   Size 24.   Med. Ill., Geo. II, 137, differs slightly in the punctuation

* As intimated in the note under 266, this is very probably a mule. These pieces of Vernon and Brown are not quite so common as those of Vernon alone, and Mr. Betts, like the Editors, was unable to identify, in every case, the reverses here given with those previously described, from the very condensed descriptions in Medallic Illustrations, which do not indicate minute die differences.—EDS.

PORTO BELLO AND CHAGRE.

275.   1740.   *Obv.* HATH . ONCE . MORE . REVIV.D . THE .
BRITISH . GLORY :·   In exergue, below a double plain line,
THE . HON . EDWARD VERNON . ESQ (N's reversed).   In the
field at right, FORT | CHAGRE   Half length figure, full face ;
his baton in his left hand ; a tree at left ; a fort, with steeple,
at right below the name ; under the fort a ship sailing to
right ; line inclosing legend.*

Rev. BY . THE . TAKEING . (*sic*) OF . PORTO . BELLO . WITH .
SIX . SHIPS . ONLY . NOV . 22 . 1739 . (N's reversed.)   In exergue,   · : I · : · W : ·   Ships three and three in two diagonal
lines rising from left to right ; five sailing to right, one to
left ; five small vessels in harbor, one outside ; one tower
and one steeple pointing to IT and between X and S ; water
lines covering harbor ; line inclosing legend.

Copper.   Size 25.   Med. Ill., Geo. II, 154.   A. J. N., II,
86, No. 16*a*.†

276.   *Obv.* VICE AD : RL : OF THE BLEW ; & COM : DER . IN
CHIEF . OF ALL HIS . MAI : SHIPS . IN THE WEST INDIES   In
exergue below a corded line, THE HON.ᴸᴱ EDWARD VERNON .
ESQ .   In the field at the right, A VIEW . | OF . FORT . | CHA-

---

* All the Medals relating to Chagre were struck in 1740 or later.—EDS.

† Mr. Betts considered this to be the same as described in A. J. N., *loc. cit.*,
but that says "ships one, two and three."   While the two descriptions are not
necessarily inconsistent, we are uncertain whether the two dies are identical or
whether another number should be added.—EDS.

GRE. Half length figure, full face; baton in his left hand; tree at left; fort and ship at right.

Rev. PORTO BELLO . TAKEN BY ADMIRAL VERNON . WITH SIX MEN OF WAR ONLY . NOV . 22 . ANNO DOM . 1739 . Ships two and four; those below being in a curve following the legend; all sailing to right; four small vessels in harbor; no line inclosing legend.

Brass. Size 24. Med. Ill., Geo. II, 152.

277. *Obv.* VICE AD : RL . OF THE BLEW : & COM : ER . IN CHIEF . OF ALL HIS . MAI : SHIPS IN THE WEST INDIES. In exergue below a corded line, THE HON . EDWARD | VERNON . ESQ In the field at right, A . VIEW . | OF . FORT | CHAGRE Half length figure, full face; baton in his left hand; tree at left; fort with steeple at right below the name; below the fort a ship sailing to right; no line inclosing legend.

Rev. Same die as the preceding.

Brass and copper. Size 24. Med. Ill., Geo. II, 153, which mentions two varieties but does not describe differences.*

278. *Obv.* VICE AD . RL OF THE BLEW COM . ER IN CHIEF OF ALL HIS MAI . SHIPS IN THE WEST INDIES. In exergue, THE HON? EDWARD VERNON ESQ In the field at right, A VIEW OF FORT CHAGRE Three-quarter length figure, three-quarter facing; his right hand on his hip; a baton in his left hand; a tree at left, a ship at right, and a fort beyond.

Rev. PORTO BELLO TAKEN BY ADMIRAL VERNON WITH SIX MEN OF WAR ONLY NOV . 22 . ANNO DOM . 1739. Six ships, three and three; harbor much curved; four small vessels and three forts.

Brass. Size 24. A. J. N., II, 86, No. 14*b*.

---

* The reverses of Med. Ill., Geo. II, 152 and 153 are apparently the same, as none is given for the latter, which is called similar to the preceding (*i. e.* 152), the differences named being on the obverse, though, as stated in the text, it mentions "two varieties." In Mr. Betts's manuscript he considered 277 as identical with Mr. Appleton's No. 15, in A. J. N., II, 48; but a comparison of the descriptions shows marked differences, and we cannot identify that with either of those here described.—EDS.

279. *Obv.* VICE . AD : RL . OF THE BLEW ; COM . : ER . IN CHIEF . OF ALL HIS . MAI : SHIPS IN THE WS : IES   In exergue, THE . HON : EDWARD | VERNON . ESQ   In the field at right, A . VIEW . | OF . FORT . CHAGRE   Half length figure, full face ; baton in left hand ; tree at left ; fort with steeple at right below the name ; below the fort a ship sailing to right ; no line inclosing legend.

Rev. PORTO BELLO . TAKEN . BY . ADMIRAL VERNON . WITH SIX MEN OF WAR ONLY   In exergue, NOV . 22 AN DOM . 1739. Ships two and four ; those below in a curve following the legend ; all sailing to right ; eight small vessels in harbor, two of them with only sterns and masts showing ; a small boat and a man standing in foreground at left ; no line inclosing legend.

White metal and brass, thick and thin planchet.   Size 25.*

280. *Obv.* Legend as 198.   In the field at right, A VIEW | OF FORT | CHAGRE   Half length figure, full face ; baton in his left hand ; small tree at left ; fort, with steeple, at right below the name ; under the fort a small ship sailing to right ; line inclosing legend ; the field chased.

Rev. Legend and exergue as 196.

Brass and copper. Size 23. Med. Ill., Geo. II, 151. A. J. N., V, 65, No. 30.

281. *Obv.* Same as the preceding.

Rev. Legend and exergue as 197, but a period after ONLY. Ships two and four ; five sailing to right, one to left ; no small

---

* This description was made by Mr. Betts from an original in his collection, and his MS. shows he thought it the same as Mr. Appleton's 16 (A. J. N., II, 48) ; the obverses are apparently the same, but the reverses differ, as that (16) places the words in the *legend* which Mr. Betts's MS. puts in *exergue*. This may be an error of his copyist ; but if not, there seems to be still another combination not mentioned by Mr. Betts. A comparison of the two pieces, which we have been unable to make, would be necessary to determine that point. The minute differences in the various dies occasionally render the verifications of attributions extremely difficult, especially as Medallic Illustrations does not attempt to give them.—EDS.

vessels or boats; two steeples and one tower pointing at second L, W and T; ornament below date; water lines below all ships.

Brass and copper.   Size 23.

282.   *Obv.*   Same as 280.

Rev. Same as reverse of 197, but the die is less worn and shows water lines below all ships.

Brass.   Size 23.

283.   *Obv.* Same die as 280, but with field smooth.

Rev. Legend and exergue as 198.   Scroll ornament.   Six ships entering the harbor.   [Positions not given.]

Brass.   Size 23.   Med. Ill., Geo. II, 150, which mentions that there are three varieties of the reverse, with this same smooth obverse, but does not describe them.   Probably one is the same as 198.

284.   *Obv.* THE . BRITISH . GLORY . REVIV . D . BY . ADMIRAL . VERNON .   In the field at left, FORT | CHAGRE   Half length figure facing left; baton in left hand; right hand extended; fort at left below the name; tree behind at right; line inclosing legend.

Rev. From the same die as 262, 298 and 301, but ONLV corrected.

Brass and copper.   Size 23.   Med. Ill., Geo. II, 146.   A. J. N., II, 48, No. 11.

285.   Legend as 198.   In the field at left, A . VIEW | OF . FORT | CHAGRE.   Full length figure standing on the shore, facing three-quarters to left; baton in his left hand; right hand pointing at fort on the left below the name; ship at right, sailing to left; no line inclosing legend.

Rev. Legend and exergue as 281. Ships one, two and three; five sailing to left, one to right; three steeples pointing at first L, W and T; two small vessels in harbor; water lines below lower ships and larger forts.

Brass and copper. Size 23. Med. Ill., Geo. II, 143. A. J. N., II, 86, No. 7a.

285a. *Obv.* Legend as 280. In the field at right, A VIEW OF FORT CHAGRE Full length figure facing three-quarters to left; baton in his left hand; a ship at left; a fort at right.

Rev. Legend and exergue as 197. Six ships entering Porto Bello harbor. [Positions not given.]

Copper. Size 23. Med. Ill., Geo. II, 141.

286. *Obv.* Same as 285a.

Rev. Legend and exergue as 212. Probably the same die.

Copper. Size 23. Med. Ill., Geo. II, 142.

287. *Obv.* Legend and inscription as 284. Full length figure facing right; a sword in his right hand, baton in left; a fort at right, below the name; a ship at left, sailing to left; shell and leaf ornament below his feet; line inclosing legend; field chased.

Rev. Same die as 230 and 261.

Brass and copper. Size 23. Med. Ill., Geo. II, 139. F. 8284.

288. *Obv.* Same as the preceding.

Rev. Same die as 260 and 300, but with one steeple omitted. Probably the original die.

Copper. Size 23.

289. *Obv.* Same as 287.

Rev. Legend, exergue and ornament as 197. [Position of ships not given.]

Copper. Size 23. Med. Ill., Geo. II, 140.

290. *Obv.* PORTO . BELLO . TAKEN . BY . ADMIRAL . VERNON In the field at left, FORT CHAGRE Half length figure, three-quarters to left ; baton in his left hand.

Rev. WITH . SIX . SHIPS . ONLY . NOV . 22 . 1739. Six ships entering Porto Bello harbor. [Positions not given.]

Copper. Size 21. Med. Ill., Geo. II, 145.

291. *Obv.* IN MEMORY OF ADMIRAL VERNON In the field at left, FORT CHAGRE and the letters I . M. Half length figure facing right ; baton in his right hand ; before him cannon, flag, sword, horn and pike.*

Rev. Legend and exergue as 207. Ships one, two and three ; one small vessel and one boat in harbor ; one boat below right hand fort, from which a man is climbing up the fort.

Copper and brass. Size 23. • Prob. Med. Ill., Geo. II, 147. A. J. N., II, 48, No. 14.

292. Legend as 291. In the field at left, FORT | CHAGRE Half length figure facing right ; baton in his right hand ; his left extended ; a fort at left above the name ; cannon balls, cannon, banner, sword, trumpet and battle-axe at right ; no line inclosing legend.

Rev. Legend as 229. In exergue, NOV 22 1739. Ships one, two and three ; four sailing to right, two to left ; small vessel and boat with two men and flag in harbor ; large boat with three men below right hand fort ; water indicated below

---

* I. M. are the initials of the unknown engraver who cut the dies for 245.—EDS.

lower ships ; one tower and one steeple pointing at right of E and left of ·W.

Copper and brass.   Size 23.   Med. Ill., Geo. II, 148.

293.   *Obv.* IN . MEMORY . OF . ADMIRAL . VERNON   A fort and the letters T . B. in the field at left.*   Half length figure facing right ; baton in his right hand ; before him cannon, flag, sword, etc.

Rev. Legend and exergue as 196.   Six ships entering the harbor.   [Position not given.]   The die closely resembles 291, but "the details vary."

Silver.   Size 21.   Med. Ill., Geo. II, 149.   Rare.

294.   *Obv.* ADM^L VERNON TOOK PORTO BELLO WITH SIX SHIPS ONLY   In exergue, NOV 22 1739   In the field at left, FORT | CHAGRE   Full length 'figure facing left ; right hand extended, pointing at fort ; baton in his left hand ; a fort at left below the name ; a ship at right, sailing to left ; water extending between the fort and ship ; line inclosing legend.

Rev. HE . TOOK . PORTO . BELLO . WITH . SIX . SHIPS . ONLY . . In exergue, NOV . 22 . 1739 .   Ships three and three ; three above sailing to left, three below to right ; two small vessels and one boat ; two steeples and tower pointing at O, W and H ; water lines below lower ships.†

Brass and copper. Size 23.   Med. Ill., Geo. II, 144. A. J. N., II, 48, No. 13.   F. 8278.

---

* The initials of some unknown engraver. It is uncertain when these "Memorial" pieces were struck. While it is possible that after his death they were muled with old reverses [in 1757 or 1758], it is more probable that "In memory of" is merely equivalent to "In honor of."—EDS.

† Mr. Betts described 285 and 294 from impressions in his own collection, and it will be observed that there are marked differences in the position of the ships, the legend, etc. : yet his MS. attributes them to Med. Ill., 143 and 144, which says the two reverses are the same and refers to Fon. (*loc. cit.*). The latter piece was not in the British Museum, and several explanations of the apparent error, either in our text or in Med. Ill., might be suggested. We allow the references to remain as Mr. Betts left them, noting the discrepancy between them.—EDS.

VERNON AND HADDOCK.

295.   1741.   *Obv.* Same as the preceding.

Rev. ADM^L H – – – K TOOK O WITH SEVERAL SHIPS ONLY.
Full length figure of Admiral Haddock wearing a hat and
facing three-quarters to left, standing on a platform ; a cannon to right, upon the muzzle of which rests his left hand ;
his right hand extended pointing to a fort at left ; a ship at
right, sailing to right ; the sea between fort and ship.

Brass.   Size 23.   Med. Ill., Geo. II, 182.

296.   1741.   *Obv.* As reverse of 295.
Rev. As reverse of 294.   (Same die.)*
Brass.   Size 23.   Med. Ill., Geo. II, 183.   F. 8276.

PORTO BELLO AND CARTHAGENA.

297.   1741.   *Obv.* THE SPANISH PRIDE PULL'D DOWN BY
ADM^L VERNON.   In the field, DON | BLASS.* Full length figure
of Vernon at left, facing right ; sword in his right hand ; he

---

* Medallic Illustrations in commenting on these pieces says : " Admiral Haddock was stationed with a fleet in the Mediterranean to prevent the junction of
the French and Spanish fleets, in which object he was twice unsuccessful. It
was very extensively believed that his instructions restricted him from activity,
and these satirical Medals were one of the modes of expressing the public dissatisfaction." The connection of the pieces with America rests on the Porto
Bello devices only, both of them being mules with Vernon dies. It will be
noticed that this mule does not mention Vernon's name, thus virtually but unin-
tentionally giving Haddock the glory of an exploit at which he was not even
present !—EDS.

receives with his left hand the sword of Don Blass,* who kneels on both knees at right, facing left, and offering sword with right hand; ornament of shell and two leaves below; line inclosing legend.

Rev. Same die as 196, 233, and 258.

Brass. Size 23.

298. *Obv.* THE SPANISH . PRIDE . PULLD . DOWN . BY . AD-MIRAL . VERNON. In the field, DON | BLASS. Full length figure of Vernon at left, facing right; sword in right hand; receiving with his left the sword of Don Blass, who kneels on both knees at right, facing left, and offering sword with left hand; ornament of shell and four leaves below; line inclosing legend.

Rev. Same die as 262, 284, and 301.

Brass and copper. Size 23½. Med. Ill., Geo. II, 165. A. J. N., II, 48, No. 17.

299. *Obv.* Same as the preceding.

Rev. Same die as 232.† Ornament of four leaves with two stems crossed below date.

Brass. Size 23.

300. *Obv.* Same as 298.

Rev. Same die as 260 and 288.

Copper. Size 23.

301. *Obv.* Same die as 298, but with a small ° over the N of DON.

---

* The placing of Don Blas de Leso, the commander of the Spanish fleet in the harbor of Carthagena, on these pieces, is incorrect. When the ships were taken it was discovered that he had made his escape, which is alluded to on a Medal below (335). He had made himself extremely unpopular in England by his insolent attitude.—EDS.

† This seems to be almost identical with 297, except in the condition of the die of the reverse which is less worn. See comments in text of 232 and 233. —EDS.

Rev. Same die as 262, 284 and 298, struck on a slightly larger planchet.*

Copper. Size 23½.

302. *Obv.* THE SPANISH PRIDE PULL'D DOWN BY ADMIRAL VERNON. In the field, DON | BLASS. Full length figure of Vernon at left, facing right; a sword in his right hand; he is receiving with his left the sword of Don Blass, who kneels on both knees at right, facing left; no ornament; line inclosing legend, except period.

Rev. Legend as 231. In exergue, NOV 22 1739. No scroll ornament. Ships one, two and three; all sailing to right; steeple and tower pointing between EL, and between WI; one small vessel and two boats.

Brass and copper. Size 17½. Med. Ill., Geo. II, 166.

303. *Obv.* Legend as 302. In exergue, G | BRADBURY. In the field, DON | BLASS. Full length figure of Vernon at left, facing right; a sword in his right hand; he is receiving with his left the sword of Don Blass, who kneels at right on both knees, facing the left, with both hands extended; line inclosing legend.†

Rev. Legend and exergue as 251. Ships one, two and three; all sailing to right; one boat at right of fort; two steeples pointing at L and between WI.

Copper. Size 22. Rare. In the collection of the New York Hist. Soc.

304. *Obv.* THE PRIDE OF . SPAIN HUMBLE.D . BY . ADMIRAL . VERNON. In the field, DON BLASS. Full length figure of

---

* This Medal seems to be identical with 298, with the exception of the ° over N on the obverse; whether this is the original die or a later alteration cannot now be determined. Mr. Betts apparently gave it a separate number merely for convenience of reference.—EDS.

† The engraver of this die is not mentioned in Med. Ill., and we have been unable to learn anything concerning him. The reverse die may be identical with that of 251, and the obverse of 303 may be merely an alteration of 302, by the addition of the name.—EDS.

Vernon at left, facing three-quarters to right, wearing hat, with his left hand extended, and receiving with his right the sword of Don Blass, who kneels on one knee at right ; behind Don Blass a large ship, stern on, bearing a large ensign with the cross of St. George ; no line inclosing the legend ; but the legend, and a light scroll ornament below, are in a depressed circle.

Rev. Legend and exergue as 197. Ships two and four, the lower line having first and third ships from the left lower than the other two ; all sailing to right ; two small vessels in harbor ; two low steeples pointing at E and I ; water lines below lower ships.

Brass and copper. Size 24. Med. Ill., Geo. II, 167.

305. *Obv.* THE PRIDE OF SPAIN HUMBLED BY ADM: VERNON In the field, DON BLASS. Full length figure of Vernon at left, facing three-quarters to right, wearing hat ; with his left hand extended, and receiving with his right the sword of Don Blass, who kneels on one knee at right, hat in hand, facing left ; behind Don Blass a small ship sailing to right ; line inclosing legend ; no ornament below.

Rev. Legend as 236. In exergue, NOV 22 1739. Ships one, two and three ; all sailing to right ; one boat in harbor ; tower and steeple pointing at first L and I ; water lines below lower ships.

Brass and copper. Size 22. Med. Ill., Geo. II, 169. A. J. N., II, 48, No. 18.

306. *Obv.* THE . PRIDE . OF . SPAIN . HUMBLED . BY . AD : VERNON. In the field, DON . BLASS (N reversed) ; the word PRIDE irregularly cut. Full length figure of Vernon, facing three-quarters to right, wearing hat ; his left hand extended, and receiving with his right the sword of Don Blass, who kneels on left knee, hat in hand, at right, facing left ; behind Don Blass a small ship sailing to right ; ornament of lion's head and leaves below ; no line inclosing legend.

Rev. Legend and exergue as 197. Ships one, two and three, all sailing to right ; a boat below right hand fort, and a man in it with both arms raised ; no boats in harbor ; short tower and steeple pointing at second L, and between W1 ; water lines below lower ship, extending faintly to middle ships ; a small leaf resembling a butterfly at beginning of legend ; break in die below date.

Brass silvered, brass and copper. Size 24. Med. Ill., Geo. II, 168.   ? A. J. N., II, 87, No. 17*a.*

307. *Obv.* THE . PRIDE . OF . SPAIN . HUMBLED + BY . AD : VERNON. In the field, DON . BLASS. Same die as last, turned down and recut, as appears by the letters AD, partly obliterated by the word BY ; the legend is inclosed by a line ; the mast of the ship is lower, and the pennon longer, and a

---

* The obverse described in A. J. N. (*loc. cit.*) does not mention that the N in DON is reversed. We should therefore consider that this reference belongs more properly to 307.—EDS.

heavier water line is under the ship; the word ʀʀɪᴅᴇ more regular.

Rev. Same die as 306.

Brass and copper.   Size 24.

VERNON AND BROWN.

308.   1741.   *Obv.* ✠ THE . ᴘʀɪᴅᴇ . ᴏғ . sᴘᴀɪɴ ✠ ʜᴜᴍʙʟᴇᴅ . ʙʏ . ᴀᴅ : ᴠᴇʀɴ . ɴ   In exergue, ᴀɴᴅ . ᴄᴏᴍ : ʀᴇ . ʙʀᴏᴡɴ.   In the field, ᴅᴏɴ . ʙʟᴀss.   Full length figure of Vernon at left, facing three-quarters to right, wearing hat, with his left hand extended, and with his right receiving the sword of Don Blass, who kneels on one knee before him, hat in hand; behind Don Blass stands Brown with baton in his right hand; no line inclosing legend.

Rev. Legend and exergue as 270.   Ships three and three, arranged diagonally upward to right; four sailing to left; two to right; two small vessels side by side, and five very small vessels in the harbor; one boat outside; tower and steeple pointing at ᴀʟ and last ɴ of ᴠᴇʀɴᴏɴ; trees at left; water lines throughout harbor; very faint above.

Brass.   Size 24.   Med. Ill., Geo. II, 173.

VERNON, OGLE AND WENTWORTH.

309.   1741.   *Obv.* No legend; in exergue, ʙʀᴀᴠᴇ : ᴠᴇʀɴᴏɴ : ᴏɢʟᴇ | & ᴡᴇɴᴛᴡᴏʀᴛʜ   Three full length figures; Vernon in the centre, full face, wearing hat, a baton in his right hand;

Ogle and Wentworth at the sides, facing right and left;
two small lions at their feet.*

Rev. Same die as 306.

Brass and copper. Size 24. Med. Ill., Geo. II, 175.

310. *Obv.* Same as the preceding.

Rev. VERNON : CONQUERD : CARTAGENA   In exergue, APRIL
1 : 1741. Perspective view of four ships sailing to right
toward a barred entrance between two forts at right; a city
and church with steeple on a hill at left; a leaf ornament
dividing water from exergue, separates APRIL   I.

Brass. Size 24. Med. Ill., Geo. II, 174.   A. J. N., II, 49,
No. 30.   F. 8190.

311. *Obv.* AD . VERNON ♥ AD . OGLE ♥ AND ♥ GEN ♥ WENT-
WORTH ♥   Three figures standing, Vernon in the centre,
facing; each holds a staff or baton : Fame, with three
wreaths, blowing a trumpet above; a ship at the right; a
banner with lion rampant at the left.

Rev. WHO TOOK CARTHAGENA   In exergue, APRILL 1741.
A harbor and three ships within it, bombarding a town; four
ships outside; soldiers on a point of land and two cannon.

Brass. Size 25. Med. Ill., Geo. II, 176.   B. N.

312. *Obv.* BRAVE : ADM : L : VERNON : OGLE & . WINTWORTH
In exergue, T . GILES.   Three full length figures standing on
a solid platform, chased; Vernon in centre, three-quarters to
left, wearing hat; baton in his left hand; Ogle at left, facing
right in coat and hair in queue; Wentworth at right, full
face, leaning on lance and wearing a plume; cannon at right;
small lions at right and left; ornament between platform and
exergue.†

---

* The obverse is the same as No. 30 in Mr. Appleton's list, but the reverse
differs. The figures on the obverse might be characters in some extravaganza,
and represent the "art" of the entire series, with scarcely an exception.—EDS.

† Mr. Betts's MS. has WINTWORTH as in the text; but as he does not note
the error, and we have found no other reference to the piece, we cannot verify
it, the original in the Yale Cabinet not being accessible to us at present. 316
and 317 also have the three figures of Vernon, Ogle and Wentworth.—EDS.

Rev. WHO : CONQUERD : CARTAGENA　In exergue, APRIL 1 1741.　Six ships sailing to right, one above, five below: two forts at right separated by narrow entrance ; city and church with steeple on a hill at left ; scroll ornament above exergue ; steeple pointing at O ; boat at left.　·

Brass and tin.　Size 23.

HAVANA AND PORTO BELLO.

313.　1741.　*Obv.*　ED : VERNON ESQ : VICE ADMIRAL OF THE BLUE　In the field at the left, HAVANAH below a castle with three turrets; full length figure of Vernon facing three-quarters to left ; sword in his right hand ; his left hand on hip ; a cannon at his feet pointing to left ; a ship at right.

Rev. Legend and exergue as 196.　Originally the same die as 306, and probably the first form of it : the same break occurring below date ; no boat below right-hand fort.

Brass and copper.　Size 23.　? Med. Ill., Geo. II, 179.*

314.　*Obv.* Same as 313.

Rev. Same die as 313, but with a butterfly in place of the W in first word of legend and O changed to E ; a boat with a man in it below the right-hand fort has been added, and the water lines extended to the width of the Medal.　Originally the same die as 306.

Brass and copper.　Size 23.　? Med. Ill., Geo. II, 178. A. J. N., II, 86, No. 14a.　F. 8277.

---

* While it would seem from the Medals bearing the word HAVANAH that Vernon had won another victory there, this was not the case ; no assault was made on that city.　The editors of Medallic Illustrations explain the pieces by stating that an attack on Havana had been suggested, before any attempt on Carthagena.　The decision was referred to the Council of War to be held in the West Indies, and Carthagena was chosen as the first place to be assaulted ; in the ensuing July (1741), and partly in consequence of orders from England, Vernon sailed for Cuba, and having landed a portion of his force, was about to proceed to Santiago and Havana.　Sickness and other difficulties, however, compelled him to re-embark and return to Jamaica.　His success had been so confidently expected that the capture was considered by the English as certain to follow, and as Mr. Betts remarks in his introduction to the chapter, the Medals were struck in anticipation of a victory which was never won.—EDS.

HAVANA AND CARTHAGENA.

315. 1741. Same die as 313.

Rev. Legend and exergue as 310. Four ships sailing to right, toward a narrow entrance between two forts at right ; a town and church on a hill at left ; leaf ornament dividing water from exergue ; steeple pointing between NC.

Copper. Size 24. Med. Ill., Geo. II, 177.*

316. *Obv.* Same as 312.

Rev. TRUE BRITISH HEROES TOOK CARTHAGENA In exergue, APRIL 1741. Two ships sailing to right toward a fort in the foreground ; two forts in the middle connected by a chain boom, behind which is a boat, above it, DON | BLASS ; in the background the city in a straight line ; flagstaff upon tower in city points at E ; coast line left and right points at B and T.

Brass. Size 23.

317. *Obv.* Same as 312.

Rev. Legend and exergue as 316. Two ships sailing to right toward a fort in the foreground ; two forts in middle connected by a chain boom, behind which is a boat ; above it, DON | BLASS ; in the background the city in a straight line ; flagstaff upon tower in city pointing between ES ; coast line left and right at E and H.

Brass. Size 24. The reverse may be that of A. J. N., V, 65, No. 71.

VERNON AND OGLE.

318. 1741. *Obv.* ✳ ADMIRAL . VERNON . AND . S^R . CHALONER . OGLE. Two full length figures ; Vernon at left facing three-quarters to right, wearing hat ; baton in his right hand ; his left hand extended ; Ogle at right facing left ; baton in his left hand ; right hand extended ; shell and leaf ornament in exergue ; line inclosing legend.

---

* Med. Ill. makes the reverse dies of [our] 310, 315 and 325 the same.—EDS.

Rev. Legend and exergue as 316. Two ships sailing to right toward a fort, below which is a boat ; two forts in the middle connected by a chain boom, behind which is a ship ; in the background the city in a straight line ; flagstaff upon tower in city pointing at o ; coast line at u and h.

Brass. Size 23. Perhaps A. J. N., V, 65, No. 70 or 71, which however is size 24. F. 8188.

319. *Obv.* ADMIRAL VERNON AND Sʀ CHALONER OGLE. Two full length figures ; Vernon at left facing three-quarters to right, wearing hat ; baton in right hand, left hand extended ; Ogle at right, facing left ; baton in left hand, right hand extended ; shell and leaf ornament in exergue ; lines inclosing legend.

Rev. Legend and exergue as 316. Two ships sailing to right toward a fort in the foreground ; two forts in the middle connected by a chain boom, behind which is a boat ; above it, DON BLASS ; in the background the city in a straight line ; flagstaff on tower in city points at E ; coast line left and right at B and T.

Brass. Size 24. Med. Ill., Geo. II, 161. ? A. J. N., V, 65, No. 70 or 71.*

320. *Obv.* Legend as the preceding. Device also similar.†
Rev. BY BRITISH COURAGE TOOK CARTHAGENA APRIL 1741. Two ships sailing into Carthagena harbor, another within a chain boom.

Brass. Size 23. See Med. Ill., Geo. II, 162.

321. *Obv.* Similar to 319, but "with ornaments after the word OGLE."
Rev. Legend as 320. Design similar to 319.
Brass. Size 23. A. J. N., V, 65, No. 72.

---

* Nos. 318 and 319 are probably the same as Mr. Appleton's 70 and 71, but we cannot certainly distinguish them by the descriptions.—EDS.

† Medallic Illustrations does not describe the obverse die, but says it is "similar to" our 319.—EDS.

322.   *Obv.* ADM VERNON AND Sʀ CHALONER OGLE TOOK CARTHAGENA   In exergue, 1741.   Vernon and Ogle at full length, approaching each other.

Rev. SPANISH INSOLENCE CORRECTED BY ENGLISH BRAVERY In the field, DON BLASS   Three ships entering one by one a nearly circular harbor on which is a town, and passing through a narrow strait guarded by four forts ; two ships and a boat in the harbor.

Brass.   Size 24.   A. J. N., II, 49, No. 29.

323.   *Obv.* THE . PRIDE . OF . SPAIN ✦ HUMBLED . BY . Aᴰ VERNON.   In exergue, AND Sʀ CHAᴸ | OGLE. In the field, DON . BLASS.   Full length figure of Vernon at left facing three-quarters to right, wearing hat ; with his left hand extended, and receiving with his right the sword of Don Blass, who kneels on one knee before him, hat in left hand ; behind Don Blass stands Ogle with a baton in his right hand, the left on his hip ; no line inclosing legend.

Rev. THEY TOOK CARTHAGENA APRIL *1741.*   Two ships sailing to right toward a fort in the foreground ; two forts in the middle connected by a chain boom, behind which is a boat ;* above it, DON | BLASS ; in the background the city in a straight line ; steeple at left pointing between CA ; tower in centre pointing at central A of CARTHAGENA ; tower at right pointing right of last A in the same word.

Brass. Size 24. Med. Ill., Geo. II, 172. F. 8189. A. J. N., II, 49, No. 28.

---

* See note on 335.—EDS.

324. *Obv.* ADM^L VERNON AND S^R CHALONER OGLE In exergue, WE LOOK FOR | DON BLASS Two full length figures approaching each other. Vernon at left facing three-quarters to right, wearing hat ; baton in his right hand, his left hand extended ; Ogle at right facing left ; baton in his left hand, right hand extended downward.

Rev. TOOK CARTHAGENA APRIL 1741. Two ships sailing to right toward a fort in the foreground, below which is a boat ; a boat above the ships ; two forts in the middle connected by a chain boom, behind which is a third boat ; above it, DON | BLASS ; in the background the city in a straight line ; flagstaff on tower in city points at N ; coast lines at T and first I of date.

Brass and lead. Size 23. Med. Ill., Geo. II, 160. F. 8187. A. J. N., V, 65, No. 69.

VERNON AT CARTHAGENA.

325. 1741. *Obv.* Same as 306.
Rev. Legend and exergue as 310, and apparently from the same die.*
Brass. Size 24. Med. Ill., Geo. II, 171.

326. *Obv.* Same as 306.
Rev. HE ○ TOOK ○ CARTHAGENA ○ APR ○ I ○ 1741. Plain view of a circular harbor, with narrow entrance, protected on the right by one fort, and on the left by two forts ; one ship passing through entrance ; four ships outside and three ships within the harbor ; houses on the shore surrounding it.
Brass. Size 24. Med. Ill., Geo. II, 170.

327. *Obv.* From the same die as 305.
Rev. HE TOOK CARTHAGENA APRIL 1741. Two ships sailing to right toward a fort in the foreground ; two forts in the middle connected by a chain boom, behind which is a boat ;

---

* The Carthagena Medals described above have Porto Bello reverses, or show one or more of Vernon's companions with him ; the following have Carthagena reverses, and Vernon alone.—EDS.

above it, DON | BLASS ; in the background the city in a straight line ; steeple at left pointing at first A of CARTHAGENA ; tower in centre pointing at A in APRIL.

Brass, size 22, and copper, size 21½. A. J. N., II, 87, No. 27b.

328. *Obv.* Same as 298.

Rev. Legend and exergue as 316. Two ships sailing to right toward a fort in the foreground ; two forts in the middle connected by a chain boom, behind which is a boat ; above it, DON | BLASS : in the background the city in a straight line ; flagstaff upon tower in city points at E in HEROES, coast line left and right at B and T.

Brass and copper.* Size 23½.

329. *Obv.* Same as 298.

Rev. Legend and exergue as 316. Two ships sailing to right toward a fort in the foreground ; two forts in middle connected by a chain boom, behind which is a boat ; above it, DON | BLASS ; in the background the city in a straight line ; flagstaff upon tower in city points between ES ; coast line left and right at E and H.

Brass and copper. Size 23½.

330. *Obv.* Same as 298.

Rev. Legend and exergue as 316. Two ships sailing to right toward a fort, below which is a boat ; two forts in the middle connected by a chain boom, behind which is a ship ; in the background the city in a straight line ; flagstaff upon tower in city pointing at O ; coast line at U and H.

Copper. Size 23½.

Of Nos. 328, 329 and 330, doubtless two correspond to 163 and 164 in Medallic Illustrations, but from the condensed descriptions there we are unable to assign them with certainty. Two of them also apparently correspond to Mr. Appleton's 27 and 27a, but the same remark applies to them also. Mr. Betts seems to have had one piece not mentioned by either authority cited ; which of his three numbers it was, cannot be determined by us.—EDS.

331.   *Obv.* Same as 224.

Rev. AD . VERNON . GEN^L . OGLE . TOOK . CARTHAGENA . BY . SEA . AND . LAND .   In exergue, AP^L : 1 : 174:1   A large fort at right ; at the left of it one large ship sailing to left, and four small ships sailing to right ; two small ships and two smaller vessels in harbor before the town in the background.

Brass.   Size 24.   Med. Ill., Geo. II, 157.   A. J. N., II, 49, No. 25.

332.   *Obv.* ADMIRAL . VERNON . THE . PRESERVER . OF . HIS . COUNTRY.   Full length figure facing three-quarters to left ; right hand extended ; baton in left ; point of sword touches the mast of the vessel behind him ; on each side of him a fort in the distance, and a small vessel before it.

Rev. TOOK . CARTHAGENA above, and 1741 at the bottom. Bird's-eye view of two points of land projecting toward the centre of the Medal ; islands above ; the point on the left having three forts marked BOCACHICA and S . PHILIPS and IAGO ; above the strait between the points an island with fort marked S . IOS ; in the foreground two ships sailing to right, and three small vessels sailing to left ; above, one small vessel sailing to left.

Brass and copper.   Size 24.   Med. Ill., Geo. II, 156.   A. J. N., V, 65, No. 64.   K., XIII, 353.   ? F., 8184.*

---

* Fonrobert (*loc. cit.*) omits BOCACHICA in the description and cut.—EDS.

333. *Obv.* I ○ CAME ○ I ○ SAW ○ I ○ CONQUERED   In exergue, CARTHAGENA.   Half length figure three-quarters to left nearly facing; his right hand extended; a baton in his left hand; line inclosing exergue which curves to conform to the lower edge.

Rev. NONE . MORE . READY . NON . (*sic*) MORE . BRAVE . APRIL 1741.   Two ships sailing to right toward a fort in the foreground; above them two boats; two forts in the middle connected by a chain boom, behind which is a boat; above it DON | BLASS; a tree behind the fort on the right; the harbor indicated by a semi-circular line; in the background the city in a straight line.

Brass.   Size 24.   Med. Ill., Geo. II, 159.   F. 8183.

334. *Obv.* ADMIRAL : VERNON : VEIWING (*sic*) : THE : TOWN : OF : CARTHAGANA (*sic*)   In exergue, 1740 : 1.   Full length figure facing three-quarters to left, wearing hat; standing on a solid platform; right hand extended; baton in left; forts at right and left in the background, before which are three ships and a tree at right, and seven trees at left.

Rev. THE FORTS OF CARTHAGENA DESTROYD BY AD^M VERNON   In exergue, 1741.   Two ships sailing to right, and two boats in the foreground; in middle distance a strait defended on the right by one fort, above which is S . IOSEPH, and defended on the left by three forts; beside the nearest is S . IAGO; in the background at left a town, above which is CARTHAGENA a steeple between A and R.

Brass, copper and lead.   Size 23.   Med. Ill., Geo. II, 155. K., XIV, 433.   F. 8285.   A. J. N., II, 49, No. 26.

335. *Obv.* ADM⁻ VERNON . VIEWING . THE . TOWN . OF . CARTHAGENA.   Full length figure facing three-quarters to left, wearing hat ; his right hand extended ; a baton in left ; a fort at right and left in the background, before each of which is a ship.

Rev. HE DESTROY D THE FORTS OF CARTHAGENA In exergue, APRIL 1741. A strait protected on each side by two forts ; between the two nearest are five ships, two and three ; the two forts in the middle connected by a chain boom, behind which is a boat ;* above it DON | BLASS ; the city in the background in a straight line.

Brass and silver.   Size 22.   Med. Ill., Geo. II, 158.   A. J. N., V, 65, No. 63.

VERNON AT FORT CHAGRE.

336. 1741. *Obv.* Legend as 198.   Full length figure of Vernon to right, standing ; a sword in his right hand and a baton in his left extended ; a ship sailing left behind him and a fort in front ; below the fort in indistinct letters FORT | CHAGRE.   Shell ornament in base.   Field chased.*

---

* As mentioned in the note on 297, Don Blass made his escape from the victorious British fleet by taking to a boat, and concealing himself, and that is alluded to on this piece.—EDS.

† This Medal should properly follow 232, but it seems to have been overlooked when the others were numbered and placed, very likely because the name of the fort is almost illegible in the piece in his collection.—EDS.

Rev. Legend and exergue as 207. Ornament of leaves with crossed stems below date. Ships two and four, all sailing left. Flag staffs pointing between o and B, and at s in six; two towers point one at o in BELLO, and the other at B. No small vessels or boats. Field plain.*

Copper. Size 24. F. 8284.

337. *Obv.* VERNON . VINDEX . PATRIÆ . MDCCXLI (Vernon the avenger of his country, 1741). Bust three-quarters to left; hair long; he wears a coat and cravat, the end of which passes through a button-hole in his coat; a ship at left; a fort at right.

Rev. Plain.

Pewter. Cast.* Size 32. Med. Ill., Geo. II, 180.

TABLE OF PORTO BELLO REVERSES.

THE following table of reverses which was compiled by Mr. Betts, in a few cases gives the position of the ships, which he did not mention in the text. As it was evidently prepared after the previous list was completed, we presume that it gave his latest notes, and that on a revision of the MS., had he been able to make it, those items would have been added. The Editors have compared it very carefully with the descriptions, and have corrected only some evident errors of the copyist. There are a few queries as to the identity of certain dies, which remain, and which we are unable to determine for reasons already given, — but if the dies thus queried are *not* identical, they resemble each other so closely in most cases, that the differences appear to have arisen from the wear to which they were subjected, or to very slight alterations made on the originals. The condition of the pieces makes it impossible to say which was an original and which an altered die. So much of an explanation seems only just to Mr. Betts, for the very great labor he bestowed on the preparation of the list has made itself so clear to us as the pages have passed under our consideration, that we can only express our regret that he could not have finished the work he had so nearly completed.

---

* The Editors of Med. Ill. (*loc. cit.*) remark that this appears to be a cast of a lead proof executed by Dassier, who did not complete his work, after the true circumstances of the expedition were known. To us it seems to more nearly resemble the Chagre than the Carthagena pieces.—EDS.

SIX SHIPS SAILING TO THE RIGHT.

176, 191, 218, 219, 220, 221, 222, 224, 226, 228, 238, 241, 248, 255, 272, 274, 276, 277, 279, 302, 303, 304, 305, 306, 307, 309, 313, 314.

Of the foregoing, 255, 302, 303, 305, 306, 307, 309, 313, and 314 arrange them one, two and three.

218, 219, 220, 221, 222, 224, 226, 238, 241, 248, arrange them two, one and three.

176, 191, 228, 272, 276, 277, 279, and 304 arrange them two and four, the lower line conforming more or less to the lower edge of the piece. On 228 the lines are nearly parallel. [The position of the ships on 176 and 291 is not noted in the text, and 304 follows the curve less closely than the others.—EDS.]

On 274 the ships are three and three.

Of the above, 218 and 219 are from the same die without alteration. 276 and 277 are from the same die without alteration. 221 appears to be the original die which was altered for 222 and 248. 306, 307, 309, 313, and 314 are from the same die at different periods, showing alterations, 313 probably being the original.

SIX SHIPS SAILING TO THE LEFT.

196, 229, 230, 231, 232, 233, 234, 235, 258, 259, 260, 261, 262, 263, 284, 287, 288, 297, 298, 299, 300, 301, 336.

Of the foregoing, 229 arranges them two, one and three.

196, 230, 231, 232, 233, 234, 235, 258, 259, 260, 261, 262, 263, 284, 287, 288, 297, 298 and 336 arrange them two and four, the right hand ship being a little above the others in the lower line.

Of the above, 196, 232, 233, 258, 297, and 299, appear to be the same die, in more or less perfect condition. 230, 263, and 287 are apparently the same. 231, 261, and 285, are the same. 260, altered, is used on 288, and 300; 288 without steeple pointing at o is probably the original. 262 is used on 284, 298, and 301.

FIVE SHIPS SAILING TO THE RIGHT AND ONE TO THE LEFT.

197, 203, 204, 205, 206, 207, 208, 209,* 227, 236, 237, 239, 240, 264, 267, 275, 281, 282. In all, it is the ship on the extreme right of the lower line which sails to the left.

239 arranges them two, one and three.

197, 203, 204, 207, 208, 209, 227, 240, 264, 267, 281, and 282 arrange them two and four.

---

* Not mentioned in the text.—EDS.

205 has them one, one and four; 236, 237, and 275, three and three, and 206 in an acute angle.

197, 240, and 282 [and possibly 256 and 265 on which the position of the ships is not mentioned] are from the same die. 208 and 227 are from the same die.

FIVE SHIPS SAILING TO THE LEFT AND ONE TO THE RIGHT.

187, 189, 190, 192, 193, 194, 199, 285. On these it is the ship on the left of the lower line which sails to the right.

187, 192, 193, 194, 199, and 285 arrange them one, two and three.

189 and 190 two, one and three.

187, 192, and 194 are the same die. 189 and 190 are the same. 199 and 285 may be the same.

FOUR SHIPS SAILING TO THE RIGHT AND TWO TO THE LEFT.

182, 183, 188, 249, 269, 270, 292.

249, 269, 270, and 292 arrange them one, two and three.

182, 183, and 188 arrange them two and four.

In 182, 183, and 188 the two right hand ships of the lower line sail to the left. In 249 and 292 the left hand ship of the second line and the right hand ship of the lower line sail to the left. In 270 the upper ship and the right hand ship of the second line sail to the left.

All are from different dies.

FOUR SHIPS SAILING TO THE LEFT AND TWO TO THE RIGHT.

212, 213, 216, 217, 270, 286, 308. In all, the two left hand ships sail to the right.

Of the above all but 270 and 308 have the ships arranged in wedge shape, — one, one, two and two. The other two arrange them diagonally rising from the left.

212 is altered for the dies of 216 and 217.

THREE SHIPS SAILING TO THE RIGHT AND THREE TO THE LEFT.

180, 186, 198, 201, 210, 211, 215, 252, 253, 254, 257, 266, 268, 294, 296.

Of the foregoing, on 180, 186, and 266 the upper line of ships sail to the right, the others to the left. On 198, 252, 253, 294, and 296, the reverse is the case. On 257 and 268 the three left hand ships sail to the right, and the others to the left.

257 and 268 arrange them one, two and three.   180, 186, 201, 210, 211, 215, 266, in wedge shape.   The others are in two lines.

186 and 266 are from the same die.   294 and 296 are from the same die, and perhaps 196.

201, 210, and 215 are alterations, of which probably 201 is the original, several houses having been added later.

THREE SHIPS SAILING TO THE LEFT, TWO TO THE RIGHT AND ONE
"STERN ON."

200 and 202, where the ships are arranged in wedge shape, and the dies differ.

Seven ships, 214 and 247*a*.

* [The differences in legend and punctuation which Mr. Betts proposed to put here, will be found in the Index.—EDS.]

CHAPTER IV.

FERDINAND VI, of Spain, surnamed "the Wise," in whose honor the Medals described in the present Chapter were struck, was the son of Philip V (some of whose Medals have been described on preceding pages), and the Princess Mary of Savoy, whose marriage took place September 11, 1711. His father's claim to the throne of Spain, under the Will of Charles II, — to perfect which was one of the objects most earnestly sought by Louis XIV, — led to the "War of the Spanish Succession," and was finally established by the Treaty of Utrecht, April 11, 1713. Ferdinand was born at Madrid on the 23d of the following September,[*] and on the 14th of February, 1714, his mother died. He ascended the throne just after the death of his father, which occurred July 9, 1746, and was proclaimed August 10, in Madrid, and at a later date in the other principal cities of the Spanish possessions, so that the exact date of issue cannot be given for the various pieces.

His father had abdicated the throne in favor of his eldest son, Louis the First of Spain, who reigned but a few months — from January 17 to August 31, 1724, — when he died, and

---

[*] Art de Vérifier les Dates. Biographie Universelle gives the date as April 10, 1712.—EDS.

Philip again resumed the crown.*　Ferdinand married the Princess Magdalena Theresa of Portugal, when he was only about sixteen years of age.　She died August 27, 1758, almost exactly a year before her husband, leaving no issue, and the crown went to his brother, Charles III, some of· whose Proclamation Medals will be given hereafter.

In the early part of his reign Ferdinand enacted many wise and just laws, encouraged manufactures, commerce, and the arts, and did much for literature and science throughout his kingdom.　In later years he was subject to melancholy, and secluded himself for considerable periods, so that his various liberal plans failed of entire accomplishment.

BUENOS AIRES.

338.　1747.　*Obv.* FERDINANDUS ✦ VI ✦ D ✦ G ✦ HISPANI- · ARUM ✦ ET . IND . REX ✦ (Ferdinand VI, by the grace of God King of Spain and the Indies.)　Armored bust of the King in profile to right, and with flowing wig.　Beaded border.

Rev. NOVILISS . FIDELISS . CIV BONAERINEI PROCLAM. 1747. (The most noble and faithful city, Buenos Aires [struck this] on his Proclamation, 1747.)　Two ships sailing to left ; an anchor on the waves in foreground ; an eagle flying above. Beaded border.†

Silver.　Cast.　Size 20.　H., Ferdinand 35.

CHIHUAHUA.

339.　1748.　*Obv.* FERDND (*sic*) VI · D . G . HISPAN . ET IND . REX. (Translated above.)　Half-length figure of the King to right in a laced coat, his left hand raised and a baton in the right.　Within a border of dots.

---

* The American Proclamation Medals of Louis have been described.—Eds.

† AM is in monogram.　NOV is an error on the piece for NON, the Latin words corresponding to the Spanish "*la muy noble y muy leal ciudad.*"　The American Proclamation pieces abound in monogram combinations of letters and have also many reversed Ns and other errors.　Hererra's engraving shows the Medal dies were poorly cut.—Eds.

Rev. CHIGUAG DIUVS · PHILIP · REGS (Chihuahua...... of*
Philip, King.) At the bottom, 17 48. Shield with royal arms
of Spain, quarterly, Castile and Leon, with an escutcheon of
pretence charged with three fleurs-de-lis, two over one (for
France); the shield is surmounted by a rude crown; its point
divides the date. Leaf-work on border and edge, on both
obv. and rev.

Silver. Cast. Size 25. H., Ferdinand 36.

CORDOVA.

340. 1747. *Obv.* FERDINAND VI . DG · HISPA . ET . INDIAR .
REX : (Translated above.)   A leaf-like ornament at the end of
the legend. Armored bust of the King to right, with full
wig and the collar of the Golden Fleece. ·

Rev. IMPERATOR ✚ IN DIARUM . [two monograms†] CORDOUA .
1747. (Emperor of the Indies, Cordova, 1747.) Crowned
shield quarterly with arms of Leon in first and fourth and
Castile in second and third quarters. No escutcheon of pretence. The cross on the top of the crown divides N and D.

Silver. Cast. Size 20. H., Ferdinand 37.

GUADALAXARA.

341. 1747. *Obv.* FERDINANDVS VI D. G. HISPANIARVM REX.
Bust of the King to right, with large medallion (?) on breast.
Beaded border.

Rev. IMPERATOR INDIARUN (*sic* and NS reversed) above,
(Emperor of the Indies) and below GVADALAXa ✚ A tree
supported by two lions. Beaded border.

Silver. Cast. Size 25. H., Ferdinand 38.

----

* Herrera gives no explanation of the letters DIUVS. As the U is singularly
formed on the Medal, it may be meant for a monogram of EJ and the letters are
possibly the abbreviations for D(edicavit) I(n) EJVS (Proclamatione). The
legend would then read in full, Chihuahua struck this in honor of his Proclamation, etc.—EDS.

† The first monogram resembles a v surmounted by a reversed v; the second
combines D and E.—EDS.

342. 1747. *Obv.* FERDIN • VI • D • G • HISP • ET IND • REX •
. (Translated above.)   Bust of the King, full face, draped, and
with flowing wig.

Rev. CIVI • GVADALAX • COL • HISP • 1747   A little tree, the
device of the city (as shown on the preceding Medal), placed
sidewise in the legend at the bottom.   (The City Guadalaxara,
of the Spanish Colony, 1747.)   The field divided by a vertical
bar, on the right of which are seven horizontal bars, and on
the left a tree supported by lions.*

Silver.   Cast.   Size 23.   H., Ferdinand 39.

343. 1747. *Obv.* UIVA . EL . SENOR . DON . FERNANDO . VI.
(Long live Don Fernando VI.)   Half length figure of the
King to the right, with broad hat ; his right hand holding a
roll ; his left hand raised.

Rev. EL COMMERCIO . DE GUADALAXARA . ⫶   (The commer-
cial community [*i. e.*, the city] of Guadalaxara.)   1747 below†
a trophy of helmet, sword, arquebus, spear and banner.

Silver.   Cast.   Size 24.   H., Ferdinand 40.

GUANABACOA.

344. 1747. *Obv.* FERNANDO . VI . D . G HISPAN . REX * *
(Translated above.)   Bust of the King to right, in flowing
wig, a star on his breast.

Rev. : SANTIAGO . DE . TORES (*sic*) . GVANA°   The letters
AN in GVANA° in monogram.‡   (Santiago of the towers.)   Below, 1747.   Two castles, each with a central gate, a tower and
two gables.

Silver.   Cast.   Size 17.   H., Ferdinand 41.

---

* This is probably intended to represent the arms of the City and (?) State,
but very rudely. . Herrera calls the tree a cypress.—EDS.

† We follow the rosettes and groups of points as nearly as may be with the
material available.—EDS

‡ Herrera, the latest and best authority, places this under Guanabacoa, a
town of Cuba; O'Crowley (p. 405) thinks it may pertain to Guayana or Guaya-
quil. —EDS.

GUATEMALA.

345. 1747. *Obv.* FERD . VI . D . HISPAN . ET IND . REX ✳
Bust of the King to right in wig and armor.

Rev. GUAT . IN . EIUS . PROCLAMATIONE. (Guatemala on his
Proclamation). The date · 1747 · at the bottom. A knight
on horseback leaping between two mountain peaks. (Arms
of Guatemala.)

Silver.   Size 20.   H., Ferdinand 42.

346. 1747. *Obv.* FERD . VI . D . G . HISPAN . ET . IND REX
Profile bust of the King to right in wig and armor.

Rev. Legend as on the preceding ; design similar, but the
hoofs of the horse rest on the mountain peaks.

Silver.   Size 15.   H., Ferdinand 43.

347. 1747. *Obv.* FERD . VI . D G . . . . IND . REX . (The
piece not being well centered the legend does not all appear.
Translated above.) Naked bust of the King to right, wearing a wig.

Rev. G . IN E . . . . MAT .   The date · 1747 · at bottom.
The legend is merely an abbreviated form of that on 345, and
has the same meaning.   Similar design to the last.

Silver.   Size 11.   H., Ferdinand 44.

HAVANA.

348. 1747. *Obv.* FERDND (*sic*) · VI · D · G · HISPAN · ET IND ·
REX (Translated above.) The date + 1747 + at the bottom.
Bust of the King to right in wig and armor ; his breast-plate
is singularly formed.

Rev. GONZALO . REZIO DE OQVENDO HAB ✳ (Havana), DO and
the last word in monogram.*   Two keys, rings above, the
wards to right below.   (The arms of the city.)

Silver.   Size 23.   H., Ferdinand 45.

---

* Rezio de Oquendo is perhaps the name of the Viceroy. The o is within
the loop of the D.

349. 1747. *Obv.* FERNANDO . VI . D . G . HISPAN . REX *
* * (Translated above.)   Profile bust of the King to right in
wig and armor.

Rev. GONZALO . REZIO DE (in monogram) OQVEND [o inside
the D] HAB? (the first three letters of the last word in monogram*) 1747 : : :   Two keys, as on the preceding.

Silver.   Cast.   Size 19.   H., Ferdinand 46.

350. 1747. *Obv.* FERDND ' VI ' D ' G HISPAN ' ET IND '
REX (Translated above.)   + 1747 +   Bust of the King to
right in armor.   Similar to 348.

Rev. GONZALO . REZIO DE OQVEND [o] (The D contains a
small o.*) ×   In the field, two keys, wards at the top and
turned to the left, and HAB (Havana) in monogram between
their tops.

Silver.   Cast.   Size 19.   H., Ferdinand 47.

HONDA.

351. 1747. *Obv.* R on left, F on right. (For Rex Ferdinandus, King Ferdinand.)   Bust of the King to right crowned,
in flowing wig, no drapery.

Rev. HONDA on left, 1747 on right.   A pomegranate with
a portion of the side cut out and showing seeds.   Edges
"rope-shaped" on both sides.

Silver.   Cast.   Size 15.   H., Ferdinand 48.

352. 1747. *Obv.* No legend.   Youthful bust of the King
to left, in a cap and wig.

Rev. 1747.   HONDA on the right, and 1747 on the left.
Similar design to the preceding.

Silver.   Cast.   Size 9.   H., Ferdinand 49.

MEXICO.

353. 1747. *Obv.* FERDINANDVS . VI . D . G . HISPANIARUM .
REX .   (Translated above.)   Half length figure of the King
to right, in a coat, within a circle of dots; he holds a roll in
his right hand and the left is raised and pointing.

---

* See note on 318.—EDS.

Rev. IMPERATOR . INDIARUM (Emperor of the Indies.)   Under the device,   MEXISI . ANNO | 1747.   (Struck at Mexico in the year 1747.)   The legend separated from the field by a circle of dots.   A castle of two stories supported by two lions, and surmounted by an eagle sitting on a cactus.   (Arms of the city.)

Silver.   Cast.   Size 24.   H., Ferdinand 50.

354.   1747.   *Obv.* JURE DU CONSULAT AU MEXIQUE EN 1747. (Allegiance sworn by the Consulate of Mexico in 1747.)*

Silver.   Size 23.   In the collection of Mr. Gustave Daniel de Loriches.   H., Ferdinand 51.

PANAMA.

355.   1747.   *Obv.* FERDINS (N reversed) ✳ VI D G HISPA ET (in monogram) ✠ INDI ✚ REX ✳ 1747 ✳   Bust of the King to right in wig, and draped, within a circle of dots.

Rev. IN C PANAMENSIS TE AMA I (*sic*) CORDE ˙ TE CLAMAT I (*sic*) ORE   ([Proclaimed] in the city of Panama which loves thee in its heart, and proclaims thee with its lips.)   A shield with border of lions and castles (for Spain), the field divided per fess; in chief a ship sailing to sinister, a six-pointed star in sinister chief; in base another, but no star.   A ducal coronet above the shield, and columns entwined with scrolls supporting globes at sides; all within a circle of dots.†

Silver.   Cast.   Size 23.   H., Ferdinand 52.

356.   1747.   *Obv.* FERDINS (N reversed) . VI DG HISPA . ET (in monogram) INDI . REX ✳ 1747 . ✳   Same design as last.

---

* This is described from Herrera, who learned of it from a Catalogue of Medals printed at Madrid in 1857, but had never seen the piece.   No other example is known.   Perhaps struck by the French Consulate out of compliment to the new King, as he was the grandson of Louis XIV of France. — EDS.

† Under each ship is a singular object, which somewhat resembles a curved sword with hilt; perhaps it is merely the die-cutter's idea of the hull.   O'Crowley, p. 403, calls this the arms of the city.   See our 152, where there are slight differences in the device.   In the legend the I after AMA is doubtless an imperfect T, and after the last I is a curved line connecting with the O, probably meant for an N in monogram.   See note on 357.—EDS.

Rev. IN C PANAMENSIS TĒ AMAT CORDE TE CLAMAT ORE ✱ Same design as last, in a circle. Translations given on the preceding number.✱

Silver. Cast. Size 22. Not in H.

357. 1747. *Obv.* FERDIN (N reversed) ✤ VI DG HISPA ET (in monogram) INDI ✤ REX ✤ 1747 ✱ Same design as 355. The letters very large.

Rev. Legend and design as 355.†

Silver. Cast. Size 23. H., Ferdinand 53.

PUEBLA DE LOS ANGELES.

358. 1747. *Obv.* FERDINANDVS (AND in monogram) VI DG . ISPANIAᴺ (*sic*) REX   Draped bust of the King to left wearing hat and wig, within a circle.

Rev. ANGELOPOLIS (AN in monogram) PROCLAMTIO (*sic*) . 1747 . (Proclamation at Puebla.) Bust of the Queen, full face, turned toward right, with collar of pearls, within circle.

. Silver. Cast. Size 18. H , Ferdinand 54.

PORTO RICO.

359. 1747. *Obv.* FERDI . VI . DG . HIS ET . IND (N reversed) . REX   Naked bust of the King to right, laureated.

Rev. PORTVS DIVES . above and AN 1747 . below. (Porto Rico, in the year 1747.) A lamb, very rudely cut, to the left, bearing a patriarchal cross and palm branch.

Silver. Cast. Size 15. H., Ferdinand 55.

✱ The letter I before N, beginning reverse legend, is omitted in Mr. Betts's MS., but from his comments we venture to insert it as on the others. See next note.—EDS.

† In his descriptions of our 355 and 357 Herrera puts at the *close* of the reverse legend the letter I which *begins* it in our text. In his engravings it is at the bottom of the piece, and equally distant from the E of ORE and the N; we see no good reason to object to the reading given in the text, which seems the only way to dispose of this letter; if it is superfluous and the legend properly begins with N as Herrera gives it, then N. C. may perhaps be the initials of NOSTRA CIVITAS, and the legend would read "Our Panama City loves thee, etc." but I would then have no meaning that we can discover.—EDS.

360. 1747. *Obv.* FERDI . VI . D G . HIS . ET IND (N reversed) . REX . Bust of the King to right, in wig, and draped.

Rev. PORTVS DIVES . above, and AN . 1747 . below. (Porto Rico, in the year 1747.) A lamb kneeling, facing the right, and bearing a patriarchal cross and a palm branch.

Silver. Cast. Size 15. H., Ferdinand 56.

SANTA FE DE BOGOTA.

361. 1747. *Obv.* . . . . RNADO (*sic*) ∴ VI D . . . . . Head of the King to left in wig, within a circle of dots.

Rev. HISPANIA . . . . . 1747 + An eagle displayed within an irregular circle of dots, with head to right, holding in each talon a pomegranate.

Silver. Cast, and very rude. Size 15. H., Ferdinand 57.*

SANTIAGO DE CUBA.

362. 1747. *Obv.* F . VI . HISP . ET IND (the last two words in monograms) REX . AN . 1747 . followed by three rosettes of seven dots, separated by colons. Bust of the King to right in wig and armor.

Rev. IOAN DE (in monogram) CAXIGAL (AL in monogram) PRO . CVB . F . VI CLAMAT (MAT in monogram) . * (John de Caxigal (?) Viceroy of Cuba, proclaims Ferdinand VI.) St. James on horseback galloping to right with a curved sword raised above his head. Dotted borders.

Silver. Cast. Size 27. H., Ferdinand 58.

363. 1747. *Obv.* Legend as preceding ; nothing after date but one rosette. Bust of the King to right, draped.

Rev. Legend as preceding, but no period after PRO. Similar design to last, but the Saint is facing, and the borders are plain.

Silver. Cast. Size 19. H., Ferdinand 59.

---

* Herrera mentions the fact that but one example of this piece is known, which is in the Spanish Museum of Archaeology, and though its attribution to Santa Fe is probable, it is not fully proved. — EDS.

364.   1747.   *Obv.* FERD . VI . HISP ET INDIARVN (*sic*) (N reversed) . REX +   Bust of the King to right, draped, and in flowing wig.

Rev. IOAN . DE (in monogram) CAXIGAL P. CUB TE (in monogram) R CLAMAT +   (John de Caxigal, Viceroy of Cuba, proclaims thee King.   R for REGEM.)   St. James on horseback galloping to left, brandishing a straight sword ; 1747 in field below the ground (which is not shown on the preceding); plain borders.

Silver.   Cast.   Size 17.   H., Ferdinand 60.

SANTO DOMINGO.

365.   1747.   *Obv.* FERDINANDUS VI D G · 1747 +   Naked bust of the King to right, in flowing hair.

Rev. HODIE APERIT ORBEM F . R . G (*sic*)   (To-day he opens the world.   Ferdinand, Most Catholic King, G for c.)   A key erect, wards at top to right, and supported by two lions, within a circle.   (The key is the device of San Domingo.)

Silver.   Cast.   Size 17.   H., Ferdinand 61.

366.   1747.   *Obv.* FERDINANDVS . VI . D . G · 1747 +   Bust of the King to left, draped, and wearing a wig.

Rev. HODIE APERIT ORBEM + F + R + G +   (Translated above.)   Same design as the last, but ruder, within a circle.[*]

Silver.   Cast.   Size 14.   H., Ferdinand 62.

SOMBRERETE.

367.   1747.   *Obv.* SOMBRE on right, and RETE on the left. Youthful bust of the King to right, in flowing wig, armor draped, and laureated.

Rev. FERDINANDVS VI . D . G . HISP . REX   Royal arms, Castile and Leon quarterly, on a crowned shield.

Silver.   Cast.   Size 21.   H., Ferdinand 63.

---

[*] The second and third stars have seven points; the type with six is nearest attainable. — EDS.

VENEZUELA.

368. 1747. *Obv.* ✦ FERDO . VI ₒ D . G ₒ HISPAN ET IND ₒ
REX ₒ 1747. Bust of the King to right, in armor and flowing
wig, draped ; waves below, and under them the date.

Rev. GVBERNATORE . PROV . VEN ZVLOAGA . ˙. (By the
Governor of the Province of Venezuela.) In the field Y over
N on the left, and SVA in similar position on the right of an
altar supporting a crown, which rests on a tasseled cushion
(for IN CORONATIONE SUA, on his coronation).* All the NS
on the Medal are reversed.

Silver. Cast. Size 20. H., Ferdinand 64.

369. 1747. *Obv.* FERDO (*sic*) VI . D . G . HISPAN ET IND .
REX. The date 1747 at the bottom. Bust of the King to
left, in wig and draped.

Rev. Same legend and design as last.

Silver. Cast. Size 14. H., Ferdinand 65.

370. 1747. *Obv.* FRO (*sic*) . VI . D . G HPA . ET IND REX .
1747, date at bottom (HP and IND in monograms.) Bust of
the King to left, draped.

Rev. PROV . VENEZ . G . ZVLOAGA. (Province of Venezuela,
etc.) A crown.

Silver. Cast. Size 10. H., Ferdinand 66.

VERA CRUZ.

371. 1747. *Obv.* FERD . VI . D . G . HISP . ET (in monogram)
. IND . R. Armored bust of the King to right, with wig, and
wearing the collar of the Golden Fleece.

Rev. NOV . VER . CRVC . PROCLAM . (Vera Cruz proclaims
him.†) ✦ A ˙ 1747 ✦ at bottom. A castle with three towers,
on waves, and surmounted by a cross. (Arms of the city.)

Silver. Cast. Size 22. H., Ferdinand 67.

---

* The capital city of the Province of Venezuela was Santiago de Leon de
Caracas (now usually called Caracas only), where the Proclamation was made,
and where the three Medals were struck. — EDS.

† NOV may be for Nobilissima as on 338.— EDS.

372. 1747. *Obv.* FERD . VI . D . G . HISPANIAR . R. (N reversed). Bust of the King to right in circle, in wig, and draped, very rudely cut.

Rev. VERA CRVCIS . PROCLAMATIO . 1747. (Proclamation at Vera Cruz.) Same design as the last, within a circle ; the cross extends to the edge of the Medal.

Silver. Cast. Size 19. H., Ferdinand 68.

373. 1747. *Obv.* FERDINAND . VI . D G HISPA . * * Bust of the King facing, turned toward right, in wig and armor, with collar of the Golden Fleece.

Rev. ENPERATO (*sic*) . INDIARVM. (Emperor of the Indies.) A castle with a single turret surmounted by a banner, and inscribed at base VERACR. A long curved line below the tower.

Silver. Cast. Size 15. H., Ferdinand 69.

ZACATECAS.

374. 1746. A medal of Zacatecas is mentioned in an anonymous pamphlet entitled "*Proclamaciones*" (as stated by Herrera, Ferd. 70), with a legend referring to the proclamation of Ferdinand VI in 1746. Its size was 17, but no other particulars are given.

UNCERTAIN.

The following pieces of uncertain mintage, are placed by Herrera among Americans.

375. 1747. *Obv.* FERNANDO . AI (*sic*) . D . G . HISPAN R. 1747. Profile bust of the King to right in wig and armor.

Rev. GONZALVER TOMASJPH. In the field 1747 ; an owl flying above.

Silver. Cast. Size 14. H., Ferdinand 71.

376. 1747. *Obv.* FERNANDO . AI (*sic*) . D . G . HISPAN . R . 1747 . ✢ The legend begins to read on the right, near the bottom, and the tops of the letters are inward. Bust of the King to right in wig and armor.

Rev. JVAN FORES VIIIAVISENCI O ⚹ . ⚹ . A tower on the centre field, with key on the left, its handle at the top, and two concentric serrated curves on the right.*

Silver. Cast. Size 14. H., Ferdinand 72.

377. 1747. *Obv.* VIVA | FERN^{DO} | VI (Long live Ferdinand VI.) Inscription in three lines, within a circle of dots, surrounded by wreath of laurel.

Rev. The same *incuse*.

Silver. Size 10. H., Ferdinand 73.

378. 1747. *Obv.* FERDINANDUS VI . OVR 1747. Bust of the King to right, draped.

Rev. FR . NUMINIS ENSEM OFERTCC. A horseman riding to the right, and holding a sword in his hand.†

Size 17. H., Ferdinand 74.

The Proclamation pieces above were struck in America; the two following were struck in Spain.

379. 1746. *Obv.* FERDINANDVS . HISPAN . REX. (Ferdinand, King of Spain.) Head of the King in profile to right, wearing a full and flowing wig.

Rev. REGNORVM SVSCEPTO REGIMINE. (The government of his kingdoms having been undertaken.) The King at left, standing; he wears a wig, ermine mantle and robes, and the collar of the Order of the Holy Spirit; his right hand holds the handle of a rudder; his left is extended towards a group of four females who are tendering their homage. The one at the right (Europe) has a mural crown, arms and hands ex-

---

* The second and third I in the last word of the reverse legend may be intended for an N, or to form a monogram with the A. Herrera, from whom Mr. Betts took this description, gives no explanation of this or the preceding. The legends of the reverses are apparently names of persons.— EDS.

† The meaning of the legend is not entirely clear, but in substance seems to imply that Ferdinand as King bears the sword of Deity. The mounted horseman may be the emblem of Guatemala. Herrera mentions it, but gives no plate or explanation. — EDS.

tended, and kneeling, with a rabbit (called by Herrera the emblem of Spain) at the right.   Behind her, a second holding an anchor· on her right shoulder, for Africa; a third with elephant head-dress and right hand extended, for Asia; and a fourth, slightly draped, wearing a panache, kneels with right hand slightly extended.   In exergue, IX JVL. M.DCC.XLVI (July 9, 1746.)

Gold (in the Spanish Archaeological Museum) and silver. Size 34.   H., Ferdinand 15.

380.   1746.   *Obv.* Legend as the preceding, but with u's for v's.   Head of the King similar to the last, but the wig differently arranged ; below the head, near the edge, I DASSIER ET FILS (I. Dassier and Son, the die-cutters.)

Rev. Legend as preceding, but with u's for v's.   Similar device to the last, but the King is in armor and sandals ; his right foot is advanced instead of his left, as on the preceding ; the four female figures are similarly arranged, but the rabbit is more nearly in front, and its ears are much longer.   In exergue, IV JUL MDCCXLVI | I D F (Initials of the die-cutters.)

Silver.   Size 25.   H., Ferdinand 16.

CHAPTER V.

T the close of what has been styled in a previous chapter "the Period of Colonization," came an interval when the efforts to protect and strengthen the American Colonies occupied a large share of the attention of the governments by which they had been established. The long wars between these governments involved, more or less directly, their possessions on this side of the ocean, so that the period from 1744 to 1775 may not improperly be called the Period of Intercolonial Wars, under which title have been grouped the Medals next to be mentioned, and a brief notice of the motive of a few of these pieces seems to be proper.

The Franco-American Jetons of Louis XV are of two classes. One was struck with special relation to commerce and the advancement of the trade between the American Colonies and France, and their designs refer to the prosperous condition of those settlements under her rule, or to the value of their products. The other, as Mr. Geo. M. Parsons says in his interesting paper published in Vol. XIX of the *American Journal of Numismatics*, "speaks of ambition, enterprise, dominion and conquest." Beginning with 1751, one of these was struck annually for a series of years, until the conquest of Canada by the British extinguished the power of France in America.

These Jetons have always been peculiarly attractive to American collectors, and so eagerly have they been sought that down to a very recent period restrikes were constantly made at the French mint, when the condition of the dies forbade their further use. For the obverse, various dies with the head or bust of Louis XV were taken from time to time, and the details here given are those of the piece under inspection. It is impossible now to decide which was the original obverse of any one piece, and it is not improbable that a new obverse was made every year; but it seems useless to describe minutely these differing dies, which always bear the portrait of the King, with his name and titles more or less abbreviated, or to assign a separate number to each of them; the different combinations that have come to my knowledge 'have occasionally ·been mentioned in the notes.

Great Britain, on the other hand, struck no coins of importance in the interest of her American possessions, and the British Medals of the period chiefly relate to her exploits in the new world, in which her own forces took prominent part, though in some, as for instance in the capture of Louisburg, the Colonists showed their loyalty and willingness to support the mother country. In addition to these she struck numerous Medals for presentation to the Indians; this was a matter of policy, to meet the liberality of France to the native tribes.

The result of the differing course of the two nations is to be seen on the one hand in the unwavering loyalty of the French Colonists, who never swerved from their allegiance, and on the other, in the jealousies constantly arising between the forces of Great Britain and those of her Colonies, due to reasons unnecessary to enlarge upon here, but which fostered the spirit which finally led to their separation. As was truly said by the writer quoted above, "the English Colonists always dreamed of independence; the French never." The Medals described in this Chapter abundantly confirm this view.

TREASURE CAPTURED AT LIMA.

381.   1745.   *Obv.* IULII · X · | MDCCXLV · in exergue.   (July 10, 1745.)   Three ships of war in action in the foreground, with letters L.E, PF and MA (the Lewis Erasmus, the Prince Frederick, the Marquis D'Antin) above their topmasts ; a row-boat in front ; in the distance, a chase between two ships, with letters ND and D (the Notre Dame, the Duke) above their topmasts.   On the lower edge, I. KIRK . F.[*]

Rev. No legend.   In exergue, VENIEBUNT (*sic*) LOND? | OCT. I . ET . II . | MDCCXLV . (They came to London October 1 and 2, 1745).   I KIRK F on the lower edge.   Two infant Fames, bearing the one on the left a trumpet, the other a laurel branch, hold two medallions, side by side, with busts facing one another of IAC. TALBOT and IOHA. MORECOCK ; below a treasure wagon disappearing at left, marked 44, followed by another, with high cover, and marked 45, drawn by six horses in line.

Silver and copper.   Size 24, nearly.   Med. Ill., Geo. II, 246. Rare.

---

[*] This Medal commemorates the capture off the coast of South America after a stubborn-action, by Captain James Talbot, in the "Prince Frederick," and Captain John Morecock, in the "Duke," of the three Spanish ships named, and about $4,000,000 in specie.   The English vessels were privateers.   John Kirk was a pupil of James Anthony Dassier, and received many premiums for his works.   He died in London, Nov. 27, 1776. — EDS.

ANSON'S VOYAGE AROUND THE WORLD.

382. 1747. *Obv.* GEORGE LORD ANSON . Below the head
VICT . MAY III MDCCXLVII. Under decollation т . ᴘɪɴɢᴏ . ꜰ. Head
of Anson to left, undraped, crowned with a laurel wreath by
Victory who holds a palm branch in her left hand, and stands
on the prow of a galley.*

Rev. CIRCVMNA VIGATION within a circular border of dots ;
at the bottom, curving to conform to the lower edge, MDCCXI.
MDCCXLIV. Surrounding the circle are six laurel wreaths inclosing the names KEPPEL, SAVMAREZ, SAVNDERS, BRETT, DEN-
NIS, CAMPBEL. On the centre a winged Victory, who holds a
wreath in her right and a trophy in her left hand, and stands
upon the back of a sea-monster over a small globe.

Gold, silver and copper. Size 28. Med. Ill., Geo. II, 325.

---

* The obverse of this Medal is an imitation, says Med. Ill., of a copper coin
of Augustus, and commemorates Anson's defeat and capture of the French fleet
off Cape Finisterre, May 3, 1747. The reverse commemorates his celebrated
voyage around the world, in which he was engaged from September, 1740,
until June, 1744. He suffered some disasters, achieved some successes, and
finally captured a Spanish galleon with treasure to the amount of a million and
a half dollars, and was promoted to be Vice-Admiral. The names are those of
the officers of his own ship, the "Centurion." He built a town called Anson-
burg, in the Carolinas, and Anson County, N. C., is named in his honor. Thomas
Pingo, the die-cutter, born in Italy, came to England about 1745, and was appointed Assistant Engraver to the Mint. He died in 1776. — EDS.

ANNAPOLIS TUESDAY CLUB.

383. 1746. *Obv.* CONCORDIA RES PARVÆ CRESCUNT ✱ (By harmony small things increase). Inscription in five lines, THE | TUESDAY CLUB | IN | *Annapolis Maryland* | MAY 14, 1746 on the field. A heart in the centre dividing the words "Annapolis" and "Maryland" which are in script letters; two hands clasped within the heart.

Rev. CAROLUS COLE ARMIGER PRÆSES . ✱ (Charles Cole, Esquire, President). Liberty as a naked boy with pole and liberty cap, seated on the grass at the right, beside an altar inscribed LIBERTAS | ET | NATALE | SOLUM (Liberty and native land).*

Copper. Size 27. Med. Ill., Geo. II, 292. Very rare.

The Tuesday Club was founded between 1740 and 1745, and existed until about 1780. An account of the Club is to be found in *Scribner's Monthly* for January, 1879.

COMPAGNIE DES INDES OCCIDENTALES.

384. 1748. *Obv.* PROTEGIT ET PASCIT In exergue, 1748. D. V. (for Du Vivier). (He protects and feeds). Two Indians with clubs supporting a shield, crowned and bearing the device of a palm tree on a field of gold, being the arms of the Compagnie des Indes Occidentales.†

Rev. DE LA MAIRIE DE Mᴿ BELLABRE PRᵀ ET SENᴸ DU PRᵗ DE NANTES ✦ A shield crowned and bearing the device of a ship, and twelve lilies in chief (? arms of the city of Nantes); the whole surrounded by a rope tied in lovers' knots.

Silver and copper. Size 18. Rare.

---

* Med. Ill., which gives a cut of this medal, says the dies were by John Kirk, but his name does not appear in their engraving. — EDS.

† This Company was the sole remnant of the schemes of John Law. Several of its earlier Medals have been already described. See note on 112 and 168. The arms as described in the text we are informed were assumed when the Company was reorganized. They gave place to another device in 1785. Jean Du Vivier, the engraver, was born at Liege in 1687, and died in Paris in 1761. The reverse legend shows that this was struck during the Mayoralty of Mons. Bellabre, a prominent civic official of the city of Nantes, the abbreviations showing his position, but they are capable of several interpretations. — EDS.

THE FRANCO-AMERICAN JETONS.

385. 1751. *Obv.* LUD. XV. REX on the left and CHRISTIAN-
ISS on the right. D. V. (for Du Vivier) under truncation.
(Louis XV, Most Christian King). Laureated bust of the
King in armor to the right; eleven laurel leaves in wreath.[*]

Rev. SUB OMNI SIDERE CRESCUNT. In exergue, COL. FR. DE
| L'AM. 1751. (They increase beneath every constellation —
French Colonies in America. 1751). An Indian with bow
and quiver, walking to left, while he looks back toward a group
of lilies; an alligator shows its head from the river near his
feet, a palm tree in the distance.

Silver and copper. Size 18. A. J. N., XIII, 67, XIX, p. 6.
McL. V.

386. 1752. *Obv.* LUD. XV. REX CHRISTIANISS. Under the
head B. DUVIV. Head of Louis, with long hair tied with ribbon and bow.

Rev. UTRIQUE FACIT COMMERCIA MUNDI. In exergue, COL.
FRANC. DE L'AM. 1752. (He creates commerce for both worlds,

---

[*] Leroux shows five different obverse dies, all with figure of Louis XV, one
without engraved name, three with D V for Du Vivier, and one with DUVIVIER in
full (Le Roux, 255 *et seq.*); the plate in Vol. XIX, Am. Jour. Numis., has another
still, with the name of " Roettier " under the truncation. Some of the obverses
have a head or naked bust with flowing hair, some have a laureated bust, and
others, one draped, or armored. Mr. Betts's MS. shows he at first contemplated
mentioning all these varieties, but he did not complete his notes, and the Editors
have made no attempt to distinguish them, for the officials of the Mint in filling
orders for the numerous restrikes of these pieces, apparently used whichever
happened to be most convenient, thus frequently making slight variations in
the size. The plate in the Journal (XIX, frontispiece) also illustrates the
reverses of 8 of these Jetons.— EDS.

French Colonies in America). Mercury with caduceus in his right hand, is flying to left over the sea. Buildings in the distance on the shore at the right under the letters C N. R. for C. N(orbert?) Roettier.*

Silver and copper. Size 18. A. J. N., XIII, 66; XIX, 6. McL. VI.

387. *Obv.* As 384, but the date in exergue is 1752.
Rev. As 386.
Silver (?). Size 18. Leroux 260.†

388. 1753. *Obv.* LUD. XV. REX CHRISTIANISS. under truncation. *J. C. R.*‡ (Jean Charles Roettier) in a cipher; diademed head of Louis to the right.

Rev. SATIS UNUS UTRIQUE. In exergue, COL. FRANC. DE | L'AM. 1753. (One enough for both). Legend separated by a line. The sun shining on two hemispheres, inscribed with initials of their names, North America being marked PA | AM . S (Pars Americæ Septentrionalis), and South America AM . M (America Meridionalis). The Equator has M. D. SUD. on the Western and M D on the Eastern hemisphere; T · ANTA · in a semi-circular line about the South pole (? for *Terra Antarctica*, the Antarctic land), and other letters in the same position on the Eastern, which may possibly be the name of Duvivier, but is not legible on the specimen examined.§

Silver and copper. Size 18. A. J. N., XIII, 67; XIX, 6. McL., VII.

---

* He was one of the famous family of the name (which we find spelled with and without a final s), so long employed in the French Mint. Leroux does not mention the obverse in text, but has one with armored and laureated bust, with D. V., and one draped, not laureated, with DUVIVIER. [His 263 and 264.] — EDS.

† Leroux does not mention the initials of the die-cutter.— EDS.

‡ Jean Charles Roettier was the son of Joseph, and engraver at the Paris Mint from 1727 to his death in 1770. — EDS.

§ This reverse is found with two obverse dies with naked bust not laureated, by F. M (Francois Marteau), one with armored and laureated bust, signed D. V., and one with draped bust not laureated, signed DUVIVIER in full. Leroux does not mention the obverse given in the text. See his 267 *et seq.* —EDS.

389. LUD. XV. REX CHRISTIANISS.   Under truncation, F M. Laureated bust of Louis in armor to the right.*

Rev. NON INFERIORA METALLIS.   In exergue, COL. FRANC. DE | L'AM. 1754. (*i. e.* [The products of the Colonies are] not inferior to the metals).   Three beavers at work on the left of a stream ; on the right Indian corn growing : underneath, the letters C. N. R.†

Silver and copper.   Size 18.   A. J. N., XIII, 67; XIX, 5. McL., VIII, IX.

390. 1758. *Obv.* LUD. XV. REX CHRISTIANISS.   Under decollation *f* | *m* in script.   Bust of Louis in lion's skin, to the right ; hair tied with a bow.

Rev. NON VILIUS AUREO.   In exergue, COL. FRANC. DE | LAM. 1755. (Not less valuable than the golden : *i. e.*, the peltry of the beavers was not less to be desired than the golden fleece sought by Jason, to which the galley alludes.)   Ancient galley, from the top of which hangs a beaver pelt.‡

Silver and copper.   Size 18.   A. J. N., XIII, 67 ; XIX, 5. McL., X.

391. *Obv.* As reverse of the preceding.

Rev. UT TOTO SERVIET COMMERCIA MUNDO.   (That commerce may be useful to the whole world).   In exergue,§

---

* F. M. for Francois Marteau, who worked at the French Mint from 1720 to about 1760. 389 is also found with several other similar obverses, viz.: Laureated naked bust, B. DUVIV. : laureated armored bust and ribbon, D. V., also one by the same artist, similar, but not laureated, and one with clothed bust and name in full DUVIVIER: laureated naked bust, F. M.: another by same engraver, naked bust not laureated, with slight drapery on edge of neck ; and still another without name. See Leroux 271, *et seq.*—EDS.

† See note on 386. — EDS.

‡ This reverse is also muled with an armored not laureated bust of the King by DUVIVIER: a laureated and armored bust, signed D. V.: with one by F. M. slightly draped on edge of the neck, and another with more drapery by the same engraver ; with a youthful naked bust by the same, and with one without engraver's name. See Leroux 278, *et seq.* — EDS.

§ Though this bears the date of 1741, it is probably a mule struck at a later date. — EDS.

MARINE | 1741.   Mercury standing on the waves with a caduceus in his left hand, and a trident in his right.

Silver and copper.   Size 17.   Leroux 281.

392.   1755.   *Obv.* SALVS IN FLVCTIBVS.   (Safety at sea). In exergue, STATVS RERVM | P PW.*   (The condition of affairs at the close of the year 1755.   The conclusion of the exergue being on the reverse).   Mercury stands facing, upon the shore, and listening, his right hand at his ear; behind him two frigates bearing upon their ensigns respectively the harp of Ireland and the lilies of France.

Rev. SED MOTOS PRAESTAT COMPONERE FLVCTVS.   (But he has power to soothe the troubled waves).†   In exergue, SVB EXITVM ANNI | MDCCLV.   An Indian warrior stands at the left, with crown and girdle of feathers, and bearing in his left hand a bow and in his right an arrow, his right foot upon an alligator; at the right a female is seated upon a sea-horse, beside the ocean, bearing in her right hand a Temple of Fame and in her left a sceptre; at her feet a cornucopia.

Silver.   Size 22.   Rare.   In the collection of D. Parish, Jr., New York.

See a full notice in A. J. N., XXIV, 7, by Mr. Geo. M. Parsons, who considers the female figure to typify Britannia, and the Indian and alligator to allude to the American Colonies of France.   "There was safety at sea," which was ruled by Britain, but the Indian (France) "was ready to adjust the arrow to the bow."   He considers the Medal "an invocation for peace, in the threatening state of affairs between the two nations."

---

* P. P. W. may be for Peter Paul Werner, a medallist of Nuremberg, 1689–1771.   Very likely struck in Germany. — EDS.

† The quotation is from Æneid I, 135. — EDS.

393.   1756.   *Obv.* LUD. XV. REX CHRISTIANISS.   Under the decollation, *m* (for Marteau.)   Laureated naked head to right.

Rev. SEDEM NON ANIMUM MUTANT.   (They change their home but not their hearts).*   In exergue, COL. FRANC. DE | L.'AM. 1756.   Two bee-hives, with the ocean between them, and a swarm of bees flying from one to the other.

Silver and copper.   Size 19.   A. J. N., XIII, 68; XIX, 25. McL., XII.

394.   1757.   *Obv.* LUD. XV. REX CHRISTIANISS.   Under decollation, R. FIL.   Bust of the King to the right, laureate and draped.

Rev. PARAT ULTIMA TERRA TRIUMPHOS.   In exergue, COL. FRANC. | DE L'AMERIQUE | 1757. (The remotest land prepares triumphs).   Mars with uplifted spear and the shield of France, and Neptune with trident in his hands, floating on a shell, both to left.†

Silver and copper.   Size 18.   A. J. N., XIII, 68; XIX, 26. McL., XIII.

---

* The legend is adapted from Horace, Epis., I, XI, 27.   The remainder of the verse, "*qui trans mare currunt*," (who cross the sea), shows the aptness of the legend.   The reverse is also found with obverse a clothed bust of the King not laureated, and hand across the left shoulder, not signed, and also with a laureated bust, edge draped, by F. M(arteau), on a slightly smaller planchet. Another has a naked and laureated bust, with *R. Filius* (Joseph Charles Roettier), beneath.   See Leroux, 285 *et seq.*, who makes the initial M refer to Mauger, which we believe to be an error, as Jean Mauger died in 1722.   See Med. Ill., II, 732. — EDS.

† This reverse is also muled with at least one other obverse having clothed bust of the King, not signed.   Leroux 286. — EDS.

395. 1758. *Obv.* LUD. XV. REX CHRISTIANISS. Under the decollation, R. DUVIV. Laureated naked bust of the King to right, with hair tied with ribbon.*

Rev. EADEM TRANS AEQUORA VIRTUS. (The same valor beyond the seas). In exergue, COL. FRANC. DE | L'AM. 1758. A sea having a rocky shore on the left, with buildings in the distance. A flock of eagles flying towards the former.

Silver and copper. Size 18. A. J. N., XIII, 68; XIX, 26. McL., XIV.

BRITISH INDIAN MEDALS.

396. 1753. *Obv.* GEORGIVS . II . D : G : MAG : BRI : FRA : ET . II : REX . F . D . (George II, by the grace of God King of Great Britain, France and Ireland, Defender of the Faith). Bust of the King, laureate, facing the left, without drapery.

Rev. The Royal Arms within the Garter and with supporters, helmet, crown and crest; upon the Garter, DIEU . ET . MON . DROIT . (God and my right).

Silver, cast and chased, with loop and ring. Size 30. A. J. N., VI, 98. Med. Ill. Geo. II, 42.

Sir Danvers Osborne, Governor of New York in 1753, brought from England thirty silver medals for presents to the Six Nations, with loop and ring, and broad scarlet watered ribbon, etc. See Hist. Mag. for Sept. 1865, p. 285.

397. 1757. *Obv.* THE RED MEN COME TO ELTONS DAILY. A trader buying skins of an Indian.

Rev. SKINS BOUGHT AT ELTONS 1757. A deer (?) lying under trees.

Copper. Size 22. A. J. N., VII, 90. Appleton collection.

---

* This has also an obverse with armored bust and ribbon, signed D. V., and another with his name in full, (see Leroux 288 and 289), and also a laureated naked bust, signed R. FILIUS. — EDS.

COLLEGE AT LIMA, PERU.

398.   1754   *Obv.* + ACADEM (ADE in monogram) ᐧ S ᐧ M ᐧ URB ᐧ REG ᐧ IN ᐧ PERU. +   (The Academy of Saint Mark in the Royal City [Lima] of Peru). Shield surmounted by a cherub's head, and having the device of a six-pointed star above s. M. (for San Marcos) and a crown below.   (The arms of the Institution).

Rev. A | 1754.
Silver.   Size 19.

399.   1754.   *Obv.* Same as the preceding.
Rev. R | 1754.
Silver.   Size 19.   F. 8907, which says they were "Premiums" or Prize Medals.   The meaning of the letters on the reverses has not been ascertained.   B. N.

KITTANNING DESTROYED.

400.   1756.   *Obv.* THE GIFT OF THE CORPORATION OF THE CITY OF PHILADELPHIA.   A shield blazoned quarterly: 1, azure, on a fess argent two dexter hands conjoined proper: 2, vert, a garb or; 3, argent, a pair of scales in equipoise, proper; 4, azure, a ship sailing to sinister proper.   These are believed to be the arms formerly used by the City of Philadelphia; the present arms are quite different.

Rev. KITTANNING DESTROYED BY COL⁰ ARMSTRONG. In exergue, SEPTEMBER . 8 . | 1756. Log cabin village in flames ; to the right a river ; in the fore-ground an officer accompanied by two men points to a soldier firing under cover of a tree ; an Indian falling on the bank of the river at the right.*

Silver, bronze and pewter. Size 28. A. J. N., VI, 17. Tancred, Historical Record of Medals, p. 45.

AMERICAN INDIAN MEDALS.

401. 1757. *Obv.* GEORGIVS · II · (pierced) DEI · GRATIA · (George II, by the Grace of God). Draped and laureated bust of the King in armor to left.

Rev. LET US LOOK TO THE MOST HIGH WHO BLESSED OUR FATHERS WITH PEACE (pierced). In exergue, 1757. A man seated beneath a tree at the right offering a pipe of peace to an Indian before him, also seated on the ground ; between them a Council fire ; the sun above at the left.

Silver, copper and pewter. Size 28. A. J. N., XII, 48. Tancred, p. 46.

This is thought to be the first Indian Medal executed in America, and is said to have been presented by the " Friendly

* Kittanning was an Indian village on the Alleghany River forty-five miles from Pittsburgh, Penn., which was destroyed in the " French and Indian War " by Colonel Armstrong, of Carlisle, Penn. Each of the commissioned officers in the engagement received one of these Medals in silver. The dies were made by Edward Duffield, a watchmaker at Philadelphia, and are now in the United States Mint. Restrikes have been made in bronze. — EDS.

Association for Regaining and Preserving Peace with the Indians by Pacific Means." *

NEW JERSEY WAR MEDAL.

402. 1758. *Obv.* Figure of an Indian prostrate at feet of Van Tile and Titfort.

Silver. Size about 25. A. J. N., X, 16. No specimen known.

The "Boston News Letter" for Sept. 28, 1756, quotes Section XXI of an Act passed Aug. 12, 1756, by the General Assembly of the Province of New Jersey, in which it was ordered that "one John Van Tile a Serjeant in the pay of" that "Colony, with a party of nine more under his command," and "a Lad aged about 17 years, sirnamed Titfort," having distinguished themselves "against the common Enemy upon the Frontiers of this Colony, the said Van Tile and Titfort" should each be presented with a silver Medal "of the size of a Dollar, whereon shall be inscribed the Bust or Figure of an Indian prostrate at the feet of the said Van Tile and Lad aforesaid, ... Which Medals the said Van Tile and Lad aforesaid shall or may wear in view, at all such publick Occasions which they may happen to attend, ... to Kindle a martial Fire in the Breast of the Spectators, etc." The reverse design is not mentioned. It was probably plain for engraving.

LOUISBURG CAPTURED.

403. 1758. *Obv.* ADM⁺ BOSCAWEN · TOOK · CAPE · BRETON Bust of the Admiral in armor facing to right ; his hair long ; mantle and ribbon across his breast.

---

* The dies for this Medal also were engraved by Duffield, at Philadelphia, who cut the dies of the preceding number. The striking was done by Joseph Richardson, a member of the Society. See "Memoirs of the Life of Anthony Benezet," by Robert Vaux, p. 79. This has been restruck several times, and the latest impressions show very bad breaks in the dies. — EDS.

Rev. LOUISBOURG   In exergue, IUL 26 1758 | ☽•☾   In the foreground, the ocean with five ships, and beyond, a very curious view of the attack on the city, with a cannon-ball just striking a high tower on a hill.*

Brass and pewter.   Size 25.   A. J. N., IX., 2.   Med. Ill., Geo. II, 411.

404.   1758.   *Obv.* Same as the preceding.
Rev. As the preceding, "and scarcely to be distinguished from it, except that there is no shell proceeding from the mortar."
Brass.   Size 25.   Med. Ill., Geo. II, 412.

405.   1758.   *Obv.* Legend as 403.   The Admiral in naval uniform at half-length, facing the right, and holding a baton in his right hand ; a sash crosses his breast from left shoulder.
Rev. Legend as 403.   Design similar, but reversed, and there are seven vessels, and no cannon-ball.
Copper.   Size 23.   A. J. N., IX, 2.

406.   1758.   *Obv.* Legend as 403, same design as 405.
Rev. LOUISBURG HARBOUR   In exergue, IUL. 26 1758.   A scene somewhat similar to the last, three hills in the town, but with only five vessels.
Copper.   Size 23.   A. J. N., IX, 3.   Med. Ill., Geo. II, 408 (which has a cut).

---

* This attack on Louisburg was the second.   A previous capture of the city when Sir William Pepperrell was in command of the Colonial forces, and was made a baronet for his services, does not appear to have been commemorated by a Medal.   Admiral Edward Boscawen, who was the second son of the first Viscount Falmouth, born 1711, died Jan. 10, 1761, commanded the fleet, and General Amherst the army.   No reason has been discovered, say the Editors of Med. Ill., why the former alone should be commemorated, and no allusion made to Amherst who commanded the army with great skill and success.   These Medals are "rare because of very inferior workmanship, and hence not thought worth preserving."   The hill shown on this and the following pieces, existed only in the die-cutter's fancy. — EDS.

407.   1758.   *Obv.* TO BRAVE ADM! BOSCAWEN.   Bust of the Admiral in armor facing the right, similar to 403.

Rev. I SURRENDER PRISONER.   In exergue, 1758.   At the left an officer (the Chevalier de Drucour, who commanded), kneeling and surrendering his sword to another officer stand-ing at the right, and waving a sword in his right hand.

Brass, copper and pewter.   Rare.   Size 16½.   A. J. N., IX, 3.   Med. Ill., Geo. II, 413.

408.   1758.   *Obv.* Legend and design as 405.

Rev. LOUISBOURG.   In exergue, IUL . 26 . 1758.   View of the harbor of Louisburg, with ships and castle on the left.

Brass.   Size 23.   Med. Ill., Geo. II, 409.

409.   1758.   *Obv.* Similar to 405, but a smaller die.

Rev. Similar to 408, "with slight differences."

Brass.   Size 15.   Med. Ill., Geo. II, 410.

410.   1758.   *Obv.* PARITER · IN · BELLA on a scroll over a globe (Equally brave in war, — alluding to army and navy as shown below).   Near the edge of the Medal, at the bottom on the left, T. PINGO. F.   A prostrate naked female figure on a rock in the foreground, pointing to an inverted fleur-de-lis. Resting on the female is a globe, inscribed, in their proper places, CANADA, AMERICA ; on the left is a British grenadier with a musket and bayonet, and on the right a sailor with his hat raised ; behind the globe is the Union Jack, and above,

Fame flying to left and blowing a trumpet ; in her left hand is a laurel wreath ; in the distance are boats and a high rock.

Rev. LOVISBOVRG ' TAKEN ' MDCCLVIII   View of the attack on the city, from the inside of a battery with soldiers, who are shelling the fortified town on the right ; a bomb just fired is seen in the air, leaving a long track.   At the left a lighthouse ; on the ocean in front of the battery are eight war vessels and a number of small boats ; one of the former is in flames [representing the cutting out of the Prudent and Bienfaisant]. ·

Gold, rare. Silver and copper.* Size 28. A. J. N., IX, 2. Med. Ill. Geo. II, 404.

411. 1758. *Obv.* O . FAIR . BRITANNIA . HAIL. Under truncation I. KIRK. F. Undraped and filleted head of Britannia to the left with a Phrygian cap before her, and a trident behind.

Rev. LOVISBOVRG . TAKEN . MDCCLVIII   Below, I ' KIRK ' F . A winged Victory marching to the right holding on her left shoulder a pole supporting a shield with a *fleur-de-lis,* an ancient cuirass, and a palm branch ; in her right hand she holds a large fish, with several small fish about its mouth.

Silver and copper. Size 26. A. J. N., IX, 2. Med. Ill., Geo. II, 407.

412. 1758. *Obv.* Same as preceding.

Rev. Legend the same as last, and design similar, except that Victory holds a cornucopia instead of a fish. (Probably the earliest die).

Copper. Size 28. Rare. See Med. Ill., Geo. II, 407.

---

* The specimen in silver in the British Museum has an engraved inscription on the edge. Mr. Parsons, commenting on this piece, remarks : " It is difficult to understand why a Medal so carefully designed and executed should represent the defeat of France by the figure of a female lying under an immense globe. A possible explanation is found by reference to the Jeton of 1753 (our 388) ; the globe on this Medal which shows . . . the Western Hemisphere, is one of the two for which the one sun of France sufficed." The motto on 388 thus becomes doubly sarcastic, — satis utrique, — sufficient for each, *i. e.,* to crush France, and to accomplish British designs. — EDS.

413. 1758. *Obv.* Similar to the last, but without the cap; a trident projecting from her neck behind; if prolonged, it would cut the H in HAIL. No name of engraver.

Rev. LOVISBOVRG TAKEN . MDCCLVIII. Victory walking to right, on the prow of an ancient war vessel; over her left shoulder she holds a palm branch and in her right hand a laurel wreath.

Copper. Size 27. Med. Ill., Geo. II, 405.*

414. 1758. *Obv.* Similar to last, except that the trident if prolonged would not touch the letter H of the legend.

Rev. Similar to last, except that the wreath nearly touches the letter M.

Lead. Size 28. Only two known, of which one is in the British Museum, and another was in the Dimsdale collection. Med. Ill., Geo. II, 406.

OSWEGO CAPTURED.

415. 1758. *Obv.* LUDOVICUS XV ORBIS IMPERATOR (Louis XV, Emperor of the world.) Under the head, 1758. Laureated head of the King to right without drapery; hair tied with ribbon.

---

* Med. Ill. says the dies were cut by Thomas Pingo, and that the wreath extends between the legend and the date. The legend on the obverse is from Dr. Akenside's "Ode on Leaving Holland." The designer of these Medals was Giovanni Battista Cipriani, who often followed types of Roman coins, but whose legends are always in English. He was born at Pistoja in 1732, came to England in 1755, and was one of the Founders of the Royal Academy. He died Dec. 14, 1785. — EDS.

Rev. WESEL, OSWEGO, PORTMAHON In exergue, EXPUG. S$^{T!}$ DAVIDIS | ARCE ET SOLO | ÆQUATA. (The fort of St. David's taken by storm, and levelled to the ground). Four forts flying the French flag ; reeded edge.*

Silver. Size 20. Rare. A. J. N., XIX, 28.

BRITISH-AMERICAN VICTORIES.

416. 1758. *Obv.* GEORGIUS · II · REX · (George II, King.) Laureated bust of the King to left, in armor, and wearing the ribbon and star of the Garter.

Rev. FŒDUS – INVICTUM · (The unconquered alliance) on a label. Below the group, MDCCLVIII · Legend in two concentric circles, the outer being names of places, the inner the names of commanders,† as follows : —

---

* Wesel, an important post in the Prussian Provinces, on the Rhine ; Port Mahon, the capital of Minorca, off the northern coast of Africa ; St. Davids, on the Coromandel coast, on the Bay of Bengal, Asia ; and Oswego, in America— places in "the four quarters of the globe," captured by Louis XV, led him to claim on this Medal the boastful title it bears.— EDS.

† Probably intended as a counterfoil to the preceding ; while it does not give a victory in Asia, it names two in Africa, Senegal and Goree ; two in Europe, St. Malo and Cherbourg ; and three in America : two years later a Medal hereafter described (427) mentions the four Continents, but no places. The names under the places here given are those of the British commanders,—Captain Marsh of the Navy and Major Mason of the Army, at Senegal ; the Duke of Marlboro' at St. Malo ; Boscawen and Amherst at Louisburg ; Commodore Howe at Cherbourg. Fort Frontenac on Lake Ontario, was a strong post destroyed by Col. Bradstreet ; Fort Duquesne, the seat of Braddock's defeat, where Washington first distinguished himself, was where Pittsburgh, Pa., now stands. Goree was taken by Admiral Keppel.— EDS.

SENEGAL . MAI . 2 .   S. MALO^s IUN . 16.   CHERBOURG . AU. 16.   LOUISBOURG . IUI. . 27
MARSH. MASON.   MARLBRO (*sic*).   HOW (*sic*).   BOSCAWEN-AMHERST.
FRONTI^c AUG. 27.   DUQUESNE . NOV . 24.   GORRE . DEC . 29. *
BRADSTREET.   FORBES.   KEPPEL.

Britannia seated in a chariot drawn by a lion, supported by the figure of Justice to the left and of Liberty to the right, drives over ground strewn with the fleurs-de-lis of France.

Silver, brass and copper.   Size 28.   A. J. N., IX, 3 ; XIX, 27.   Med. Ill., Geo. II, 416.

GUADALOUPE.

417.   1759.   *Obv.* GVADALVPE · SVRRENDERS   In exergue, MAY · I · MDCCLIX   Britannia stands leaning upon her spear, and facing to the left ; on her right side a shield with the British crosses ; with her right hand she raises a kneeling figure, who holds a cluster of sugar canes.

Rev. MOORE on the left, BARRINGTON on the right, in perpendicular lines, reading upward.   In exergue, SOC · PROM · ARTS | AND · COMMERCE   Pallas helmeted, facing to left, with a trident in her right and an antique standard in her left hand ; her right foot upon the prow of a galley.*

Silver and copper.   Size 25.   Med. Ill., Geo. II, 427.

---

* The dies of this Medal were cut by Pingo from designs furnished by Stuart, under the direction of Mr. Thomas Hollis, who had charge of the issue of a large number of Medals of this period.   The Society named, which was established at London in 1754, offered prizes for the best designs of Medals commemorating British victories, etc., and struck numerous pieces, one of its earliest being intended "as an honorable encouragement to young gentlemen and ladies of fortune and distinction."— EDS.

QUEBEC, NIAGARA, ETC.

418. 1759. *Obv.* Same die as 416.

Rev. Legend in three circles, the outer giving the names of six places; the next, of commanders, and the inner the date of the victories; over the arms is the seventh of the groups below : —

GUADALOUPE	NIAGARA	QUEBEC	CROWN POINT
BARINGT? MOORE	IOHNSON	WOLFE	AMHERST.
MAY . I	JULY . 25	MONCK? TOWNS?	AUG . 4
		SEP. 13 & 18	
LAGOS	MINDEN	HAWKE	
BOSCAWEN	FERDINAND	QUIBERON.	
AUG . 19	AUG. I	NOV . 20.	

A shield bearing a fleur-de-lis reversed, surrounded by a garter inscribed PERFIDIA EVERSA.   (Treachery overthrown.) Supporters: a crowned lion to left for England, and a horse to right for Hanover; on a ribbon below, W. PITT AUSP. GEO. II PR. MI. (William Pitt, Prime Minister, under the auspices of George II); under the arms, MDCCIX.

Silver, brass and copper.* Size 28. A. J. N., VIII, 45 ; IX, 3 ; XIX, 28.   Med. Ill., Geo. II, 444.

---

* Of the victories commemorated on this Medal four belong to America : Guadaloupe has been mentioned above; Niagara was taken by General Johnson after a most vigorous assault, in which Provincials and Indians participated; Crown Point was abandoned by the French, on the approach of the English under General Amherst; Wolfe's capture of Quebec, when he "fell in the arms of Victory," is commemorated on others described below. The horse may be intended for a unicorn. — EDS.

419. 1758, 1759. *Obv.* Same die as the reverse of 416.
Rev. Same die as the reverse of 418.
Silver, copper and brass. Size 28. A. J. N., IX, 3. Med.
Ill., Geo. II, 445.

420. 1759. *Obv.* As 416, but on a smaller planchet.
Rev. QUEBEC | WOLFE | SAUNDERS | SEPT. 13 & 18; the
remainder of the legend the same as 418. Struck from the
same die as the last, but altered by cutting out the words
under QUEBEC and substituting SAUNDERS for MONK! TOWNS?
and used on a smaller planchet.*
Brass. Size 27. Rare.

421. 1759. *Obv.* BRITANNIA. SAVNDERS to left, WOLFE to
right in the field. Head of Britannia to the left, her hair
bound with a fillet; underneath is a laurel wreath, over an
antique standard at right and trident at left, crossed.
Rev. QVEBEC. TAKEN. MDCCLIX. In exergue, SOC. P. A. C.
(Society for promoting Arts and Commerce.) Victory on tip-
toe with a palm branch in her left hand to the left crowns with
laurel a military trophy, in which appears the shield of France.
Bound to the foot of the stump on which the trophy is suspended is a captive; behind the stump is the prow of a galley.
Silver and copper. Size 25. Rare. A. J. N., IX, 3. Med.
Ill., Geo. II, 439.

DEATH OF WOLFE.

422. 1759. *Obv.* IACOBUS WOLFE ANGLUS. (James Wolfe,
the Englishman). Below the truncation, GOSSET. M. KIRK. F. Bust
of Wolfe in armor, draped, to the left, with flowing hair tied
in bow.
Rev. IN VICTORIA CÆSVS. In exergue, QVEBECÆ | SEPT. XIII
| MDCCLIX. (Slain in the moment of victory at Quebec, Sept.
13, 1759.) A funeral urn, surmounted by a laurel wreath, on
a high pedestal inscribed PRO | PATRIA. (For fatherland.)

---

* Saunders commanded the Naval forces at the capture of Quebec. — EDS.

Surrounding the monument are flags, cannons, drums, battle-axe, sword, shield, helmet, powder-barrel, and other implements of war.*

Silver, copper and lead (the reverse only in the latter metal, and probably a trial impression). Size 23. Rare. A. J. N., IX, 3. Med. Ill., Geo. II, 440.

BRITISH COMMANDERS.

423. 1759. *Obv.* GEORGIUS · II · REX. (George II, King.) Bust of the King to left, laurcate, in armor, and wearing the ribbon and star of the Garter.

Rev. GLORIA ET HONOR BRITANNICIS PRÆFECTIS in an outer circle and FINIS CORONAT OPUS within. In exergue, MDCCLVIIII (Glory and honor to the British commanders. The end crowns the work, 1759). A lion rampant, for England, devouring and trampling upon the lilies of France.†

Silver. Size 21. Extremely rare. Med. Ill., Geo. II, 442.

424. 1759. *Obv.* As the preceding.
Rev. Similar to the last, but from a different die.
Silver. Size 22. Very rare. Med. Ill., Geo. II, 443.

425. 1759. *Obv.* · · · KING GEORGE · THE · II ·　　FRED · KING · OF · PRUSSIA · At the bottom, 1759. Bust of the two Kings facing each other, laurcate, in armor, and with ribbons across their breasts ; crown above.

Rev. Six medallions with portraits arranged around that of of H. WILM. PITT ; the others are of PRINCE FERDINAND, PRINCE

---

* Kirke, the die-cutter, has been noticed above. Isaac Gosset, who modelled the head on the the obverse, if not the design of both dies of this Medal, was of French Huguenot descent, and born in 1712. He came from Jersey, and died at Kensington, England, Nov. 28, 1799. Gen. Wolfe, born in 1726, was appointed by Pitt to command the British forces in America. He was with Amherst and Boscawen at the siege of Louisburg. His victory at Quebec over Montcalm, and the death of both commanders in that battle, are familiar to every reader. We differ from Med. Ill. as to the rarity of this piece.— EDS.

† While this commemorates all the recent victories in America and elsewhere, it probably refers most directly to Hawke and his associates who vanquished the French fleet off Belle-Isle, in what is called on a preceding Medal the battle of "Quiberon," when De Conflans, the French Admiral, commanded. — EDS.

HENRY, DUKE BRUNSWIG (*sic*), ADM. BOSCAWEN, COL. CLIVE and GEN. L. AMHERST.*

Brass.   Size 29.   Med. Ill., Geo. II, 438.

VICTORIES OF GUADALOUPE, CAPE BRETON, ETC.

426. 1760. *Obv.* GEORGIUS · II · REX · Bust of the King to right, in armor, with ribbon, and hair long and tied : NON · OMNIS · MORIAR · (I shall not wholly die) on a band below ; around are views and the names GADALUPE (*sic*), GOREE, SENE-GAL, CAPE BRETON, QUEBEC, MONTREAL. †

Rev. Plain.

Silver.   Size 38.   Very rare.   Med. Ill., Geo. II, 452.

427. 1760. ' GEORGIUS · II · D · G · MAG ·   BR · FR · ET · HIB · REX ' (George II, by the Grace of God, King of Great Britain, France and Ireland.)   Under truncation, J. DASSIER F. Bust of the King to left, laureate, in armor, draped, and long flowing wig. ‡

Rev. TRIUMPHA   UBIQUE. In exergue, I. D. F.   (? Triumphs everywhere. J. Dassier, fecit).   A winged Victory seated, facing left, upon a cannon on a pedestal supporting a trophy of standards, weapons, etc. ; she is inscribing a shield ASIA | AFRICA | AMERI | EUR | ; behind her is a pyramid dec-orated with laurels and a medallion of GU : PITT DICTATOR : (William Pitt, etc.) with bust to right ; Fame at the left, with trumpet, removes a curtain from the medallion ; the pedestal is inscribed NATUS : 10 NOV : 1683 | COR : 22 OCT : 1727 | OBIIT

---

* William Pitt was "the inspiring genius" of the war. Prince Ferdinand commanded at Minden (see 418); Prince Henry was the brother of the Prus-sian King ; the Duke of Brunswick was the son of the reigning Duke. Clive had distinguished himself in India, and enlarged the British dominion there. Amherst and Boscawen have been noticed above. — EDS.

† This was struck on a very thin plaque of silver, probably intended as an ornament for the top of a box. It was issued about the time of the death of the King. — EDS.

‡ This obverse was cut by Dassier in 1731 as the "Dedicatory Medal " of his series on the English Sovereigns, and struck with another reverse die. The present reverse (which apparently contains an error in the Latin, not noticed in Med. Ill.), was cut after the King's death. — EDS.

25 OCT : 1760. (Born Nov. 10, 1683 ; crowned Oct. 22, 1727 ; died Oct. 25, 1760), and bears a skull encircled by roses and and thistles.

Copper. Size 25. Rare. Med. Ill., Geo. II, 454.

428. 1760. *Obv.* SALUS POPULORVM . B . P . D . M . L . T . G . H . W . A . N . B . H . (The safety of the peoples.) Bust of George II to right within a wreath.*

Rev. AT MONTREAL MDCCLX in the exergue. A figure representing Canada kneeling before Britannia and pointing to burning buildings in the distance.

S., Suppl. 76.

429. 1760. *Obv.* THE CONQVEST OF   CANADA COMPLEATED A laureated male figure (typifying the St. Lawrence) to the right, reclining, with his right arm resting on the prow of a

* The description follows Sandham's somewhat meagre account of the piece (*loc. cit.*), who gives neither metal nor size. He does not attempt to explain the letters in the legend, and we have not been able to decipher them. It has been suggested that they may be the initials of the officers of the British forces, and among them are several that might be so interpreted — Boscawen, Pocock, Monckton, Townsend, Wolfe, Amherst, Bradstreet — but this omits the names of several equally prominent, such as Saunders, Johnson, Forbes, Otway, etc.

We have found no reference to this curious Medal in McLachlan or in any English authority which we have been able to consult, and it is difficult to understand the connection of the device on the reverse — the burning buildings, which were the result of British invasion — with the *safety of the peoples* under the British King, proclaimed on the obverse ; if the burning buildings refer to the Indian raids on British Colonies, Britannia would point to them. If correctly described it is apparently a most incongruous combination of dies. — EDS.

galley; in his left hand he holds a paddle, while a dog-like beaver is climbing up his left knee. In the background is a standard on which is inscribed the name AMHERST within a wreath of laurel, and surmounted by a lion, which divides the legend at OF ; in exergue is the shield of France charged with fleurs-de-lis, surmounting a tomahawk, bow and quiver.

Rev. MONTREAL TAKEN MDCCLX. In exergue, SOC. PROMOTING ARTS | AND COMMERCE. A female figure to the right seated on the ground; behind her is a coniferous tree, and an eagle with expanded wings standing on a rock ; before her is the shield of France,* with club and tomahawk behind it.

Silver. Size 26. A. J. N., IX, 3. McL., CXXVI. Med. Ill., Geo. II, 447.

430. 1760. *Obv.* GEORGE · II · KING Laureated naked head of the King to left in flowing wig.

Rev. CANADA SUBDUED. In exergue, MDCCLX | S · P · A · C (Society for Promoting Arts and Commerce). A female figure, weeping, to the right, seated on the ground beside a pine tree ; behind on the left is a beaver climbing up a bank.†

Silver and bronze. Borders dotted. Edge plain, (one inscribed WILLIAM PITT ADMINISTRING.) Size 24. Rare. A. J. N., IX, 45. Med. Ill., Geo. II, 448. McL., CXXVII. .

---

* The shield has the Bourbon lilies and another charge, perhaps a dolphin. — EDS.

† The dies of this Medal were by Pingo, and the design, evidently suggested by the Roman coins of "Judaea Capta," very likely by Cipriani.— EDS.

INDIAN MEDALS, MONTREAL.

431.   1760.   *Obv.* MONTREAL.   In exergue, D C F, the maker's initials, in depressed oval.   View of a fortified town with five steeples and five bastions and with a river flowing

in front; on the right is a fort from which flies a flag with St. George's cross.

Rev. *Tekahon waghse* at the top; ONONDAGOS across the field, and below, in three lines, *Taken from an Indian | Cheif (sic) in the AMERICAN | WAR,* 1761.

Silver.   Size 29.   The obverse cast and chased; reverse engraved.   A. J. N., XVIII, 85.*   Bushnell.

432.   1760.   *Obv.* Same as last.

Rev. MADOGHK   MOHICKANS.

Silver; obverse cast and chased; reverse engraved.   Size 29. Rare.

---

* A very full account of this and the following Medal, and of their history, will be found in the Journal (*loc. cit.*), reprinted from the Proceedings of the American Numismatic and Archaeological Society (New York, 1884), written by Mr. McLachlan.   D. C. F(ecit?) he takes to be the initials of some unknown engraver which appear counterstamped on another Indian Medal of 1764, described in a subsequent chapter, and who was, as he thinks, a New York work-man, from the counterstamp on that piece.   The lines at the bottom were scratched on the Medal at a later date.   "The Indian who received it is nowhere mentioned in history," says McLachlan, but he gives some particulars concerning him, without referring to his authority.— EDS.

433.   1760.   *Obv.* Same as 431.

Rev. Tank alkel at the top ; MOHICKANS on the field*.

Pewter.   Size 32.   The obverse cast and chased ; reverse engraved ; with ring for suspension.   A. J. N., XVIII, 85. S., Suppl., 75, with plate.   Rare.

The three preceding are British war medals presented to members of the tribes who assisted at the capture of Montreal, 1760.

FRENCH PRIVATEERS REPULSED.

434.   1760.   *Obv.* A brigantine under full sail bearing seven guns, sailing to the left, and displaying the banner of England.

Rev. This Medall | Given by the Underwriters | to the Bearer Captain James | Weir of the Mars for his | Brave defence against | Two French privateers | April & July | 1760.

Gold, oval.   Size 25 x 30, with loop for suspension.   Engraved.   A. J. N., XIV, 24.   Its history is unknown.

BRITISH INDIAN MEDALS.

435.   1762 (?).   *Obv.* GEORGIUS III DEI GRATIA.   Youthful bust to right in armor and wearing the ribbon of the Garter ; seven rivets on the front of the breast plate ; hair in a double curl over the ear.

Rev. The Royal Arms upon an oval shield in high relief, surrounded by the Garter and surmounted by a crown ; a lion at left and unicorn at right as supporters ; HONI . SOIT . QUI .

---

* The description in the text is taken from Mr. McLachlan's paper, as printed in the Proceedings mentioned in the preceding note.   In his account of this piece in "Canadian Numismatics," CXXXI, the name of the recipient is given as "Tankilkel," and that of the tribe is twice spelled "Mohigians."   An inspection of Sandham's engraving which Mr. Betts follows, shows that these are errors, although Sandham himself, in his description, has Mohigrans.   Mr. McLachlan was in doubt whether to assign it to the time of the capture of Montreal, 1760, or to its defence in 1777.   Only one specimen is known, which was formerly in the collection of Mr. I. F. Wood, of New York. — EDS.

MAL . Y . PENSE upon the Garter, the paw of the lion touching N in HONI ; upon a ribbon below is the motto DIEU . ET . MON . DROIT ; behind the ribbon a rose and thistle ; the quartering of the arms shows that of England and Scotland in the first, France in the second, Ireland in the third, and Hanover in the fourth quarter. (The legends have been translated above.)

Silver. Size 50. Thickness of edge, 2. Very rare.

McLachlan, No. CCXCII, states that a crack appears across the shoulder on the obverse. A specimen in the author's collection [now in the Yale University Cabinet] shows no crack.

This Medal and the five following are supposed to have been struck for distribution among the Indian chiefs in Canada at the close of the French and Indian war. The specimen in Mr. McLachlan's collection in Montreal, as he states in his " Canadian Numismatics," was obtained from the widow of one of the tribe called " Lake of the Two Mountains," and was given to her husband's grandfather for services rendered during the Conquest of Canada. Our 436, of the same size, is in the British Museum, and is a dotted shell of silver. The third, nearly as large (size 48), our 438, was obtained by Mr. McLachlan (his CCXCIII) from the Caughnawaga Indians, and a second specimen is in the author's collection. The smaller Medal, No. 439, was also obtained from an Indian, but no tradition is preserved from which its date could be learned ; but the Medal No. 440 gives a clue to the time when all these medals were struck, for it has the same reverse as No. 439, and on the obverse it has the busts of the King and Queen, and was struck as a gift to friendly Indians, who sent an address of congratulation upon their marriage. As this marriage took place September 8, 1761, and several months must have elapsed before the delivery of the address, we assign the date 1762 for all those medals bearing the youthful bust. A copy of the address is in the Haldimand papers in the Government archives at Ottawa.

436. 1762. *Obv.* Same die as the preceding.
Rev. Similar to the last, but from a different die.
Silver, shell, with loop for suspension. Size 50. Mus. Brit.

437. 1762. *Obv.* Same legend as 435 and similar design, but from a different die ; seven rivets on the front of the breast-plate ; hair in a single curl over the ear ; a crack in the die extends across the shoulder and half way toward I in GEORGIUS.

Rev. Same die as 435.

Silver.   Size 49.   McL., CCXCII (see comments under 435).

438. 1762.   *Obv.* Same legend as last, and similar design, but with eight rivets upon breast-plate.

Rev. Similar to the last; the paw of the lion touching I in HONI.

Silver; size 50.   Another, silver; size 49.   Another, silver; size 48, with traces of gilding.   Another, lead; size 48.   Rare. N. Y. State Library, Albany.   McL., CCXCIII.

439. 1762.   *Obv.* GEORGIUS III DEI GRATIA.   Bust of the King to right in armor, similar to last; six rivets on front of breast-plate.

Rev. Similar to last, but with the shield in much lower relief; the lion and unicorn thinner and more erect; and the whole design larger in proportion to the size of the piece.

Silver.   Size 24.   S., Suppl., 60.   McL., CCXCIV (who, however, does not mention the differences).

440. 1762.   *Obv.* No legend.   Bust of George III to the right and of Queen Charlotte to the left, facing each other; above their heads a curtain, tied up, the cords and tassels falling midway between the heads.

Rev. Same die as 439.

Silver.   Size 24.   Pierced for suspension.   McL., CCXCV.

VICTORIES IN WEST INDIES AND NEWFOUNDLAND.

441. 1762. *Obv.* GEORGIUS · TERTIVS · REX   Youthful bust of the King to left in armor, draped; wig, hair tied with a bow, and flowing locks below.

Rev. On the field, PAX | AUSPICATA | NOV . 3 (Peace foretold*), within a circle formed by a serpent devouring its tail, and holding scales, and an anchor below; under the circle, MDCCLXII.   Surrounding the circle are four groups, the upper and lower in compartments; in that at the top PR of WALES Bo | AUG · 12   Under this, HERMIONE | MAY 31   In the group at the right, The HAVANNAH | ALBEM⸢ & POCOCK . AUG 14 | NEWFOUNDLAND SEP 18 | AMHERST | ALCANᵗ CASSEL &C &C   At the left, MARTINIĠO | MONCKᴺ & RODNEY FEB. 4. | Sᵗ LUCIA Sᵗ VINCENT | TOBAGO GRANADA &C | MARCH 1·5 &C   In the bottom compartment, GRÆBENSTEIN | FERDᴰ & GRANBY | IUNE 24

Gold, silver, copper and brass.   Size 26.

---

* This Medal commemorates various British victories which were regarded as the harbingers of peace (pax auspicata). That at Havana was gained by Lord Albemarle and Admiral Pocock (see 443); the place had been thought impregnable, and its fall produced a deep impression at Paris.   We have not found any special account of the attack on Newfoundland, but it may have been by Gen. Sir Jeffrey Amherst, who had been in command in Canada.   Martinique was taken Feb. 4, 1762, and Tobago and the Leeward Islands about the same time by the expedition which sailed from New York in November, 1761, under General Monckton and Admiral Lord George Brydges Rodney; the Marquis of Granby was commander-in-chief of the British troops in the Seven Years' War, during which he won the battle of Graebenstein; for Ferdinand, see note on 425. — EDS.

442. 1762. *Obv.* EVROPAE ALMAM NE TARDET PACEM. In exergue, MDCCLXII. (May it not delay the fair peace of Europe). An Indian with bow and quiver supporting a cupid who is placing a figure of Peace on a column which bears the Imperial Eagle of Germany, and on its breast a shield with the fir cone of Augsburg ; at base rest the shields of England and France and an anchor.

Rev. DVRET VSQVE AD EXTREMVM. (May it endure forever). In exergue, BELG. FOED. (The United Netherlands). Mercury seated upon the Belgian lion who supports in right paw a staff with bundle of arrows and cap of liberty ; boxes, cornucopia, etc. ; in background on the right a vessel, and on the left the ocean, ships, etc. On sockel (or line separating the exergue), J. G. HOLTZHEY. FEC.[*]

Silver.   Size 28.   V. L., Sup. 365.

CAPTURE OF THE MORRO CASTLE, HAVANA.

443. 1762. *Obv.* LVDOVICO DE (in monogram) VELASCO ET VINCENTIO GONZALEZ Accolated busts in profile to right, of the two Spanish officers named in the legend. They are dressed in the costume of the time, with coats having straight lapels, ruffled shirts, mantles thrown back, etc. Velasco wears a wig tied with a ribbon behind, and locks flowing on his shoulder ; Gonzalez wears a medal on his breast which bears a small cross. Under the drapery at the right, PRIETO.

Rev. IN · MORRO · VIT · GLOR · FVNCT · (They ended their lives in glory in the Morro Castle.) In exergue, in four lines, ARTIVM ACADEMIA | CAROLO REGE CATHOL. | ANNVENTE CONS · | A MDCCLXIII (The Academy of Arts, Charles the Catholic King consenting, has consecrated this [to their memory] in the year 1763.) View from the harbor of the final assault on

---

[*] John George Holtzhey was the son of Martin Holtzhey, born at Amsterdam in 1729, Master of the Mint in Zealand in 1754, and died in 1808. This Medal appears to have been struck in the Netherlands in the hope of the speedy return of peace. V. L. (*loc. cit.*) seems to imply that it was hoped that the events in America, typified by the Indian, would not delay it. The Seven Years' War was closed by the Treaty of Hubertsburg, Feb. 18, 1763 (see 445), and the Treaty of Paris was signed a few days earlier (see 444). — EDS.

the Morro Castle, Havana, and the explosion of the magazine, which carries into the air the bodies of its defenders; at the left are three large men-of-war; at the right, another in sinking condition; a small boat is leaving it, and a larger one is rowed to the right; the British soldiers are storming a breach in the walls, and bodies of troops are seen in the background at the left, and the city and a small vessel in the distance at the right.

Bronze. Size 31, nearly. A. J. N., IV, 49. Bolzenthal, p. 262. This very rare Medal is described from an impression in the Parish collection.* It commemorates the storm and capture of the Morro Castle at Havana, by a British fleet of 200 vessels and an army of upwards of 14,000 men, under Lord Albemarle and Admiral Sir George Pocock, in August, 1762. The city fell after a stubborn defence, in which the officers named on the Medal lost their lives.

THE PEACE OF PARIS.

444. 1763. *Obv.* LUDOVICUS XV REX CHRISTIANISS. Laureated bust of the King to right, undraped. B . DUVIVIER . F . on edge of decollation.

---

* The very full and interesting account of this Medal in the Journal (*loc. cit.*) by the late Prof. Anthon, shows that this expedition sailed from New York, where the troops engaged had been encamped for some months on Staten Island. It was commanded by the Governor of the Province, General Monckton. The artist was Don Tomas Francisco Prieto, "who was also a painter and engraver, and received from Charles III the supervision of all coins in the entire kingdom, with the order to improve the dies."— EDS.

Rev. PAX   UBIQUE VICTRIX.   In exergue, GALLORUM ET
BRITANNORUM | CONCORDIA | MDCCLXIII.   (Peace everywhere
triumphant.   Harmony [or peace declared] between France
and Great Britain, 1763.)   At the left near the edge, J. C. H (for
Holtzhey.)   Peace standing, holding in her right hand extended an olive branch, and in her left a caduceus.   At her
feet on the left a nude male figure is seated on a battering
ram, with flags and implements of ancient warfare.*

Gold, silver and copper.   Size 26½.

445.   1763.   *Obv.* ADES PAX ET TOTO MITIS IN ORBE and
separated from the preceding words by the dome of the temple,
MANE.   (Be present, Peace, and let thy gentle influence remain throughout the world).   In exergue, MDCCLXIII.   A circular temple surmounted by the double head of Janus over
the Russian arms, crowned with olive ; upon its right side a
flying Genius attaches the arms of Saxony ; within, Neptune
holding a trident extends his hands to Apollo beside an altar ;
approaching the temple on the left is Mars in antique armor,
his foot upon the lower step, which bears the words SVVM
CVIQVE (to each one his own) ; he hands his sword to Minerva
at the left ; an Amazon accompanying her, holds an oar (the
emblem of Holland) in her right, and a standard on which
is IMP. ROM. (the Roman Empire) surmounted by a double-
headed eagle in her left ; the arms of Sweden (three crowns)
hang near the top of a column at the left of the entrance ;
near the Amazon in the left foreground lies the shield of
Austria (gules, a fess argent, for Hapsburgh).   On the sockel,
or line which separates the exergue, I. G. HOLTZHEY. FEC.

Rev. ALMA PACE | INTER | RVSSIAM ET BORVSSIAM | D. 5
MAJI MDCCLXII. | BORVSSIAM ET SVECIAM | D. 22 MAJI MDCCLXII |
ANGL · | FRANC · | HISP · | ET PORTVGAL | D ${}^{10}_{16}$ FEB. MDCCLXIII.
| AVSTR. BORVSS. ET SAXON. | D. 18 FEB. MDCCLXIII. | RECON-
CILIATA.   (Sweet peace concluded between Russia and Prus-

---

* By the Peace of Paris, signed Feb. 10, 1763, between France, Spain, Portugal and England, all the French possessions in America, to the Mississippi were
ceded to England. — EDS.

sia, May 5, 1762 ; Prussia and Sweden, May 22, 1762 ; England, France, Spain and Portugal, Feb. 10–16, 1763 ; Austria, Prussia and Saxony, Feb. 18, 1763).

Silver.   Size 31.   V. L., Sup. 368.*

446.   1763.   *Obv.* NUNCIA PACIS (The messenger of Peace.) In exergue (?), D . 15 . FEBR . MDCCLXIII (The 15th day of February, 1763), and below, ŒXLEIN.   View of the Stadt house ; Peace flying above with trumpets.

Rev. IAM REDIRE AUDIT.   In exergue, GERMANIA PACATA . (Now she dares return.   Germany at peace).   Peace standing, holding a sceptre and a spear of wheat ; a landscape in the background and a man ploughing.

Silver.   Size 28.

447.   1763.   *Obv.* Same legend, and design as the preceding, but with maker's name, LOOS.

Rev. Same legend, and design similar to the preceding, but with a circle of clouds around the head of Peace, and with the signs of Leo and Virgo above her head †

Silver.   Size 14.

---

* This is one of the most elaborate Medals of the series. The arms of Saxony can be distinguished with great difficulty, and the Editors would not have been able to mention them, but for the explanation in V. L. (Sup. p. 408), which further says the arms of Spain are beside Apollo, and those of Portugal beside Neptune.   These were countries involved in the long war, but the arms and some other details mentioned in V. L., but not given in our text, cannot be made out in the engraving.   The explanation there given shows that the figures typify the various powers who united in the Treaties of Peace : Neptune denotes England ; Apollo, France ; Mars, Frederick the Great, King of Prussia ; Minerva, Holland ; the Amazon, Maria Theresa, Empress of Austria ; the other Powers, Spain, Portugal, Sweden and Saxony, are indicated by their arms. — EDS.

† We have seen neither this nor the preceding Medal, nor have we been able to find a description by which to verify the MS. left by Mr. Betts, which does not clearly give the obverse.   The allusion is to the Treaty of Hubertsburg, and relates only indirectly to America. — EDS.

CHAPTER VI.

THE death of Ferdinand the Wise made his brother Charles, who was the second son of Philip V and his second wife, Elizabeth Farnese, the successor to the Spanish crown. He was born January 20, 1716, and had been created Duke of Parma and Placentia in 1731. His father ceded to him the Kingdom of the Two Sicilies, and Charles was crowned at Palermo, July 3, 1735. He married the Princess Maria Amelia, of Poland, on the 9th of May, 1738. His reign in Sicily was peaceful, and devoid of any events of special interest. He became King of Spain, August 10, 1759, and soon after declared his son, Don Fernando, to be his successor in the Sicilian Kingdom. Entering Madrid December 9, 1759, where he had been proclaimed on the 11th of the previous September, as "Charles Third, Catholic King of Spain and the Indies," he at once assumed the government. His proclamation in his various American possessions was made in the following year, except in a few instances, where it was delayed until 1761. All the Medals described in this Chapter therefore belong to the former date, unless otherwise noted.

His judgment as a ruler was sound, and his reign was beneficial to his country. He restricted the power of the Inquisition, and expelled the Jesuits from Spain and all his dominions in 1767, but his people often resisted his reforms, and he is reported to have said: "My subjects are like infants, that cry when one goes to wash them." In 1779 he declared war against England, thus becoming an ally of the struggling Colonies in the Revolution, and was one of the signers of the Declaration of Peace at Versailles, in 1783, which acknowledged the Independence of the United States. He died at Madrid, December 14, 1788.

BAYAMO.

448. 1760. *Obv.* CARL (AR in monogram) . III . D ✦ G . HISP . ET ˙ IND . R.   (Charles III, by the grace of God, King of Spain and the Indies.)   Clothed bust of the King to right, in wig with long flowing locks.

Rev. BAY ✦ ANNO : DNI ✦ 1760 ✦ (Bayamo, in the year of our Lord 1760.) Two keys crossed in saltire, handles at the left.

Silver.   Cast.   Size 14.   H., Charles III, 50.

BEJUCAL.

449. 1760. *Obv.* CAROLVS ˙ III ˙ D ˙ G ˙ HISPAN ˙ REX   Bust of the King to right in armor, draped, and wig with flowing locks.

Rev. Inscription in four lines on the field, BEJVCALI | PER MIC . RODZ . | PROCLAMATVS | MDCCLX.   (Proclaimed at Bejucal by Michael Rodriguez (?), 1760.)*

Silver.   Cast.   Size 21.   H., Charles III, 51.

BUENOS AIRES.

450. 1760. *Obv.* CAROLVS . III . G . HISPAN ET IND . REX. (Translated above).   Draped and armored bust of the King to right, in flowing wig; he wears the Order of the Golden Fleece.   [The D which should be given before G. is omitted.]

Rev. PROCLAMATVS ˙ BON ˙ AER ˙ 1760.   (Proclaimed at Buenos Aires.   1760).   Two ships sailing in opposite directions; an eagle displayed above; an anchor in the waves in the foreground.   [Device of the city.]

Silver.   Cast.   Size 22.   H., Charles III, 52.

---

* The full name of the representative of the King abbreviated on the Medal is not given by Herrera, and the piece was unknown to O'Crowley. — EDS.

CHIHUAHUA.

· 451.   1760.   *Obv.* Legend similar to the preceding.   Bust
of the King.

Rev. PRINCIPIS LAUDIUS IGNE CLES . MIHUAG . EXALT MDCCLX.
Arms of the Cathedral Chapter.   Our description is taken
from the Catalogue of the collection of Don Pedro Alonso
O'Crowley (Madrid, 1794), p. 409.   Herrera knew it only
from that authority (his 53), and does not give any further
description, nor the size or metal.   He, however, states that
with other authorities, he believes the M in MIHUAG should be
CH, for which reason he places the Medal under Chihuahua.*

H., Charles III, 53.

CHILE.

452.   1760.   *Obv.* CAROLUS . III . D . G . HISPAN . ET IND .
REX ✦ 1760 ✦   Bust of the King, laureate, to right, with
epaulet and ribbon ; the Order of the Golden Fleece upon
his breast ; a circle of laurel leaves surrounds the bust, close
to the legend.

Rev. AUGUSTIS . IMPERAT . IUSIURAND . S . P . Q . CHI . ✦   (The
Senate and people of Chile [take] the oath [of fidelity] to the
august rulers,† [the King and Queen]).   A shield surmounted
by a ducal crown, and bearing a lion rampant who holds a
sword surrounded by a border on which are eight cockle-shells.
The columns of Hercules at right and left, with a scroll inscribed PLUS on that at the left, and one with VLTR. on the

---

* We are disposed to go still further and suggest that the Latin, which is
untranslatable as it stands, is incorrectly given, certainly as to the second, third,
and fourth words. It seems more probable, in view of the curious monograms
and careless work of the die-cutters of this city (see note on 339, p. 155, *supra*),
that the legend may read PRINCIPIS LAUD(es) INSIGN(es) ECLES(ia) CHIHUA(hua)
EXALT(at), The Church at Chihuahua exalts the high praises of the Prince ; or
if we read INSIGNE (as on other Medals of this series), ECCLES(iæ) CHIHUAH(unae)
EXALT(ans), Token of the Church at Chihuahua, exalting the praises of the
Prince. Whether our theory is correct, must be left till some more accurate
description of the piece can be obtained. — EDS.

† Or, more probably, " takes the oath to the Emperor with imposing cere-
monies," though the other translation is allowable. — EDS.

other. (More beyond). The dexter or left column is surmounted by a royal crown, and the other by that of an Arch-
duke. Below the shield a flaming heart, its point on a small
platform, divides the word AM – AT. (It loves).
Silver. Size 25. H., Charles III, 54.

CORDOBA.

453. 1760. *Obv.* CAROL . III . ANTQ . ET NOV . HISPA . REX .
(Charles III, King of Old and New Spain.) Draped and
armored bust of the King to right in flowing wig.

Rev. INSIGN FIDELIT ET PVBLIC LAETITIA (*sic*) VILLÆ DE
CORDU (The token of the fidelity and public joy of the City
of Cordoba.) Royal arms (Castile and Leon) quarterly on a
decorated shield surmounted by the royal crown.*
Silver. Size 21. H., Charles III, 55.

FLORIDA.

454. 1760. *Obv.* CARLOS . (AR in monogram) III . D. G
HISPAN . REX. Bust of the King to right in armor, and flowing hair.

Rev. JVAN . ESTEVAN . DEPENA . FLORIDA . 1760 . (Date at
bottom, reversed, in line with the legend.) A full blown rose,
with a single leaf on the right and a bud on the left.†
Silver. Cast. Size 19. H., Charles III, 56. Rare.

GUADALAXARA.

455. 1760. *Obv.* Legend, and bust of the King (not described).

---

* Herrera begins this legend with LAETITIA, but we concur with Mr. Betts,
in thinking the proper order is that given in the text, as PVBLIC clearly quali-
fies the word LAETITIA, which should, correctly, read LAETITIAE.— EDS.

† An impression of this singular piece was once in the Mickley collection,
and later in that of Mr. H. W. Holland, of Boston [See A. J. N., IX, 93]. Dick-
eson has some comments on it in his "American Numismatic Manual." Some
attempts have been made to show that it is not an American piece, but it is
placed among them by Mr. W. S. Appleton and other authorities.— EDS.

Rev. S . P . Q . GUADALAX . IN . NOV . GAL (?) . PROCL . 1760
(The Senate and people of Guadalaxara, New Spain, proclaim
him, 1760.)   Arms of Guadalaxara (see 341).
   O'Crowley, p. 409.   H., Charles III, 57.*

456.   1760.   *Obv.* CAROLVS III . VET . REX . ET NOV . HISP .
IMPERAT . (Charles III, King of Old Spain and Emperor of
New Spain.)   Below the bust, 1760.   Bust of the King to
right in armor and draped ; his wig tied with a bow of ribbon.
   Rev. EPIS . ET CAP : S . CATHED . GVADALAX . ECCLES . (The
Bishop and Chapter of the Cathedral of the Holy Church in
Guadalaxara.)   In exergue, A . B . MADERO | F. (the die-cutter).
On the field at the left an ornate shield surmounted by a
Bishop's hat, a crozier behind, and bearing "the five wounds"
of St. Francis ; on the right a double-headed eagle displayed,
each head crowned and having in its beak a key ; on the
breast of the eagle is a flaming heart with a patriarchal cross ;
the Papal tiara above the eagle.
   Silver.   Size 25.   H., Charles III, 58.

457.   1760.   *Obv.* CAROL . III . D . VOCAT . INDIAR . IMPER
F . P . A . TRIVMPH .   Under the decollation, separated by a
short circular line, CASANOVA . F. (the die-cutter).†   Naked bust
of the King to right, in long flowing locks tied with a ribbon.
   Rev. IVDICES VECTIG COLLIGVND . GVADALAX . EXACTOR
PROCL . A . MDCCL (*sic*).   (The officers charged with collecting
the taxes at Guadalaxara proclaim him who has power to
impose them.   In the year 1760).   The Virgin of Guadaloupe

---

   * Herrera gives no further description, but quotes from O'Crowley (*loc. cit.*).
— EDS.
   † The meaning of the abbreviations can only be conjectured, but perhaps
the legend in full should be Carolum III, Dei Vocatione Indiarum Imperatorem,
Fidelis Provincia Americana Triumphat (or triumphans clamat); *i. e.,* His Faith-
ful American Province exultingly proclaims Charles III, by the call of God
Emperor of the Indies.   F. P. is used on some Medals for FAUSTE PROCLAMAT,
and if that be the intention here, the final abbreviations may signify Fauste Procla-
mant Atque Triumphant; *i. e.,* They happily proclaim and triumph in Charles
III, as Emperor, etc.   "They" being the officers who issued the Medal, see *rev.*
The words JUDICES and EXACTOR on the reverse allude to Isa. LX: 17. — EDS.

upon a mantle tied in two knots above, and falling over two palm branches crossed; the whole surmounted by a royal crown.

Silver.　Size 25.　H., Charles III, 59.

GUANAXUATO.

458.　1761.　*Obv.* CAROL • III • D • VOCAT • INDIAR • IMPER • F • P • A • TRIVMPH.　Draped and armored bust of the King to right, wearing the Order of the Golden Fleece.*

Rev. Inscription, LACTA FIDE UERAM | SUAM ESSE FIRMAT | GUANAXUAT | AN • MDCCLXI • in four lines, below a rock upon which rests a "monstrance" or a chalice supporting the wafer, from which rays proceed.†

Silver.　Size 25.　H., Charles III 60.

----

* For explanation of the legend, see note on the preceding number. — EDS.

† This Medal is as good an example as could be selected to show the uncertainty attending attempts to decipher the abbreviations, whether of letters or words, which mark this particular group, more than those of any other Medals described in this volume. The inscription on the reverse, as it is given by Herrera in his text and in his engraving, has several difficulties. That author gives no explanation, neither does he allude to the possible existence of any error in the Latin; yet, if correct as they stand, the uncertainty as to the words which should be supplied makes the meaning obscure. If LACTA FIDE, as printed, be correct, the expression may be taken to mean "in the nourishing faith," and in connection with VERAM, suggesting the text "sincere milk of the word" (I Peter, ii: 2); but we learn by inquiry from the Rev. L. J. Morris, Pastor of the Church of St. Mary of the Assumption, Brookline, Mass., and from the Clergy of St. John's (R. C.) Ecclesiastical Seminary, at Brighton, Mass., who have most kindly aided us in our attempts to explain the inscription, that they can recall no such use of the term. They incline to the opinion that there may be an error in the die, and that LACTA should read LAETA (joyful); whether FIDE should be taken as an abbreviation of FIDEM (or possibly FIDELITATEM) is also uncertain; and again the allusion in SUAM VERAM is also in doubt, as some qualifying word must be implied, — such perhaps as loyalty; this may be the loyalty of the city, or of the Roman Church, and the latter seems to be indicated both by the device and by the source from which the Medal emanated. The Editors, therefore, give as conjectural translations, reading LACTA as LAETA, either "The Church at [or the City of] Guanaxato rejoicing in the faith [whether of the Catholic King, or the Christian Church generally] declares its true [? loyalty];" or reading FIDE as if for FIDEM, "The City of Guanaxato joyfully declares its true [allegiance to King Charles]." The latter rendering is that

GUATEMALA.

459. 1760. *Obv.* CAROLUS · III · D · G · HISPAN · ET · IND · REX **+** Naked bust of the King to right, rudely executed.

Rev. GUAT . IN . EIUS . PROCLAMATIONE · Date, 1760 at the bottom, in legend, but reversed. A mounted knight, armed with a sword, leaping to the right over two conical mountains; this is the device of Guatemala, and the knight typifies St. James, the Patron Saint of Spain.

Silver. Size 21. H., Charles III, 61.

460. 1760. *Obv.* Same legend and similar bust.
Rev. Same legend and design, but the horse not so erect.
Silver. Size 17. H., Charles III, 62.

461. 1760. *Obv.* Same legend terminating with a period instead of a rosette; similar bust, but draped.
Rev. Same legend and design as 460.
Silver. Size 14. H., Charles III, 63.

462. 1760. *Obv.* Same legend as last, but no period after D and G; naked bust of the King.
Rev. Legend and date as the preceding, but G instead of GUAT. Same design as last, but the horse is disproportionately long.*
Silver. Size 11. H., Charles III, 64.

HAVANA.

463. 1760. *Obv.* CAROLVS . III . D . G . HISPAN . ET IND (ND in monogram) REX Draped and armored bust of the

---

preferred by the Clerical gentlemen consulted. If it is to be read with LACTA, — "The city of Guanaxuato declares its [? reliance] in the nourishing faith to be true [or sincere];"—the reverse seems entirely foreign to the character of a Medal proclaiming a new King. — EDS.

* These Medals of varying size (459-62) were circulated as coins,—for they corresponded in value very nearly to pieces of 4, 2, 1 and ½ Reales,—and the Colony thus evaded the royal prerogative, while virtually striking its own money. — EDS.

King to right, wearing a flowing wig and the Order of the Golden Fleece.

Rev. • GONZALO REZIO DE OQVENDO • HABANA   Date 1760 in legend at bottom reversed. Three castles (one over two) and a key erect, the handle at top.*

Silver. Cast. Size 26. H., Charles III, 65.

464. 1760. *Obv.* CARLOS . (AR in monogram) III . D . G . HISPAN . REX   Bust of the King to right, similar to the preceding.

Rev. • GONZALO . (AL in monogram) REZIO . DE (in monogram) . OQVENDO • (VE and ND in monogram) HABANA (AB and AN in monogram) and date 1760 as on preceding. Same design as last.

Silver. Cast. Size 22. H., Charles III, 66.

465. 1760. *Obv.* Bust of the King to right.

Rev. Three towers and a key.

Silver. Size 18. H., Charles III, 67. Collection of Garcia de la Torre, No. 6800.†

466. 1760. *Obv.* CAROLO III . HISP ET IND . IMPERIUM AUS-PICANE (*sic*), probably for AUSPICANTE, but neither the N nor E is in monogram with a T. (Charles III beginning his reign over Spain and the Indies under happy auspices.) Bust of the King to right in robe, with very full wig, and a ribbon over his breast.‡

Rev. NEGOTIATORES HAVAN . OPTIMO PRINCIPI . (The backers of Havana to the best Prince.) The date 1760 at bottom, in the circle of the legend, but reversed as to that, as on most of the preceding. Mercury facing, with petasus and talaria,

---

* For Oquendo see note on 348. This device of the castle and key alludes to the arms of the city, which bore those emblems, but is given somewhat differently at different times.— EDS.

† Herrera takes this description from a Catalogue published in 1852, which gives no further description.— EDS.

‡ Herrera mentions that the King wears the Order of the Golden Fleece, but we can not see it in his engraving, from which this is described. — EDS.

a purse in his right hand and a caduceus in his left, is advancing over a bag of money.

Silver.   Cast.   Size 19.   H., Charles III, 68.

IZINTZLINTAN.

467.   1760.   *Obv.* Bust of the King, etc.

Rev. IZINTZLINTAN CAPITAL DE MIHUACAN 25 DE DICIEMBRE. (1760.)

Silver.   H., Charles III, 69.*

JALAPA.

468.   1761.   *Obv.* CAROLUS III . D . G . HISPAN . ET IND REX. ⁕ 1760 ⁕   Bust of the King to right, in armor and draped, with a small wig.

Rev. XALAPA ⁕ ⁕ ⁕ ⁕ D . L . F . ⁕ ⁕ ⁕   (Jalapa de la Feria.) A shield bearing quarterly Castile and Leon ; an escutcheon of pretence for Granada ; surmounted by the royal crown.†

Silver.   Cast.   Size 19.   H., Charles III, 70.

LIMA.

469.   1760.   *Obv.* CAROLUS ⚫ III ⚫ HISPAN ⚫ ET IND ⚫ REX ⚫ LIMA (IMA in monogram) ⚫ 1760 ⚫   (The date is in the

---

* Herrera takes this from O'Crowley, p. 409, who gives no further description, merely remarking that the obverse is similar to those previously described. The legend of the reverse is simply the name of the place, and the date, December, 1760. — EDS.

† The Proclamation Medals were struck on silver mined near the places where they were issued, and scattered among the populace. See Herrera, p. 92. The proclamation here took place May 30, 1761. The piece has the old name of the city. The rosettes on the reverse are quite large.— EDS.

legend.) Bust of the King to right, robed, within corded circle; he wears a full wig, a band across his breast, and the Order of the Golden Fleece.

Rev. OPTIMO ● PRINC ● PUBL ● FIDELIT ● JURAM ● ◆ ● (Publicly we swear [juramus] allegiance to the best Prince). A double-headed eagle bearing the coronet of a Marquis, and on its breast and oval shield with a comet, its tail dividing the letters K I crowned, and touching a pomegranate crowned. At the sides the columns of Hercules crowned, twined with a scroll bearing the words PLUS on one and ULTR on the other (more beyond); waves below, above which in the field are the letters SUP VND below the eagle's feet.*

Silver. Size 24. H., Charles III, 71.

LUJAN.

470. 1760. *Obv.* CAROLVS . III . G . HISPAN . ET IND . REX . (The D before G is omitted.) Draped and armored bust of the King to right, with flowing wig, band and Order of the Golden Fleece.

Rev. PROC LAMATVS . LUJAN . (UJ in monogram) 1760 (Proclaimed at Lujan, 1760.) The date in the legend. A shield bearing the arms of Spain quarterly, Castile and Leon, and crowned; its base between C and L.

Silver. Cast. Size 23. H., Charles III, 72.

---

* There may be a double significance in the words SUP VND which primarily allude to Don Joseph Manso de Velasco, Count of Superunda, Viceroy at the time of Peru and Chile, the city of Lima being regarded as the "Royal" or capital city of the South American possessions of Spain (see Herrera, p. 92); the place of the words resting on the waves (SUPER UNDAS) suggests the other meaning. The arms are those of the city of Lima. Its name was confirmed in 1537 by a special edict of Charles I of Spain, afterwards the Emperor Charles V of Germany, and the crowned K and I we take to be the initials of that Prince and his Queen, Isabella of Portugal. The allusion of the comet we have not ascertained; but a rare Medal of Cardinal Hippolyte de Medici, who died in 1535, has a comet upon it (see Walter's "Medallic Memorials of the Great Comets," A. J. N., XXIV, 49,) and perhaps these may refer to some celestial visitant of that period. The double-headed eagle is the well known imperial device of Germany. The coronet is called that of a Marquis by Herrera; it differs somewhat from that used in English Heraldry for that rank.— EDS.

MATANZAS.

471. 1760. *Obv.* CAROLVS . III . D . G . HISPAN . ET IND
'ND in monogram) REX .   Draped and armored bust of the
'...g to right, with flowing wig and Order of the Golden
Ki'... the base of the bust on lower edge of the Medal.
Fleece ; '...N DE DIOS MOVEJON MATANS Date, 1760, at bot-
    Rev. • JVA.... h three turrets, and a central portal.*
tom.   A castle w.... .g.   H., Charles III, 73.
    Silver.   Cast.   Size 2..

                              III . D . G . HISPAN . REX *
472. 1760. *Obv.* CARLOS '.. and band, but no Order.
Bust of the King to right in armon ..
He wears a flowing wig.   inversed.) Date 1760,
    Rev. * JVAN DE DIOS MOFEJON (last N re, th three towers,
at bottom, in legend, reversed.   A castle wip.
very rudely made.   'n
    Silver.   Cast.   Size 19.   H., Charles III, 74. '.

MEXICO.   \ MEXIC .

473. 1760. *Obv.* CAROL . III . D . G . HISPAN . REX .'raped
PROCL Date 1760, at bottom, in legend, reversed.   D 9ow-
and armored bust of the King to right, with band and 1
ing wig.   'd
    Rev. INSIGN FIDELIT ET PVBL. LÆTI (Token of fidelity an '
public rejoicing).   In exergue, A . B . MADRRO | F. (The die-cutter.,
A bridge with three arches above waves, defended by a tower
supported by two lions, and surmounted by an eagle seated
on the nopal (arms of the city) ; the whole enclosed by an
ornamental shield bordered by shells and branches of palm
and laurel.
    Silver.   Size 28.   H., Charles III, 75.

474. 1760. *Obv.* CAROL . III ANTIQ . ET NOV . HISPAN (AN
in monogram) REX . MEXIC PROCLAM (Charles III, proclaimed
King of Old and New Spain at Mexico).   Below the truncation, A . B .MADRRO Draped and armored bust of the King to

---

* Probably the name of the Governor of Matanzas.   The V (?) in MOVEJON
on this Medal somewhat resembles a Y, and on the next is still ruder.   The words
are run together.— EDS.

right, with band and Order of the Golden Fleece, the emblem falling near the edge between MEXIC and PROCLAM.

Rev. ✳ INSIGN . FIDELIT . ET PVBLIC LAETITIAE ✳ (Token of fidelity and public rejoicing.)   The date 1760, at the bottom. Similar design to last, without the ornamental shield.

Bronze.   Size 24.   H., Charles III, 76.

475.   1760.   *Obv.* As the preceding?
Rev. As the preceding?
Edge. CONSIDERATE LILIA NEC SALOMON IN OMNI GLORIA SUA (Consider the lilies, not even Solomon in all his glory).

Silver.   Size 24.   H., Charles III, 77.   His description*
is from a Medal in the Rivadeneira collection.

476.   1760.   *Obv.* CAROL . III ANTIQ . ET NOV . HISPAN . REX ME   XI . PROCL (Translated in 474).†   MADENO below truncation.   Draped and armored bust of the King to right ; he wears a smaller wig, a band and the Order of the Golden Fleece, which separates E and X in MEXI.

Rev. Legend and design as 474.
Silver.   Size 22.   H., Charles III, 78.

---

* Herrera has only this, but it is clear from his notes on his 79, that the Latin is an edge inscription, and that otherwise it was from the same dies as the preceding.   The allusion to Solomon probably refers not merely to the title of "the Wise" given to his father, but to a publication entitled "The Solomon of Spain," etc. by Don Jose Castillo, published in 1768, in Mexico (see Herrera, p. 93), from which it may perhaps be inferred that the edge inscriptions on this and others described below, were added at some later time.   The *lilies* were the emblem of France, under the Bourbon Kings, from whom this Prince was descended.   The motto on the edge is from St. Luke, XII: 27.— EDS.

† Herrera has Q in ANTIQ in his plate, and C in his text.— EDS.

477.   1760.   *Obv.* From the same die as the preceding.
Rev. Same as the preceding.
Edge. As 475.
Silver.   Size 22.   H., Charles III, 79.   In the Royal (Span-
ish) Historical Collection.

478.   1760.   *Obv.* CAROLO TER MAX . HISP ET IND . REGI .
R . ACP . M . A . D . C . O .   (To Charles Third, the greatest,
King of Spain and India, etc.*)   Date 1760, in the legend, but
reversed.   Draped and armored bust of the King to right.

Rev. NOVUS MIHI NASCITUR ORDO.   (A new order springs
for me.)†   In exergue. A . B . MADBRO | F .   Arms of Spain (Castile
and Leon quarterly) in a shield ornamented with shells and a
palm branch on the left and a laurel branch on the right, and
surmounted by a triple crown.
Silver.   Size 27.   H., Charles III, 80.

479.   1760.   *Obv.* CAROL · III · VET · ET NOVAE HISP · REX
MEX . PROCL.   (Charles III, King of Old and New Spain, pro-

* Herrera mentions (p. 94), that this was struck by the University of Mexico,
from which we suppose the letters to signify R(egalis) AC P(ontificalis) M(exicana)
A(cademia), etc.   Several suggestions for D. C. O. might be made, (*e.g.*, Dedicavit
cum Obedientia), but having no actual knowledge we leave the reader to supply
them.   So far as given above the meaning is, The Royal and Pontifical University of Mexico [? dedicates to] Charles the Third (Tertio) the greatest, King of
Spain and of the Indies, etc. — EDS.

† Adapted from Virgil, Eclogue IV, lines 5 and 7.   O'Crowley, p. 407, says
these arms are those of the Cathedral Chapter of Mexico. — EDS.

claimed at Mexico.)   In exergue, separated by a curving line,
v.casanova. v   Naked bust of the King to right, in wig with
flowing locks tied by a ribbon.

Rev. EMAN ' ARCHIEP MEX CONSEN ' LAETIT ' SACRIS CELE-
BRAV. (Emmanuel, Archbishop of Mexico, joyfully consenting,
celebrated [the event] with sacred rites.)*   In exergue, mdcclx.
Upon an ornate shield, the Virgin standing on clouds in front
of two keys crossed in saltire, wards in chief; above the shield
appear the tops of a cross at the left and an ornate crozier
at the right, staffs below, in saltire; ribbons float on either
side from the top of the shield.

Silver and copper.   Size 26.   H., Charles III, 81.

480.   1760.   *Obv.* CAROL III ' D ' G ' HISPAN ' REX MEXIC .
PROCL   (Charles III, King of Spain, proclaimed at Mexico).
Below the truncation is the date, 1760.   Draped and armored
bust of the King to right; he wears a smaller wig.

Rev. IMPERATOR INDIARUM.   (Emperor of the Indies.)   In
exergue, A . MADPRD F and below, curving, CONSVLATUS.   (The
Consulate.)   An ornate shield surmounted by the royal crown
and ornamented on each side with palm and laurel branches ;
it is blazoned, per pale ; dexter, or, a vase with three lilies,
proper ; sinister, or, the five wounds of St. Francis (gules ?
color not indicated).

Silver.   Size 27.   H., Charles III, 82.

481.   Herrera mentions and gives a separate number to a
Medal of silver in the Rivadeneira collection, which is "like
the preceding," apparently from the same dies, but has an
inscription around the edge, MERCIBUS MERCEDIBUS CONSVULIT
(*sic*) UIRGA AEQUITATIS VIRGA REGNI SUI.   (He has regard to

---

* This Medal was struck by order of Don Manuel Rubio y Salinas, the Archbishop of Mexico (see Herrera, p. 93. foot note).   The proclamation took place
there on the 25th of June, and a Triumphal Arch was erected by the Archbishop
in honor of the event.   The arms are said by O'Crowley, p. 407, to be those of
the Archbishop.—Eds.

goods and to rewards.   The sceptre of his kingdom is a right
sceptre.)

Silver.   Size 27?   H., Charles III, 83.*

482.   1760.   *Obv.* CAROL · III · D · G · HISPAN (AN in monogram) REX MEXIC PROCLAM . (Charles III, by the grace of
God King of Spain, proclaimed at Mexico.)   The date ✦ 1760
is in the legend at the bottom, reversed.   Under the truncation A . D . MADERO .   Draped and armored bust of the King to
right, wearing a small wig, and a ribbon across his breast.
The jewel of the Order of the Golden Fleece falls nearly to
the edge after PROCLAM.

Rev. IMPERATOR INDIARUM ✦ above, and CONSVLATUS below.
(Translated above.)   Arms as on the preceding, but differently garnished, and the shield smaller.

Silver.   Size 24.   H., Charles III, 84.

483.   1760.   This Medal exists in the Rivadeneira collection
with edge † inscription CONSIDERATE LILIA . NEC SÀLOMON IN
OMNI GLORIA SUA.   (Translated above.)

NUEVA CANTABRIA.

484.   1760.   *Obv.* CAROL · III · D · VOCAT INDIAR · IMPER ·
F · P · A · TRIVMPH (Translated in 458‡).   Draped and armored
bust of the King to right ; wig tied with a bow ; the Order of
the Golden Fleece on his breast.

Rev. ECCLESIÆ NOUÆ CANTABRIÆ EPISCOP . ET CAPITULUM
○ ✦ ○ (The Bishop and Chapter of the Church of Nueva Can-
tabria.)   On the centre of the field in large letters MAR in

---

* This and the preceding were struck by "the Consulate."   CONSVULIT is
either for CONSVLUIT, or CONSVLIT, and the allusion in the closing portion of the
inscription (literally, a rod of equity) is clearly to Psalm XLV: 6 (A. V., verse 47
in the Church Psalter).   Father Fischer commenting on this Medal as described
by O'Crowley (p. 407) who has CONSVLIT, says the arms are those of the Consulate. — EDS.

† See note on 475. — EDS.

‡ See note on 458 for the abbreviations. — EDS.

monogram (for the Blessed Virgin's name) ; a crown above it surmounted by a Cardinal's hat, the cord and tassels of which drop on either side ; at the left of the monogram is a ladder with a cock on its top ; below the tassels on the left the sun, and on the right the moon ; under the point of the M are two seven-pointed stars ; below are various ecclesiastical vessels, the chalice and paten, thurible, chrismatory, pyx, monstrance and tabernacle ; crossed behind the crown are an olive branch at the left and a palm at the right.

Silver.   Size 25.   H., Charles III, 85.

PACHUCA AND REAL DEL MONTE.

485.   1761.   *Obv.* CAROLUS III BORB REX CATHOL (Charles III, of the House of Bourbon, Catholic King.)   Near the lower edge, P . CASANOVA F .   Laureated bust of the King to right, with a very full wig and flowing locks ; drapery on the edge of the bust.

Rev. FIDELIT ' ÆTERN ' POP ULOR ' PACHUQ ' ET REG ' MONTANI (The eternal fidelity of the people of Pachuca and Real del Monte.)   In exergue, IN PROCLAMAT . REGIA | MDCCLXI (In Royal Proclamation, 1761.)   Danae with slight drapery, a part of which floats behind her to the left, is stepping forward over a scythe and winged hour glass, the emblems of time ; she turns backward to the left to catch in her right hand the shower of gold [*i. e.*, Jupiter], and holds in her left the banner of Castile and a diadem ; in the distance a mountain peak rising from the sea.

Silver.   Size 28.   H., Charles III, 86.

PUEBLA DE LOS ANGELES.

486.   1760.   *Obv.* CAROLVS III REX CATHOQ . HISPANIARVM ET INDIARVM.   (Charles III, Catholic King of Spain and the Indies).   Bust of the King to right, in flowing wig.

Rev. CIVITAS ANGELOP . PROCL . ANNO 1760 REGNAT UBIQVE SOL (The city of Puebla de los Angeles proclaims him in the year 1760. His sun rules everywhere.*) The sun in the zodiac illuminating a globe over the waves.

Silver.   Size 21.   H., Charles III, 87 (p. 244).

487.   1760.   *Obv.* CAROLVS III REX CATHO · HISPANIARVM ET INDIARVM.   (Charles III, Catholic King of Spain and the Indies.)   Naked bust of the King to right ; he wears a very full wig with short curls.

Rev. CIVITAS ANGELOP · PROCL · ANNO 1760 REGNAT UTRIQUE SOL •   (The city of Puebla de los Angeles proclaims her, in the year 1760 ; her sun reigns over each [continent]).   Draped bust of Queen Amelia, full face.

Silver.   Cast.   Size 20.   H., Charles III, 88.

488.   1760.   *Obv.* CAROLVS III . D . G HIS 1760 P TE (in monogram) IND . REX *   (The city proclaims thee, Charles III, King of Spain and the Indies).   Bust of the King to right, robed, and wearing a full wig.

Rev. D . MARIA (AR in monogram) AMELIA (ME in monogram) HISP · ET · INDI (ND in monogram) · R · G · D.   Bust of Queen to right, draped.†

Silver.   Cast.   Size 16.   H., Charles III, 89.

Herrera (90) gives a brief description of a Mining Real of Raboileca, taken from O'Crowley (p. 409), but as it is rather a coin than a medal, we omit it.   There is nothing in the legends or devices to indicate that it refers in any way to King Charles, unless the date (1761) be so considered.

---

* Herrera describes this in his Appendix (see his p. 243-44), from an impression in the collection of the Marquis de Molens, and gives UBIQUE, but it would seem that this was probably an error of the die-cutter for UTRIQUE as on the next, signifying that his power as monarch extended to each hemisphere, and suggesting the device and motto of his ancestor, Louis XIV, on 388. — EDS.

† The heads of both monarchs represent them as old.   Herrera in his description, places the D at the beginning, here given at the *end* of the legend ; we consider the arrangement in the text better, and read it Donna [Domina] Maria Amelia, of Spain and the Indies, Queen [Regina Gratia Dei] by the grace of God. — EDS.

SAN LUIS POTOSI.

489. 1760. *Obv.* CAROL . III VET ET NOVA HISP . REX POS . PROCL.   (Potosi proclaims Charles III King of Old and New Spain.)   Naked bust of the King to right, his hair curiously arranged.   Under the decollation in a bow-shaped panel illegible letters, perhaps F. FUN, the die-cutter's name.

Rev. EN LA CIVDAD . DE SAN LVIS POTOSI ✿   At the bottom in the legend reversed, ANO 1760 (N's reversed).   (In the city of San Luis Potosi. 1760).   St. Louis with crown and mantle, trampling under his feet a monster, typical of heresy ; on each side of him are two placards.*

Silver.   Cast, very rude.   Size 20.   H., Charles III, 91.

SAN MIGUEL.

490. 1761. *Obv.* CAROLUS III BORB REX CATHOL.   (Charles III, Bourbon, Catholic King).   Under the decollation, near the edge, F . CASANOVA F.   Draped and laureated bust of the King to right ; very full and flowing wig, the locks tied with a bow of ribbon.

Rev. Inscription in seven lines, CAROLI III | HISPANIAR . ET IND . REGIS | PROCLAMATIO AVGVSTA | MICHAELOPOLI ˙ IN NOVA HISP ˙ | XIX APRILIS MDCCLXI | A JOSEPHO MARIA CANAL | MAGNO VEXILLIFERO.   (August Proclamation of Charles III, King of Spain and the Indies, at San Miguel, April 19, 1761, by Joseph Maria Canales, Grand Standard Bearer).

Silver.   Size 29.   H., Charles III, 92.

SANTA FE DE BOGOTA.

491. 1760. *Obv.* CAROLO III ˙ HISP ˙ CATH ˙ REGI ˙ ET IND ˙ IMP ˙   (To Charles III, Catholic King of Spain and Emperor of the Indies).   Bust of the King to right, in armor, draped and

---

* The ornament at the end of reverse legend is floral. We use the nearest available character, though it is not exact. The "placards" [Spanish *cartelas*] are oblong figures of different sizes, placed perpendicularly in the field. We have no theory to offer as to their significance, if they possess any.— EDS.

laureated ; with the Order of the Golden Fleece ; on the truncation of the arm, BENTOF.

Rev. SANCTA FIDES PRAESTAT FIDEM. (Santa Fe excels in loyalty). In exergue, OCT . IDUUM AUG . | M . DCC . LX. (The eighth before the Ides of August [*i. c.,* Aug. 6], 1760.) An eagle displayed, crowned, head to left, and holding a pomegranate in each talon.

Silver. Size 25. H., Charles III, 93.

492. 1760. *Obv.* CAROLO III HISP ' ET IND AVG . REG. (To Charles III, August King of Spain and the Indies.) Naked and laureated bust of the King to right.

Rev. Same legend, exergue and design as the preceding.

Silver. Size 21. H., Charles III, 94.

SANTIAGO DE CUBA.

493. 1760. *Obv.* CAR (AR in monogram) JUSTE (TE in monogram) AC SAPER (AP in monogram) IMPERAT (IMP and AT in monogram) ORBEM. (Charles III justly and wisely rules the New World.) N̄o on the left and VM on the right of the bust of the King, who is robed, and wears a singular wig ; his hands hold two globes before his face.

Rev. JOSEPH RONDONS (ND in monogram) . PAPLO DE JISVAN (VA in monogram and N reversed) 1760. Saint James on horseback galloping to left with drawn sword in hand, within a circle of twenty-one flowers, rosettes and crosses.*

Silver. Size 26. H., Charles III, 95.

SANTO DOMINGO.

494. 1761. *Obv.* CAROLO III D G . HISP ET IND . OFF 1761. (They offer this to Charles III, King of Spain and the Indies.) Laureated bust of the King to right in armor, robed, with band, ruffles, full flowing wig, and Order of the Golden Fleece.

---

* We presume the name to be that of some public official of the place. The piece is extremely rude, and from the engraving would seem to be a cast, but Herrera does not call it such.— EDS.

Rev. PRAESES · ET REGII HISPANIOLÆ QVÆSTORES · F · O ✠ (The Presiding Officer and Magistrates of Santo Domingo).* A shield bearing, gules, a bend argent between two lion's heads; a border argent, charged with five castles and five lions rampant (color not indicated), and surmounted by the coronet of a Count. Probably the arms of the Viceroy, but his name has not been ascertained.

Silver. Cast. Size 21. H., Charles III. 96.

495. 1761. *Obv.* CAROLO III D G . HISP . ET IND . R . OFF 1760. Bust of the King to right, similar to the preceding.

Rev. Legend and device as the last, but the shield has no coronet. (Legends translated above.)

Silver. Cast. Size 21. H., Charles III, 97.

496. 1760. *Obv.* CAROLO III . HISP . ET . IND . R . F O . 1760. (Translated above). Bust of the King to right, in armor, and very full wig.

Rev. HISPANIOLA OFFERT (RT in monogram) . PRIM . POST CASTELL. A key erect, wards to left, supported by two lions and surmounted by the coronet of a Count.†

Silver. Cast. Size 16. H., Charles III, 98.

497. CAROLO III . D . G . 1760. Bust of the King to right, robed, and with full wig; the head much larger in proportion than the preceding.

Rev. HISPANIOLA. Same design as the preceding.

Silver. Cast. Size 16. H., Charles III, 99.

498. 1760. *Obv.* No legend. Draped bust of the King to right in smaller wig.

Rev. No legend. Same design as last.

Silver. Cast. Size 9. H., Charles III, 100.

---

* Hispaniola, or "Little Spain," was the early name of the Island. — EDS.

† The reverse legend apparently means that St. Domingo was the first to issue a Proclamation piece "after Castile ;" *i. e.*, of the American Provinces.— EDS.

TABASCO.

499. 1760.   *Obv.* CARLOS III D G · HISPAN · ET IND REX date 1760 in legend, reversed as to letters.   Bust of the King to right, draped, in armor, and with flowing wig.

Rev. DON CLAVDIO LANDERO . TAVASCO ✦ ✦   A shield bearing an eagle displayed, crowned, his head to left : in field at right and left of shield an inverted exclamation point.[*]

Silver.   Cast.   Size 19.   H., Charles III, 101.

TACUBA.

500.   1761.   *Obv.* CAROL . III HISP ET IND REX   Draped and armored bust of the King to right, with the Order of the Golden Fleece, the jewel falling near the edge.

Rev. UILLA DE TACUBA above, and ● 1761 ● below.   (Town of Tacuba, 1761.)   A bridge of three arches above waves, and defended by a tower supported by two lions ; upon the tower is an eagle displayed, seated on a nopal.   These are the arms of the State of Mexico, in which Tacuba is situated.

Silver, with loop and ring for suspension.   Size 21½.   H., Charles III, 102.

TASCO.

501.   1761.   *Obv.* CAROL . III HISPANIAR · ET IND · REX Below decollation, separated by a curving line, F . CASANOVA F. Naked bust of the King to right, with flowing locks tied by a bow of ribbon.

Rev. Inscription in nine parallel lines, CAROLI III | PROCLA-MATIO | AUGUSTA | TASCHI IN NOVA HISPAN | ARGENTI . FOSO-RUM (*sic*) P. Q | CONSENSU ET LAETITIA | A IOSEPHO MARTINI | VIEDMA | AN · MDCCLXI . (August Proclamation of Charles

---

[*] The name on the reverse is probably that of the governor of the place, but we have learned nothing of him. On the shield at the right and left of the eagle's head are small charges, which we are unable to name from Herrera's engraving, and he does not mention them in his description. On each side of the shield outside is the mark ¡ — as it is used in Spanish printing at the beginning of an exclamation. — EDS.

III at Tasco, in New Spain, by Joseph Martinez Viedma, with the consent and rejoicing of the silver miners and people, in the year 1761.)

Silver.   Size 23.   H., Charles III, 103.

TEPEACA.

502.   1760.   *Obv.* CAROL III . D . G . HISPAN . (N reversed) REX TEPEACA PR.   (Tepeaca proclaims Charles III by the grace of God King of Spain.)   Draped and armored bust of the King to right in a wig.   The letters of the legend have their tops inside towards the field.

Rev. INSIGN . FIDELIT ET PVBLI . ÆTIA (*sic*) D 1760.   (Token of fidelity and public rejoicing, 1760).   Letters arranged as on the obverse.*   Device similar to 500, but the lions are omitted.

Silver.   Cast.   Size 17½.   H., Charles III, 104.

VALLADOLID.

503.   1760.   *Obv.* Bust of the King with his titles.

Rev. VALLISOLETI MICHOACAN . 24 NOVEMB . (1760)   (Struck at Valladolid [Capital of the State of] Michoacan.)   Arms of Valladolid.†

Silver.   Size not given.   H., Charles III, 105, from O'Crowley, p. 407.

504.   1761.   CAROLVS . III . D . G . HISPA . ET . INDIARVM . REX.   Armored bust of the King to right.

---

* D probably for *dedicavit, i. e.,* dedicated, or struck in honor of the King. — EDS.

† Neither O'Crowley nor Herrera give any further particulars; the latter, however, has descriptions of two other Medals struck by this city, one in 1791, for Charles IV, and another in 1808, for Ferdinand VII, both of which have on their reverses armorial devices, almost identical, and which we therefore infer are the arms of the city.   This device is an ornate elliptical shield with drooping palm branches on each side, and the royal crown above; on the shield is a sort of bracket or shelf on which are two busts draped, and wearing Roman helmets, turned towards a third in the centre between them, which is facing, clothed, but with uncovered head.   It seems probable, from O'Crowley, that this or a similar device is on this Medal. — EDS.

Rev. REGAL SIGN . . DE . and on the field the inscription, in five lines, JURADO | EN | VAIIADO (*sic*) | AÑO | 1761. (Token of the oath of fidelity, taken at Valladolid in 1761).
Silver.   Size 17½.   H., Charles III, 106.   F. 6,928.

VERA CRUZ.

505.   1760.   CAROLVS III D . G . ✦ ✦ HISPAN . E IND . R . Draped and armored bust of the King to right, in flowing wig, with Order of the Golden Fleece.

Rev. NOV VER . CRVZ PROCLAM .   At bottom, A 1760 in legend, reversed as to the rest.   (Proclaimed at New Vera Cruz.)   Resting on waves is a tower with central portal, three circular windows, and three turrets; the central turret is surmounted by a large cross.   (Device of the city).
Silver.   Size 25.   Cast.   H., Charles III, 107.

506.   1760.   Same as the preceding except that in the field on the reverse are the letters on right and left of castle ZAB —ALETA (AL in monogram), — the name of the Royal "Alferez," or principal officer.
Silver.   H., Charles III, 108.   F. 7,045.

CHAPTER VII.

FROM THE PEACE OF PARIS TO THE REVOLUTION.

N the brief period between the Peace of Paris and the beginning of the American Revolution, there were few events which were of sufficient importance in the popular mind to call for Medals to perpetuate their memory. Yet the limited number which were struck seem to form a group by themselves. Two alone relate to British American victories. Some were for presentation to the Indians; one or two were issued by local societies for the use of their members; and there are a few others, which can be called Personal Medals; most of the latter class, the exceptions to which are given in their chronological order, relate to William Pitt, whose opposition to the odious Stamp Act made him extremely popular in America. These will form the subject of the present Chapter. A few are added at its close, which probably belong to this period, but whose dates have not been definitely determined.

HIBERNIAN SOCIETY OF CHARLESTON, S. C.

507. (1763?). *Obv.* HIBERNIAN)I(SOCIETY above, and CHARLESTON · SC · below. A harp of six strings formed of a winged female figure with fish's tail; the legend on an oval band surrounding the harp, which is in skeleton.

Rev. The harp in skeleton, and engraved as on the obverse ;
no legend.*

Silver. Elliptical, with ring for suspension.   Engraved.

CHARLESTON (S. C.) SOCIAL CLUB.

508. 1763. *Obv.* VINCTI AMICITIA. (Bound in friendship.)
Two men in the costume of the last century, shaking hands ;
a tree at the left ; in the back-ground at the right, a church
and buildings.

Rev. Inscription in six lines, SOCIAL CLUB | INSTITUTED
| CHARLES TOWN | SOUTH CAROLINA | VI OCTOBER | MDCCLXIII.

Silver, quite rare, and bronze (probably restrikes).†

Size 23 x 21½, elliptical.   B. 331.

INDIAN MEDALS.

509. 1764. *Obv.* GEORGIUS III. D. G. M. BRI. FRAN. ET HIB.
REX. F. D. (George III, King of Great Britain, France and
Ireland, Defender of the Faith.)   Bust of the King in armor,
to right.

---

* Mr. Betts did not mention the size of this Medal, and we have found no
other account of it. Apparently it was made like many of the English Masonic
Medals of the last century, with a die in very low relief, and afterwards portions
of the field were cut out, leaving the device "in skeleton." Strictly speaking,
it can hardly be called a *medal.* — EDS.

† This Medal is mentioned in the American Journal of Numismatics, V, 7
and 39, as having been struck "on the Social Club being instituted in Charles
Town, South Carolina, 1763," and an impression in the Hollis Sale, 1817, brought
£2 14s. See also A. J. N., XVII, p. 66. It appeared in the Bushnell Sale (331)
where it was illustrated, and was bought by Mr. W. S. Appleton ; another, in
Chapmans' sale of the Warner Collection, brought $17. — EDS.

Rev. HAPPY WHILE UNITED. In exergue, 1764. An Indian holding a pipe, seated near an officer upon a roll of tobacco. In the back-ground the city and harbor of New York (?).

Metal and size not given. Loop for suspension formed by a pipe and an eagle's wing. For presentation to the Indians. A. J. N., II, 110. B. N.*

510. 1764. *Obv.* GEORGIUS III. D. G. M. BRI. FRA. ET. HIB. REX. F. D. (Translated above.) Bust to right, laureate, in armor, with ribbon of the Garter.

Rev. HAPPY WHILE UNITED. In exergue, 1764. In the field N | YORK and DCF counterstamped.† Landscape, representing in the foreground an officer and at the right an Indian, seated on a rustic chair on the bank of a river. On the right a house on a rocky point, at the junction of the river with the ocean, and three ships, under full sail, at sea. The Indian holds in his left hand a pipe. With his right hand he grasps the hand of the officer who is seated on his left. At his right a tree, at the left a mountain range.‡

Silver. Cast. Size 46, with loop for suspension, formed of a pipe and an eagle's wing. A. J. N., VII, 90; Appleton cabinet.

511. 1764. *Obv.* Legend as 510. Laureated bust of the King to right, clothed, and wearing a broad band of ribbon from the left shoulder across his breast; on his head he has

---

* This description is from the American Journal of Numismatics (*loc cit.*), which quotes Mons. Vattemare's work "Collection de Monnaies et Medailles de l'Amerique du Nord de 1652 a 1858." Vattemare's notice, however, is substantially a translation from Schoolcraft's "History of the Indian Tribes," where an engraving is given (see p. 79 and plate 70). The description in Vattemare apparently applies equally well to No. 510. The difference between 509 and 510 as described, is in the object on which the two are sitting, and we incline to believe that these two are identical. — EDS.

† See note on 431. — EDS.

‡ What is called in the text "a mountain range" is apparently the same triangular object, which is evidently the gable of a building, on the next Medal.— EDS.

a sort of skull-cap, but this is very likely intended to show the hair smooth; below the wreath the hair is tied with a ribbon, the ends of which float back.

Rev. Legend as the preceding. The design is similar to the last:—the Indian and officer (?) being seated on a rustic settee; the latter has a cocked hat in the style of the period; behind the tree at the left, is the gable of a building; a village at the right. The foreground is separated by a line from the ground on which the seat is placed, but there is nothing to show it is intended for a river, and there are no ships; the field and exergue are plain.

Silver. Size 34. Tancred (illustrated), p. 49.

512. 1764. *Obv.* GEORGIUS III. DEI GRATIA. Youthful bust of the King, in armor.

Rev. The Royal Arms, quarterly: 1, England impaling France; 2, Scotland; 3, Ireland; 4, Hanover.

Silver. Size not given. Tancred, p. 50.*

513. 1764. *Obv.* Legend as on 510. Laureated bust of King George "in full costume" and wearing a wig tied with a bow.

Rev. Similar to 510, but there are several houses at the junction of the river with the ocean, and only two ships on the latter.

Silver. Size 36. Loop of pipe and eagle's wing, as on 510. A. J. N., X, 54.†

---

* From Tancred it would seem that several of these Medals were struck, of substantially the same design, but varying in size — some as large as 48.— EDS.

† This Medal was found in a grave with other relics, at old Fort Loudon, in October, 1875, by Mr. J. J. Snider. Its present owner is unknown. A full account of the discovery is given in A. J. N. (*loc. cit.*). The Rev. Horace E. Hayden, of Wilkesbarre, Pa., reprinted in 1885 a small monograph on Indian Medals, from the Proceedings of the Wyoming Historical and Geological Society, Vol. II, part 2 (see a notice of same in A. J. N., XXI, 23), which gives an interesting account of many of these pieces. See also a paper by Mr. R. A. Brock on Indian Medals, including 45, 46 and 47 in this volume, and others of 1754 (perhaps 396), in A. J. N., XXI, 88. Several Indian Medals with bust of George III are in private collections, of which meagre accounts have from time to time

WILLIAM PITT.

514. 1766. *Obv.* RIGHT HONOVRABLE WILL.^M PITT ESQ. Bust of Pitt to left.[*]

Rev. Inscription in seven lines, THE MAN | WHO . HAVING | SAVED THE | PARENT . PLEADED | WITH SUCCESS | FOR HER | CHILDREN.

Brass.   Size 20.

515. 1766. *Obv.* GVLIELMVS PITT.   Bust of Pitt to left.
Rev. Same inscription as the preceding.

Silver and bronze; two varieties of each die with slight differences, in bronze.   Size 26.

516. 1766. *Obv.* Legend and device as the preceding, but the wig is fuller and the letters heavier.   Beneath bust, T. PINGO, F.

Rev. Similar to 514.
Silver and bronze.   Size 26.

----

been published in the A. J. N., [*e. g.* one in VII, 50, impressions of which are in Mr. W. S. Appleton's cabinet and that of Mr. M. Moore, of Trenton Falls, N. Y.,] but they all seem, from the descriptions we have obtained, to correspond with some of those described by Mr. Betts, and further reference to them is needless.   See also 534 below, which probably should follow 513. — EDS.

[*] The date assigned to this and the three following is conjectural, there being none on the piece, as will be observed.   William Pitt was born at Boconnoc, Cornwall, Nov. 15, 1708; he began his political life in 1735, as a member of Parliament for Old Sarum.   In 1756 he had become the most popular statesman in England, and in 1760, he was almost idolized by the people who called him the "Great Commoner," and he was regarded even by his opponents as one of the ablest, if not the foremost, Englishman of his time.   His argument in 1765 and 1766 against the Stamp Act, and the right of England to tax the Colonies, endeared him to America, and his famous speech in 1775 on the America war and the Boston Port bill, and that against employing Indians to fight the American Colonies in 1777, are too well known to Americans to need comment.   He became Earl of Chatham in 1766.   He was seized with an apoplectic fit, as he was rising to speak in the House of Lords, and died a few weeks after, in May, 1778. Copley, the eminent American artist, painted a picture of this distinguished statesman, as he fell in the arms of his friends, which hangs in the National Portrait Gallery in England. — EDS.

517.   1766.   *Obv.* Similar to the preceding, except I. W. beneath bust.*

Rev. Similar to 514.

Brass.   Size 25.

518.   1766 (?)   *Obv.* RT HONOURABLE Wᴹ PITT   Bust to left, similar to 515.

Rev. WHO ROUZE (*sic*) THE BRITISH LION   A lion to left, looking backward, a sword in his right paw, and his left resting on a globe.   An ornament in exergue.

Copper.   Size 20.   Num. Chron. [London], 1890.

519.   1766.   *Obv.* THE . RESTOREʀ OF . COMMERCE 1766 : Below, completing the circle, NO . STAMPS :   Clothed bust of Pitt to left, in wig and long cue.

Rev. THANKS ' TO ' THE ' FRIENDS ' OF ' LIBERTY ' AND ' TRADE.   Ship sailing to right, with AMERICA on the field diagonally across her bow, which has a lion figure-head.†

Silver, copper and tin.   Size 17½.

520.   1766.   *Obv.* IHE ' RESIORER (*sic*) ' OF ' COMMERCE ' 1766 : NO STAMPS :   Bust of Pitt to left dressed in coat, with full wig.   (Similar to the preceding.)

---

* These initials may be those of the engraver of several of the Vernon dies (see 268 and others, *supra*) struck about twenty years earlier, but the name has not been ascertained with certainty to our knowledge. Many of these Medals of Pitt were little, if at all, superior in execution to the Vernon pieces. The Numismatic Chronicle says this "with I. W. on truncation is always cast."—EDS.

† The allusion on the reverse is clearly to his efforts for the repeal of the Stamp Act, which was designed to restrict the trade of the American Colonies. — EDS.

Rev. Same legend and design as the preceding.
Brass and copper.   Size 15½.   Very rare.*

521.   1766.   *Obv.* LIBERTATIS VINDEX (N reversed) and below, completing the circle, GUL: PITT. (Wm. Pitt, the defender
of Liberty.)   A group of three leaves after the x.   Bust of
Pitt three-quarters to right, nearly facing.

Rev. BRITANNIA ET AMERICA IUNCTÆ · (the NS reversed).
(Britain and America United.)   Hands clasped in front of a
sword, upon the point of which is a liberty cap ; the whole
between two olive (?) branches, which spring from the sword-
guard.†

Brass.   Size 21.

522.   1773.   *Obv.* No legend.   Bust of Pitt facing to the
right, dressed in coat.   Under the bust KIRK. F.

Rev. Inscription in three lines, LORD | CHATHAM | 1773.
Copper ; (some were silver-plated).‡   Size 15.

523.   1778 (?)   *Obv.* GVL . PITT . COMES . DE· . CHATHAM .
PATRIÆ . DECVS . ET . DELICIÆ .   KIRK. F.   (William Pitt, Earl of

---

* This is called "a rough copy" of 519 in Numismatic Chronicle, London,
1890.— EDS.

† Probably struck soon after the repeal of the Stamp Act.— EDS.

‡ For the title given to Pitt on this Medal see note on 514.   He had retired
from the Government in October, 1768, but in 1771 returned to public life, and
was opposed to the course of the Ministers until his death.   For *Kirk* see note on
381.   This, says the Numismatic Chronicle (1890, p. 54), is one of a series of
thirteen Medals given away with as many numbers of a magazine called "The
Sentimentalist," published 1773-75, which explains the date.   Some were struck
in silver and given as prizes.— EDS.

Chatham : the glory and the beloved of his country.)   Bust of Pitt to right ; over his shoulder, a toga fastened with a brooch.

Rev. QVIS . DESIDERIO . SIT . PVDOR . AVT . MODVS . (Freely, Why should there be any shame or limit to our regret at his loss.*)   In exergue, NAT . NOV . XV. MDCCVIII . OB . MAII . XI . MDCCLXXVIII .   (Dates of birth and death.)   A female figure weeping, and resting her right elbow and hand on an urn placed on a pedestal, against which rests the British shield, and inscribed KIRK. F. ; her right hand supports her head.†

Silver and bronze.   Size 24.

PITT AND HOWE.

524.   1773.   *Obv.* THE RIGHT HONO⁵ WILLIAM PITT.   Bust three-quarters to left.

Rev. THE RIGHT HONO⁵ COMMODORE HOWE.   Bust of Howe three-quarters to right, holding a baton.‡

Brass.   Size 15½.

DEATH OF WHITEFIELD AT NEWBURYPORT.

525.   1770.   *Obv.* THE ' REV ' GEORGE   WHITEFIELD ' A.M   Under the bust, T. HOLLOWAY. F.   Bust three-quarters to right nearly full-face; he wears a singular wig, with bunches at the sides, and the bands and robes of an Anglican clergyman.

Rev. A tablet inscribed : TO THE MEMORY OF | THE REV: GEO: WHITEFIELD. A. M. | WHO, WITH UNRELUCTANT GRANDEUR | GAVE, NOT YIELDED UP, | HIS SOUL SUBLIME. | AT NEWBURY

---

* This is the first line of Horace's Ode to Virgil (I : xxiv). — EDS.

† There are others of Pitt,—one with reverse, bust of Lord Thurlow, another, "The Supporters," etc., struck about 1789, and many of later date, mentioned in Numismatic Chronicle, not properly to be included here.— EDS.

‡ The date of this Medal is uncertain, but it probably belongs to this period. Commodore Richard Howe, born in 1725, died in 1799, was "regarded as the first sea officer of his time;" he was in command of the British fleet on the coast of the United States, early in the Revolution, as an Admiral, and in 1788 was created Earl Howe.   He won distinction in the Seven Years' War, and later by his operations against the French in the Revolution; and in 1794 he gained a decisive victory over their fleet.— EDS.

P. N. AMERICA. S. 30. 1770 | IN THE 56 YEAR OF HIS AGE. | HIS CONDUCT IS A LEGÁCY FOR ALL   Above the tablet a draped figure is reclining, his right arm leaning on a large book, and an urn in front ; his left hand pointing to a church in the distance.   Below the tablet on a garland, an oval shield bearing dexter, argent on a bend gules (?), a small device, not distinguishable : sinister, a lion rampant.   Crest, Out of a coronet a stag's head.   The tinctures are not clearly indicated.*

Silver and bronze.   Size 23.

526.   *Obv.* REV? GEORGE   WHITEFIELD   Bust of Whitefield facing, similar to preceding, but from a smaller die.†

Rev. AN ISRAELITE INDEED, A GOOD SOLDIER OF IESUS CHRIST ·   A figure of Faith, standing at the right, supporting a cross and leaning upon a tomb, on which is an urn ; on the tomb, DIED 30 | SEP · 1770, | ÆT 56; on a scroll behind the figure BY GRACE | ARE YE | SAVED.

Copper.   Size 20.   Appleton Cabinet.   Conder, 209, No. 59.

---

* By the kindness of Mr. A. Van Name, of Yale University, we have been allowed to examine this Medal, in the hope of giving a blazon of the arms, and thus determining its origin, as Whitefield himself was not entitled to any armorial device.   The bend on dexter seems to have some device above it (perhaps a lance bend-wise), and a row of fusils conjoined fess-wise below, but these are not sufficiently distinct to be stated with certainty ; nor can we distinguish the charge which is placed on the bend.   It has been suggested that they were those of the Countess of Huntingdon, who was an earnest supporter of Whitefield, but that is not the case, as the device of the Earl was a "maunch;" another has suggested that they are the arms of some one connected with the Colony of Georgia, in which Whitefield was deeply interested, but we cannot place them. Whitefield, whose father was an Inn-keeper, in very moderate circumstances, was born at Gloucester, England, December 16, 1714, and died at Newburyport, Mass., Sept. 30, 1770.   His labors as a Revivalist in America are too well known to need mention here.   There are other Mortuary Medals of Whitefield, beside those mentioned in the text, with bust on obverse, and reverses (1) Tomb, with inscription ; (2) "The Funeral Sermon."   These are mentioned in the Numismatic Chronicle (London), Third series, VI, pp. 318-19, and will no doubt be given in time among the English Personal Medals, of which descriptions are now publishing in that magazine.   These had not been seen by Mr. Betts, and the Editors have not obtained full descriptions.   See also Catalogue Bushnell Sale, p. 25, 332-336.   Thomas Holloway, who cut the dies of this Medal, was born in London, in 1748, and died in 1827.   He was a skillful workman, and was "engraver of History to the King."— EDS.

† The die shows a slight fracture near the top. — EDS.

527. *Obv.* Similar to 525.

Rev. B. 16. D. 1714. D. 30. S. 1770. (Dates of birth and death.)   An urn ; a cherub with a skull above.

Silver and bronze.   Size 23.   B.

WILLIAM AND MARY COLLEGE, VIRGINIA.

528. 1772. Two gold Medals, one for the best Class ical scholar, the other to the best scholar in Philosophy, were awarded to students of the College of William and Mary, Virginia.   These were "purchased annually" with the income of a gift to the College made by Lord Botetourt (Norborne Berkeley), Governor of the Province from 1768 until his death in 1770.   The names of eight of the recipients are given in the "History of the College of William and Mary," (p. 42) and in A. J. N., XIII, 47.   No description of the Medal has been found ; it was probably engraved.

ST. VINCENT REBELLION SUPPRESSED.

529. 1773. *Obv.* GEORGIVS · III · M B · REX   (George III, King of Great Britain).   Bust of the King in profile to right, clothed, and wearing a broad band across his breast ; on his head is a sort of fillet, or band, the ends of which, with curls, fall behind him, on his shoulder.   On the truncation, MOSER F.

Rev. PEACE AND PROSPERITY TO S.ᵗ VINCENTS   In exergue, MDCCLXXIII.   Britannia standing at the left, her right arm on a shield which bears a union of the British crosses ; with her left hand she offers a sprig of olive to a vanquished Carib ; various weapons on the ground between them.*

Silver.   Size 36.   A ring attached at the top of the planchet.   Tancred (illustrated), p. 47.

---

* This commemorates the suppression of the rebellion at St. Vincent, com‑
pleted by Major‑General Dalrymple, Feb. 20, 1773.   Moser, who made the dies
for this piece, we have not certainly identified, but it seems probable from such
information as we have been able to obtain, that he was George Michael Moser‑
a Swiss artist, born at Schaffhausen in 1705, who went to London in 1726, where
he acquired a high reputation for his ornamental gold work and enamelling.   In
1768 he was appointed Keeper of the Royal Academy of Arts, and was praised
by Sir Joshua Reynolds for his knowledge of painting and sculpture. — EDS.

530. 1775. *Obv.* ST. VINCENT'S BLACK CORPS. Victory with palm branch and sword standing over a vanquished Carib.

Rev. BOLD LOYAL and below, OBEDIENT. H.G FEC A negro soldier with musket.

Bronze. Size —.*

WILLIAM PENN AND PENNSYLVANIA.

531. 1775. *Obv.* WILLIAM PENN. Below, B · 1644 D . 1718 and at the right, L. P. Clothed bust of Penn to right, with compact wig, plain coat without collar, and cravat.

Rev. BY DEEDS OF PEACE In exergue, PENSYLVANIA | SETLED (*sic*) | 1681 A "Friend" (perhaps Penn) at the left, advancing and shaking hands with an Indian, who stands with a bow in his left hand.†

Silver and bronze. Size 26. Med. Ill., Geo. I, 40.

Mentioned in a letter from Lady Juliana Penn, wife of Governor Thomas Penn, to Rev. Wm. Smith, dated May 30, 1775: "I send a silver medal just struck, of the first Proprietor of Pennsylvania."

---

* This description we have been unable to verify, and its size is not given in Mr. Betts's MS. This and the preceding were struck for presentation to the officers and soldiers who served in the "Carib War," but the engraver's name we have not learned. This seems to have escaped the notice of Tancred. — EDS.

† L. P. is for Lewis Pingo, a son of Thomas, appointed Assistant Engraver in the Royal Mint at London in 1776, on the death of his father. He was Chief Engraver, 1779–1815, and died Aug. 26, 1830. The Editors of Medallic Illustrations were unable to fix the date of this Medal, but place it "about the middle

There is another Medal of Penn, by Rogat, in Durand's "Series Numismatica" of a later date than to entitle it to mention here. The dates of striking the following have not been definitely determined.

PROPRIETORS AND GOVERNORS OF PENNSYLVANIA.

532. *Obv.* IOHN • PENN • JUN.ᴿ & • IN.ᵒ • PENN • PROPRIE.ᴿˢ & • GOVERN.ᴿˢ • OF • PENNSYLVAN.ᴵᴬ •   An ornamental shield bearing a fess with three plates ; above it as a crest, a lion rampant to left ; a garland of roses surrounds the shield ; around the legend a beaded circle.

Rev. Plain.*

Electrotype.   Size 23.

TRISTRAM COFFIN, NANTUCKET, MASS.

533. *Obv.* TRISTRAM COFFIN THE FIRST OF THE RACE THAT SETTLED IN AMERICA.   Full length figure standing, facing, in doublet, cloak, ruff and hat, upon a pedestal inscribed 1642.

---

of the last century," and believe it was executed by direction of Thomas Hollis, as the legend was his favorite motto. Penn died at Ruscombe, Berkshire, England, July 30, 1718. The portrait on the Medal might be thought a caricature, but it closely resembles the bust of Penn in the Loganian Library, Philadelphia, the work of Sylvanus Bevan, and claimed to be an excellent likeness. An engraved portrait copied from this bust, and also one taken in his younger days, will be found in Watson's Annals of Philadelphia, I, p. 111, the sharp-pointed nose being plainly shown in each. — EDS.

* This description appears to be made from an electrotype copy of a Medal, no original of which has come under our notice, and we are not aware whether the reverse was plain, or bore some device which is lacking in the copy. John Penn was the son of Richard, fifth child of William the founder of Pennsylvania by his second wife, Hannah Callowhill. He arrived in America about Nov. 1, 1763, and was Deputy Governor till May 6, 1771, and again from August, 1773, till Sept., 1776. John Penn, Jr., — so called to distinguish him from the preceding, — was the eldest son of Thomas, the second son of the founder. His mother was Juliana, a daughter of the Earl of Pomfret. He was born Feb. 23, 1760, and died at Stoke Poges Park, Bucks, England, in June, 1834. He resided for many years in America, and was "Hereditary Governor" of Pennsylvania, though never actually holding the office. The arms of William Penn were argent, on a fess sable three plates [roundlets of silver]. Crest, a demilion rampant, argent, gorged with a collar sable charged with three plates. The motto accompanying the arms on the Governor's seal was MERCY AND TRUTH.— EDS.

His right hand rests on his hip, and in his left he holds a staff.

Rev. DO HONOR TO HIS NAME. BE UNITED. Four hands united to form a cross. [Punctuated with stars.]

Copper, (silver-plated,) and lead. Rare. Size 34. Med. Ill., Chas. I, 121, which says it may have been struck at the time of the War of Independence.*

FRENCH COMPANY OF·GUIANA.

534. *Obv.* LUDOVIC · XVI · REX CHRISTIANISS · (Louis XVI. Most Christian King). Under the truncation ᴅᵁᵛᴵᵛ. Bust of the King to right in civic dress, with ribbon and wearing a wig.

Rev. No legend. In exergue, COMPAGNIE · DE | LA · GUY· ANNE | FRANCAISE (Company of French Guiana.) A negro naked, but for a cloth around the waist, standing before the door of a hut among bales and barrels, and, while leaning upon his spade, sowing seed among tobacco plants in front of

---

* This Medal was undoubtedly struck under the direction of Admiral Sir Isaac Coffin of the British Navy, who was born in Boston, Mass., in 1750. While it bears the name and an imaginary likeness of one of the early settlers of the Island of Nantucket, we believe the date of its issue was much later than that ascribed to it in Med. Ill., and that it was struck about the beginning of the present century. If we are correct, it cannot fairly be placed in this list; but Mr. Betts included it, following the authority cited, and we therefore allow it to remain. Sir Isaac is said to have presented impressions to all male descendants of Tristram bearing his name. [Thacher, Am. Med. Biog., I, 229. See also A. J. N., X, 80.] — EDS.

him ; in the middle ground men carry merchandise to a boat, and in the distance are ships at sea.

Silver and copper, octagonal.* Size 21.

BRITISH INDIAN MEDAL.

535. *Obv.* GEORGIUS III DEI GRATIA (George III, by the grace of God). Armored bust of the King to right, wearing the ribbon of the Garter.

Rev. No legend. The British lion reposing under a small tree at the left ; a wolf barking at him at the right ; in the background, at the left, behind the lion, a church and two houses ; at the right, behind the wolf, trees and shrubs.†

Silver. Size 38. McL., 297. S., Supp., 62. Tancred (illustrated), p. 50.

---

* Mr. Betts notes in his MS. that a "silver piece of Louis XVI, for the Colony of Cayenne is mentioned in Med. Rep., 1805, iii, 357." He was uncertain whether the piece he describes was identical with that to which he refers. Cayenne is the principal city in French Guiana, and it seems probable that the two pieces are identical. — EDS.

* In the Historical Magazine, X, 158 (1866), is a note to the editor, dated March 27, 1860 (*sic*), from Toledo, Ohio, signed H. H., asking for an explanation of the device on the reverse of this Medal, of which he had an impression, "taken from the grave of Otussa (a son of the celebrated Pontiac), on Presque Isle, at the mouth of the Shawnee river:" the note further mentions that it had been originally worn by Pontiac himself. As there described, the lion is "complacently watching a barking cur....behind the lion are houses and all the evidences of civilization.... behind the cur seems to be an unbroken wilderness." The query was not answered, we believe, certainly not in that year; but if the statement is true that Pontiac wore the Medal, and we see no reason to doubt it, it enables us to fix the date of striking it as about the close of the French and Indian war; Pontiac made peace with the English in the summer of 1765, and July 23, 1766, he was presented by Sir William Johnson, at Oswego, N. Y., with numerous gifts (see Parkman's "History of the Conspiracy of Pontiac," chap. XXXI), among which we may believe, was this Medal, and that others from the same dies were bestowed on his chiefs. This also serves to explain the device; the lion represents Great Britain, who had completed the conquest of the French possessions in America, which are typified by the wilderness and the snarling wolf, that animal having not unfrequently been used to symbolize France. The Medal has been a troublesome one to explain. McLachlan says: "I have been at a loss to know on what account this was struck, but in a Catalogue of British War Medals....sold in London about four years ago, it is described as an

SPANISH INDIAN(?) MEDAL.

536. *Obv.* CARLOS III REY D'ESPANA E DE LAS INDIAS. (Charles III, King of Spain and the Indies.) Bust of the King.

Rev. POR MERITO (For merit) within a wreath of cactus. Silver. Size 36. Rare.

This Medal was discovered at Prairie du Chien about 1864, and is now in the Wisconsin Historical Society's Cabinet. It is supposed to have been given by Don Francisco Cruzat, the Spanish Governor, to Huisconsin, a Mitasse chief of the Sauks and Foxes.

MEXICAN ACADEMY.

537. *Obv.* CARLOS * III * REY * DE * ESPANA *. EMPERA-DOR * DE * INDIAS (Charles III, King of Spain and Emperor of the Indies). Under truncation, GIL Bust of the King to right, undraped, laureate.

Rev. AL | MERITO (To merit), within a wreath of laurel.*
Copper. Size 26.

Indian Chief's Medal....It is likely that the design represents the American wolf frightened away from Canada, represented by the Church, by British vigilance, the lion." McLachlan's explanation, though ingenious, can hardly be accepted; the wolf is not the symbol of "America" — (by which expression here the United States alone can be meant) —and at the time this was struck the Anglo-American Colonies were still under the British crown. A specimen is in Mr. McLachlan's collection, and another is reported to be in the Mint Cabinet (possibly the same as the Toledo piece *supra*, as it is said to have been "found in the grave of an Indian warrior "), and one or two others are known.— EDS.

* This was a Prize Medal of the Academy in the City of Mexico. "Gil" was an engraver at the Mint in that City, but its date we have not found. [Gaillard, 7068.] — EDS.

CHAPTER VIII.

THE PERIOD OF THE REVOLUTIONARY WAR.

OT many Medals directly referring to the events of the Revolutionary War have an English origin, and the resources of the struggling Colonies did not often permit them to honor the gallant deeds of their leaders by numismatic monuments before their independence was attained. Such as were struck by order of the Continental Congress were engraved abroad. Yet the sympathy for the cause of America, and the resentment which was generally felt at the course of Great Britain, made itself manifest by several Medals issued on the Continent, and especially in Holland, where a number of historic interest to American collectors were struck.[*]

Nearly one hundred years before, in 1677, the City of Amsterdam had ordered a Medal to be issued, referring directly

---

[*] There are Medals of Lord North, the British Minister who endeavored to conquer the Colonies, of Lafayette and Kosciuzko, and many more of Washington and Franklin,— beside those given in the text, — which were unquestionably known to Mr. Betts, but were intentionally omitted by him, since they evidently were not struck in the period of which he wrote. He has described a few Medals which for the same reason might have been excluded, although bearing dates which apparently entitle them to a place in this volume, or which have no date to show when they appeared; this he may have done for the sake of completeness, following the example of " Medallic Illustrations," or it may have been his intention to omit them in the final revision, which it must be remembered his death prevented his completing. These the Editors have commented on, as they occur.— EDS.

to the Peace of Breda, which bears the Batavian lion and a commemorative inscription, and which has sometimes been classed among American Historical Medals from the indirect influence which the cession of New York to Great Britain by the Netherlands, under that Treaty, had on the final result,* but which seemed to have rather too remote a connection to give it a place in this volume. As early as 1777 the King of Prussia declared his willingness to recognize the independence of the United States, refraining from doing so lest he might injure their cause rather than aid it ; and Catharine of Russia bluntly told the English Ambassador that England "could in a moment restore peace, by renouncing her colonies " — a remark which is said to be the foundation of the traditional friendship between America and Russia.

The League of "Armed Neutrality" between the various European powers in 1780, who united in a compact to resist the maritime claims of Great Britain, involved several of them in war with that country ; and all were hostile, either actually or by their avowed sympathy with the young Republic, thus aiding the cause of American liberty. Several of the Medals described below refer to this Treaty, and to events consequent upon it. The active aid of France is commemorated by Medals described in the next and concluding Chapter. There are a few others, which by their dates are properly included in the period now to be considered, though having no reference to the Revolution.

BATTLE OF BUNKER HILL.

538. 1775. *Obv.* A · TESTIMONY · OF · PUBLIC · REGARD ✠ G. R. in script, crowned, on the field.

Rev. Inscription in seven lines ; By Order | of the King | with 300 Pound | for the Wound | Capt. Ewing Receiv'd | the 17 of June, | 1775.

---

* See a valuable paper by Geo. M. Parsons, LL. D., on the subject, in A. J. N., **XXIII**, pp. 4 and 5, where the obverse is illustrated. — EDS.

Silver.   A circle on the centre of a diamond-shaped planchet, with flames issuing between the points.   Engraved.*
Size 32 point to point.   Unique.   "The Antiquary," London,
1871, p. 189.   Hamilton Sale, London, 1882, 446.   Tancred
(illustrated), p. 48.

LOYAL REFUGEES.

539.   1776 (?)   *Obv.* VIVANT ✦ REX ✦ & ✦ REGINA ✦ (Long
live the King and Queen!)   Clothed busts of King George
III and Queen Charlotte, conjoined, to the right.   The
King wears a wig, tied with a bow behind; the Queen
has a small coronet.

Rev. LOYAL ASSOCIATED REFUGEES on a ribbon at the top
of the planchet ; a chain (?) from each end completes the circle around the device.   Britannia seated on a platform at the
right, presenting an olive branch to an Indian with her right
hand; her left rests on a shield with the British crosses ;
behind the Indian, who wears a crown of feathers, is a palm
tree and hogshead ; behind Britannia, who is armed with a

---

* An engraving of both obverse and reverse is given the London Antiquary,
Dec. 2, 1871, *loc. cit.*, and also in Tancred.   Capt. Ewing " received his wound
while gallantly leading the Grenadier Company " at Bunker Hill.   See A. J. N.,
VII, 44.   The Medal subsequently passed into the collection of J. W. Fleming,
F. R. C. S., Edin., Surgeon-Major late 4th Dragoon Guards.   The Medal is engraved, as stated in the text, but has so frequently been mentioned in Numismatic periodicals that Mr. Betts decided to include it in his list.— EDS.

spear, is a fort, or possibly the stern of a ship, with a curious flag flying to the left from a staff.

Copper gilt, and brass, with ring for suspension struck with the Medal. Size 21. Rare.* A. J. N., VII, 61.

UNION OF THE COLONIES.

540. *Obv.* + CONFEDERATIO + AMERICANA . JUVENUS (*sic*) (The youthful American Confederation). A radiated star, formed by thirteen angular rays terminating in a circle surrounded by dots; on its centre is a triangle of thirteen stars enclosing the letter G.

Rev. TYRANNIS . IN PERPETUUM . ABEIT . TERRA (Let the earth be forever free from tyrants). An Indian at the right, with a tobacco leaf in his left hand, and extending his right to a dove flying toward him with an olive-branch in its beak; a wigwam at the left; a circle of dots surrounds the device within the legend.

Copper. Size 18 nearly. Rare.† B., 49, No. 885.

---

* Nothing seems to be known of the history of this Medal, and we have not learned why Mr. Betts placed it under 1775, to which we add the query. The Loyalists who left when Howe evacuated Boston, in 1776, or those who founded St. John, New Brunswick, at the close of the Revolution, may perhaps be alluded to, but if the latter, the piece must have been struck more than ten years later.—Eds.

† From an account of this Medal in Hist. Mag., V. p. 340, it seems to have been first noticed at a meeting of the Boston Numismatic Society, in October, 1861, where it was shown as "a remarkable piece lately found in Philadelphia," and the description there differs, reading JUVENIS and ABIET: it does not mention the *triangle*, and places the leaf in the Indian's *right* hand while his *left* is extended. The Medal in the Bushnell Sale was from the Mickley cabinet, and the text follows the [Chapmans'] description in that Catalogue (*loc. cit.*), which says only two are known, and that the die was cracked. Mr. Betts assigned no year to it in his description, and as we have been unable to fix its date with certainty, we leave it in the order where his MS. placed it, but believe it to be of a much later period than its position here would indicate. While the *thirteen* stars enclosed in a large single star of rays and the obverse legend suggest the "Confederatio" coins of 1785, the letter G, probably for the emblem of Deity, instead of the All-seeing Eye used on the "Constellatios," would lead us to assign it to the present century. An impression of what may have been the same Medal was shown at the meeting of the same Society in March, 1874, by Mr. Appleton (see A. J. N., VIII, 87), but the account there given differs from each

PENNSYLVANIA COUNCIL OF SAFETY.

541. 1776. *Obv.* • PENNSYLVANIA • COUNCIL • OF • SAFETY • 1776 | THIS • IS • MY • RIGHT & I • WILL • DEFEND • IT | in two circles surrounding a liberty cap upon a pole; the outer legend between two beaded circles.

Rev. Plain.

Copper. Size 32. A. J. N., II, 72; X, 94.* •

WASHINGTON:—SIEGE OF BOSTON.

542. 1776. *Obv.* GEORGIO WASHINGTON SVPREMO DVCI EXERCITVVM ADSERTORI LIBERTATIS and below the bust, COMITIA AMERICANA (The American Congress to George Washington, General-in-Chief of the Armies, the Defender of Liberty). Naked bust of Washington to right, his hair dressed with a cue tied with a bow of ribbon; under the decollation, DUVIVIER PARIS F.

Rev. HOSTIBUS PRIMO FUGATIS (The enemy for the first time put to flight). At the left a group — Washington with four officers, all on horseback; with his right hand he points

---

of the others : it gives the legends as in the text, but instead of the "triangle" "in the centre [is] a G in a circle of *fifteen* stars round which are *fifteen* rays, pointing inwards.....The number of stars and rays has suggested a possible connection with the Southern Confederacy." We are unable to harmonize these descriptions. Whether that in Bushnell is incorrect, or whether there are two differing dies of the reverse, we cannot now determine, but of the accuracy of Mr. Appleton's description we have no doubt. It appears from his record of the meeting, that it was given from an impression in *silver*, which was in his own collection. If its reference is to the Confederacy, which the blunder in the die has been thought to indicate, the engraver anticipated that all the slave-holding States would secede from the Union, which was not the case.—EDS.

* An impression of this piece was in the collection of Mons. Alex. Vattemare, as appears from A. J. N. (*loc. cit.*). The "Council of Safety" was an association of patriotic citizens, and similar organizations existed in the various Colonies throughout the war. The following note printed in A. J. N., X, 94, explains the piece, which may be an impression of a seal and not a Medal :—
"Philadelphia, Aug. 31, 1775. At a meeting of the Committee of Safety, held this day, *Resolved*, That Owen Biddle provide a Seal for the use of the Board, about the size of a dollar, with a cap of Liberty, with this motto : 'This is my right, and I will defend it.'"—EDS.

to a city in the distance; at the right a fort, and near it two cannon, on one ᴅᴜᴠɪᴠ. and cannon-balls lying on the ground; in the middle distance soldiers under arms; beyond is a view of Boston, lying near the water, on which are several vessels sailing away. In exergue, ʙᴏsᴛᴏɴɪᴜᴍ ʀᴇᴄᴜᴘᴇʀᴀᴛᴜᴍ . xᴠɪɪ ᴍᴀʀᴛɪɪ . ᴍᴅᴄᴄʟxxᴠɪ . (Boston recovered, March 17, 1776.)

Gold (unique), silver and bronze. Size 43. A. J. N., VII, 73; VIII, 27; XV (with plate*), 1. B., p. 88. Loubat.

543. 1776. *Obv.* From the same die as the preceding.

Rev. As the preceding, from the same die, with the erasure of one leg of a horse, in the group of mounted officers.

Bronze, in the Appleton collection. Size 43. A. J. N., VII, 74. Loubat.

WASHINGTON.

544. 1777. *Obv.* ɢᵘ. ᴡᴀsʜɪɴɢᴛᴏɴ ᴇᴿ. ɢᴇɴᴇʀᴀʟ ᴏғ ᴛʜᴇ ᴄᴏɴᴛɪɴˡ. ᴀʀᴍʏ ɪɴ ᴀᴍᴇʀɪᴄᴀ. Head of Washington (?), facing the right.

Rev. ᴡᴀsʜɪɴ. ʀᴇᴜɴɪᴛ ᴘᴀʀ ᴜɴ ʀᴀʀᴇ ᴀssᴇᴍʙʟᴀɢᴇ. ʟᴇs ᴛᴀʟᴇɴs ᴅᴜ ɢᴜᴇʀʀɪᴇʀ & ʟᴇs ᴠᴇʀᴛᴜs ᴅᴜ sᴀɢᴇ (Washington combines by a singular union the talents of a warrior and the virtues of a philosopher). A military trophy, consisting of a

---

* This Medal, commemorating the evacuation of Boston by the British, after its siege by the American troops under Washington, was struck in France by order of Congress; a full account will be found in A. J. N., XV, 1. The original, in gold, presented to Washington, by a Committee of the Continental Congress (the Hon. John Adams, Hon. John Jay, afterwards Chief Justice of the U. S., and Hon. Stephen Hopkins, of Rhode Island,) was purchased from the widow of George Lafayette Washington, whose husband was a descendant of an elder brother of Gen. Washington, and presented to the City of Boston by a number of gentlemen resident in that city, on the Centennial Anniversary of the evacuation. An impression in silver is in the Cabinet of the Massachusetts Historical Society, which once belonged to Washington and subsequently to Daniel Webster, and another, in bronze, is in that of Mr. W. S. Appleton. Though dated 1776, it was struck several years later. Pierre Simon Du Vivier, the engraver, was born in Paris, Nov. 5, 1731; engraver-general of the Paris Mint prior to 1793, and died June 10, 1819. He was a grandson of Jean, the first of the famous family of French Medallists of the name. — ᴇᴅs.

cannon, a mortar, balls, a drum, a trumpet and flags, resting on the ground, and surrounded above by a halo of rays.

Silver, rare, in the Appleton collection, and bronze. Size 25½. A. J. N., VII, 74.*

BENJAMIN FRANKLIN.

545. *Obv.* BEN^{N} FRANKLIN L. L. D. Bust of Franklin to left in wig and coat.

Rev. Plain.

Bronze. Size 24 nearly. Num. Chron., 1891, p. 101.†

546. 1776. *Obv.* LIGHTNING AVERTED TYRANNY REPELL'D Bust of Franklin, facing the right.

Rev. An oak tree, at the trunk of which a beaver is gnawing, and at the right a bunch of reeds. In exergue, 1776.‡

Silver, Appleton cabinet, and bronze. Size 26. A. J. N., VII, 49. B., p. 80.

---

* Mr. Appleton, in his list of Washingtons, in A. J. N. (*loc. cit.*), says: "This Medal appeared in France during the Revolutionary War, and is probably first mentioned in April, 1778, by Samuel Curwen, who says in his Journal that it had been lately struck for M. Voltaire." A correspondent of A. J. N. (see IV, 34), mentions that the head on this Medal bears no resemblance to Washington, but is believed to be a likeness of Jeremy Bentham, "which Voltaire thought proper to use in the absence of any portrait of Washington himself, and the lines on the reverse may be presumed to have originated with the author of the Henriade, in which poem they are perhaps to be found....Its historical value is enhanced by the fact that Voltaire died in the month following its issue,— May 30, 1778." See also Snowden's "Medals of Washington." Only two are at present known in silver.— EDS.

† The Numismatic Chronicle says that "the dies of this Medal were probably cut by Wm. Mossop." This was the elder Mossop, of Dublin, one of the most distinguished Medallists of his time, who died, we are informed, in 1804. The date of this Medal is not determined; the authority quoted thinks it may have been struck on the occasion of his reception of the Doctorate of Laws at St. Andrew's, Edinboro, and at Oxford, or previous to 1762. If so, it is probably the earliest of the Franklin Medals. He had been elected a member of the Royal Society, and presented with the Copley Medal in 1753. — EDS.

‡ Although this Medal is dated 1776, it was struck at the United States Mint early in the present century, and is often spoken of as the Sansom Medal, from the gentleman under whose direction the dies were prepared by Jacob Reich. The device of the beaver (which symbolizes America), gnawing the oak-tree (the emblem of Great Britain), was used on the Continental money.— EDS.

547.   1777.   *Obv.* B. FRANKLIN OF PHILADELPHIA L.L..D. & F.R.S.   Young bust facing, turned toward left, wearing a loose cap, and drapery about the neck.

Rev. NON IRRITA FULMINA CURAT (He cares not for the ineffectual thunderbolt).   In exergue, 1777 +   A tree struck by lightning from a cloud at the left.*

Bronze.   Size 28½.   A. J. N., VII, 49.   B., p. 80.

548.   1777.   *Obv.* B . FRANKLIN . AMERICAIN .   (B. Franklin, the American.)   1777 (date *incuse*).   On truncation, NINI . F . 1777 Clothed bust to left in a fur cap.†

Rev. No legend ; a ring of chased work.

Bronze, cast and chased, and reverse turned in lathe.   Size —.   Dr. Thos. A. Emmet's collection.   See A. J. N., V, 89.

---

* The date of this is somewhat uncertain.   The Numismatic Chronicle (1891, p. 101) thinks it may have been struck on the occasion of the Inquiry of the Privy Council of England, relative to certain political papers, which it was charged he had clandestinely obtained and forwarded to America.— EDS.

† In A. J. N. (*loc. cit.*) will be found an account of a large medallion by the same artist, of similar design, which was exhibited at a meeting in March, 1871, of the Boston Numismatic Society.   That was " of a red tile, four and a half inches across the face, and the portrait is raised from the surface nearly a quarter of an inch.   The coat is collarless, the waist coat is buttoned close up to the throat, and the ends of what we presume is a white handkerchief, are knotted under the double chin.   His head is crowned with a fur cap — fez style — with a tassel on the top.   The features are strongly brought out, and the delicate lines about the eyes are plainly discernible....A coat of arms, the design of which we fail to discern, appears under Franklin's shoulder where the clay is

WASHINGTON AND FRANKLIN.

549. 1776. *Obv.* No legend. Busts of Washington and Franklin, facing the left.

Rev. As reverse of 546.*

Bronze.   Size 26.   A. J. N., VII, 74.

CONTINENTAL ARMY.

550. 1776. *Obv.* FRANGIMUR SI COLLIDIMUR (We are broken if we clash).   Two vases swimming on the water.

Rev. Legend, if any, not mentioned.   Four hands clasped together; a dove above, and a serpent cut in pieces below.

Silver and copper.   Size not given.   A. J. N., XXI, 22.†

---

cut off square." Dr. S. A. Green showed this medallion at the meeting mentioned, and said that it was probably the one alluded to by Franklin in a letter to his daughter, Mrs. Bache, dated Passy, June 3, 1779, where he says: "the clay medallion of me....was the first of the kind made in France. A variety of others have been made since of different sizes; some to be set in the lids of snuff boxes, and some so small as to be worn in rings." The Medal described in the text appears to be one of the smaller reproductions. "The coat of arms, so called," said Dr. Green, "is undoubtedly the private mark of Nini....The fur collar and lining were the habitual badge of the Master Printer of the olden times, and a fur cap would naturally go with them. An engraving of this Medal of reduced size, is to be found in Lossing's 'Field Book of the Revolution, II, 855.'" Jean Baptiste Nini was born at Urbino, Italy, in 1717. He resided in Paris, and died at Chaumont in 1786; he was noted for his skill as an engraver on glass, and his work in terra-cotta. A still larger medallion, even rarer than the above, by the same artist, is in Mr. Appleton's collection. — EDS.

* The note on 546, applies equally to this. — EDS.

† No impression of this Medal is known to us. The description in A. J. N. (*loc. cit.*), is quoted from a newspaper article of Aug. 12, 1776, which further states: "The Congress have struck a number of silver and copper Medals, which are distributed among the officers of the Army, who wear them constantly....These Medals were designed or executed by P. E. Du Simitiere." Mr. M. A. Stickney, of Salem, Mass., who furnished the Journal with the above cutting, further mentions that the Journals of Congress, Nov. 29, 1776, p. 485, have:—"Paid P. E. Du Simitiere for designing, making and drawing a Medal for Gen. Washington, $32." The artist was a painter from Geneva, who resided in Philadelphia for many years and was living there in 1782. The device of the floating jars, with its accompanying motto, is quite an old one (several Medals bearing it being given by Van Loon); it was used on the Continental paper money. That of the serpent divided into thirteen pieces, each part lettered with the initial of one of the Colonies, and the motto "Join or die" was also a favorite Continental emblem.— EDS.

LORD NORTH.

551. (1776?) *Obv.* FRIDERICUS ' BARO : NORTH ' ORD : PERISCEL : EQVES (Frederick, Baron North, Knight of the Order of the Garter). Profile bust to left ; he wears a wig tied with a bow, and an embroidered coat. Below the truncation, GOSSET M. KIRK F.

Rev. SU : ÆRAR : PR : CANC : SCACC : ET : ACAD : OXON : MDCCLXXV (First Lord of the Treasury, Chancellor of the Exchequer, and of Oxford University). On a mantle surmounted with a Baron's coronet an elliptical shield, bearing azure a lion passant or between three fleurs-de-lis argent ; in chief a label ; the shield is surrounded with a ribbon bearing the motto of the Order of the Garter (Honi soit, etc.), and the collar and George are suspended below : a palm-branch and caduceus at the right, crossed by a mace at the left, beneath the shield.

Silver. Size 24. Lossing (illus.) *

CAPTAIN JAMES COOK.†

552. 1776 (?) *Obv.* GEORGE . III . KING . OF . GR . BRITAIN . FRANCE . AND IRELAND . ETC . Head of the King, laureated, to right ; on the decollation, B. F. (Barnet fecit.)

---

* Frederick, Lord North (second Earl of Guilford), born April 13, 1733, was a son of Francis, who died in 1790—the 'label' on the arms on the Medal showing that he was the eldest son, and that his father was living when that was struck. He became one of the "Lords of the Treasury" about 1760 : he was subsequently Chancellor of the Exchequer, and was made Prime Minister by George III in 1770. During his administration he prosecuted the war against the United States with great pertinacity, holding his office until the surrender of Cornwallis at Yorktown terminated the Revolution. He became Earl of Guilford in 1790, and died Aug. 5, 1792. Lord Brougham has said that "The American War was the great blot on his fame." The obverse was modelled by Isaac Gosset, an eminent artist of Huguenot descent. He invented a composition of wax, in which he modelled portraits of several of the Royal house. He was born in 1712, and died at Kensington, Nov. 28, 1799. — EDS.

† Captain James Cook, whose explorations in the Western Hemisphere and his voyage around the world have immortalized his name, was born at Marton, Yorkshire, England, Oct. 27, 1728; he served as Master of a vessel at the capture of Quebec, by Wolfe, in 1759, and was Marine Surveyor of Newfoundland

Rev. RESOLVTION . ADVENTVRE . [The names of his ships.] In exergue, SAILED . FROM . ENGLAND . MARCH . M DCC LXXII. Two ships on the sea.

Gold, silver and bronze.	Size 27.	Num. Chron., Third Series, X, 72.

553.	1776 (?). *Obv.* IAC · COOK OCEANI INVESTIGATOR ACER-RIMVS (James Cook, the most ardent explorer of the Ocean). Profile bust of Cook to the left, wearing a naval uniform and tied wig.	Below, in two lines curving to conform to the edge, RRG · SOC · LOND · | SOCIO SVO (The Royal Society, London, to their Fellow).*	Under truncation, L. P. F. (Lewis Pingo, fecit).

Rev. NIL INTENTATVM NOSTRI LIQVERE (Our [associates] leave nothing untried).	Fortune, typified by a female figure, stands facing left, and leaning against a rostral column; in her right hand she holds a rudder, which rests on a globe; in her left is a spear; at the right of the column is an oval

and Labrador, 1764-68.	This Medal commemorates his arrival home from his second voyage, when he was elected a Fellow of the Royal Society (on Feb. 29, 1776, or by some authorities in March of the previous year), and the Society's Copley Medal, struck in gold, was presented to him for his discoveries.— EDS.

* This is the Royal Society's Medal for Capt. Cook.	"As a special honor" says Num. Chron. (*loc. cit.*) "this had Cook's head on the obverse, instead of the regular die."	The reverse legend is from Horace, Epistola ad Pisonem, 285, where the word which follows is *Poetae,* for which we have supplied "Asso-ciates."	For Pingo, see Note on 531.	The accounts of the date of striking are conflicting: A. J. N. (*loc. cit.*) says it was not struck till 1784. — EDS.

shield with the British crosses. In exergue, in three lines,
AVSPICIIS | GEORGII | III (Under the auspices of George III).

Gold, silver and bronze. Size 27. A. J. N., II, 38; Num.
Chron., Third Series, X, 73 (illus.).

554. 1779 (?) *Obv.* CAPT. JAMES COOK. Bust of Cook to
right, in naval uniform and tied wig.

Rev. Inscription in four lines, KILL'D BY THE INDIANS AT
O'WHY'HEE, FEBRUARY 14, 1779. The words are separated by
rosettes of six leaves. In exergue, an oak branch .

White metal. Size 24. Num. Chron., Third Series, X, 73.

555. 1779 (?) *Obv.* Similar to the preceding.

Rev. Inscription in three lines, COURAGE | AND | PERSEVER-
ANCE A flower above. In exergue, BORN 1728, DIED 1779.

White metal. Size 24. Num. Chron., Third Series, X, 73.†

BATTLE OF GERMANTOWN, PA.

556. 1777. *Obv.* GERMAN | TOWN | OCT. 4 · 1777 in a
laurel wreath.

---

* Cook sailed from England on his third voyage July 12, 1776. He discovered the Sandwich (or Hawaiian) Islands in 1778, and was killed by the natives
of Owhyhee (or Hawaii) in Kealakeakua Bay, on the west side of that Island,
Feb. 14, 1779.—EDS.

† There is another Medal of Cook (in the Series Numismatica), of later
date. — EDS.

Rev. No legend.   View of the battle at the Chew house ; the building in the background and troops with cannon in the foreground.   In exergue, J. MILTON F.

Sometimes engraved on obverse with the words "40TH REG." above the word "Germantown," and on the reverse "*Reward of merit*" (in script) with a soldier's name above the house.

Silver, rare, and copper.   Size 28.   Usually pierced.   Tancred (illustrated), p. 332.*

BURGOYNE'S SURRENDER AT SARATOGA.

557.   1777.   *Obv.* HORATIO GATES DUCI STRENUO and in exergue, COMITIA AMERICANA (The American Congress to Horatio Gates, the valiant Commander).   Profile bust of Gen. Gates in uniform to left ; at the right, below the decollation, N. GATTEAUX.

Rev. SALUS REGIONUM SEPTENTRIONAL. and in exergue, HOSTE AD SARATOGAM | IN DEDITION. ACCEPTO | DIE XVII. OCT. MDCCLXXVII. (The safety of the Northern Regions secured by the surrender of the enemy received at Saratoga, Oct. 17, 1777.)   Gen. Gates at the right receiving the sword of Gen. Burgoyne ; behind Gates are soldiers under arms, and near them an olive branch ; behind Burgoyne are soldiers laying down their arms ; on the ground between the officers are a drum, flag, mortar and cannon-balls ; in the distance are hills ; below, at the left, GATTEAUX F.

---

* This is an English Medal on the Battle of Germantown, Pa., and commemorates the occupation and defence of Chew's house at Shippock Creek, near that place, by troops of the 40th British Regiment, under Lieut. Col. Musgrave. Lossing, in his " Field-book of the Revolution " (II, 114), says that though the Americans retreated from almost certain victory, no blame was attached to Washington and his officers, by Congress, who when his letter was read describing the battle, passed a vote of thanks "for his wise and well-concerted attack upon the enemy's army near Germantown," and to " the officers and soldiers of the army for their brave exertions upon that occasion."   A " Medal was ordered to be struck and presented to Gen. Washington.   It was never executed."   [See A. J. N., V, 62.]   John Milton, the engraver, was an assistant at the Royal Mint from 1789 to 1798; his works date from 1760.   He was also Medallist to the Prince of Wales.   [See Med. Ill.]   An impression of this Medal in copper, pierced, was in the Balmanno Sale, June, 1885, and brought $18.25.   See A. J. N., XX, 21.— EDS.

Gold (presented to Gen. Gates), silver (Webster collection, in the cabinet of the Mass. Hist. Soc.), and bronze.* Size 36. A. J. N., IX, 27. Loubat. Wyatt.

FRANCE PREPARES TO AID AMERICA.

558. 1777. *Obv.* LUDOV. XVI. REX CHRISTIANIS. (Louis XVI, Most Christian King.) Bust of the King to right.

Rev. PACEM ARMA TUENTUR. (Arms preserve peace.) In exergue, EXTRAORDINAIRE | DES GUERRES | 1777. (This may be understood to mean Special issue of the War Department.†) Mars reposing at the right with spear and shield ; Peace at the left lays one hand upon his shoulder and with the other points him away.

Silver. Size 18.

---

* An impression in gold was by Vote of Congress, Nov. 4, 1777, presented to Gen. Gates, Commander-in-chief of the Northern Department, through its President, in the name of the United States, in recognition of his victory over Burgoyne at Saratoga, which secured the alliance of France. The dies were cut in France (according to Wyatt, under the direction of Thos. Jefferson), by Nicolas Marie Gatteaux, an eminent French Medallist, who was born in Paris Aug. 2, 1751, and died there, June 24, 1832. He was appointed Engraver of Medals by Louis XVI, and executed several by request of the American Government. The silver Medal mentioned in the text, and others in silver of this series presented to American officers, were struck by the French Government, and presented to Washington ; from his estate they passed into the hands of Daniel Webster, and thence to their present ownership. Mr. J. F. Loubat's magnificent work has engravings of all the U. S. Revolutionary Medals, and Lossing's Field Book of the Revolution has illustrations of several of those described in this chapter. Gen. Gates was born in Malden, England, in 1728 ; he served with the British army, under Braddock, and in consequence of a wound received in battle, resigned and settled in Virginia. His military experience procured for him a high rank in the Continental army, but after his defeat by Cornwallis at Camden, S. C., in 1780, he was superseded, and though honorably acquitted by an "inquiry," he took no further part in the war, and died April 10, 1806.— EDS.

† It was the custom of the different Departments of the French Government to issue jetons occasionally, having reference to some special event in their administration, and this piece belongs to that class. From its device it seems to allude to the fact that France was preparing to take an active part in the alliance with the Colonies against Great Britain ; hence, although it bears no direct allusion to America, Mr. Betts included it in his list.— EDS.

ADMIRAL HOWE.

559. 1777. *Obv.* ADMI^L EARL HOWE. Bust to right, in cocked hat and naval uniform.

Rev. BRITAN   NIA . Below, 1777. Figure of Britannia seated and facing the left.*

Brass. Size 14.

GERMAN PEACE MEDAL.

560. 1778. *Obv.* 𝕭etracht die 𝕮laag 𝕾ie bringt am 𝕮ag 𝕱reud oder 𝕻lag (*sic*) (Consider the balance, it brings each day joy or trouble). A balance supported by a hand projecting from the clouds, and holding in one scale crossed swords and in the other branches of palm and olive; below the balance a globe inscribed AMERICA EVROPA ASIA AFRICA; behind and around the globe, standards, cannon, sword, drums, trumpets, cannon-balls, etc.

Rev. 𝕱aſt will die | 𝕲anze 𝕮𝕮elt Geweʒte | 𝕾chwerder ſieben ! 𝕳𝕰𝕽𝕽 | laſſe 𝕶ron und 𝕮hron die | 𝕱riedens 𝕻almen bluhen 𝕾prich | ʒu der ganʒen 𝕮𝕮elt 𝕾prich | ʒu den 𝕮eutſchen REICH | dies groſe 𝕾egens 𝕮𝕮ort | 𝕱𝕶ein 𝕱ride ſep mit 𝕰uch In exergue, 1778. (Nearly the whole world have whet their swords ! O Lord,

---

* Admiral Howe was Richard, second son of Lord Emmanuel Scrope Howe; he became Viscount (with an Irish title), in 1758, on the death of his elder brother. His English title of Earl was gained in 1788, as mentioned in note on 524; this Medal, from the date on the reverse, seems to have been struck not long after he was appointed to the command of the British fleet, on the coast of the United States.

let Crown and Throne blossom with palms of peace. Speak Thou to all the world—speak Thou to the German Empire this great word of blessing, My Peace be with you. 1778).
Tin. Size 24.*

RHODE ISLAND.

561. 1779. *Obv.* D'Vlugtende AMERICAANE^N van ROHDE YLAND Aug! 1778 (The flying Americans of Rhode Island, August, 1778). View of the island, with troops crossing to right; three ships at left and thirteen boats at right; palm branches crossed below.

Rev. DE ADMIRAALS FLAG van ADMIRAAL HOWE 1779 and below VLUGTENDE (Admiral Howe's flagship flying, 1779). Flagship, with sails furled, to right.
Brass. Size 20. Rare. A. J. N., II, 54, 80; XXI, 13.†

---

* This Medal, the history of which has not been learned, is not mentioned in Van Loon's Supplement. It evidently alludes to the unsettled state of affairs at the time of striking, and the apprehension of coming war, in which the European powers were soon to be involved. France had recently signed the Treaty of Alliance with the United States, and was preparing to lend them active aid; England had secured the assistance of Hessian troops, while the antipathy to Great Britain, caused by her maritime claims, which soon after led to the League of Armed Neutrality to resist them, (referred to in the introduction to this Chapter), was already creating a sympathy for the United States, only half suppressed. The legend on the obverse is a rhyming triplet. The reverse legend, it will be noticed, is a stanza of eight lines. "Am Tag" might perhaps be rendered "from day to day," *i. e.*, alternately, now joy, now trouble.— EDS.

† This piece has been somewhat of a puzzle to American collectors, as it was to Muller, the editor of the Supplement to Van Loon. That writer remarks "Although the Medal has Dutch inscriptions, the spelling and design indicate an English or Anglo-American origin....It may have been a mere speculation." It was almost unknown to American collectors, until an impression was sold in Woodward's Fifth Semi-Annual Sale, June 21, 22 (Seavey collection), 1864, for the remarkable price of $40, the result of two unlimited bids having been sent to dealers. It was then attributed to Dutch sympathizers with the British side; but the bravery of the Americans which attended their retreat, after an encounter, which Lafayette declared to be the "best fought action of the war" [See Arnold's History of Rhode Island, II, 428], was a matter of pride, and Mr. Bushnell first advocated the opinion that it was not unfavorable to the Colonial side. He thought that while the obverse commemorates the retreat of the Americans, on the night of August 30, 1778, and may perhaps have been intended to ridicule the Continental troops, yet the inability of the British to hold the fruits of their

562. 1779. *Obv.* Same die as the preceding.

Rev. Same as preceding except that the word "vlugtende" has been removed.

Brass. Size 20. A. J. N., II, 54, 80. V. L. Supp., 537.

563. 1779. *Obv.* Same as last.

Rev. Same as preceding except that scroll work is substituted for the word "vlugtende" below the ship.

Silver, copper, brass and pewter. Size 20. A. J. N., II, 54, 80.*

KEPPEL VINDICATED.

564. 1779. *Obv.* THE HON[BLE] AUGUSTUS KEPPEL ADMI[RL] of ⸴ Blue. Bust facing three-quarters to right.†

victory was equally satirized by the reverse, their fleet sailing away from Narraganset Bay, and their troops evacuating Rhode Island in October of the following year under orders from the British Ministry, to which the same word *vlugtende* is applied under the Admiral's ship on one of the varieties. Mr. Geo. T. Paine, in a communication to the A. J. N., II, 80, takes the ground that it was struck in Holland, by some sympathizer with the Americans, who intended by the obverse to compliment the Americans on their successful retreat, and by the reverse to ridicule the English on their inability to hold their possessions. The Medal, it must be confessed, is sufficiently ambiguous to satisfy both parties, and we think that was its original design.— EDS.

* See a paper on these Medals by Dr. H. R. Storer, of Newport, R. I., in A. J. N., XXI, 13.— EDS.

† Admiral Keppel, born in Suffolk, England, April 2, 1725, was an eminent English Commander. He accompanied Anson on his voyage around the world [see 382], and won distinction in several engagements with the French. He was appointed Admiral in command of the British Channel fleet on the outbreak of hostilities between England and France, after the alliance of the latter with the American Colonies; and an indecisive action between the French and British

Rev. JUSTICE TRIUMPHANT and MALICE DEFEATED In exergue, Feb : 11 : 1779. Justice standing with sword and scales, and trampling Malice under foot ; a ship of war at left.
Brass. Size 22.

STORMING OF STONY POINT, N. Y.

565. 1779. *Obv.* ANTONIO WAYNE DUCI EXERCITUS and in exergue, COMITIA AMERICANA (The American Congress to Anthony Wayne, General of the Army). An Indian Queen, symbolical of America, at the left, holds a mural crown in' her left hand, and with her right presents a laurel wreath to Gen. Wayne ; she wears a cap, and a skirt of feathers ; at her feet are an alligator, a rope, and the shield of the United States ; below the General, GATTRAUX.

Rev. STONEY-POINT EXPUGNATUM (Stony Point taken by storm). In exergue, XV JUL. MDCCLXXIX. (July 15, 1779.) A view of the assault, including both sides of the Hudson river ; the fort in the distance, a battery and troops in the foreground at the right ; below at the left, GATTRAUX.

Gold (presented to Gen. Wayne*), silver (Webster collection, in the cabinet of the Mass. Hist. Soc.), and bronze. Size 34. A. J. N., IX, 27. Loubat. Lossing. Wyatt.

---

fleets off Ushant, July 27, 1778, led Sir Hugh Palliser to accuse him of neglect of duty, and he was tried by Court Martial, Jan. 7 to Feb. 11, 1779, and acquitted. This piece commemorates that fact. He held various high positions under the King, and was raised to the Peerage as Viscount, April 8, 1782. He died at Suffolk, Oct. 3, 1786. Another with different reverse, which may refer to the same event, was in the Bushnell Sale, but the description is too meagre to enable us to judge. — EDS.

* Gen. Wayne, one of the most daring and distinguished officers in the American army, whose exploits won for him the epithet of "Mad Anthony," for his impetuous valor, was by no means deficient in prudence and judgment. His assault on Stony Point, which had been strongly fortified by the British, and which was taken at the point of the bayonet, the American troops having been forbidden to load their pieces, was one of the most brilliant events of the War. He was born in Chester Co., Pa., in January, 1745; he was a friend of Franklin, and distinguished himself as a soldier, not only in the Revolution, but subsequently against the Indians in Ohio. He died at Presque Isle, on Lake Erie, December, 1796. The Medal described above, in gold, was presented to him by Vote of Congress.— EDS.

566. 1779. *Obv.* VIRTUTIS ET AUDACIÆ MONUM. ET PRÆ-MIUM; in exergue, D. (*sic*) DE FLEURY EQUITI GALLO | PRIMO SUPER MUROS | RESP. AMERIC. D. D. (A monument and reward of valor and bravery; to M. de Fleury, a French officer, the first to mount the walls, the American Republic presented this gift [dono dedit].) De Fleury, in ancient armor, standing in the ruins of a fort, with a short sword in his right hand, and in the left a flag, on which he places his right foot; on a stone of the fort DU VIVIER F.

Rev. AGGERES PALUDES HOSTES VICTI and in exergue, STONY-PT. EXPUGN. | XV. JUL. MDCCLXXIX. (Fortifications, marshes and enemies overcome. Stony Point taken by storm July 15, 1779.) A bird's-eye view of the fort; beyond is the river with six vessels.*

Silver, rare, and bronze. Size 29. A. J. N., IX, 28. Loubat, 4. Lossing.

567. 1779. *Obv.* JOANNI STEWART COHORTIS PRÆFECTO and in exergue, COMITIA AMERICANA (The American Congress to John Stewart, Commander of the [storming] party). An

---

* Major François Louis Teisseidre de Fleury, born at St. Hippolyte, France, Aug. 28, 1749, had been an "Aid-major" in the French army. He offered his services to the American cause, and was appointed to duty at Fort Mifflin. as an Engineer May 22, 1777; he was wounded in the attack on that post; he distinguished himself in the Battle of Brandywine, and after the affair at Red Bank was promoted to be a Lieutenant Colonel in the army. Later, at the recommendation of Baron Steuben, he was assigned to duty as Inspector; in the assault on Stony Point he commanded the right van of the storming party: he was the first to gain the walls of the fortress, and struck "the enemy's standard with his own hand." [Wayne's Report.] The approach was difficult, and the way led over marshes, to which reference is made on the Medal. An impression in silver was presented to him as a reward for his gallantry, by a unanimous Vote of Congress, July, 1779. After the arrival in America of the French allies, he resigned his commission in the Continental Army, but served with the French, under Count Rochambeau. There is reason to believe that an impression of this Medal found at Princeton, N. J., in April, 1850, was the original intended to be presented De Fleury. Congress was in session there, at one time, and it is thought that this may have been sent there, and lost by the person having it in charge. De Fleury is said to have returned to France before his Medal had reached America. This is the only one of the three which spells Stony Point correctly. The dies are lost.— EDS.

Indian Queen at the right, presents a palm branch to Major
Stewart ; her left hand rests on and supports the shield of
the United States ; a quiver hangs at her back ; she wears a
crown of feathers and slight drapery, clasped with a fleur-de-
lis at her waist ; at her feet are an alligator and a rope ;
below the officer GATTEAUX.

Rev. STONEY–POINT OPPUGNATUM and in exergue, XV JUL.
MDCCLXXIX (Stony Point assaulted, July 15, 1779). A view
of the assault, a charge by the troops in the foreground led by
Stewart, who waves his sword above his head ; below, at the
left, GATTEAUX.

Silver (Webster collection, in the Mass. Hist. Soc. cabinet),
and bronze. Size 29.* A. J. N., IX, 28. Loubat. Lossing.

JOHN PAUL JONES.

568. 1779. *Obv.* ✦ JOANNI PAVLO JONES   CLASSIS PRAE-
FECTO. ✦ Below, completing the circle, COMITIA AMERI-

---

*An impression in silver was presented to Major Stewart, an infantry officer,
under the Vote mentioned in the preceding note. He commanded the left van
of the advanced parties in the assault, and was commended by Wayne, in his
official report, for his prudence and bravery. Thomas Wyatt, in his work on
"The Generals and Commodores of the American Army and Navy," which has
engravings of a number of these Medals, says he was killed by a fall from his
horse, near Charleston, S. C. The Medals for Wayne, de Fleury and Stewart
were struck in France, under the direction of Franklin.— EDS.

CANA. (The American Congress to John Paul Jones, Commander of the fleet.) ' Profile bust of Jones to right, in naval uniform, the buttons showing an anchor; his hair is tied in a queue, the ribbons floating behind.   On truncation, DUPRÉ. F.

Rev. HOSTIVM NAVIBVS   CAPTIS AVT FVGATIS.   And in exergue, AD ORAM SCOTIAE XXIII. SEPT. | M.DCC LXXVIIII ' (The ships of the enemy captured or put to flight on the shores of Scotland, Sept. 23, 1779.) Below, separated by a line, DUPRÉ. F.   A naval combat, the American ship, but little injured, sailing to the right; the British ship crippled, sailing to the left; her side is badly injured and flames are breaking out at her bow: another British ship in the distance at the left. Two sailors in the sea at the left, clinging to a spar.*

Gold and silver.   Size 36.   [Rare, in perfect condition, as the die cracked.]   V. L., Supp., 547.   Loubat.   Lossing.

---

* From a letter of John Paul Jones to Thomas Jefferson, found in "Sherburne's Life of Jones, pp. 303, 304," we find that Houdon, the famous sculptor, designed the bust, for which, says Loubat, he furnished a plaster mould. From the same letter it appears that impressions in gold were presented to the King of France and to the Empress of Russia. He mentions that another medallist, [Renaud,] had executed for him three Medals in wax, one of which showed this battle between the Bon Homme Richard and the British frigate Serapis [see A. J. N., IV, 45], but we do not find that the dies from these models were ever engraved. Jones was born in Scotland July 6, 1747; he went to Virginia

569. *Obv.* No legend. Bust of Jones in uniform to the right ; similar to the preceding.

Rev. Plain, with deep depression, behind the bust.

Soft metal, bronzed. A cast. Size 56.*

INDIAN MEDAL, VIRGINIA.

570. 1780. *Obv.* REBELLION TO TYRANTS IS OBEDIENCE TO GOD. On a label in the upper part of the field, VIRGINIA. Arms of Virginia ; a woman in armor, with a sword in right hand and a spear in her left, presses her right foot on a man lying prostrate, and with her left foot secures a chain, which he clutches with his left hand ; on the ground is a crown.

Rev. HAPPY WHILE UNITED In exergue, 1780. At the right is a strange sort of tree, under which an Indian at the left and a white officer at the right, are seated; the Indian holds a pipe; at the left is an open sea, on which

---

and entered the naval service of the Colonies in 1775; he was appointed Captain in August, 1776, and the following year sailed for the British coasts, where he obtained some successes, and alarmed the enemy by his boldness. In the month of September, 1779, he took the Serapis, to which he transferred his flag, his own ship, the Bon Homme Richard, being so much damaged that she sank a few hours later. For this exploit he was voted a gold Medal by Congress. The King of France honored him with the Order of Merit and the Empress with the Cross of St. Anne. During the battle (which was off Flamborough Head, and witnessed by many spectators on shore) the flag of the American ship was shot away, and recovered by one of Jones's officers who leaped into the sea after it. Captain Jones, in the letter cited above, criticised the drawing of the action as not giving the positions of the vessels, etc., correctly. He subsequently entered the Russian service as Vice Admiral, but did not long remain in that position, and died in Paris, July 18, 1792. Augustin Dupre was born at St. Etienne, France, Oct. 6, 1748; he was an engraver at the French Mint for many years, and Engraver-general from July, 1791, until 1801, when he was dismissed by Bonaparte. He died at Armentieres, Jan. 31, 1833. See an account of his works, etc., by Mr. W. S. Appleton, in the Proceedings of the Mass. Hist. Soc., second series. V. 348, *et seq.* — EDS.

 * This is probably the first essay from Houdon's bust for the Medal, by Dupre. Only a single impression is known, which is in the cabinet of the Public Library, in Boston. The description of this piece, which is almost unknown to collectors, is added by the Editors. — EDS.

are three vessels ; near them is a rocky point with a
house.*

Copper, rare (Appleton collection), and pewter, rare. It
has a loop, formed of a pipe and eagle's wing. Size 46. A.
J. N., II, 110 ; VII, 90 (copper) ; Brit. Mus. (pewter).

TREATY OF NEUTRALITY.

571.　1780.　*Obv.* CATHARINA MAGN : D. G. IMP. AVTOCR. RVS-
SOR. (Catharine the Great, by the grace of God Empress
and Autocrat of All the Russias.) Draped and armored bust
of the Empress Catharine II to the right, laureated, and in
profile ; she wears a low-necked dress, and a veil on the
back of her head falls on her shoulder. Below, at the left,
I. G. HOLTZHEY FEC.

Rev. MARE LIBERVM. (A free ocean). On the sockel, or
line beneath the device, I. G. HOLTZHEY FEC. In exergue, MDCCLXXX.
Neptune with a trident in his uplifted right hand, which also
catches a scarf, floating upward, and his left hand extended,
is standing turned to the right, in a shell, at the seaside ; on
the back of the shell hangs a group of four shields ; that of
Russia above, bears a double-headed eagle ; Sweden, at the

---

* The device differs slightly from the arms of Virginia, in which the figure
has her left foot on the breast of the tyrant. The device of the reverse is similar
to that of 510, but the figures are at the left and the sea at the right on that,
or exactly opposite to their position on this.— EDS.

right and below, three crowns ; Denmark, at the left, three
crowned lions, passant, and Holland beneath, with rampant
lion holding a clump of arrows. A sailor with folded arms
stands at the right, his hat lying on the ground, and before
him a rudder and flag ; at the left, Mercury with caduceus,
seated on a cornucopia, addressing Neptune, and pointing to
the rudder ; ships in the distance. A star, emitting rays
(said in Van Loon to be typical of the new constellation of
America), between the words of the legend.*

Silver. Size 31½. A. J. N., XXIII, 5 (plate) ; V. L., Sup.
549.

572. 1780. *Obv.* GEWAP ENDE NE UTRALI TEIT. (Armed
Neutrality.) A mailed arm holding a sword and four shields
united by a chain ; that in the centre bears the device of
Russia, gules, St. George and the dragon ; Sweden, on the
right, azure, three crowns, two over one ; Denmark, at the
left, or, semee with hearts, three crowned lions passant ; and
Holland below, gules, a crowned lion rampant, holding a
sword in his dexter and clump of arrows in his sinister paw.

Rev. Inscription in eight lines, JEHOVAH | WREEKER | DER
| VERBONDEN | STAAF KATHARINA'S | HULPVERDRAG ; | ZOO
BLYF'T ONZYDIG | ZEEGEZAG, | TOT HEYL DER VOLKEN | ON-
GESCHONDEN : (Jehovah, the Avenger of Treaties, confirms
Catharine's Treaty of assistance, so that the commerce of
the neutral powers remains intact for the benefit of their
people.) The All-seeing Eye in a glory of rays at the top,
and in exergue, in two lines, the lower curving to the edge
of the Medal, M.DCC.LXXX. | A. V. BAERLL.

Silver. Size 20. V. L., Sup. 548.†

---

* The Treaty of Armed Neutrality, commemorated by this Medal, was made
between the Powers whose shields are shown on the reverse, to resist the claims
of England, and indirectly to aid the American Colonies. The first convention
to arrange its provisions was held between Russia, Denmark and Sweden, July
and August, 1780 ; Holland acceded in December, and Prussia and the German
Emperor in the following year. For Holtzhey see note on 442. — EDS.

† These dies were by Adriaan Van Baerll, an engraver in Holland. His
works are not numerous. V. L., Sup., mentions that there are two slightly

573. 1781. *Obv.* PROC : SCOP : BONO : VOT : REIPU : NERV : (*i. e.*, *Procerum scopus; Bonorum votum; Reipublicae nervus;* The aim of Princes, the desire of good men, the life of the republic.) In exergue, curving upward, I. M. LAGEMAN. A sailor, standing, wearing a naval crown, and holding in his right hand a rudder on which is the rampant lion of the United Provinces, and resting his left upon a column on which is the "hat" of the Netherlands; an anchor at its base on the right, and the shields of Denmark, with lions, Russia, with St. George, and Sweden with the three crowns, united by a line symbolizing the Neutrality "Band," and tied with a bow, hang from the top; ships in the distance at left.

Rev. Inscription : DE KOOPVAARDY | GETERGT DOOR BRIT- | SCHEN EUVELMOED : | BIND EEN NEUTRAALE | BAND OM NEERLANDS | VRYEN HOED. | 17-81 (The merchant trade provoked by British arrogance, binds a neutral band around the free hat of the Netherlands, January 5, 1781. A rhyming couplet in the original). A garland below.*

Copper. Size 20. F., 328. V. L., Sup. 553.

ESCAPE OF THE DUTCH FISHING FLEET.

574. 1780. *Obv.* TER BEVEYLIGING VAN SCHEPEN EN VOLK. In exergue, IACOB VAN DER | WINT (For the safety of ships and the people. — Jacob Van der Wint). A cutter sailing to left; its flag separates C and H.

---

differing dies of the reverse — one having a comma after Jehovah and Vol. For an interesting treatise on the history of the events commemorated by the Medals of this period, especially those of the Netherlands, see the paper by Hon. Geo. M. Parsons, LL.D., in A. J. N., XXIII. — EDS.

* This was struck in Holland, and indicates the same spirit of resistance to the demands of Great Britain that is shown by the Medals previously described; "The desire of the Princes," etc., as stated on the obverse, is more fully explained by the inscription on the reverse to be a determination to carry on their maritime affairs without interference. *Nervus*, therefore, might be rendered "the moving principle." Lageman, who engraved a number of excellent Medals, was a citizen of Amsterdam, where he lived on the "Papen-bridge" street; he was a dealer in gold and silver (*goud-kashouder*), and eked out his income by the manufacture and sale of toys, and by engraving cards for weddings, balls, visiting, etc. See Wap, *Astrea*, IV, 193, as quoted in Van Loon, Sup., p. 72. Concerning the date on the reverse, see V. L., Sup., p. 142. — EDS.

Rev. 1780 | DEN 29 DEC : | VAN | VLAARDING | UYT GEZEILT | OM ONSE VLOOT VAN | DEN OORLOG KENNIS | TE GEVEN . EN OP TE | ONTBIEDE . | BEHOUDE BINNE | GEKOOMEN | DEN XI . JAN : | 1781 | and below, curving, A . V . B (Dec. 29, 1780, sailed from Vlaarding in order to communicate the state of war to the fleet, and to recall the same ; safely returned Jan. 11, 1781. A. Van Baerll).*

Silver. Size 20. Two varieties of reverse. V. L., Sup. 554.

MAJOR HENRY LEE, FOR PAULUS HOOK.

575. 1779. *Obv.* HENRICO LEE LEGIONIS EQUIT. PRÆFECTO and below, completing the circle, COMITIA AMERICANA (The American Congress to Henry Lee, commanding a battalion of cavalry.) Bust of Lee in profile to the right, his hair tied with a bow ; he wears a military uniform. On the truncation J. WRIGHT.

Rev. Inscription in ten lines, the ends of the eighth curving upward, NON OBSTANTIB. | FLUMINIBUS VALLIS | ASTUTIA & VIRTUTE BELLICA | PARVA MANU HOSTES VICIT | VICTOSQ. | ARMIS HUMANITATE | DEVINXIT. | IN MEM PUGN AD PAULUS | HOOK DIE XIX. | AUG. 1779. (Notwithstanding rivers and ramparts, with a small band of men he conquered the enemy by his sagacity and valor, and bound to him by his humanity those whom he had overcome by arms), within a wreath of

---

* When the British Government found the Continental powers determined to resist its maritime claims, it used its utmost endeavors to prevent Holland from uniting in the League of Armed Neutrality; these having proved unavailing, and while negotiations were still in progress at the Hague, its cruisers seized two hundred merchant vessels, whose cargoes were valued at fifteen millions of guilders. Englared declared war against Holland Dec. 20, 1780, and the news reached that country on the night of the 28th. The fishing fleet of the Netherlands, with nearly one hundred and fifty vessels, was at sea, and Van der Wint sailed out in his cutter, the "Red Rose," to call them home. Nearly all returned in safety, and this piece commemorates his conduct. The Provinces had not yet taken any notice of the communications of the Colonies, but the conduct of England in the events which immediately followed, commemorated by other Medals described in this Chapter, made the Netherlands actual, though not avowed, allies of the United States, and within a few months its navy was actively engaged against the British fleets. — EDS.

laurel, open at the top, and crossed and tied with a bow of ribbon at the bottom.

Gold, and bronze (restrikes from recut reverse die*).　Size 29.　Loubat.　Wyatt.

CAPTURE OF ANDRE.

576.　1780.　*Obv.* FIDELITY.　A heart-shaped shield with ornamental border, the legend upon a scroll above it, the whole enclosed within a wreath formed by two branches — fleur-de-lis on the right, terminating in a flower, and laurel on the left, crossed and tied at the bottom by a ribbon.

Rev. VINCIT AMOR PATRIÆ (Love of country conquers). A wreath formed by two branches of fleur-de-lis, terminating in flowers, crossed and tied with ribbon at the bottom, enclosing a space between them, for engraving.†

Silver.　Elliptical.　Size 27 x 36, with loop for suspension. Loubat 7.　Coll. Mass. Hist. Soc., III series, IV, 304. A. J. N., XXVI, 21.

---

* The original obverse die is in the U. S. Mint, but that of the reverse has been lost, and another was cut several years ago by Wm. Barber.　Henry Lee, familiarly known as 'Light Horse Harry,' from his having had command of the first Legion of Cavalry in the Revolutionary Army, was born at Stratford, Va., Jan'y 29, 1756.　He graduated at the College of New Jersey in 1773, and when only twenty years old was appointed captain of a company of cavalry raised in Virginia, which in consequence of Washington's urgent request, was shortly afterwards incorporated into the army.　He was soon made Major, and distinguished himself on many occasions, particularly in the battles of Guilford Court House and Eutaw Springs.　For his prudence, skill and bravery, in the successful surprise and capture of Paulus Hook — now Jersey city — near New York, Congress ordered a gold Medal to be struck and presented to him.　After the Revolution he was a Delegate to the Continental Congress until the adoption of the Constitution; he was also Governor of Virginia 1791-4, and a Member of Congress in 1799, and at the request of that body pronounced the Eulogy on Washington, in which he embodied the words so familiar to every American,— " First in war, first in peace, first in the hearts of his countrymen."　He died on Cumberland Island, Ga., March 25, 1818.　Joseph Wright, who cut the dies, was born at Bordentown, N. J., in 1756.　He was the first draughtsman and die-engraver in the United States Mint, and died in Philadelphia in 1793.— EDS.

† This was struck under a vote of the Continental Congress of Nov. 3, 1780, for presentation to the captors of Andre after his interview with the traitor Arnold; three bore, engraved within the wreath on the reverse, the initials of

MEXICAN MEDAL: BIRTH OF A SPANISH PRINCE.

577.   1780.   *Obv.* CARLOS · III · REY · DE · ESPANA · Y · D · LAS · INDIAS · CARLOS · Y · LUISA · DE · BORBON · PRINCIPES · DE · ASTURIAS ✦ and below, GERONIMO · A · GIL.   (Charles III, King of Spain and the Indies. Charles and Louisa of Bourbon, Princes of Asturias. Jerome A. Gil [Die-cutter]). Bust of Charles III to right undraped, with the Order of the Golden Fleece ; and bust of the Prince and Princess of Asturias conjoined to left, and facing that of the King.

Rev. CARLOS · DE · BORBON · NACIO · EN · EL · PARDO · EN · 5 · DE · MARZO · DEL · ANO · DE · 1780 In exergue, in two lines, GRABADA † EN † MEXICO † POR † GERON | † ANTONIO † GIL †   (Charles of Bourbon, born in ' El Pardo,'* March 5, of the year 1780 : engraved in Mexico by Jerome Anthony Gil). An Indian queen (Mexico) at the right, with a crown of feathers, and with bow and quiver at her back, kneeling on her left knee and with hands outstretched to receive an infant from Spain who stands at left wearing a helmet, and draped in a garment embroidered with lions and castles ; behind the Indian queen is a shield with the arms of Mexico : and at her feet is a cornucopia ; behind Spain is a blazing altar bearing a shield, and at her feet is a rabbit.†

Copper. Size 33. B. N.

---

three men, John Paulding, David Williams, and Isaac Van Wart, and were given them in the presence of the army, the following year, by Washington. It has erroneously been said that only three were struck. Mr. Charles Pryer showed one at a meeting of the Amer. Numis. and Arch. Soc., November, 1891, with *no* letters in the wreath ; one was in the Vattemare Collection, and others are known. The vote of Congress ordering the Medal and prescribing the devices is printed in Hist. Mag., I, 314. Loubat who gives an engraving, says it is not struck, but is *repoussé* work by a silversmith. Wyatt and Lossing also have engravings. — EDS.

* El Pardo was a shooting-box or country house, about six miles north of Madrid. It was built by the Emperor Charles V, burned in 1604, rebuilt for Philip III, and enlarged by Charles III. Our thanks are due to Prof. Addison Van Name, of Yale University, for kind assistance as to this point. — EDS.

† This Medal apparently commemorates the birth of an heir to the crown of Spain. The bust of Charles III on the obverse, is that of the King of Spain in whose honor the Proclamation Medals described in Chapter VI, were struck ;

BRITISH REGIMENTAL MEDAL.

578. 1780. *Obv.* The Irish harp in an open wreath of laurel; on a scroll below, CONCITAT AD ARMA (It calls to arms); on another scroll beneath, VOLUNTEERS OF IRELAND.

Rev. Inscribed, *Conferred by Colonel Lord Rawdon upon Sergeant Hudson for bravery in the battle fought near Camden on the 16 of August, 1780.*

Silver. Engraved.* Tancred (illus.), 353.

CAPTURE OF ST. EUSTATIA.

579. 1781. *Obv.* G. B. RODNEY. Bust to right in naval uniform.

Rev. THE HERO WHO HAVING SPENT HIS YOUTH IN THE SERVICE OF HIS COUNTRY, IS AMPLY REPAID BY THE CAPTURE OF ST. EUSTATIA, FEB^Y 3^D, 1781.†

Brass. Size —. See A. J. N., 23, 6.

---

those facing him are of his son, Charles, born at Naples, Nov. 11, 1748, created Prince of Asturias in 1759, who succeeded as Charles IV, on the death of his father,—and of his Princess, Maria Louisa, of Parma, to whom he was married Sept. 4, 1765, when not yet seventeen years old. The Charles whose birth is commemorated on the reverse, we have not found mentioned in any authority accessible to us, but he appears to have been the first-born of the Prince, some fifteen years after his marriage. As Ferdinand VII, born Oct. 13, 1784, was proclaimed Prince of Asturias and heir to the crown in 1790, we conjecture that the infant whose birth is commemorated by the Medal died in childhood, since the next younger brother of Ferdinand, who was born Mar. 29, 1788, received the name of Charles, and is known as "the Pretender, Don Carlos," who incited an insurrection against Queen Isabella, daughter of Ferdinand VII, when she was proclaimed in 1833, and continued his attempts until September, 1840. The rabbit is called by Herrera [see 379 *supra*] the emblem of Spain; it was not an uncommon symbol in Mexican decoration, even in Aztec times. — EDS.

* This is hardly entitled to be included here, as it is an engraved Medal. Lord Rawdon was the eldest son of the Earl of Moira, and commanded a Regiment recruited in America from Irishmen who were loyal to the King. It was afterwards known as the 105th Regiment. — EDS.

† Lord George Brydges Rodney was born at Walton-upon-Thames, England, in 1718. He was an admiral in the British Navy, and distinguished himself by defeating the Spanish fleet off Cape St. Vincent, 1780. He captured St. Eustatia, in 1781, as noted on the Medal, only a short time after England had declared war against the Netherlands, and the following year he gained a victory over the French fleet, under Count de Grasse, in the West Indies. He was raised to the Peerage as Baron Rodney, and died in 1792. See also 441, *supra*. — EDS.

580.   1781.   *Obv.* Same as last.

Rev. THE | GLORIOVS MEMO? OF THE 3ʳᵈ OF FEB? 1781 | WHEN HE SURRELY PUNISHD (*sic*) THE DUTCH AT S? EUSTATIA TAKING | UPWARDS OF 3 MILLIONS | OF VALUE WITH 300 | SAIL OF SHIPS.*

Pewter.   Size —.

581.   1781.   *Obv.* WILH CRUL TOPARCHA BURGST PRÆF. CLASS • HOLL • & W-F.   Under truncation, ᵢ·ɢ·ʜ·ʄ.   (William Crul, Heer Van Burgst, Admiral of the Fleet of Holland and West Frisia).   Bust of Crul nearly facing, dressed in a laced coat, his hair tied in a bow, and his body turned toward the right.

Rev. VI INFERIOR NON VIRTVTE.   In exergue, PUGN. OCCUB. IV FEB. | MDCCLXXXI   (Inferior in strength, but not in valor. He fell, fighting, Feb. 4, 1781).   A pedestal with tablet representing a battle. between three frigates ; upon the pedestal is an urn with garland of cypress ; upon the right side stands Mercury weeping ; his left hand extended, holds a caduceus turned downward, his right covers his face ; and upon the left are grouped a cannon, anchor, standard and shield with the arms of Crul (or, a mast vert, entwined [om krulde] with a serpent (tincture not indicated) impaling Burgst (azure, a tower [berg] argent ?) ; the arms show "canting heraldry" ;

---

in the distance at the right a ship at sea ; a radiant starry crown divides the legend over the monument ; beneath the feet of Mercury, on the sockel, or line separating the exergue,

I. G. HOLTZHEY FEC.

Silver.   Size 28.*   V. L., Sup. 556.   F. 5700.

582.   1781.   *Obv.* OPE DEI ET CVRA PATRVM   (By the help of God and the efforts of our fathers).   The Netherlands, personified by an armed and helmeted maiden, standing at the right, displays a shield on which are the seven arrows of the United Provinces bound in a sheaf, before a youth who is seated at the left, supporting with his right hand the arms of the city of Amsterdam ; his left, which holds a coil of rope, points to the shield of Holland ; behind the maiden is the lion of the Netherlands ; in the foreground at the left, a beast of prey is gnawing at the base of the shield of the city.   In exergue, 1781.

Rev. Inscription in eight lines, OCH, DAT DER VADREN | EENDRAGT S' BAND | BESTENDIG BLYVE | IN NEDERLAND, | DAN SLAAN WY T' | ROOFSIEK ALBION | VAN DE OP' TOT DE ON | DERGANG DER ZON.   (Oh that the band which united our Fathers still remained in the Netherlands.   Then should we smite rapacious Albion from the rising to the setting of the sun.)   Festoons above, below, and on the sides of the inscriptions.†

Silver.   Size 21.   V. L., Sup. 555.

583   1781.   *Obv.* VIS VI FORTITER REPULSA.   (Violence bravely repelled by force.)   A sea fight between the Nether-

---

* William Crul, born at Harlem, Nov. 25, 1721, was the Dutch commander in the naval engagement with Rodney, at St. Eustatia, in which he lost his life.   A full account of the event, and of Crul himself, is given in V. L., Sup. pp. 145, 6. — EDS.

† This Medal belongs to the series on the Armed Neutrality, which as has been remarked, conduced to the aid of America, in her struggles with England. It was struck in the hope of promoting a general feeling of harmony in sustaining that Treaty, especially in Holland.   The reverse is a stanza of four lines. — EDS.

lands ships Briel and Castor, and British frigates Flora and Crescent, off Cadiz, the Briel and the Crescent in the foreground, the others in the distance. In exergue, in two lines, PROPE GADES XXX MAY | MDCCLXXXI. (Near Cadiz, May 30, 1781.)

Rev. ANTIQUA VIRTV TE DVVM VIRI (By the old time valor of two men). The trident of Neptune standing erect in the open ocean ; the sun setting in the distance at the left ; from the top of the trident hangs the shield of the Admiralty, gules, a lion rampant or, holding a sword in his dexter and a sheaf of arrows in his sinister paw ; in chief are the letters A R (for Rotterdam Admiralty), and the shield is surmounted by a naval crown ; two anchors crossed in saltire behind the shield. Below, at the left, is a shield bearing or, three cushions gules, charged with a crescent argent [the arms of Melvill], and at the right another, per fess ; in chief argent, a house between two trees proper ; in base, argent, a dexter arm, couped at the shoulder, vambraced and grasping a falchion proper [for Oorthuys]. From the top of the shield at the left rises a staff, from which falls a .pennant, inscribed P. MELVILL NAVARCHUS (Capt. P. Melvill), and from the other a similar staff and pennant, with the name G. OORTHUYS NAVARCH (Capt. G. Oorthuys). In exergue, a double festoon of two laurel wreaths, and between them a lion's head, facing. On the sockel, or separating line, I. G. HOLTZHEY . FEC. (The die cutter.)*

Silver. Size 28. A. J. N., XXIII, 6 (illus.). V. L., Sup. 559.

---

* This commemorates the action off Cadiz, between two Dutch and two British ships, in which the Dutch were victorious; the English frigate at the left foreground is dismantled, while her adversary is comparatively unharmed; the reverse legend is a continuation of that on the obverse. The device of the house (Dutch, Huys) is of the class known as *Arma parlantes*, or canting heraldry, and alludes to the name of the Captain [Oorthuys]. This Medal is mentioned by Mr. George M. Parsons, in his paper in A. J. N. (*loc. cit.*), as properly to be placed among these relating to America, and like several others in the text, alludes to the events growing out of the League of Armed Neutrality. — EDS.

BRITISH RESENTMENT.

584.   1781.   *Obv.* GEORGIUS III REX ANG.   (George III,
King of England.)   Bust of the King to left, laureated, in
armor and cloak ; his hair tied behind, floats on his shoulders.

Rev. INDOCILIS PATI ∘   In exergue, in two lines, IN PERPET.
MEMOR. | MDCCLXXXI ·   (Never taught to submit.   In perpetual
memory, 1781.)   A rampant lion advancing to the left, burst-
ing his bonds.*

Silver and copper.   Size 34.

---

* The lion struggling with the rope in which he is entangled, shows the resentment of Great Britain at the League of Neutrality, typified, as on Medals
already described, by the cord. — EDS.

BATTLE OF DOGGERSBANK.

585.   1781.   *Obv.* PAX QVAERITVR BELLO.   (Peace is sought by war.)   In the field at the right, v. AVG. | MDCC | LXXXI. A winged Victory to the right, holding in her right hand outstretched a wreath of laurel, and in her left palm and olive branches ; she is standing on the prow of an antique galley, from the front of which project the seven arrows of the United Netherlands ; its terminal is a lion's head.   On the prow, DOGGERS | BANK.*   Under the prow s for Schepp, the engraver.

Rev. MVNIFICENTIA PRINCIPIS AVRIACI   (By the liberality of the Prince of Orange).   A laurel wreath of two branches crossed and tied with ribbon at the bottom and close at the top, encloses the inscription EXI | MIAE | VIRTV | TIS | PRAEM | IVM   (The reward of distinguished valor.)

Gold and silver.   Elliptical, with ring for suspension.†
Size 24 by 18.   V. L., Sup. 567 A.

586.   1781.   *Obv.* As the preceding, but the figure of Victory varies slightly in the drawing.
Rev. As the preceding.
Silver and bronze.   Elliptical, with ring.   Size 11 by 7 nearly.   V. L., Sup. 567 B.

587.   1781.   *Obv.* WOLTER JAN   BARON BENTINCK   In exergue, in four lines, als Kapitein den gewond 5– | als Schout

---

* The battle of Doggersbank, which took place on Aug. 5, 1781, was fought between an English fleet under Admiral Keith Stewart, and a Dutch fleet under Admiral John Arnold Zoutman.   The Doggers [or Cod] bank in the North Sea was the resort of the fishermen of both nations, and the fleets sent out for their protection encountered each other, with no decisive result according to the English authorities, though the Dutch claimed a victory, and struck several Medals to commemorate the event. — EDS.

† The gold Medal was presented to Rear Admiral J. A. Zoutman, the commanding officer, and those in silver to the captains of the other vessels participating in the action. — EDS.

by nagt en Adjud | overl. den 24–begr. | 28. Aug. 1781.
(Walter John, Baron Bentinck; wounded as Captain on the
5th, died as Rear Admiral and Aide on the 24th; buried Aug.
28, 1781.) A funereal urn with a cypress wreath, on a square
pedestal; at the foot of the urn on the right, the cap and
caduceus of Mercury; on the face of the monument is a
tablet bearing the arms of Bentinck, which are azure, an
"anchor-cross" argent; the shield is surmounted by a Baron's
coronet; on the left of the monument is a trophy of arms
— a lance with a wreath of laurel on its point, an elliptical
shield, cannon, flag, etc.; on the right, on the sea, the
Admiral's ship, the Batavier, its flags at half-mast; the spear
point and a crown of stars separates the words JAN and
BARON of the legend.

Rev. DEUGDS BELONGING (Recompense of valor). A circular monument, having on its top a shield surmounted with
a naval crown, and bearing in dexter and sinister chief the
letters A A (for Admiralty of Amsterdam), with two anchors
crossed in saltire; the device is surmounted by a smaller
shield bearing gold, a demi lion rampant, crowned and holding a sword in his dexter and a cluster of arrows in his sinister paw; the tinctures cannot be distinguished; the latter
shield is also surmounted by a coronet. The front of the
monument has a circular tablet on which an angel is flying,
holding a palm branch in his left hand and trampling on the
English roses; around the bottom of the tablet OP DOGGERS-
BANK (For Doggersbank), very small; on either side of the
monument are flags, cannon, muskets, and other weapons; on
the line separating the exergue, I. G. HOLTZHEY FEC. In the exergue,
an ornamental tablet on which, in two lines, OP | HOOG GEZAG.
(By high authority.)*

Silver.   Size 28.   V. L., Sup. 565.

---

* Wolter Jan Gerrit, Baron Bentinck, who commanded the Batavier in the
battle of Doggersbank, was born July 30, 1745. He was mortally wounded in
the fight, having distinguished himself by his bravery, and was made Rear
Admiral a few days before his death. Van Loon, Sup., *loc. cit.*, gives a full
sketch of his life. The arms on reverse are those of the Admiralty. — EDS.

588.   1781.   *Obv.* HOEZEE! DE BRIT RUIMT ZEE (Huzza! Britain abandons the sea!) in a curving line above the mast of the ship at the right.   Two full-rigged ships, Dutch and English, stern on, in action.   In exergue, in three lines, OP DEN VYFDEN | OOGSTM. | 1781.   (On the 5th August, 1781.)

Rev. Inscription in eight lines, O BATAVIER · | GOD STAAFT UW REGT! | DAAR ZOUTMAN MET | ZIJN HELDEN VEGT, | HERSTELT HIJ DE EER | DER VRIJE VLAG, | TROTS OVERMAGT, | IN EENEN SLAG.   (Oh Batavians, God sustains your right; Zoutman, by his heroic valor, has restored the honor of the free flag, and overcome arrogance in this battle).   Over the inscription is a small rostral crown, and beneath it a wreath of laurel.   At the bottom, A · V · B · (for Adrian Van Baerl, the engraver), curving to conform to the edge.*

Silver.   Size 19.   V. L., Sup. 563.

A large and beautiful medallion, having on the obverse the arms and supporters of the United Provinces, with the legend, CONCORDIA RES PARVAE CRESCUNT (By concord small things increase), and on the reverse the arms of the House of Orange-Nassau, surrounded by those of the seven Provinces, entwined with orange leaves and fruit, and the legend DISCORDIA MAXI-MAE DILABUNTUR (By discord great things are destroyed), was struck in gold for presentation to the Admiral of the fleet engaged in the battle of Doggersbank; of this there is an

---

* Struck in honor of the same battle.   John Arnold Zoutman, who commanded the Dutch fleet in this battle, was the son of an eminent jurist of the same name, and was born May 10, 1724.   The eight lines of the inscription, it will be noticed, make a rhyming quatrain. — EDS.

engraving and description in Van Loon, Supplement, No.
566; as, however, it was virtually the same in design with
others struck to reward patriotic services to the United Provinces, more than a century and a half previous (see Van Loon
II, 53, where others — which were struck in 1609, similar but
without the central arms — are described, and engravings of
three different sizes are given), it seems hardly proper to include it among Medals relating to America.

589. 1781. *Obv.* INJVRIIS COACTA (Compelled by in-
juries). In exergue, in two lines, IN VADO ASELL. V AVG. |
MDCCLXXXI. (On the Doggersbank, August 5, 1781.) Holland, symbolized by a crowned female, standing, looking
towards the left, and advancing to the right; she holds a
lance in her right hand, and her left uplifted points to a glory
which divides the legend at the top; at her left is a blazing
altar from the top of which hang by ribbons three medals,
and on its front is the free hat of the Netherlands; behind
the altar a barrel and box of merchandise; at the right is the
Batavian lion, springing forward over an anchor and cannon,
and casting lightnings; two ships in the background; on the
line separating the exergue, at the left, i. g. holtzhuv. fhc.

Rev. IMMORTALIBUS BATAVVM GLORIÆ VINDICIBUS (To
the immortal defenders of the glory of the Netherlands).
On the field a glory of rays, surmounted by seven laurel
wreaths; that on the centre has two anchors crossed behind
it and the letter A on each side (for Amsterdam Admiralty);

from each wreath hangs a ribbon and medal. On the wreath at the top, SALOMON | DEDEL ; on that at the left, WILLEM | VAN BRAAM ; opposite, at the right, I. H. VAN | KINSBERGEN | EQVES ; on the central wreath, IOH. ARN. | ZOUTMAN ; on the lower left, W. J. BARON | BENTINCK ; opposite, ADRIAN | BRAAK ; and on that at the bottom, EV. CHR. | STARINGH.[*]

Silver. Size 29. Illus. in A. J. N., XXIII. V. L., Sup. 562.

590. 1781. *Obv.* VII . HOLL : TEGEN IX ENGEL : SCHEEP : VICTOR : BEVO :   In exergue, 5 AUG : 1781 . | (Seven Dutch vessels won a victory over nine English ships, Aug. 5, 1781.) The lion of Batavia holding a sword in his right and a caduceus in his left paw, beside an altar upon which lies the free hat, and against which leans a shield with the arms of Amsterdam ; an eye in a triangle above at right emits rays.

Rev. Inscription in eight lines, PAS KOOMT DE | VLOOT IN ZEE | MET NEER LANDS | HELDEN STOET, | OF S'VYANDS TROTS

---

[*] The names are those of the Dutch Captains ; Salomon Dedel, born at Amsterdam, Dec. 18, 1736, commanded the ship Holland of 64 guns, which sunk soon after this action ; he died Oct. 15, 1801 : Willem Van Braam, born at Werkhoven, Utrecht, Nov. 10, 1732, commanded the Piet Hein, of 54 guns ; he died Feb. 21, 1807 : Jan Hendrik van Kinsbergen, born at Doesburg, May 1, 1735, commanded the Admiraal Generaal, of 74 guns ; he subsequently greatly distinguished himself, and was ennobled, taking his title from this battle ; he died May 22, 1819 : Bentinck has been mentioned above ; his ship, the Batavier, carried 54 guns ; Adrian Van Braak, commander of the Erfprins, also of 54 guns, was later Vice Admiral, and died in Surinam in 1796 : Evert Christiaan Staringh commanded the Argo, of 40 guns. Admiral Zoutman's ship was the Admiral De Ruyter, of 68 guns. The Dutch fleet was composed of seven vessels, mounting 408 guns, and the English fleet of the same number, mounted 446 guns. *Vado Asellino*, on the obverse, is the Latin equivalent for the Cod or Doggers bank. *Eques* on the reverse is the equivalent of the Dutch Ridder, or Knight. The battle had great influence in leading the Netherlands to acknowledge American Independence. — EDS.

| HEYD ZWIGT | VOOR VATERLAND | SCHE MOED   (Liberally,
Hardly had the fleet got to sea, with its brave sons of the
Netherlands, when the arrogance of the enemy sank out of
sight before their patriotic courage.*)   A garland of flowers
above; at the bottom, curving beneath, two palm branches,
J. M. LAGEMAN.

Copper.   Size 17.   V. L., Sup. 564 A

591. 1781.   *Obv.* Same as the preceding, but 5 AU: in
exergue.

Rev. Same as the preceding, except the apostrophe is omitted in S VYANDS, and three lines are used in place of the palm
branches.

Copper.   Size 17.   V. L., Sup. 564 B.

ADMIRAL ZOUTMAN.

592. 1781.   *Obv.* ZOUTMAN curving upward, beneath a
large ship under full sail, with flags flying, sailing to right.
A corded edge.

Rev. Plain.

Copper.   Size, as engraved, 12.   V. L., Sup. 568.†

BATTLE AT COWPENS.

593. 1781.   *Obv.* DANIELI MORGAN DUCI EXERCITUS and
in exergue, COMITIA AMERICANA (The American Congress to
Daniel Morgan,‡ General of the Army).   Near the edge,

---

* This boastful Medal is hardly sustained by the facts.   Van Loon's Supplement, II, pp. 161-2, gives the names of seven Dutch line-of-battle ships (see
note on preceding number) and two frigates, the Bellona and Dolphin, as com-
posing the fleet of the Netherlands, and of only seven British vessels; so that it
would appear from that authority, that the vessels participating in the battle
were the exact reverse of the numbers given on the Medal.   V. L., Sup. 564,
p. 156, however, describing it, makes no reference to the error. — EDS.

† This is a scarce little piece, which seems to have been struck to wear on
the watch chain. — EDS.

‡ Daniel Morgan was born in New Jersey, in 1736; he served in Braddock's
Expedition, and when the Revolution began, was early in the field.   He was

dupre f. At the left America, as an Indian queen, slightly draped, advancing; she wears a coronet of feathers, and a quiver at her back, and places a laurel wreath on the head of Gen. Morgan, who stands at the right, and bends to receive it; his right hand rests upon his sword; before him, on the ground, the American shield is leaning against a cannon, with an olive branch, flags, a drum, trumpet, etc., in the background; at the right is an open landscape.

Rev. VICTORIA LIBERTATIS VINDEX. (Victory the vindicator of liberty.) In exergue, FVGATIS CAPTIS AVT CÆSIS | AD COWPENS HOSTIBVS | XVII JAN. MDCCLXXXI. and separated by a line, DUPRE INV. ET F. (The enemy put to flight, captured, or slain, at Cowpens, Jan. 17, 1781.) Gen. Morgan mounted, leads a body of troops bearing the American flag, from the right; in the background the enemy is seen flying, and a combat between a foot soldier and a dismounted officer in the foreground at the left.

Gold, silver (in the Webster collection) and bronze. Size 36. A. J. N., IX, 28. Loubat. Wyatt.

594. 1781. *Obv.* GULIELMO WASHINGTON LEGIONIS EQUIT. PRÆFECTO and in exergue, COMITIA AMERICAN · (The American Congress to William Washington, Commander of a Regiment of Cavalry.) Col. Washington mounted, leads a charge of cavalry at the battle of Cowpens; he holds a sword in his

---

Captain of one of the first two companies of "expert riflemen," raised in Virginia in June, 1775, and marched his command from Frederick County, in that State, to Boston, a distance of nearly six hundred miles, in three weeks, to aid in the siege of that place. In October he was detached with his company to join Benedict Arnold, in the expedition against Quebec, where his bravery was highly commended, and where he was taken prisoner. Throughout the war he was distinguished for his activity and efficiency, and was promoted to the rank of Colonel, and Brigadier-General. To him was chiefly due the victory at Saratoga, and though Gates did not give him due credit, it was ascribed to his conduct in the British accounts of the battle. At Cowpens he was in command of the forces which won the brilliant victory over Tarleton, and March 9, 1781, Congress voted that a gold Medal should be presented to him, and silver Medals to his associates, Lt. Cols. Wm. Washington and Howard. He served as a Member of Congress 1795-9, and died July 6, 1802. — EDS.

right hand; before him a body of cavalry are flying to the left; a dismounted soldier in the foreground; in the air above is a figure of Victory, with a laurel wreath in her right and a palm branch in her left hand; at the right, below the horse, DUVIV.

Rev. Inscription in seven lines, in a wreath of laurel, tied by a bow at the top and bottom, QUOD | PARVA MILITUM MANU | STRENUE PROSECUTUS HOSTES | VIRTUTIS INGENITÆ | PRÆ-CLARUM SPECIMEN DEDIT | IN PUGNA AD COWPENS. | XVII JAN. MDCCLXXXI. (Because with a small band of soldiers he energetically pursued the enemy, and gave a distinguished example of native valor in the battle at Cowpens, Jan. 17, 1781.)

Silver and bronze. Size 29. A. J. N., IX, 28. Loubat. Wyatt.*

595. 1781. *Obv.* JOH. EGAR HOWARD LEGIONIS PEDITUM PRÆFECTO and in exergue, COMITIA AMERICANA (The American Congress to John Egar Howard, commanding a Regiment of Infantry). Col. Howard on horseback to right, with uplifted sword, pursuing a standard-bearer who flees before him, his cap having fallen on the ground; above and between them a flying figure of Victory, with a laurel crown in her left and a palm-branch in her right hand; below, at the left, behind the horse's heels, DU VIV.

Rev. Inscription, QUOD | IN NUTANTEM HOSTIUM ACIEM | SUBITO IRRUENS | PRÆCLARUM BELLICÆ VIRTUTIS | SPECIMEN

---

* The dies of this Medal are in the French Mint. This was presented to Wm. Washington by vote of Congress of March 9, 1781, for his conduct "on that memorable day" (Jan. 17, 1781). His company of cavalry on that occasion numbered only 80. William Augustine Washington was the eldest son of Baily Washington, of Stafford County, Virginia, where he was born Feb. 28, 1752; he was a distant relative of George Washington, and early in the Revolution was appointed to command a company of infantry in the Third Regiment of Virginia troops; he served with distinction in various engagements, chiefly in the cavalry, in North and South Carolina, especially in the battles of Guilford Court-house and Cowpens. After the close of the Revolution he was a member of the South Carolina Legislature, residing on his plantation at Sandy Hill, S. C. He died March 6, 1810.

DEDIT | IN PUGNA AD COWPENS | XVII. JAN. MDCCLXXXI. (Because suddenly rushing upon the wavering line of the enemy, he gave an example of distinguished martial valor, in the battle at Cowpens, Jan. 17, 1781), in seven lines, within a wreath of laurel tied at top and bottom by bows of ribbon, the ends of which fall within the wreath.

Silver.   Size 29.   A. J. N., IX, 28.   Loubat.   Wyatt.*

BATTLE AT EUTAW SPRINGS.

596.   *Obv.* · VIRTUTE · ET JUSTITIA · VALET ·   (He prevails by valor and justice.)   An officer pointing with his sword to the enemy (seven soldiers) retreating to left, and beckoning to his men (five soldiers) to advance; above, a figure flying and holding the scales of Justice, crowns him with a wreath of laurel.†

---

* John Egar Howard was born in Baltimore County, Md., June 4, 1752. He was second in command of the Fourth Maryland Regiment in the battle of Germantown, Lieut.-Colonel of the Fifth Regiment in 1779, and subsequently was a Colonel in the Continental Army, and distinguished himself at the Battle of Cowpens, Guilford Court House and Eutaw Springs; in the last named battle commanding the Second Maryland Regiment. After the close of the Revolution he was Governor of Maryland, 1789-92, and was offered the position of Secretary of War, by Washington, which he declined. When the attitude of the French Directory led the United States to consider the formation of a Provisional Army, in 1798, Washington, who had been appointed Commander-in-Chief, nominated him as a Brigadier-General. He served as U. S. Senator, 1796–1803. Not long before his death, which occurred Oct. 12, 1827, at Baltimore, he wrote an interesting account of the Battle of Germantown, which is published by Sparks in his "Writings of Washington," V, 468. His middle name is frequently spelled Eager. — EDS.

† This Medal is mentioned in an article in Niles' Register, printed Oct. 16, 1824, and reprinted in A. J. N. (*loc. cit.*). It was then in the possession of J. Howard McHenry, of Baltimore, Md., and is no doubt still owned by the descendants of Gen. Howard, whose grandson (Mr. McHenry) describes a dinner party at which Lafayette was present when this Medal, suspended to a ribbon with the colors of the Order of the Cincinnati, with that described above (595) was exhibited. Mr. McHenry believed that this was presented to his grandfather by Congress, but on what occasion he was unable to say; but nothing to sustain this has been adduced, and it has been conjectured that it may have been presented to him by his native State, whose troops he had commanded in several engagements, and very likely alludes to his gallantry in the battle at

Rev. • VINCULIS • SUIS • VINCTUS • (Bound in his own fetters.)   An officer treading with his left foot on the British lion and flag, and with his right hand piercing the lion with a spear, while with his left he holds a chain that binds him ; below, around the edge, thirteen five-pointed stars.

Silver, engraved.   Size 33 ; with loop for suspension supported by two wings.   A. J. N., XII, 15 ; Mag. Am. Hist., III, 377.

597.   1781.   *Obv.* NATHANIELI GREEN EGREGIO DUCI COMITIA AMERICANA.   (The American Congress to Nathaniel Green, the distinguished leader.)   Profile bust of Green in uniform, to left.*

Rev. SALUS REGIONUM AUSTRALIUM.   (The safety of the Southern territories.)   Victory to left, nearly facing, alighting on a trophy of arms ; her left foot rests upon a broken shield, near which is another shield, and flags, fasces, a broken sword, helmet, spear point, and laurel branch.   In exergue, in

---

Eutaw Springs, when his regiment encountered the " Buffs," who offered such an obstinate resistance, that " many of that regiment and the Marylanders were mutually transfixed with each other's bayonets."   This conjecture is the only reason known to the Editors for placing this Medal beside that of Gen. Green, which was presented for that battle, under the same head of " Eutaw Springs." It has been frequently described in Magazine articles, and being so well known, though an engraved piece, Mr. Betts thought it proper to deviate from his general plan and include it here. — EDS.

* Nathaniel Green was born in Warwick, R. I., May 27, 1742.   His father was an " approved preacher " in the Society of Friends.   The son began the study of law in 1772, but at the prospect of difficulty with the mother-country, he joined a military company called the Kentish Guards, for which offence against Quaker principles he was excluded from the Society.   At the outbreak of the Revolution he was commissioned Brigadier-General of Rhode Island troops, and marched to take part in the siege of Boston.   The following year he was made Major-General by Congress, and subsequently Quartermaster-General, but retaining his position or right to command when in action.   He participated in numerous battles, at Trenton, Germantown, Monmouth, Camden and Eutaw. For his victory at the last named place, which forced the enemy to abandon the Carolinas, Congress, Oct. 29, 1781, ordered a gold Medal to be struck and presented to him.   After peace was established he resided on his plantation in Georgia until his death, which resulted from the effects of a sunstroke, June 19, 1786. — EDS.

three lines, HOSTIBUS AD EUTAW | DEBELLATIS DIE VIII SEPT. | MDCCLXXI. (The enemy vanquished at Eutaw, Sept. 8, 1781.) near the sword-hilt, DPRR.

Gold and silver (in Webster collection). Size 35. A. J. N., IX, 29, 31. Loubat. Wyatt.

GEORGE CLINTON, GOVERNOR OF NEW YORK.

598. *Obv.* Head of George Clinton to right, without drapery, his hair tied in a cue; within a beaded ellipse; no legend.*

Rev. Head of Mrs. George Clinton to left, without drapery; within a beaded ellipse; no legend.

Brass, shell, silver-plated; elliptical. Size 20 x 17; with a loop for suspension struck with the medal and projecting from a bow tying two branches of laurel, which extend around the upper edge.

LOSS OF ST. EUSTATIA BY THE DUTCH.

599. 1782. *Obv.* EN LEIT ONS NIET IN VERZOEKING MAAR VERLOST ONS V. D. BOOZEN (Lead us not into temptation, but deliver us from evil.) In exergue, 1782. Holland typified by a female figure, kneeling, to right; she supports a staff sur-mounted by the hat of the Netherlands, with her right hand, while her left is extended towards a horn of plenty and other emblems on the ground before her; above at the right is a long cloud from which rays illumine the field.

Rev. Inscription in six lines, MYNE ERFDEELEN | ZYN TOT ANDERE | OVERGEGAAN | EN MYN EYGEN | DOMMEN AAN DE | VREEMDE (My inheritance has gone to others, and my

---

* George Clinton, born in Ulster County, N. Y., in 1739, was an active patriot in the Revolution. A lawyer by profession, he was the leader of the opposition to the King in the Colonial Assembly. Although he voted for the Declaration of Independence, his name does not appear among the signers, as he was called away on military duty. He was Governor of New York for eighteen successive terms, and Vice-President of the United States from 1804 to 1812, dying in April of the latter year. — EDS.

property to strangers.*)   Above the inscription an anchor leaning against a corner-stone, and below is a double festoon. At the bottom, curving to conform to the edge, t. m. lachman. (the die-cutter.)

Silver.   Size 23.   B., p. 22, No. 297.   V. L., Sup. 569.

BRITISH INDIAN MEDALS.

600.   *Obv.* GEORGIUS III DEI GRATIA (George III, by the grace of God).†   Bust of the King to right in armor, wearing

---

* This commemorates the loss by Holland of St. Eustatia, captured by the English the preceding year.   See 579–581.   The obverse legend is from the Lord's prayer, and the reverse inscription, slightly altered from Lamentations, v: 2, shows the national grief. — EDS.

† During the Revolutionary War the British Ministry often employed Indians to aid their troops, notably in 1777, under Burgoyne in his march on Albany, etc., and the preceding year at the West, in what afterwards became the States of Illinois, Kentucky, etc., where the cruelties of their barbaric warfare aroused the deepest indignation in the mother country, and elicited the famous protest by William Pitt, in the House of Commons, against the action of the British Ministry.   The Medal described as 600, which is apparently a mule, and the following number, Mr. Betts seems to have inserted, following McLachlan, who states that they were struck for presentation to the Indian allies of Great Britain, and are known as Chief's Medals, [see his note under CCXCVIII] ; several

the ribbon of the Garter; the face somewhat older than on
the Indian Medals of 1762.

Rev. The Royal Arms surrounded by the Garter, and surmounted by a crown; lion at the left and unicorn at the right
as supporters; HONI · SOIT · QUI · MAL Y · PENSE upon the

---

of this character, doubtless struck for such uses, are described in our preceding
chapters, [see pp. 194–6, 226–8, and 238]. No date appears on either of these,
but it seems probable, if they were issued for that purpose, that *this* was minted
as early as 1777 or 1778. With regard to the next number, the Editors are
convinced it does not properly belong in this series, notwithstanding McLachlan
says [ccxcvi] it "was struck for distribution among the Indians who took
part in the war with the United States, during the Revolution . . . . and at its
conclusion wore these Medals proudly, as mementoes of having nobly helped
[*sic !*] to drive the invaders from Canadian soil:" and we base our opinion on
Mr. Betts's description of the arms on the reverse; it was not until 1801 that
the fleurs-de-lys of France were removed by Royal Proclamation from the arms
of the British Kings; this difference in the armorial devices is the chief dis·
tinction between the two Medals, clearly fixes the date of the latter, and proves
that it could *not* have been worn as McLachlan asserts, as a memento of the
"noble help" of the Indian allies of Great Britain in the Revolution. The close
resemblance between these two, and the possibility that 601 was struck for a
similar purpose, though many years later, has decided us, though not without
much reluctance, to retain the description of 601 as given by Mr. Betts. — EDS.

Garter, and DIEU · ET · MON · DROIT upon a ribbon below ; behind the ribbon a rose and thistle, *two* leaves appearing upon each stem above the ribbon ; the quartering of the arms shows England impaling Scotland in the first, France in the second, Ireland in the third and Hanover in the fourth.

Silver. Size 38, with loop for suspension. The reverse die shows a crack extending across the shield. Oby. McL., CCXCVI ; Rev. *ib.* CCXCII.

601. *Obv.* Same die as the preceding, but the planchet is a little larger.

Rev. Same general design as the last, but the mottoes are not punctuated ; the word QUI is partly concealed by the crown, and the letters V and P by the leg of the unicorn ; *four* leaves appear on each stem above the ribbon, and the quartering of the arms shows England in the first and fourth, Scotland in the second and Ireland in the third, that of Hanover, with a crown, being placed over them on an escutcheon of pretence.

Silver. Size 39, with loop). McL., CCXCVI. [See note on preceding number.]

CHAPTER IX.

THE successful issue of the Revolutionary War, in 1783, terminated the "Colonial History" of the larger part of the British possessions in North America; and the renunciation of their allegiance to King George the Third, by the Colonies whose efforts had achieved that result, sounded a note of warning to the other European rulers to prepare to relinquish their power on this side of the Atlantic. In 1803, Napoleon sold Louisiana to the young Republic — the last of those Franco-American possessions which in the previous century extended from the St. Lawrence to the Mexican Gulf. The Treaty for the cession of Florida to the United States was signed by Spain on the birthday of Washington in 1819. Mexico rebelled in 1810, and its independence dates from a few years later; the bonds which held the greater portion of South America subject to the Spanish crown were broken not long after, by Bolivar and his companions: a branch of the royal family of Portugal held sway over the broad Empire of Brazil until the recent dethronement of Dom Pedro, and while Denmark yet clings to the icy shores of Greenland, England alone, of all the powers of Europe, retains her hold on North American territory, although the islands adjacent to the coast, and Guiana, in South America, still display foreign flags. But the self-reliant Provinces of Canada, though still forming a "Dominion" of the sovereign of Great Britain, are no longer colonies, and conduct their internal affairs with little interference from the mother-country; indeed, the finger of destiny seems to point to their independence and possible union with their Southern neighbor at no distant period.

The recognition of the independence of the United States by the Continental powers, the end of the

> " Good old Colony times
> When we lived under the King."

therefore fixes the most suitable point at which to close our descriptions of "Medals relating to American Colonial History."   Of those remaining to be considered nearly all refer directly to the birth of the new nation; a few are personal Medals in honor of Adams, Franklin and others, which were struck about the same period, and therefore may be properly included, and these form the subject of our concluding Chapter.

RECOGNITION OF THE INDEPENDENCE OF THE UNITED STATES BY FRISIA.

602. 1782. *Obv.* No legend.   Three standing figures; the one in the centre is a Frisian in ancient armor, who grasps with his right hand the right hand of a maiden in Indian cos- tume, with plumed head-dress, symbolizing America; her left rests upon an elliptical shield on which, in nine lines, is DE | VER | EENIG | DE | STAATEN | VAN | NOORD | AMERI | CA (The United States of North America); at her feet are the links of a broken chain and she tramples on a sceptre; the Frisian warrior turns his back on another female figure, whom he repels with his left hand extended and pointing downward; the latter figure offers with her right hand an olive-branch to the Frisian, and her left rests on a similar shield inscribed, in three lines, GROOT | BRIT | TANJEN (Great Britain); at her right, partly concealed, is the leopard of England, and in the grass at her feet is coiled an adder, towards which the Fris-

ian points : above him an angel flies in a radiant cloud, to
present the free hat of the Netherlands to America : in exergue, at the right, B. C. V. CALKER F.

Rev. Inscription in eight lines, AAN DE STAATEN VAN
FRIESLAND | TER DANKBAARE NAGEDACHTENISSE | VAN DE
LANDSDAGEN IN FEBR. EN APR. | MDCCLXXXII | TOEGEWYD |
DOOR DE BURGER SOCIETEIT | DOOR VRYHEID EN YVER | TE
LEEUWARDEN (To the States *i. e.* the Legislature, of Friesland, in grateful recognition of the Acts of the Provincial
Assembly, held in February and April, 1782. Dedicated by
the Civic Society " For Liberty and Glory," at Leeuwarden.)
Above the inscription a right hand from the clouds holds the
arms of West Frisia, on a crowned shield, which are azure,
billety of seven pieces gold (alluding to the seven Provinces),
two lions passant gold.

Silver. Size 28. A. J. N., II, 64 ; XXVI, 18. V. L.,[*]
Sup. 572.

In the " Diplomatic Correspondence of the American Revolution " is a
letter of John Adams, from Amsterdam, Feb. 27, 1782, in which he says :
" Friesland has at last taken the provincial resolution to acknowledge the

---

[*] Van Loon in his Supplement, has some very full and interesting notes on
this Medal, the earliest of the so-called Peace Medals of the United States ; he
remarks that the Frisian in ancient armor is intended to symbolize that the
States of Holland originally sought after Liberty, and their purpose to maintain
it was still unchanged : he calls the animal a leopard ; others have called it a
bull-dog and a lioness. As it is a Dutch Medal Mr. Betts followed the Dutch
description. In the A. J. N., XXVI (*loc. cit.*), are also extensive comments on

independence, of which United America is in full possession." The symbol of the snake in the grass shows the doubt existing as to the sincerity of Great Britain, which was felt not alone in Holland, but in France, as is proved by the letter of caution written by Count de Vergennes to Franklin, at this time.

HOLLAND RECEIVES JOHN ADAMS AS ENVOY.

603. 1782. *Obv.* LIBERA SOROR   In exergue, in two lines, SOLEMNI DECR. AGN. | 19 APR. MDCCLXXXII. (A Free Sister, acknowledged by solemn decree April 19, 1782.)   At the left an armed woman, personifying Holland, with her right hand grasps that of an Indian Queen, while on a pole in her left hand she holds the free hat over the head of the Indian, who stands at the right, with a plumed head-dress, and bearing in her left hand a sword, a shield charged with thirteen stars in five rows three and two, and a chain which holds a lion, on

the Medal, an impression of which, it is there stated, is preserved in the "Museum of Antiquities and History" of Leeuwarden; the dies are also still in existence, and a few impressions in silver were re-struck in 1891. The State of Friesland, or West Frisia, was the first of the States of the Dutch Republic to recognize officially, Feb. 26, 1782, John Adams as an Ambassador of the United States; 'one by one the other States followed the example of the most northern Province, and on the 19th of April (eventful day in American history), the vote in the States General was taken welcoming the new Republic. The following day Mr. Adams presented his credentials, and was warmly greeted.... At Fraenker, the students of the University celebrated the event by special manifestations of joy; some of the Latin orations, etc., delivered on the occasion are printed in the history of the University, in one of which it is said "One day's freedom is worth more than a century passed under a tyrant's yoke."' — EDS.

whose head she presses her left foot ; between the figures is a round altar, on which fire is burning ; on its face is a caduceus between cornucopiæ erect ; and above the figures are rays of the sun.

Rev. TYRANNIS VIRTUTE REPULSA In exergue, SUB GALLIÆ | AUSPICIIS. (Tyranny repelled by valor under the auspices of France) : on the sockel, I. G. HOLTZHEY FEC. A landscape with a high rock at the left, at the base of which lies a unicorn, one of the supporters of the arms of England, with a crown encircling his throat, who has broken his horn against the precipitous face of the rock.

Silver. Size 28½. A. J. N., II, 64 ; XXIII, 32.* V. L., Sup. 573.

On Friday, April 19, 1782, their "High Mightinesses, the States-General of the United Provinces," passed this resolution :

" It has been thought fit and resolved, that Mr. Adams shall be admitted and acknowledged in quality of Envoy of the United States of North America to their High Mightinesses, as he is admitted and acknowledged by the present."

TREATY OF COMMERCE BETWEEN HOLLAND AND THE UNITED STATES.

604. 1782. *Obv.* FAVSTISSIMO FOEDERE JVNCTÆ. 'Below, completing the circle, DIE VII OCTOB ' MDCCLXXXII ' (United by a most auspicious treaty, Oct. 7, 1782.) Fame seated on the clouds, supporting with her right hand two elliptical shields, one of Holland with the rampant lion, and the other charged with thirteen stars for the United States ; above them is a naval crown, and below, the club of Hercules and lion's skin ; her left hand holds to her lips a long trumpet.

Rev. JUSTITIAM ET NON TEMNERE DIVOS In exergue, in two lines, S. P. Q. AMST. | SACRVM (Learn justice and not to

---

* Mr. Parsons, in commenting on this Medal, A. J. N., XXIII, 32, notes that "the hind-quarters of the lion are still upright," as if to intimate that the British power was not entirely subdued, the King not yet having consented to acknowledge American independence. An autotype of the Medal accompanies his paper in the *Journal.* — EDS.

despise the gods.   By the Senate and people of Amsterdam):
on the sockel at the right, ı. ɢ. ʜᴏʟᴛᴢʜᴇʏ ꜰʀᴄ.   At the left is a
pyramidal monument ; around its base are hung garlands of
flowers, and on its front a scroll inscribed ᴘʀᴏ | ᴅʀᴏ | ᴍᴠꜱ (a
forerunner) ; on the front of the monument the crowned shield
of Amsterdam (as engraved, gules, on a pale sable three sal-
tires argent) rests against crossed fasces ; Mercury flying

through the air is about to place a wreath on the crown ;
in the foreground are a basket of fruit and an anchor, on
which stands a cock typifying France, clapping his wings and
crowing ; in the distance is the ocean, on which are several
vessels.*

Silver.   Size 29.   V. L., Sup. 575.   A. J. N., II, 64.

605.   1782.   *Obv.* The same legend and design but a much
smaller planchet.

Rev. Similar legend and design.

Silver.   Size 21.   A. J. N., II, 64.   V. L., Sup. II, p. 178.

---

* The treaty of commerce commemorated by this Medal, was signed at the
Hague, October 7, 1782.   The legend is from the Æneid, VI, 620, the full line
being the warning words of Phlegyas, heard by Æneas in Hades : —
    "Discite justitiam moniti, et non temnere divos."
The cock has in his left claw an object which we cannot distinguish in the engraving, but called in Van Loon a "wichelroede," perhaps an augur's staff.

606.   1782.   *Obv.* EN DEXTRA FIDESQUE (Behold, here is my right hand, and the pledge of my good faith).   In exergue, in three lines, DEN. 7 OCTOBER. | 1782. | I : V : B.   At the right a woman sits on a bale of goods, resting her left arm on the shield of Holland ; behind her leans a pole, on the top of which is the free hat ; her right hand is extended to receive an olive branch from a man in classic dress standing at the left, who offers it with his right hand, and with his left supports a staff, from which flies the "Stars and Stripes" ; near him is a barrel, filled to overflowing with Indian corn.

Rev. Inscription in eight lines, HEIL, VRIJGESTREEN | AMERIKAAN ! | GANSCH NEERLAND NEEMT | UW VRIENDSCHAP AAN. | GODS GUNST VEREEN   TWEE VRIJE LANDEN, | TOT WEERZYDS NUT, | DOOR VASTE BANDEN : (Hail to you, American, who have fought out your freedom : All Netherlands accepts your friendship.   God's grace unite two free lands, to mutual good, through solid ties) ; below is a caduceus between a branch of olive at the left and a branch of palm at the right, crossed at the bottom.*

Silver.   Size 20¼.   A. J. N., II, 65.   V. L., Sup. 576.

Mr. Adams's letters state that on Oct. 8 "were executed the Treaty of Commerce and the convention concerning recaptures," and that Oct. 7, the date on the Medal, was originally appointed as the date of signing.

---

* The obverse legend, separated between DEXTRA and FIDESQUE by the flag, is from the Æneid. IV, 597, where the words are used by Dido, sarcastically, as she sees the ships of Æneas departing from Carthage. I. V. B. are the initials of J. Van Baerll, concerning whom see Van Loon, Sup. II, p. 155, note 7. The inscription on the reverse is a rhyming quatrain. Van Loon mentions that ships

HOLLAND DECLARES AMERICA FREE.

607. 1782. *Obv.* NEDERLAND VERKLAARD AMERICA VRY. (Netherlands declares America free.) In exergue, I. M. LAGRMAN. A woman in classic dress stands facing, her head turned to the right, holding in her right hand a bundle of seven arrows, the emblem of the United Provinces, and supporting a lance, on the top of which is the free hat ; in her left is a caduceus ; at her feet are a cactus and a horn of plenty, and in the distance are fortifications, buildings and a range of hills.

Rev. DE ALGEMEENE WENSCH. (The universal desire.) In exergue, 1782. A group of bales and barrels, a boat at the left with a single mast, and a tall trident-headed staff, from which hang the flags of Holland and the United States.

Silver and copper.   Size 21½.   A. J. N., II, 65 ; XXIII, 32 (illus.).   V. L., Sup. 574.*

PEACE OF VERSAILLES.

608. 1783. *Obv.* LIBERTAS AMERICANA (American Liberty).   In exergue, MDCCLXXXIII ; in field, C F or C.R.   Louis XVI at the left in royal robes, adorned with lilies, and seated

---

under the American flag were early at Amsterdam, and cites a "song made by a Dutch lady at the Hague for the sailors of eight American vessels at Amsterdam, June, 1779."— EDS.

* Van Loon, Sup. II, p. 176, commenting on this Medal, says the city in the background was intended by the die-cutter (as appears by his printed description) for Philadelphia, then the capital of the United States, but it bears no resemblance to that city. The same authority calls the merchandise a barrel of sugar and a canister of tobacco. The bale is marked H. I., which he does not explain. — EDS.

on his throne, facing the right, points with his left hand to a shield charged with thirteen bars, azure on a silver field, which a woman, representing Liberty, has just hung on a column surmounted by the free hat.

Rev. COMMVNI CONSENSV. (By common consent). Pallas standing, facing the right, supporting with her right hand a spear, at the foot of which an olive springs up ; her left hand holds a ribbon, tied in a bow, from which hang the shields of France with its lilies at the left above, Great Britain at the right, Spain below, at the left, with Castile and Leon quarterly, and Holland at the right, the rampant lion with sword and arrows ; on the ground lies a shield with the head of Medusa.

Silver, and tin with copper plug inserted. Size 29. A. J. N., II, 65 ; XXIII, 32. V. L., Sup. 593.*

THE TREATY OF PARIS.

609. 1783. *Obv.* NVLLA SALVS BELLO. (No safety in war.) A small olive tree, with a banner, drum, cannon and balls at the right, and an anchor and cornucopia full of coins at the

---

* The initials of the die-cutter are indistinctly engraved, and V. L., Sup. II, p. 209. is unable to decipher them. The arms of the various countries show the heraldic charges, but as they have been so frequently given, it seems unnecessary to repeat them. The Medusa head is the familiar device of Pallas. The Treaty of Peace was signed at Versailles, Sept. 3, 1783, between Great Britain and the United States. — EDS.

left ; a ship in the distance. On a tablet curving to conform
to the lower edge, ı ʍ ʟᴀɢᴇᴍᴀɴ · ꜰ ·

Rev. Inscription in six lines with an ornamental dash below, FVNDAMENTA · | PACIS · A . BRITANN · | ET · BELGAR · |
LEGATIS · POSITA · | PARIS · II SEPTEMBR · | MDCCLXXXIII ·
(The preliminaries of peace settled by ambassadors of Great
Britain and the Netherlands at Paris, Sept. 2, 1783.)

Silver. Size 20 nearly. V. L., Sup. 591.

610. 1783. *Obv.* SIC HOSTES CONCORDIA IVNGIT AMICOS
(Thus concord unites enemies as friends). At the left is
Peace advancing with an olive branch in left hand, with her
right grasping that of America who holds in her left hand a
pole, on which is the free hat ; at her feet a shield, charged
with bars as on the preceding ; behind Peace is a horn of
plenty, and between the figures the shields of Ireland, with a
harp, used as the emblem of Great Britain, France with its
lilies, and Spain symbolized by the castle of Castile ; behind
the first figure is the shield of the Netherlands with the rampant lion ; the shields are tied with a triple bow of ribbon ;
in the field at each side is a battle between a fort and several
vessels, with MAHO on the left, and GIBR. on the right, referring to the loss of Port Mahon and defence of Gibraltar ;
above the figures a triangle, from which proceed rays ; in the
exergue is a view of a large fortified town on the water side,
intended (says V. L., Sup. II, p. 208) for Paris, where the

treaty was signed, over which PRUDENTIA & FATIS (By Prudence and the Fates).

Rev. ENSIBVS EX MARTIS LVX PACIS LÆTA RESVRGIT (From the clash of arms [or the weapons of war, literally the swords of Mars], the joyful light of peace rises again). In exergue, in two lines, OPE VVLCANI | 1783. (By the aid of Vulcan, *i. e.* hard labor or industry.) Peace, with an olive branch in her right hand and a horn of plenty in her left, tramples on War lying prostrate, with a broken sword in his right hand ; in the distance a view of Gibraltar and vessels besieging ; above, at the left, is the sun in splendor over hills, and an angel flying to the right, with a wreath in left hand, and in right a trumpet through which he sounds the words FIAT PAX. (Let there be peace.)

Silver and tin. Size 27½. A. J. N., II, 65 ;* XXIII, 33 and plate. V. L., Sup. 592.

611. 1783. *Obv.* LVD XVI REX CHRISTIANISS · (Louis XVI, Most Christian King.) Under truncation, GATTBAUX. Bust of

---

* Mr. W. S. Appleton, commenting on this rare Medal, in A. J. N., *loc. cit.*, mentions that "reference is here made to the English loss of Port Mahon, with the island of Minorca, and their successful defence of Gibraltar, both which events occurred during the War of American Independence." Its history and origin have not been ascertained, and V. L., Sup. II, pp. 208-9, describes it without remark. Mr. Parsons thinks "from its rude execution it may reasonably be inferred that it was designed and struck in America. From the variety of designs and inscriptions which are crowded upon the two sides of the Medal, it seems as if the author proposed to write a poem in celebration of the Peace, but finally concluded to publish a Medal." From certain peculiarities in the

Louis XVI, in profile to right, in royal robes and wearing the Order of the Golden Fleece.*

Rev. PAX FRANCIAM INTER ET ANGLIAM and in exergue, in two lines, VERSALIIS | MDCCLXXXIII (Peace between France and England, at Versailles, 1783). Near the sockel at the left, DUVIV. Peace standing, with an olive branch in her right hand, and a horn of plenty in her left, resting her left foot on the prow of a galley.

Silver. Size 27. A. J. N., II, 63.

612. 1783. *Obv.* LUD . XVI . REX CHRISTIANISS [Translated above]. Under truncation, B. DUVIVIER. Bust of the King to right in plain drapery.

Rev. Same as the preceding.

Gold. Size 27. B. N., Paris.

613. 1784. *Obv.* A draped female figure partially facing to the left, standing on a square pedestal ; in her right hand are a caduceus and three heads of grain ; in her left hand a cornucopia, the upper portion of which rests against the shoulder. On the front of the pedestal is a circular disc, or shield, with the inscription RES | PUBLICA | AMERI | CANA (American Republic), in four lines : from behind the disc, arising diagonally towards the left, a trident, and towards the right, a pole with the free hat ; from either side of the field, pendant from a bow, is a festoon or garland, from which are suspended four shields : at the left, Spain, quarterly Castile and Leon, an escutcheon of pretence with the Bourbon lilies ; next the pedestal on the left, the arms of Great Britain, quarterly, 1. England impaling France ; 2, Scotland ; 3, Ireland ; 4, Hanover ; next the pedestal on the right, the rampant lion of the Netherlands, and above at the right, the lilies of France. In the exergue, H. C. V. CALKER, F.

---

dies, we incline to think it was struck in Holland or Germany. The Treaty of Paris was that between Great Britain and the other powers who had been at war with her during the Revolution. — EDS.

* For Gatteaux see note on 557. — EDS.

Rev. RESTAURATA MDCCLXXXIII | & MDCCLXXXIV. (Peace restored, 1783 and 1784.)   A hand issuing from a cloud on the right above, returns a sword to its scabbard, point downward ; the hand holds also an olive branch, extending towards the left ; across the scabbard and occupying the centre of the field, a ribbon or scroll bearing the word PAX (Peace).   The legend is at the bottom of the Medal, and the second line is over the first.

Lead and tin.   Size 26.   A. J. N., IV, 19 ; XXV, 89.   V. L., Sup. 609.*

614. 1783.   *Obv.* FELICITAS : BRITANNIA : ET : AMERICA (Literally, Happiness, Britain and America).   In exergue, in two lines, MDCCLXXXIII | SEP^T. 4   At the right Britannia seated, facing the left ; by her side a shield with the crosses of St. George and St. Andrew; in her left hand is a spear, and her right is extended towards an Indian Queen, who is advancing with a bow in her right hand, and a quiver behind her back ; between them flies a dove with an olive-branch ; in the distance is a view of London, in which appear St. Paul's Cathedral and the Monument.

---

* The heraldic tinctures are shown on the various arms by the conventional lines, but the arms have been blazoned so frequently it seems unnecessary to repeat them.   The final arrangements for peace between the European powers were completed at Paris in May, 1784.   The Treaty is frequently termed "The Peace of Versailles," the place at which England recognized American inde. pendence, on which fact the subsequent action of the powers depended. — EDS.

Rev. AMERICAN : CONGRESS ✦ on a ring, from which extend thirteen rays; beyond the rays a chain of thirteen rings inscribed MASSCHS N. HAMPS CONNCT R. ISLAND N. IORKE N. JERSEY PENSILVA DELAWARE MARYLAND VIRGINIA N. CAROLI S. CAROLI GEORGIA On the centre, WE | ARE | ONE.

Tin or pewter; rude. Size 25; very rare. Edge with ornamental milling, in the Appleton collection; inscribed CONTINENTAL CURRENCY on the specimen formerly in the possession of Dr. Charles Clay, of Manchester, England, and later in that of Henry W. Holland, Esq., of Boston.* A. J. N., II, 65; X, 21. C., 370.

615. 1781. *Obv.* LIBERTAS AMERICANA (American Liberty). In exergue, 4 JUIL. 1776 (July 4, 1776). Beautiful head of Liberty with flowing hair, and staff with liberty-cap behind it.†

---

* Of this Medal only two impressions are at present known, and it seems to be a mule,—the reverse of the well-known "Continental Currency" combined with the obverse described. The execution, like the Latin of the legend, is poor. The engraving is not quite correct. Dr. Clay's impression was sold in New York, in December, 1871, for $31. (See A. J. N., VI, 70.) With regard to the reverse die, see also A. J. N., XXI, 89 and Crosby. — EDS.

† The *Libertas Americana*, the dies of which were cut by Dupre, is universally considered by far the most beautiful of the Peace Medals. Its spirited head of Liberty was imitated on some of the earliest coins of the new nation. The Phrygian cap now takes the place of the free hat of the Netherlands. The reverse design is peculiarly suggestive. This, as Mr. Parsons remarks in A. J. N., XXIII, 31, "conveys a very adroit compliment to the French nation;" the infant Hercules, type of the young Republic, has strangled the two serpents which attacked him, symbolizing the victories of Saratoga and Yorktown, but he is still exposed to the relentless rage of the British lion, whose tail between his legs, — "coward" as the heralds style it, — shows his power is baffled by Minerva, whose lily-shield shows her to be the emblem of France, springing to protect him. The legend is taken from the beautiful Ode "Descende coelo," [Horace III: IV. 20]. The mottoes were supplied to Franklin by Sir William Jones—see Sparks' Works of Franklin, Vol. IX, *passim*, as quoted by Mr. Appleton, A. J. N., II, 63. See also A. J. N., XV, 76, where Franklin's letter suggesting the reverse is printed. The dates in exergue are those of the two victories over Burgoyne and Cornwallis. The dies were engraved in 1782. With reference to the change in the style of the hair, in the design on our early coins originally taken from the charming head on this Medal, some interesting notes and references will be found in A. J. N., XXI, 95. — EDS.

Rev. NON SINE DIIS ANIMOSUS INFANS. (The infant is not bold without divine aid.)   In exergue, ¹⁵⁄₁₀ OCT. ¹⁷⁸³ DUPRE F. The infant Hercules on his shield-shaped cradle, strangling a serpent in each hand ; Minerva, representing France, stands over him, repelling with lance, and shield blazoned with lilies, the attack of the British lion.

Silver and bronze.   Size 30.   A. J. N., II, 63 ; XXIII, 33, and plate.   Loubat.

616.   *Obv.* Similar to the preceding, but cut in the United States.

Rev. 1783.   An eagle, with an olive-branch in his beak, and lightnings in his talons, hovering over a part of a sphere, inscribed UNITED STATES.*

Bronze.   Size 26.   See A. J. N., VII, 49 for reverse.

617.   1783.   *Obv.* As obverse of 549 (same die).
Rev. As reverse of 616.
Bronze.   Size 26.   A. J. N., VII, 74.†

BENJAMIN FRANKLIN.

618.   1783.   *Obv.* BENJ. FRANKLIN MINST PLENT DES ETATS UNIS DE L'AMERIQ., SEPT. MDCCLXXXIII (Benjamin Franklin Minister Plenipotentiary from the United States of America, Sept., 1783.)   Profile bust of Franklin, clothed, facing the left.   Below, NERNIER.

Rev. DE LEURS TRAVAUX NAITRA LEUR GLOIRE (From their labors will spring their glory).   In exergue, DES NEUF SŒURS (Lodge of the Nine Sisters).   At the right, F. N. ; on a rocky hill a circular temple, within, and near which are the Nine Muses at work.‡

Silver and bronze.   Size 19.   Rare.   Marvin's Medals of the Masonic Fraternity, LVIII.   A. J. N., VII, 49; XI, 62.

---

* This is a mule, the reverse die having also been struck with the obverse of 547 as well as 617 and 621, and is of much later date than properly to have a place here, although the date might seem to allow it. — EDS.

† This mule is of the same period as the preceding. — EDS.

‡ This famous Masonic Lodge of Paris numbered among its members Franklin, Bernier who cut the dies of this Medal, Houdon who carved the

619.   1748.   *Obv.* BENJ. FRANKLIN NATUS BOSTON XVII JAN. and MDCCVI at the bottom (Benjamin Franklin, born at Boston Jan. 17, 1706). Clothed bust in profile, of Franklin, facing to the left; on the edge of the bust, DUPRE F.

Rev. ERIPUIT CŒLO FULMEN   SCEPTRUMQUE TYRANNIS (He snatched the thunderbolt from heaven and the sceptre from tyrants*). In exergue, in three lines, SCULPSIT ET DICAVIT | AUG. DUPRE, ANNO | MDCCLXXXIV (Aug. Dupre engraved and issued this, in the year 1784.) On an open plain a winged genius stands facing; his right arm raised,

---

busts· of Franklin and Washington, Lalande the astronomer, Voltaire, and many others distinguished for their eminence in science, literature and art. — Eds.

* The famous epigram which forms the legend, was first applied to Franklin by M. Turgot, who is supposed to be its author; although Pres. Sparks, in his "Writings of Franklin," remarks that it was probably suggested by a line in the Astronomicon of Manilius (Lib. I, 104), where the Poet is speaking of Epicurus: —

> "Eripuit Jovi fulmen, viresque tonandi."

The motto was translated into English by Mr. Elphinstone,

> He snatched the bolt from Heaven's avenging hand,
> Disarmed and drove the tyrant from the land.

It has also been rendered,

> From heaven he snatched the burning levin-brand,
> And wrenched the sceptre from the tyrant's hand.

For Dupre see note on 569. In the portrait of Franklin on this Medal, says Charles Blanc, "he has indicated the flat parts, the relaxation of the muscles, and as it were the quivering of the flesh, so as to convey an exact idea of the age of the model. He has conscientiously represented the lines which the finger of time imprints upon the countenance, but above all he has given us with wonderful fidelity, the physiognomy of the American sage, his shrewd simplicity, his sagacity, and his expression of serene uprightness." See a paper on "The Engravers of the Revolutionary Medals," in A. J. N., XXVIII, 1. There are numerous Medals of Franklin, and a very full list compiled by Mr. W. S. Appleton will be found in A. J. N., VII, 49, and subsequent numbers (see also XXIV, 10), but those described in this and the preceding Chapter are, we believe, all that are entitled to mention in this volume. It may be proper to add here that the rare "Diplomatic Medal" by Dupre, a full description of which is given in A. J. N., IX, 65 and 78, and sometimes improperly called "The Medal Commemorative of American Independence" from its date "IV JUL. MDCCLXXVI" was not struck until 1791, and is not "Colonial." — Eds.

points to a circular temple on a hill at the left, protected by
a rod from a flash of lightning which darts from a cloud ;
with his left he points to a crown and sceptre, both broken,
on the ground before him.

Silver and bronze.   Size 29.   A. J. N., VII, 49.   Loubat.

620.   1786.   *Obv.* From the same die as the preceding.

Rev. Inscription in four lines, ERIPUIT CŒLO | FULMEN |
SCEPTRUM QUE | TYRANNIS [Translated above] within a wreath
of oak, close at the top and crossed and tied at the bottom
with a bow of ribbon.   Below the stems of the wreath,
in three lines, SCULPSIT ET DICAVIT | AUG. DUPRE ANNO |
MDCCLXXXVI. [Translated above, but the date (1786) differs.

Silver and bronze.   Size 29.   A. J. N., VII, 49 ; IX, 29.
Loubat.

Although this was struck after the close of the Revolution,
it has so close a connection with the other Revolutionary
Peace Medals, that it seems fitting to include it among
them.

621.   1783.   *Obv.* As the obverse of 547 (from the same
die.)

Rev. As the reverse of 616 (from the same die.[*])
Bronze.   Size 26.   A. J. N., VII, 49.

---

[*] A mule of later date.   See note on 616. — EDS.

VAN BERCKEL, MINISTER FROM HOLLAND.

622. 1783. *Obv.* No legend. Within a wreath of laurel, clothed bust nearly facing, of Van Berckel; he wears a close wig with the cue stiffly falling at the side. A ring at the top for suspension.[*]

Rev. Plain, or not described.

Silver, elliptical. Size 14 by 9 nearly. V. L., Sup. 583.

AMERICA FREE.

623. *Obv.* O MANES HEROUM VESTRA LIBERA EST PATRIA (O shades of heroes, your country is free). WAREN (*sic*) WOOSTER MONTGOMERY MERCER inscribed upon a funeral monument at the foot of which lies a weeping female with a feather-wrought girdle. The monument stands in a wooded landscape.

Rev. Not described.

A. J. N., IV, 45†. No specimen known.

---

[*] This little Medal was struck to be worn as an ornament. Pieter Johan Van Berckel, who was appointed by the Netherlands as Plenipotentiary [Gevolmachtigde], to America in 1783, was a native of Amsterdam, where he was born in 1725. His business relations with America and knowledge of the affairs of the Colonies made his services of considerable value to the Netherlands, for which reason he was appointed by the States General to represent them. His son succeeded him, with the title of Resident. He died in New York, Oct. 27, 1800. The Medal is said to be quite rare, and seems to have been first noticed in the catalogue of an auction sale of the collection of H. Westhoff, Jr., in 1848, in which it is No. 3139. — EDS.

† All that is known of this Medal, if it be a Medal, is given in A. J. N. (*loc. cit.*), where it is said that the obverse described in the text is a copper-plate engraving on the title page of the first volume of "Lettres d'un Cultivateur Américain, Paris, 1787." The work seems to have been originally published in English, in 1782, at London, under the title "Letters from an American Farmer." Its author was Hector St. John Crevecœur, a native of Normandy, who settled in America in 1754, and was French Consul at New York 1783-93. It seems extremely doubtful if such a Medal was ever struck, since no impression of it is known. The names commemorated are those of Gen. Warren, who fell at Bunker Hill; of Gen. David Wooster of Connecticut, mortally wounded in the battle at Ridgefield in that State in 1777; of Gen. Richard Montgomery who served under Wolfe in Canada, and was killed in December, 1775, in an assault on Quebec when in command of the American forces, and of Gen. Hugh Mercer, who was mortally wounded in the battle at Princeton, N. J., in Jan'y, 1777.—EDS.

There are several Medals relating to individuals prominent in this country in connection with the War of Independence, or active abroad in behalf of the cause of the Colonies; among them we may name one of Cornwallis, and six or seven which are described and engraved in the Supplement to Van Loon, struck in honor of Johan Derk, Baron Van Capellen, — including three on the death of the latter.* He was an ardent sympathizer with the cause of the American Colonies, and in frequent correspondence with the famous Governor Jonathan Trumbull of Connecticut, and with Gov. William Livingston of New Jersey, during the Revolution. From the notices of his services in the "Life of Gov. Trumbull," as well as in Van Loon's Supplement, the importance of what he did for America is clearly apparent. It was probably owing to his suggestion that John Adams was sent to Holland, secretly to advance the cause of the struggling Colonies; and to the influence of the Baron, so energetically yet discreetly used, it was largely due that the Dutch were ready so early to recognize the Colonial Agent as an Ambassador of a sovereign State. One of the Medals struck in honor of Capellen was given by him to Adams, and is still preserved by his descendants. But they all were either struck to commemorate events occurring after the period at which our descriptions close, or their bearing on American affairs is too slight to entitle them to a place in this volume.

Nearly three centuries elapsed between that autumn morning when the sunny islands of the New World rose from the sea to greet the wistful eye of the weary voyager across the Atlantic, and that day of earlier autumn when the starry flag of the new Republic, no longer a cluster of Colonies, but a "free sister" among the nations, was saluted by the guns

* The Medal of Cornwallis, 878 in V. L., Sup., commemorates the Treaty of the Peace of Amiens; those of Baron Van Capellen, are 578 to 582 A, and 611-13, in the same work. None of these have any relation to America. On retiring from his mission to the Netherlands, Adams was presented with the Diplomatic Medal of that country, an account of which, with an engraving, is given in A. J. N., 85, and in the "Works of John Adams," Vol. VIII. — Eds.

which had failed to bring her-rebel will to submission. Yet
the history of that long and eventful period, with its romance
of discovery, its patient toil in subduing the wilderness and
the savage, its ceaseless strife for the mastery of those mighty
rivers and vast domains, the struggle between the roses of
England and the lilies of France on the fertile prairies of the
West and the rock-bound shores of the ocean, the story of
valorous deeds, and heroic combats, and of final triumph,
may be read as truthfully on these little medallic monuments
whose legends and devices we have endeavored faithfully to
describe, as on the pages of the most careful and painstaking
historian. It would be folly to claim that in this, the first
adventure into a field of such surpassing interest to an
American, nothing has escaped us ; if the reader shall have
been stimulated to glean for himself among these memorials
of the past, our task will have been accomplished.

CORRIGENDA.

HERE are a few matters concerning which further information has been obtained by the Editors, since the preceding pages were printed, which it seems proper to mention, and we also note the errors which have been discovered.

In addition to what is said in the Editorial Note on page 2, on early numismatic references to America, we may mention that it is stated by Herrera that Cortez struck coins in Mexico, but what inscriptions they bore has not been established with certainty; these seem to have been issued as early as 1522 (see A. J. N., XVI, pp. 2 and 25); it is also a matter of record that Mints were ordered to be established in Mexico and Hispaniola (St. Domingo), in 1528 and 1530, but it does not appear that they were in operation in either of these places before 1535 or 1536, since renewed orders were sent from Spain, under date of May 11, 1535, to begin the coinage of silver, etc., in Mexico (ibid., p. 3), in Santa Fe, and Potosi (see Report of Gutierrez, Secretary of State, Mexico, 1849, p. 4). The mint of Mexico was doubtless in operation for many years before 1555, and specimens of very early coins, known to have been struck there, bear the title REX INDIARVM; as they have no date, authorities differ as to the exact time when they were issued; when the St. Domingo Mint began work is very uncertain: but this is a subject the discussion of which would be out of place in this volume.

Page 7, No. 16. The engraving in M. H. has the date in exergue, on the obverse.

Page 7, No. 18. The arms of the Marine Council are simply those of West Frisia on a shield surmounting two anchors crossed in saltire.

Page 11, No. 23. In the engraving of this Medal in M. H., EADEM has the line over the A.

Page 12, No. 24. The engraving of this Medal in M. H. has *C. P.* in place of *Cum Privil.* The Medal itself we have not seen.

Page 20, No. 34. See A. J. N., III, 29 and 60.

Page 22, No. 22. The reverse inscription, in the engraving in M. H., differs from the text, in having V for U throughout; PRÆSTATISMO in the third line: ARCIS *begins* the *sixth* line, and instead of SZEWSKI REB, *etc.*, as printed, it is SZEWSKI · REBVS · IN BRASILIA The seventh line begins PER and ends with FORTISS: the last two lines are HOC · MONVM · ESSE · VOLVIT | A° CHTI · 1637.

The larger capitals, except in CHRISTOPH, are not given. The differences in the engravings are so marked that there may have been two dies. We have not seen the Medal.

Page 32, Note. For a paper giving reasons why the Varin and Richelieu Medals are not properly included among those relating to America, see A. J. N., XXVII, 29.

Page 58, No. 114. In the last line of exergue of the obverse, for 13 read 12. In a description of this piece, given in A. J. N., XIII, p. 96, at that time in Mr. Benjamin Betts's cabinet, it is said to be XII on the Medal; we have been unable to see one. Cicero uses *putarem*, not *judico*, in the texts which we have examined, and attention is called to this discrepancy in the descriptions in A. J. N., (*loc. cit.*). The quotation from Horace, on the reverse, begins with the word QUICQUID.

Page 60, No. 116. The difference, WEXEL, mentioned, we believe to be on the obverse, and not as printed.

Page 60, No. 117. In the chronogrammatic legend of the obverse the M in MELAC should be a full capital and the S in next word should be a small capital.

Page 63, No. 121. For "these" at beginning of last line but five of the text, read "four."

Page 64, No. 122. The obverse legend is in two circular lines, the second beginning with the word CONSEILS; the word DE is on the left and FRANCE on the right of Law's hat. On the reverse, the legend ends with BOURSES; the remainder forms an *inscription* in eighteen lines, as follows: LUNDI : | NOUS ACHETTONS | DES ACTIONS, | MARDI : | NOUS AVONS | DES MILLIONS, | MECREDI : (*sic*) | NOUS REGLONS | NOTRE MENAGE, | IEUDI : | NOUS NOUS METTONS | EN. EQUIPAGE, | VENDREDI : | NOUS ALLONS | AU BALL, (*sic*) | ET SAMEDI : | A L'HOPI-TAL. | 1720. This is as given on Plate III, of V. L. Sup., I, 31.

Page 67, No. 128. An autotype of this Medal in the London *Numismatic Chronicle*, Series III, Vol. 8, "Medals of Scotland," plate, has KLUGSTEN instead of THOREN. We therefore conclude that there was an altered or second reverse die.

Page 69. No. 131, 73. No. 137, and 74, No. 140. The size is by an oversight given in millimetres; by the American scale (always used elsewhere in the volume) it would be 16 on each.

Page 70, Note. Eighth line from bottom, for PAVVLM read PAVLVM.

Page 72, No. 135. In the chronogrammatic inscription on the reverse, for LAQVEOS read LAQVEOS.

Page 74, No. 140. There is a variety of this Medal, viz.: —
140*a*. *Obv.* As obverse of 140.
Rev. As reverse of 131, but MAAS for MAASS; WOL ' LEN in the fifth line; FALLEN forms the sixth and IN the seventh line of the inscription, and there are periods after VERSUCHUNG. i. TIMOT. V. 9. and 10. Size 16.

Page 124. The cut with No. 272 is incorrectly engraved; it should be as above.

Page 149. Omit the asterisk in the fifth line; the reference to the foot-note belongs with 337.

Page 159, No. 354. On page 240 of Herrera we find a more complete description of this piece: *Obv.* FERDINANDVS. VI. D. G. HISPANIARVM REX. Bust of the King. *Rev.* IMPERATOR INDIARVM. MEXI. CONSVLATVS. (Emperor of the Indies: Mexican Consulate.) Crowned arms of the Consulate.

Page 160, No. 356, rev. It is suggested that if the I which begins the legend as printed, closes it, as mentioned in the note, it may be the initial of Imperator.

Page 166. The rabbit called by Herrera the emblem of Spain, may possibly have an allusion to her Mexican possessions, as it is not an uncommon emblem in Mexican decoration.

Page 174, No. 390. The date at the beginning should be 1755.

Page 175, No. 392. PRAESTAT translated " He has power," may here be better rendered " It is incumbent first of all."

Page 180-1. The Louisburg Medals are described by McLachlan in his work on Canadian Numismatics, and also in his paper on "Annals of the Nova Scotia Currency." For convenience we refer the reader to his article in A. J. N., XVIII, pp. 16, 17. Mr. Betts followed the descriptions in Med. Ill., which are not always so minute, and the Editors are therefore unable to identify his numbers with McL. in all cases. The planchets varied slightly in size in different impressions from the same dies, so that the size does not certainly serve as a guide. From McL. it appears that there are differing dies of the obverse of our 405, varying in the number of buttons on the coat, and one has the erroneous date, 1768. Probably these correspond to 404 and 408, one of which, if this be the case, has only four vessels in the harbor. It was impossible for us to compare these various descriptions with originals, and we therefore did not notice these differences in the text since we could not positively place them. McL. also mentions that these were most, if not all, "manufactured for Mr. Pinchbeck, in London," whose name is chiefly remembered for its association with a peculiar metal.

Page 196, No. 439.   The obverse cut is of an older bust, and may have belonged to one of the later Medals struck for the same purpose.

Page 197, No. 441.   For GEORGIUS read GEORGIVS.

Page 200, No. 444.   McLachlan, in "Annals of the Nova Scotia Currency," No. 54, mentions a curious mule, the reverse of our 444 combined with that of our 142, received from the Musee Monetaire, and evidently a piece of carelessness.

Page 205.   The note on 454 may not be sufficiently definite.   While the piece may have been struck for some of the Spanish American colonies, *Florida* is the name of a person and not of a place.   There are others of the same family.

Page 230, No. 518.   The design and dies were probably by Paul Revere, of Boston.

Page 237, No. 533, rev.   For HONOR read HONOUR.

Page 257.   In note on 564, another Medal of Keppel is mentioned.   Possibly it may be that given in Conder's "English Tokens," among "Farthings not Local," p. 250, viz. : —
Obv. ADMIRAL AUGUSTUS KEPPEL.   A head facing.   *Rev.* VICTORY.   A man-of-war, sailing, firing guns.   Brass.   The occasion when this was struck does not certainly appear; it may have reference to the victory at Goree, which he won December 29, 1758, and in honor of which a Medal was struck, (see Med. Ill., Geo. II, 415), differing apparently from our 413 only in having GOREE for LOUISBURG.   There is however a possibility that the piece has a much closer relation to America, as it may allude to the attack on Belle-Isle by the fleet under Keppel, and land forces under Gen. Hodgson, in April, 1761, when the British forces gained a victory [see 416].

Page 268, No. 578.   A list of the officers of Lord Francis Rawdon's Volunteers is printed in Hist. Mag., VIII, 322.

Page 295, No. 609.   The obverse legend is from the Æneid, XI, 362.

INDEX.

I. LEGENDS AND INSCRIPTIONS.

NOTE. — In the following Index the beginning of every Legend and Inscription is given with sufficient fullness and minuteness of punctuation to enable the reader to turn to any Medal described, but some abbreviations have been found necessary; several dots at the close denote that one or more words are omitted there; several inserted in the legend itself signify that the words and the punctuation omitted, are the same as in the Legend next preceding. Of the references it may be said that if the Legend sought is not printed in full on the page given, the *first* page-reference should be consulted; *e. g.*, in the legend ADMIRAL VERNON AND COMMODORE BROWN the Legend is printed in full on page 117 (the first reference), in No. 249; the second reference is to page 119, where under Nos. 254 and 255 will be found "Legend as 249."

It should also be borne in mind, in attempting to identify the Vernon Medals with the descriptions in the text, that the dies of these Medals were often used till nearly worn out; and then retouched or even altered (*e. g.*, see No. 314), so that a punctuation mark which might appear on an early impression did not show on a later one. The use of the Table of Reverses on p. 149, *et seq.*, in connection with this Index, will, it is believed, enable one to assign to its proper number any Vernon described.

II. DIE SINKERS AND ENGRAVERS.

NOTE.— We find that the letters on obverse of 608, taken by Mr. Betts to be " C. F. or C. R.," and which the editor of Van Loon Sup. was also unable to decipher, are Œ, the initial of Oexlein, who engraved No. 446. Johann Leonhard Oexlein, born at Nuremberg in 1715, was a die-cutter in that city, 1740-87.— EDS.

III. PERSONS, PLACES AND SUBJECTS.

Page 4.   No. 9, in first line, for 1557 read 1577.

Page 150.   In first paragraph, line 10, for 291 read 191.

Page 302.   In the date assigned to No. 619, for 1748 read 1784.

Since page 303 was printed, we learn from Mr. W. S. Appleton that while Mr. Betts's description of 621 conforms to his list of Franklins, as given in A. J. N., VII, 49 (No. 111), the description there is erroneous, and the obverse of our 621 should read "As obverse of 546, with legend, LIGHTNING AVERTED, etc.," and *not* of 547, as now. — EDS.